...ky Cheese Bread • Pain Pesto • Outstand...
• Open-Hearth Cinnamon... ...utter
...ago-and-Cheddar Potato Rolls • Onion ...
...Old-Fashioned British Crumpets • Butter...
...at-Honey-Walnut Buns • Golden Corn R...
...esy Garlic Twisty Bread • Pancetta Layered
...ion Focaccia • Double-Garlic Fougasse • ...
... Pepperoni Pizza Rolls • Traditional Irish
...lueberry-Blackberry Honey Butter-Glaze...
...Buttermilk Scones • Mr. Darcy's Wheat M...
...cones • Kitchen Sink Cookies • Triple-Th...
...ranberry Cream Scones • Marcy's Legenda...
...cones • BLT Bread • Classic Southern Bu...
... Cheese, Jalapeño, and Tomato-Pesto Bisc...
... Cashmere Muffins • Blueberries-and-Cr...
• Smash Apple Pie • Tender, Buttery Cho...
...ti • Garlic Bubble Bread • Pizza Blanca • ...
...ckberry Streusel-Topped Muffins • Mexica...
...Marvelous Marble Cream Cheese-and-Ch...
...ega-Butter Sugar Cookie Jam Sandwiches...
...es and Cream Cookies • White Chocolate...
...ookies • Deluxe Sticky Ooey-Gooey Pean...
...ookies • Candy Bar Shortbread • Double-...
...ip Almond Biscotti • Blueberry Biscotti •...

a *passion* for Baking

by Marcy Goldman

Text and recipes ©2007 by Marcy Goldman
Images ©2007 by Oxmoor House, Inc.
Book Division of Southern Progress Corporation
P.O. Box 2262, Birmingham, Alabama 35201-2262

ISBN-13: 978-0-8487-3179-3
ISBN-10: 0-8487-3179-4
Library of Congress Control Number: 2007930131

Printed in the United States of America
Second Printing 2008

Oxmoor House, Inc.
Editor in Chief: Nancy Fitzpatrick Wyatt
Executive Editor: Susan Carlisle Payne
Art Director: Keith McPherson
Managing Editor: Allison Long Lowery

A Passion for Baking
Author: Marcy Goldman
Editor: Julie Gunter
Senior Copy Editor: L. Amanda Owens
Copy Editors: Donna Baldone, Jacqueline Giovanelli, Diane Rose
Editorial Assistant: Rachel Quinlivan, R.D.
Proofreader: Vanessa Rusch Thomas
Senior Designer: Melissa Jones Clark
Photography Director: Jim Bathie
Senior Photo Stylist: Kay E. Clarke
Associate Photo Stylist: Katherine Eckert
Test Kitchens Director: Elizabeth Tyler Austin
Test Kitchens Assistant Director: Julie Christopher
Food Stylist: Kelley Self Wilton
Test Kitchens Professionals: Kathleen Phillips,
   Catherine Crowell Steele, Ashley T. Strickland
Director of Production: Laura Lockhart
Production Manager: Theresa Beste-Farley
Production Assistant: Faye Porter Bonner

Contributors:
Copy Editor: Dolores Hydock
Editorial Assistant: Laura K. Womble
Indexer: Mary Ann Laurens
Interns: Amy Edgerton, Amelia Heying, Lucas Whittington
Photographers: Beau Gustafson, Lee Harrelson
Photo Stylists: Melanie J. Clarke, Lydia DeGaris-Pursell
Test Kitchens Professionals: Jane Chambliss, Ana Kelly, Mary Long, Debby Maugans

a *passion* for Baking

by Marcy Goldman

To my sons, Jonathan, Gideon, and Benjamin:
I love you more than words can say and far more than infinite
fields of golden wheat. You are the gold of my heart.

• • •

I also dedicate this to my yet-to-be grandchildren with the
hope that one day they too will also discover a passion
for baking. May someone always remember to bake
or bring the bread and share it with those they love.

Oxmoor HOUSE®

cont

ents

Dear fellow baker,

Welcome to a cookbook that is my personal invitation to you to a very special baking class. We are going on a baking adventure—a never-ending passion for the flour arts. Consider this a coffee klatch between friends who meander through many topics of sweet things, pausing to chat and lingering over what we bake and enjoy.

This book is my personal and professional harvest of all my baking seasons to date—a collection that is truly a mother lode of great baking. It is about both **what** to bake and **how** to bake it better.

Home baking is the sensory bouquet of all these things—scents, sounds, touches, and visions—but most of all, it is a feeling born of a desire to create, nurture, nourish, and give. Within such magical things, there is a feeling or a unique energy that is, in turn, a taste. It is a taste that cannot be bought, sold, borrowed, or imitated.

Homey stuff may not always be picture-perfect, but it is absolutely, undeniably beautiful. It is food created with care that is meant to nourish in every way. That said, I intend to share with you each and every trick "in the book" on baking, to make your recipes foolproof and beautiful.

A passion for baking is like falling in love with life again and again. We recommit to those things we love as a matter of choice that seems innate. So it is each time you take out a block of butter, find a recipe, and choose to create something home baked for yourself and those in your circle.

It is with great delight and warmth that I invite you to join me in the kitchen and become part of the conversation and celebration that will ensue. For all of you, my baking readers, who patiently asked for years when I was going to do another book—here, at last, is the book I promised.

As always, I wish you sweet times in the kitchen and sweeter times in life.

Consider this a coffee klatch between friends who meander through many topics of sweet things, pausing to chat and lingering over what we bake and enjoy.

—Marcy Goldman
September 2007

baking
secrets

Baking, much like fashion, changes as tastes change. It is true that we like things sweeter than our ancestors may have, and we are more aware of better fat choices; also, we might like to visit the notion of whole grains in some of our baking. Some things in the baker's kitchen, however, are eternal: Taste, specifically *great* taste, is one of them. Great taste in baking is founded on three things: superb ingredients, proper handling, and a balanced recipe. That said, the best vanilla extract, superb flour, unsalted butter, rich chocolate, fragrant spices, fresh baking powder, and pure salt are things that always impact home baking and never seem to change.

Baking is about craftsmanship. It is a process—a series of building blocks—just as is crafting an heirloom rocking chair from the best maple you can find, using the best tools, as well as considering the gifts of time, expertise, and love involved. Memorable baking thrives on the same criteria.

Innate care and attention to detail make the difference between good baking and memorable baking. The oven can do magic, but it cannot transmute poor ingredients or remedy poor handling into a baking symphony; only your care and consideration can do that. In the end, good taste in all foods, and particularly in home baking, is *everything*.

If you have a beautiful recipe—the baking blueprint before you—all you have to do as the baking contractor is do it justice by contracting out, in turn, the best ingredients, techniques, and execution. And add your personal energy, of course. It all results in the incredible, memorable taste that is the crowning touch.

I call this the "bliss factor": When people take a bite of your baking, perhaps based on my recipes, you want to witness closed eyes, a smile, no talking for a second more than it takes to munch whatever it is, and then that sigh—in short, the bliss factor. That's how you know you've done your magic.

To help you craft that magic, you will find on these pages my best advice regarding essential ingredients, equipment, and techniques—all with a common goal in mind: successful and inspired baking.

Techniques: My Tricks of the Trade

When I create a recipe, I am always thinking the same thing: how to distill something spectacular into bakery "haiku," as it were, so that the average home baker can replicate the same success. I consider the end user as well as the time and expertise people have as I'm streamlining the process and factoring in baking logic. Whether for a cookie, a muffin, or a stately loaf of bread, a super baking recipe is worth its weight in gold, for it will bring pleasure over and over; it renews itself in every fresh batch.

Here is a glimpse of some of my best tips and techniques that will enhance your confidence in the kitchen and make baking fun. You'll see these tricks and more with the recipes they accompany throughout the book.

My Signature Tips

• First and foremost, I recommend double sheeting. It is my method of stacking two baking sheets so that there's a cushion for even baking and no risk of scorched bottoms.

• Throw a large clear plastic bag over your entire mixer full of dough in order to proof dough.

• My recipes often feature more vanilla than you might expect. Don't be timid here. It is, in fact, enhanced flavor with no extra effort.

• Shred cold butter with a box grater if you forget to take the butter out to soften. You can also shred apples for a quick-and-easy fruit pie. And you can shred frozen pastry dough for an easy alternative to a lattice pie topping.

• Get great results by blending citrus zest with sugar in a mixer or food processor before adding it to a recipe. The citrus flavor will be dispersed evenly and with maximum impact.

• Learn to bake mammoth muffins my way—use an ice-cream scoop to deposit gobs of thick batter easily into muffin pans.

shredding butter in lieu of softening it

proofing dough under a large plastic bag

scooping batter for mega muffins

Ingredients

Aroma is key to ascertaining freshness. Before you use ingredients, *smell* and *taste* the ones you can. Get into the habit of sniffing your spices, sampling a nut from its bag, and checking the date on your milk to guarantee fresh flavor and the best taste for baking. Other than that, use the best ingredients—or simply what the "best" is to you. If *Lindt* chocolate is what you love, use it. If you prefer to bake with imported French butter, choose that. *Your* taste counts. That is part of the autonomy of baking. Once you have the basics down and have set a standard as a baker, your own preferences factor into the final taste. If something is not good for plain eating (outside of overripe bananas), by the way, it is not great for fine baking, either. So make sound choices.

Here are some recommendations regarding ingredients for success with recipes in this book. More information on ingredients is given throughout the book via the tips and tricks in each chapter.

Flour

There are several common brands of all-purpose and bread flour—the primary flours used in this cookbook—on the market. There are those that are milled and treated traditionally (most recognizable national brands), as well as unbleached flours (naturally aged without bleaching agents) and organic flours made from wheat grown per the code of organic standards. Find a brand of flour that you prefer and that performs per your expectations.

Different wheat harvests produce slightly different flours. In response, flour companies aim to keep flours consistent by careful blending. That

Read the Recipe

To start, I advise you to first thoroughly read a recipe. It is the difference between good baking and superlative baking. It gives you the lay of the land, and surprises and glitches are minimized. Prepare all ingredients beforehand—this is the basic credo of my pastry-chef-in-training days, and it makes even more sense for a rushed, multi-tasking home baker. You will be amazed by how much more success great organization brings to your efforts. In addition, reading a recipe beforehand and having ingredients at the ready are small musts that make the whole endeavor calming, which in turn contributes to the final outcome.

said, some recipes, especially those for breads and sweet yeasted things, might require a bit more or less flour than the recipe specifies. Be somewhat flexible about this and learn by becoming accustomed to the dough or batter in different stages and by watching the results. Wherever possible, I have indicated what a dough or batter should look or feel like.

When measuring flour, I recommend whisking or stirring it a bit in its canister first; then simply scoop it using a metal dry measuring cup and level off the top. There's no need to sift it unless the recipe calls for sifting.

• **Unbleached All-Purpose Flour, Unbleached Bread Flour** Unless otherwise stated, all my recipes call for unbleached all-purpose flour, which is readily available in the supermarket. *Unbleached* means the flour is naturally aged (versus having been bleached with chemicals, a process that strengthens the flour as it hastens its aging). When flour is untreated, it naturally bleaches and matures, and many bakers prefer it so as not to include or ingest extra chemicals they don't need. Some bakers can actually *taste* the bleaching agent in flour.

Side by side, you can generally discern a subtle color difference between bleached and unbleached flours. I feel better knowing that the slightly creamier color of the unbleached flour comes from the flour's natural aging process.

When measuring flour, I recommend that you lightly whisk or stir it a bit in its canister first; then simply scoop the flour using a metal dry measuring cup and level it off.

Most flours, bleached or not, are enriched with vitamins and added nutrients. This is a good thing, for flour becomes a carrier for nutrients we need in our diet, as well as being the core baking ingredient.

When I bake breads, my recipes specifically call for unbleached bread flour. Freshly milled unbleached bread flour also needs to age before being used in baking in order for it to strengthen. If you cannot find unbleached bread flour, you can use regular enriched flour in these recipes and still have success.

• Whole Wheat Flour

You have a choice between using stone-ground or regular whole wheat flour, as well as white whole wheat flour. I prefer stone-ground whole wheat flour because it features all of the nutritious

whole wheat flour

components of "whole" wheat (the full wheat berry). Often, supermarket brands of regular whole wheat flour are simply white enriched flour with traces of bran added. In the industry, this is called "restored" whole wheat flour, meaning it is stripped of much of its goodness and then some of the bran is added back. It is a cosmetic sort of whole wheat flour, meaning it looks the part but it isn't nutritionally equal.

White whole wheat flour—available from *Hodgson Mill* or *King Arthur Flour*—is sweet, nutty, and nutrient dense. I like it for exactly these two traits: great taste *with* great nutrition. It is the perfect flour if you are encouraging your family to eat better without compromising taste. For bread, whole wheat flour (alone, or in part) is ideal, but when baking cookies, muffins, or scones—when you want the more tender mouthfeel and taste of white flour but with more nutrition—white whole wheat flour is the perfect choice. You can also experiment by replacing some white all-purpose flour with white whole wheat flour if you prefer the idea of adding fiber without affecting the taste.

• Spelt, Kamut, Rye, Cornmeal, and Multigrain Flours

Occasionally, recipes in this book call for flours other than all-purpose or whole wheat. Such flours as spelt and kamut usually come via organic companies because they are ancient grains and are not mainstream. For rye-based bread recipes, you can choose regular supermarket rye flour or organic; in either case, as with whole wheat flour,

rye flour

opt for stone-ground rye. It has all the good stuff of the rye berry and, consequently, just tastes better. The same choices for cornmeal, multigrain cereals, and mixed-grain flours also apply. You can choose organic varieties, but be sure to go with stone-ground. Rye flour is also sometimes referred to as pumpernickel flour.

Store rye flour (as well as any stone-ground flour or cornmeal) in the fridge or freezer because the oils in the bran of the rye berry hasten spoilage. As a general rule, unless you bake regularly with these flours, buy them in small amounts and store them up to three months.

Sweeteners

• White Sugar

Also known as granulated sugar, white sugar is the basic sweetener used throughout most of this book. Occasionally, my recipes call for superfine sugar. This is simply white sugar that is pulverized a bit finer in a food processor. To measure white sugar, just scoop it using a metal or plastic measuring cup for dry ingredients and level it off with a knife. Do not use a glass or liquid measuring cup with a pouring spout for dry ingredients, such as sugar, because it does not always measure the same.

• Brown Sugar: Light and Dark

Brown sugar is granulated sugar with traces of molasses in it. It offers a special flavor and a slight caramel kiss to baked goods. When called for, light brown sugar is usually the preferred choice, but dark will work if it is what you have. To measure light or dark brown sugar, scoop the sugar into a metal or plastic dry measuring cup and pat it down; this is known as *firmly packed*. Since brown sugar is a moist sugar and is coarser than white sugar, packing it down ensures that you have an accurate measurement.

• Confectioners' Sugar

Confectioners' sugar (or icing sugar, as it is called in Canada) is white sugar pulverized with cornstarch. It is used in butter-based icings or for dusting on top of cakes and pastries as a finishing touch. It also can be mixed with extract, food coloring, butter, and/or liquid (water, juice, coffee—per the recipe) if you are making a quick glaze or fondant. If you are whipping heavy cream, use confectioners' sugar instead of regular white sugar to whip a more stable cream.

• Honey

Honey helps baked goods brown, contributes to keeping baked goods extra moist, and offers a slight toffee/caramel/floral sweetness. When baking with honey, watch out for browning: The baked product can go from having a golden glow to being scorched very quickly. To measure honey, use a glass measuring cup sprayed with nonstick cooking spray. The cooking spray aids in easy release when pouring out sticky honey.

Baking Fats

• Butter

I use unsalted butter, also called sweet butter, in 90% of my baking, unless otherwise stated. Unsalted butter is considered the premium, freshest-quality, best butter choice available.

In home baking, unsalted butter is queen. Nothing tastes or performs quite like it. Butter choices available are salted, semi-salted, unsalted, and whipped, but the fat content is usually the same, regardless of the manufacturer. *Land O' Lakes, Cabot, Lurpak, Plugra,* and *Celles Sur Belle* all offer butter variations wherein the water and air contents are even less than what is in regular butter—and the bright taste is evident. If you can find a butter that advertises better baking, give it a shot. When you find unsalted butter on sale, stock up. It freezes well for months and is fine in the refrigerator for several weeks. I always keep several pounds in the freezer and about two pounds in the fridge.

In home baking, unsalted butter is queen. Nothing tastes or performs quite like this classic choice, prized for its pure flavor that sings through with utmost clarity.

cold butter, in chunks (in background); softened butter (in foreground)

Here is one of my favorite tips: Butter is typically softened and creamed with sugar as a basic step in baking cakes or cookies. This imports air and lightness into a recipe. But you can also often use melted butter, or, better yet, shredded butter, which is handy if you are baking against the clock and your block of butter is hard. Melted butter must be cooled, but then it can be blended with sugar in most recipes. The resulting baked item will be a touch less light, but this tip is a convenient option.

Butter is measured in cups for my recipes (not by sticks or by weight):

> **1 pound butter = 2 cups**
> **$\frac{1}{2}$ pound butter = 1 cup**
> **$\frac{1}{4}$ pound butter = $\frac{1}{2}$ cup**
> **$\frac{1}{8}$ pound butter = $\frac{1}{4}$ cup**

When a recipe calls for melted butter, allow the butter to cool down a few minutes before using it. I use the microwave to melt butter, heating in 1-minute increments on High power until the butter is melted.

Cold butter works best in scones, biscuits, and many pastries. Room-temperature butter is best for blending into cookies, cakes, and yeasted recipes.

• Oils: Canola, Vegetable, Corn, Olive, and Safflower

Unless otherwise stated, you can use canola or vegetable oil to replace butter in cakes, muffins, and quick loaves if you prefer. This might reduce concerns about dairy fats and increase the shelf life (foods made with oil last longer), but nothing is added as far as taste goes when using oil. Oil is not, however, a recommended replacement fat in scones, biscuits, pie dough, or most cookies.

Olive oil offers a distinct taste and is used, in either virgin or extra virgin varieties, in the pizzas and some of the breads in this book. I do not recommend olive oil for sweet baking, but you can use light olive oil to replace melted butter or vegetable or corn oil in some muffin and biscotti recipes.

• **Margarine** Margarine is the most evolving fat on the market, for manufacturers are forever reformulating margarine products according to tastes and nutritional studies. It is OK for toast, but it is rare that I use it for cooking and particularly not for baking. At the very least, it is unusual to find a hard (unwhipped) margarine that is also unsalted. Usually margarine is whipped (with air, water, chemicals, and emulsifiers) and is quite salty. Be aware that even stick margarine does not measure the same as a solid fat, such as butter, or a liquid fat, such as oil, because it is inflated with water and air. Overall, avoid margarine for baking unless it is necessary for dietary reasons.

• **Shortening** Shortening is a solid fat that is made from vegetable oil that has been hydrogenated. On occasion, it is recommended in pastry (such as in pie dough) or for doughnuts. The trans-fatty acids in shortening have been a health concern in recent years, but shortening, like margarine, has been improved and can be found without trans fat—read the labels closely. I do not use shortening often, except when I want a particularly flaky piecrust, and I generally use it in conjunction with butter even then.

Shortening can be stored for a year at room temperature; however, it is better to store shortening in the fridge. It is easier to cut and measure when it is cold, and it will be ready for use in pastry and pie dough.

Other Dairy Ingredients

• **Eggs** Eggs—which provide flavor, color, leavening, and tenderness to recipes—are part of the structure in baked goods. All recipes in this book call for large eggs. Results will not be the same using extra large, jumbo, or medium eggs. Brown or white eggs are both fine to use. You can also bake with the omega-3-enriched eggs now on the market. They perform well and provide a convenient way for people to improve their omega-3 intake and achieve better health. All baking profits from using room-temperature eggs because they whip up with maximum volume. Take them out of the refrigerator about 20 to 30 minutes before baking or dunk them in hot water in a bowl for a minute before cracking them open and using them in a recipe.

• **Milk** Whole milk is a regular companion in my kitchen, but you can use milk of any fat percentage without a discernable difference in flavor. Milk assists with browning and tenderizing in baked goods, and, as with all liquids in baking, it greatly expands the crumb of a cake, scone, or cookie. By *crumb,* we bakers refer to the interior texture and structure of anything from cakes to muffins to yeast breads. Milk is best used at room temperature in baking, so let it sit out 20 to 30 minutes, also.

• **Cream** Depending on the recipe, I use a variety of creams. I always specify which sort of cream, and it can be anything from half-and-half (what Canadians call light cream) to whipping cream to heavy whipping cream, which has a fat content of 36%. Because cream has more fat than milk, it is ideal in scones, tart doughs, cakes, and such applications as icings or ganache. Some creams, such as half-and-half or evaporated milk, can be substituted for each other; however, when a recipe calls for whipping cream, it is best to use that specific cream.

• **Buttermilk, Sour Milk, Sour Cream, Yogurt, and Buttermilk Powder** Buttermilk is one of the nicest additions to baking and plays a role in many of my recipes. Buttermilk was originally the liquid by-product of churning butter. It made for a refreshing drink on a hot day, but more often than not, it was dispatched into biscuits, cakes, and other sorts of baking, since the

The biggest myth about using buttermilk in baking is that you must mix it first with baking soda. Not true. Not necessary.

slightly acidic nature of this dairy product married well with baking soda to produce exceptional light and tender baked goods. Nowadays, buttermilk is made from skim milk, with a bacterial culture introduced to sour it. It still offers acidity—the better to interact with baking soda (which, in turn, helps bread rise). It also adds vitamins, calcium, and a subtle but tasty tang. If you don't have buttermilk on hand, you can use sour milk (1 cup of milk mixed with 1 tablespoon of lemon juice or white vinegar) or slightly liquidy plain yogurt.

Saco Foods offers all-natural, pure Buttermilk Blend, which is a dry, natural buttermilk powder that is also a fine substitute in recipes calling for buttermilk. Remember that buttermilk powder goes in with the flour, and you'll need to substitute water for the buttermilk in the recipe (conversion is ¼ cup buttermilk powder and 1 cup water to replace 1 cup of real buttermilk).

The biggest myth about using buttermilk in baking is that you must mix it first with baking soda. That advice came from the old days, when baking soda was coarse and hardly the consistent fine powder it is today. The step of stirring soda into buttermilk helped break up the soda in those early days. Of course, that is no longer necessary, but that old counsel is often still seen, even in some contemporary buttermilk-based recipes. All this does, actually, is start the leavening action instantly (you can see the buttermilk foam), and you lose that precious leavening before the buttermilk is even incorporated into your batter. For the best results, my recipes call for baking soda to go in with the dry ingredients rather than with the buttermilk.

Sour cream and plain yogurt are interchangeable in most recipes, although sour cream offers far more fat (unless it is a low- or no-fat variety) than standard yogurt. Yogurt and buttermilk are also interchangeable; both are similar in

fat content and in how loose they are (versus sour cream, which is considerably thicker). All three are acidic dairy products that perform in similar ways, offering that subtle but characteristic tang and helping cakes, muffins, and quick breads to rise.

Leaveners

There are many things that help baked goods to rise: steam, air, chemicals (baking soda and powder), gas (produced by yeast), and eggs (which provide expansion as well as structure in a recipe). Some recipes use one leavener, and some use a combination. Here are the basics.

• **Yeast** Yeast is better, more powerful, and more reliable than ever. Dry yeast is easily available, and you have choices of instant (also known as bread machine, rapid-rise, and quick-rise) or active dry yeast, as well as fresh yeast.

All my recipes use rapid-rise yeast. If you prefer active dry yeast, you can use it with no change in the recipe method; just expect a 15% to 30% longer rise. *Fleischmann's Yeast* and *Red Star Yeast* are most commonly available, or you can use yeast from *Saf* or *Fermipan,* both available from specialty bakery-supply online catalogues or at local bakery suppliers.

Rapid-rise yeast is good for all baking and is especially helpful in sweet yeast baking, as it is more resilient and tolerant of mishandling or contact with fat or sugar.

Rapid-rise yeast can be mixed with the flour, as the package directions specify, but I prefer to mix the yeast with the warm water of the recipe. The water needs to be slightly warmer than room temperature (100°F to 110°F).

Rapid-rise yeast rules in my recipes. The best feature: It can tolerate inexperience.

You only need to mix the yeast and water together to hydrate the yeast, not wait for it to proof as you do with active dry yeast.

Since my recipes call for varying amounts of yeast, it is easier to buy it in jars or one-pound brick packs instead of the traditional packets that hold about 2½ teaspoons of yeast. Store unused yeast in the fridge in a well-sealed container. It lasts three to four months.

Yeast is not as mysterious as some people think, but its primary enemies are direct contact with icy-cold ingredients, whether it be cold water, milk, or refrigerated butter, or sugar or salt. If you whisk the warm water and yeast together and then promptly and briskly add these other things, there should be no problem. However, a neat trick is to mix the water and yeast and then cover the mixture immediately with 1 cup of flour from the recipe as a "shield" to protect it from the onslaught of these potential foes.

Find more on yeast in "Loaves, Large & Small" (beginning on page 29).

• **Baking Powder** Baking powder is essentially baking soda mixed with an acid and some cornstarch as a carrier. Once baking powder is mixed with a liquid, its rising action (leavening) begins. Continuous action, or the "second action" (hence the term *double acting* on the can), ensues with the heat of the oven.

Baking powder should be as fresh as it can be. To ascertain whether baking powder is fresh, mix 1 teaspoon baking powder with ½ cup warm water and 1 teaspoon lemon juice. The mixture should immediately start to bubble and foam. If it doesn't, the baking powder is no longer active, and it is time to buy a new can.

All recipes in this book were tested with *Clabber Girl, Rumford, Davis,* or *Magic* baking powder (available in Canada). Since baking powder is an integral product in baking, buy a brand name you know will guarantee consistent results. Unopened baking powder usually has a six-month shelf life; once opened, it is optimal for about three months.

Salt is the 'little black dress' of baking in terms of how essential and effective it is.

• **Baking Soda** Unlike baking powder—which is a combination of cornstarch, baking soda, and an acid—baking soda is simply one element: soda. It is called for when there is more than the usual acid in a recipe than the baking powder alone can neutralize (like when the recipe calls for buttermilk, for example). Some recipes, such as soda breads and some cookies, only rely on baking soda. Baking soda does not lose potency over time like baking powder does. A can of baking soda includes an expiration date, but, technically speaking, there is no past-due date. The real threat is using baking soda that has ingested odors over a period of time or using baking soda that has been used for deodorizing your fridge. And if you taste a soapy or "off" taste in your baking, chances are you have used too much baking soda.

Flavorings

• **Salt** Salt is used to counterbalance the sweetness in a recipe or to enliven dough that is otherwise bland. In yeast doughs, salt not only offers flavor but also contributes to browning and performs a crucial role in regulating a steady, sedate rise of the dough.

Salt is a somewhat humble ingredient, yet it has maximum impact on a recipe. People sometimes regard it as unimportant, yet too much or too little salt vastly affects a recipe. If you can, find fine kosher salt in supermarkets or online. Kosher salt is an iodine-free, lightly salty, pure salt that is ideal for baking. Regular table salt is saltier than kosher salt and has a telltale taste of iodine. It, as well as fine sea salt, does the job, but nothing beats kosher salt in quality home baking. But even with kosher salt, brands differ. Taste it before using it in baking. Salt, as much as any other ingredient, must be measured accurately.

• **Vanilla** Another core ingredient and a default flavor note in baking is vanilla. What you want in vanilla is

Pure vanilla, like true love, changes everything for the good.

its purity but also a warm, resounding, full flavor. I recommend using pure vanilla, specifically *Nielsen-Massey Vanillas,* available in some supermarkets, gourmet stores, or online. *McCormick* is another fine brand. The definition of *pure, natural,* and *artificial* in the vanilla industry is a heated subject. Suffice it to say—and this is so important—the flavor of artificial vanilla is not subtle. Moreover, when freezing baked goods, items baked with artificial vanilla can go "off" in flavor, as opposed to goods made with pure vanilla, which stays true. Pure vanilla, like great coffee beans, can have up and down years as per crops and pricing, but it is one more linchpin in quality home baking. My sons, who are discerning tasters, can easily detect when I have used inferior vanilla.

• **Other Flavors and Extracts** Orange, lemon, tangerine, and lime oils are fairly new and vibrant flavorings in the marketplace. *Boyajian* is a leading citrus-oil company offering all-natural, intense citrus oils. If you use oils, use half as much as you would use of extracts. *McCormick, Nielsen-Massey Vanillas, Boyajian,* and

other companies offer wonderful, pure extracts that—as much as fresh orange juice, lemon zest, or toasted almonds—lend yet another flavor dimension to baked goods. Use the finest quality extracts you can find. I recommend using almond, orange, and lemon extracts often in baking. Use them in conjunction with vanilla or on their own for added taste dimension, depending on the recipe.

• **Chocolate** Dark, semisweet, and bittersweet chocolate are the most common chocolates used in baking. These *real* chocolates contain at least 35% chocolate liquor and 27% cocoa butter. Because they are sold under a variety of names, including special dark, dark sweet, and German sweet, buying them can be confusing. Tasting them is the best way to become familiar with brands of choice for baking.

Unsweetened chocolate is pure chocolate, without any added sugar or vanilla. By and large, recipes that call for unsweetened chocolate can also be made with semisweet chocolate without adjusting the recipe. Those baked goods will be a wee bit sweeter.

On the other hand, never substitute unsweetened chocolate for bittersweet or semisweet chocolate in a recipe.

Milk chocolate contains less chocolate liquor, as it also contains added sugar, milk, and vanilla.

White chocolate does not contain any pure chocolate liquor. Instead, it is made with cocoa butter or fat, milk, and sugar. While it is called white chocolate, it is more accurately defined as a chocolate confectionary product. It has its own place in the baker's chocolate repertoire and is a great boost in many recipes. The words white chocolate simply sound divine and the taste is unparalleled in baking, offering a smooth, mellow bouquet.

White chocolate in particular is quite tricky to melt. *Callebaut, Lindt,* and *Valrhona* are recommended brands. White chocolate disks from confectionary-supply stores may melt easily, but they have very little taste and are not really chocolate.

Chocolate chips—whether semisweet, milk, or white chocolate—should be real chocolate. Make sure you pick up a package marked as real chocolate, not "chocolate-flavored" chips. You can also use chopped chocolate in baking, upgrading a typical chocolate chip cookie. That said, *Nestlé, Hershey's,* and *Baker's* do an admirable job whenever chocolate chips are called for.

Butterscotch or caramel chips are largely artificially flavored baking chips. They, along with cinnamon, toffee, and mint chips, are fun and tasty additions in your baking, much like raisins or nuts are.

Melt chocolate slowly in a glass bowl in the microwave (20 to 30 seconds at a time) at Medium power or in a small bowl set over simmering water. Slow and steady is the rule for properly melted chocolate—especially in the case of white chocolate, which can be quite a prima donna. Stir to cool before adding it to a recipe to keep it from melting the butter or cooking the eggs in the recipe. For melting all types of chocolate, make sure no water or steam comes into contact with the chocolate, or it will seize.

• **Cocoa** Cocoa powder is a pure chocolate product that has no added milk, sugar, or vanilla and contains no cocoa fat. To me, it makes little difference whether you use cocoa with alkali treatment in it (otherwise known as Dutched or Dutch process) or untreated (non-Dutch cocoa), although Dutch cocoa generally produces darker-hued chocolate cakes. Some also purport (as I do) a subtler but distinct pure chocolate taste when using Dutch-process cocoa.

Measure cocoa by first stirring it only slightly in its container to break up any big clumps; then scoop, measure, and level it off. Generally, you will add cocoa to the dry ingredients of a recipe, whisking with a hand whisk to blend it into the flour and leaveners. See my trick for making chocolate paste using cocoa powder on page 230.

• **Nuts and Dried Fruit** As with all ingredients—but particularly with nuts—taste before you use them. Fatty and natural, nuts can turn rancid before they ever arrive in your pantry for baking. Store nuts in the freezer six months to one year. Toast nuts lightly for best flavor.

Dried fruit varies in quality; for the most part, however, dried fruit—be it dried cherries, cranberries, or apricots—profits from being allowed to plump in boiling water for several minutes before being added to a recipe. To use, drain, dry fruit well, and then proceed.

Plumping Dried Fruit

In all my recipes using dried fruit, the term *plumped and dried* means to cover the fruit, such as raisins, with very hot water and let the fruit stand 5 to 10 minutes; then drain and pat dry with paper towels before using in a recipe.

• **Spices** Buy high-quality fresh ground spices in small amounts and taste or smell them before adding them to a fresh batch of scones or cookies or to a fruitcake. There are many places to find specialty spices (see "Source Guide"), but never assume that all brands of cinnamon, cloves, or allspice are equal. Spices are not only why Columbus ended up discovering America, but they are also the core of superb home baking, as are all other baking essentials. Store spices in the freezer or otherwise sealed and away from heat and light in your kitchen.

baker's caramel

Miscellaneous Ingredients

• **Baker's Caramel** Also known as **blackjack,** baker's caramel consists mainly of burnt sugar and water and is used to add color and a depth of flavor to foods. Recipes for pumpernickel bread, for example, often call for baker's caramel. It is available from *Golda's Kitchen* (see "Source Guide") or some professional bakery suppliers. It lasts seemingly forever and it is essential for my Christmas Black Cake ("Holiday Baking," page 283). Store it at room temperature in your pantry.

• **Malt Powder** This light beige powder comes from dried barley. It is also referred to as malt flour. Malt adds a tiny flavor boost and aids in coloring breads and such rustic items as bagels. It is my secret ingredient in homemade pancake and waffle mixes. It is not imperative in my recipes, but it does add that special professional taste we associate with artisan bakeries. It is available at health-food stores and online from *King Arthur Flour.* Beer-brewing stores offer liquid malt syrup; if you find that, use unhopped malt syrup in the same quantity as dry malt powder.

• **Nonstick Cooking Spray** There are a few cooking sprays on the market: *Baker's Joy,* and, of course, *Pam* (sprays with and without flour in them). I recommend you forgo the domestic route in this case and head online or to a bakery-supply store for *Everbake.* It offers excellent release and is what the pros use. It tends not to deposit a shortening or butter-and-flour greasy buildup that, while invisible, compromises the whole release of cakes and breads. And the greasy buildup is close to impossible to wash off metal, especially nonstick bakeware. Cooking spray plays a major role in one of my baker's tricks for breads: Spray rising breads with cooking spray to keep the breads moist as they rise without adding undue fat to their surface. I also find it helpful to spray zip-top plastic bags with cooking spray before storing dough in the bags.

Some favorite equipment—Marcy's tapered rolling pin, a Danish dough whisk, a metal brownie pan, an offset spatula, and stacked baking sheets lined with parchment and ready for baking.

Equipment

Bakeware

Consider all sorts of bakeware sizes and shapes for well-rounded baking. Your local restaurant-supply store is the best bet to find bakeware, second to your favorite gourmet kitchen-supply store and then such places as the housewares section of *Wal-Mart, Kmart,* and *Sears,* etc. In "Source Guide" on page 316, you will find places to mail order specialty bakeware if you do not have a comprehensive retail store near you. For exclusive or hard-to-find items, online retailers are the way to go. *All-Clad Metalcrafters,* renowned for their incredible cookware, has a superb line of bakeware that offers durability, performance, design, and aesthetics. There is little finer in basic bakeware pans, nor any style that lasts as long or needs as little care as *All-Clad. Chicago Metallic* and *ECKO* bakeware, available through some of the mail-order references in "Source Guide," are also good choices.

Metal bakeware is most often offered in aluminum, glazed commercial aluminum, anodized aluminum, and varieties of nonstick finishes on metal. I prefer glazed commercial aluminum. It is not pretty, but it is durable and solid and offers great results.

Anodized bakeware is a chemically treated aluminum genre of bakeware that features a slightly dull finish. It touts nonstick attributes, but this is not always the case. It has only some of the nonstick properties of true nonstick bakeware and some of the qualities (even heat distribution) of aluminum, glazed or not. Being somewhat dark cast, anodized

rimmed baking sheets

loafpan lined with parchment

brownie pans

bakeware also can promote undue browning of many baked goods.

Nonstick bakeware ranges greatly in price and type of manufacture. It offers unrivaled easy release, but being dark hued (most times) there is a tendency for it to darken the crust of cakes, bars, or squares and to produce a hard crust. For specialty shaped pans (Bundt and other fluted pans), nonstick would seem like a great idea because of the release factor, but do be careful not to produce overly browned baked goods. To prevent this, place all nonstick pans on doubled-up baking sheets, with the top sheet lined with parchment paper.

Glass or *Pyrex* bakeware is good for seeing how the baking is moving along (such as on the bottom of a pie), but you do have to remember to reduce the oven temperature by 25°F if the original recipe specifies a pan. And take care that the product, once baked, does not "sweat" in the dish. Anytime baked goods sweat (as with *Pyrex* and/or when items are not properly cooled on a wire rack), this can promote premature staling of baked goods. I do like *Pyrex* bakeware for deep-dish pies and for its nostalgic appeal, easy washup, and affordability.

Baking Pans

I recommend metal bakeware in general. For most recipes, the newer silicone bakeware is fine (super for gelatin molds and meat loaves), but the lack of structural rigidity on most of them calls for more careful handling. In addition, release is great with this bakeware, but browning is not.

Well-selected bakeware is at the center of the overall investment toward quality home baking. You will find the experience of simply handling finely crafted bakeware makes baking a pleasure.

Essential Bakeware

For flexibility in your baking, collect the following pans:

4 large baking sheets (21" x 15" or 18" x 10") Make sure these fit your oven. This is what is meant by large baking sheets. I recommend baking sheets with rimmed edges.

4 (15" x 10") jellyroll pans As above, these are pans with rimmed edges that are commonly used as baking sheets.

- 1 (13" x 9") rectangular pan
- 1 (9" x 9") square pan
- 2 (9") piepans or pieplates
- 1 (9") springform pan
- 1 (10") springform pan
- 1 (9" or 10") deep-dish quiche pan

1 (12" x 5") loafpan This is a commercial-sized pan and can be found at professional baker-supply stores. This is an essential size to have in making large family-sized loaves of bread or yeasted coffee cakes.

- 2 (9" x 5") loafpans
- 2 (8" x 4") loafpans
- 1 (9" or 10") tube pan
- 1 (9" or 10") angel food cakepan
- 1 Bundt pan (12 cups) or
  (9" to 10") fluted cakepan
- 2 or 3 (9") round cakepans

• Other Pans Various other loaf sizes and shapes, including miniature 5" x 3½" loafpans

Various dollar-store round cakepans and springform pans (which come in smaller sizes for mini cheesecakes), and other decorative pans

Foil (disposable) loafpans and novelty pans for the holidays. Such companies as *Nordic Ware* and *Wilton* offer great options for whimsical baking pans for seasonal use.

• Angel Food Cakepan This is a high-sided pan with a center tube that bakes up lofty cakes and is also good for yeasted items, such as bubka. Avoid the models with removable bottoms—they sometimes leak. I prefer angel food cakepans instead of tube pans for the high-standing cakes they yield. Given the choice, I prefer angel food pans over Bundt or other fluted pans for their ease of release and overall height. But, of course, a Bundt pan is beloved for its festive shape and that "aura" of a Bundt cake. Standard measures are 9- or 10-inch angel food cakepans. Aluminum angel food pans, in conjunction with a generous coating of nonstick cooking spray, are ideal.

• Springform Pans Look for heavy-duty aluminum models that either feature a clip on their "collar" or a push-up bottom pan. The best odd-sized cheesecake pans for the price are often found at the dollar store. I keep tons of new ones in various odd sizes on hand, for I use them often, aware that they do not last but will be fine for a few months. No matter which pan, batter leakage can occur. If you suspect your pan might leak batter, wrap the exterior snugly in foil (shown below), especially if baking a cheesecake in a water bath. Springform pans are also wonderful replacements for 13- x 9-inch pans, turning a low-slung coffee cake into a pretty round affair.

springform pan wrapped in foil

• Deep-Dish Quiche Pan This 9-inch fluted pan can be hard to find, but *Beryl's Cake Decorating & Pastry Supplies* furnishes them, as does *Golda's Kitchen* in Canada. Usually imported from Germany or France and made of nickel or tin, this pan is deep (about 3 inches) and also works for coffee cakes, cheesecakes, and tarts. It also offers instant nice edges to pastries if you are uneasy about shaping them. A holiday pecan pie is gorgeous in this pan (see page 272).

• **Loafpans** I prefer commercial pans that have a special commercial coating or glaze on them. These pans offer great release, and their heavy weight helps them bake thoroughly without scorching. Look for such brands as *Lockwood, ECKO,* and *Chicago Metallic,* all marketing pans made of reinforced steel and aluminum or reinforced steel and tin. Smaller loafpans are used for quick breads or small yeasted breads; larger loaves are great for family-sized breads and coffee cakes.

Small Wares

• **Muffin Pans** Heavy-duty professional muffin pans coated with industrial glaze are best. Second to that, nonstick muffin pans are recommended if you use paper liners, which ensure release. With liners, the muffin batter is not in direct contact with the dark finish, which otherwise could make the muffins brown too fast or cause their bottoms to get slightly crusty.

There is not much standard in muffin pans—even a regular pan varies in the cup dimension of the muffin wells. If you have extra batter, put it into another pan, using the outer cups instead of the center ones, where more heat congregates. Keep an assortment of mini, standard, and Texas-sized muffin pans to vary the size of your muffins. You might want lots of little muffins for a potluck supper or as a pretty gift, or you might prefer large Texas-sized muffins to impress.

Texas-sized muffin pan

• **Piepans or Plates** Aluminum is one of the most ideal materials for piepans. It might not be pretty, but it features a retro diner appeal and is great for even heat distribution and overall pastry browning. Especially pretty ceramic piepans are available from *Emile Henry* from France, *Le Creuset,* and *Chantal Cookware.* If you can find it, my first choice is tin-coated graniteware, with its speckled-color enamel. Pie tins are fun bakeware to collect, and a range of sizes and types will suit all

heavy-duty cutter

your baking needs, as well as provide a simple, cheery pie presentation. Glass pieplates offer a great view of a browning crust, but I tend to use *Pyrex* ware either for cobblers and deep-dish pies or for general cooking.

Baking Tools

• **Cookie, Doughnut, and Biscuit Cutters** *Matfer Bourgeat, Inc.* from France; *Wilton;* and *Ateco* offer nested cookie-cutter sets. They all stock a plain-edged cutter set and a serrated-edge cutter set, both in nine nested sizes. It is good to have both plain-edged cutters and serrated ones. *Rochow* cutters, from the *Rochow Swirl Mixer Company, Inc.* in Rochester, New York, are the best choice for heavy-duty biscuit cutters as well as well-stylized gingerbread men, teddy bear, scone, doughnut, and heart cutters.

• **Knives** Cooking requires a bevy of knives; baking demands but a few flatware essentials. You need an 8-inch chef's knife, an 8- to 10-inch bread knife, a thin serrated knife (for slicing cake layers), a regular straight-edged paring knife, and a curved bird's beak paring knife. *Cutco* makes the best long serrated slicing knife (ideal for 1,001 pastry and baker's tasks); *Cutco* and *LamsonSharp* offer very fine paring knives and chef's knives. A good-quality knife, which needs a certain heft and a full tang, is made of fine-grade stainless or carbon steel. Have your knives sharpened by a professional every four to six months. Between visits to the pro, keep your knives in shape by honing them on a knife steel.

• **Measuring Spoons** Look for long-handled measuring spoons that enable you to reach into cans without your hands getting in the way. Dishwasher-proof stainless steel keeps its gleam and usually features strong handles that will not bend with repeated use.

Just double up on a few sets so that when you are doing a lot of baking you won't have to dig around in the sink or dishwasher for your one-and-only set.

• **Measuring Cups** Use glass or plastic measuring cups with a pouring spout for liquid measures (such as honey, milk, water, and oil) and nested metal or plastic measuring cups for dry ingredients.

• **Professional Scoops** For best results, scoop muffins into muffin pans using a professional ice-cream scoop, which you can find at any restaurant-supply store or kitchen-supply store. This simple tool gives a rounded finish to muffins and is what muffin-shop owners use. Note that scoops are calibrated by a number indicating how many portions of ice cream per quart they furnish. For example, a #16 scoop produces 16 scoops of

ice cream per quart. Scoops can be as large as a 10 or 12 or go down to a melon-baller size of 80 or 100 (excellent for cookies and meatballs). Sizes 12, 14, and 16 are good choices for standard muffins.

• **Rolling Pins** A good rolling pin is a baker's best friend, but it needn't cost the earth. I like a tapered pin without ball bearings (a French rolling pin)—so much so that I designed my own, called the *Cuisine d'Or French* tapered rolling pin. See the "Source Guide" for ordering information. A tapered pin without handles is ideal for pie doughs, pastries, and cookies; a tapered pin gives you more control over the dough. Larger pins are the best choice for working with yeasted doughs or heavier loads of cookies. Pins from *Thorpe* or *Vic Firth Gourmet, Inc.* are about the best options in ball-bearing pins. I like both styles of

Home bakers tend to reach for a wooden spoon, but a whisk is often the better choice for a lion's share of work in our kitchens.

tapered rolling pin for evenly rolled dough

balloon whisks and Danish dough whisk

pins for almost all jobs and recommend you have at least one of each. Make sure that the ball-bearing model is 15 inches, not 12 inches, wide. You need that width so that your knuckles do not get entrenched in the dough you are rolling. Kids, of course, can use a 12-inch pin. A higher price usually indicates a better-quality wood, such as dense northern maple versus softer imported boxwood. Better wood in a well-crafted pin pays for itself in its naturally nonsticking attributes. Porous soft-wood rolling pins can stick unduly to the dough, fat, or flour, or else they absorb these things.

dough scraper

• **Whisks** Home bakers tend to reach for a wooden spoon, but a whisk is an underutilized, indispensable tool as well. It's a good idea to stock a few sizes of oblong and balloon-shaped whisks. Domestic whisks are fine, but I recommend such commercial ones as *Best,* which are easy to find, and *Vollrath.* These whisks are marked as approved by the NSF (formerly National Sanitation Foundation), meaning that batters will not clog the whisk tines (clogging leads to the formation of bacteria)—a very good attribute to look for. You can use a whisk for any number of tasks—to blend dry ingredients, an egg wash, or a glaze and to help chocolate melt evenly.

• **Danish Dough Whisk** This utensil, which looks like an old-fashioned rug beater, has a flat wired configuration on the end of a wooden stick. This is the ideal tool for blending quick breads and carrot cake batter or for pulling together scones or blending muffin batter. It works best with gloppy or heavy batters, since the

citrus zester

batter falls between the wide wires instead of getting caught as it would in a fine balloon whisk. *Danesco* imports these from Denmark, and they are usually available from *Golda's Kitchen, King Arthur Flour,* and *Hodgson Mill* online stores.

• **Dough Scraper** A dough scraper, also known as a bench cutter, is a basic tool that becomes a wonder tool. It is used for cutting dough into sections, for dividing scones, and, finally, for scraping a work surface clean of dough. Dough scrapers feature plastic, wood, or urethane handles and a wide metal blade that has an edge but is not as sharp as a knife. Like whisks, NSF dishwasher-safe dough scrapers are especially handy, but you can keep a few types on hand. Like measuring spoons, you will use this blade often, so have a backup or two.

• **Zesters**

You can use a traditional citrus zester as shown below to produce long shreds and follow up with a chef's knife to finely mince the zest, or you can use the fine-toothed side of a box grater. There is also a newer item on the market—a long sticklike affair with fine slots on it—called a Microplane® (originally known as a rasp). I prefer a true citrus zester for zest, but I rely on the Microplane for grating chocolate and hard cheese. Whichever zester you choose, a good-quality one is essential. Price point is generally an indicator of quality, performance, and durability. *Lee Valley Tools Ltd.* is said to be the inventor of the Microplane, and they sell some of the best.

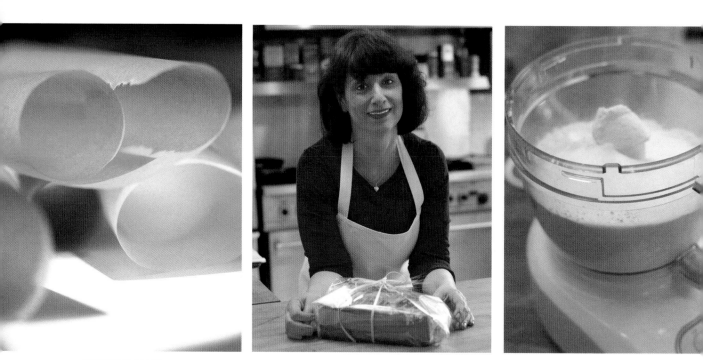

parchment paper

food processor

• **Parchment Paper** This heatproof paper is essential to consistent quality baking. It is available at gourmet shops, some supermarkets, and via mail order. I happen to get mine in stacks of 1,000 sheets through a bakery supplier in a size that fits my baking sheets. This is worth stocking up on and makes the difference between scorched bottoms and not; rolled edges on cookies and thin, ragged edges; and most importantly, messy baking sheets to clean versus none. (Parchment is different from wax paper, which smokes in the oven if used to line baking sheets.)

• **Baking Mats** These are synthetic, burnproof, heatproof mats available in different sizes that many bakers use to line baking sheets. While expensive, they are durable and indisputably nonstick. That said, you would have to invest in several of these to ensure you have enough on hand for a big baking session. Although many pros prefer these, I prefer to use parchment paper.

• **Paper Products** Avid bakers like to share the fruits of their labor. If you're going to bake well, plan to present well. Leave the foil, cling wrap, and plastic tubs at home. Visit a kitchen- or bakery-supply house or check your local phone book or warehouse store; then stock up on commercial cake boxes, cellophane bags, wax paper sheets, and other odds and ends. Your baked goods will look far better dressed up. Add a ribbon and a gift or business card, and you have a gift like no other. *Sweet Celebrations* is a good source for these items, as are warehouse shopping outlets and party centers. You can also find paper muffin liners and parchment paper from this source.

• **Plastic Bags (for rising bread dough)** Large, clear trash or leaf bags, available in supermarkets, are indispensable for proofing bread doughs. They are large enough to drape over an entire mixer, making your mixer into a home proofer or proofing tent. Although these bags are not designed for food or officially considered "food-grade" plastic, I carefully place them over my mixer so that they never have direct contact with the dough. More recently, *Ziploc* introduced extra-large resealable bags, which might also fit over your mixer. They are also more durable. Otherwise, plastic wrap works fine to loosely cover and protect a rising dough.

Appliances

• **Stand Mixers** I test many mixers and always return to *KitchenAid* simply because of its design, capacity, and reliability, as well as being assured that the company stands behind its products. However, there are other great mixers out there—*Kenwood, Hamilton Beach, Viking,* and *Jenn-Air.* Look for a model you like, but make sure the work bowl is at least a 5-quart capacity. The largest *KitchenAid* is a whopping 6-quart machine, which does great work with double batches of cookies and cakes and comfortably kneads the largest of doughs. You can also check out a 7-quart *Kenwood* or *Viking.* This is wonderful added capacity, but on days when you are making a small batch of cookies, it is a less optimal work bowl, since much of the batter stays clustered in the center well.

A 5-quart mixer is a wonderful all-purpose machine. For frequent, well-rounded bakers, however, I would advise the 6-quart *KitchenAid.* There are various references to wattages in mixers, but in my experience, wattage generally does not play out as faster, stronger, or more durable in home baking performance. Choose the style and capacity you prefer.

• **Food Processors** *KitchenAid* offers 7-cup, 9-cup, and 12-cup models. Most other brands are around an 8- to 10-cup capacity. Most of the recipes in this book depend on a machine with a larger bowl. If you have a smaller-capacity machine, you might have to divide the recipe in half and process things in two batches.

If you are considering your first machine or a new one, the 12-cup is the only way to go. It makes pureeing soups a snap, too. I also use a food processor to make many types of icing; it is less messy than a mixer, and it frees your mixer to prepare the cake, but you can only do all this providing your processor has a decent capacity. When you have smaller amounts to work with, even a large processor handles that job more than adequately. *KitchenAid* machines are about the easiest to use in baking, and their larger machines are invaluable for scones and pie dough. *Cuisinart* makes superb food processors, though I still find the safe but cumbersome feed tube impedes my baking efforts. The quality, however, is unrivaled, as is the sheer stability of the machine on the counter. *Viking* is another fine choice; other brands, such as *Braun* and *Hamilton Beach* offer good starter machines for the price. If you buy a top-of-the-line machine to begin with, a processor will serve you for years to come, offering durability, capacity, and reliability. Few people appreciate how a food processor is as much help to a baker as a stand mixer.

• **Bread Machines** I only use and recommend bread machines for preparing and rising dough, and they do a grand job for such. I prefer *Zojirushi* for its performance and quiet ways; *Cuisinart* also has a good-quality machine. Almost any 1½- to 2-pound bread machine will nicely knead or handle a dough.

• **Ovens** Real bakers don't need tons of bells and whistles with their ranges. They want capacity and reliability in a basic heat source. My recommendation is to go for the largest double oven you can afford that fits in your kitchen—good if it is electric, better if it is gas (it heats faster), and convection only if you can turn off the fan. The convection option seems to bake things marginally faster—but it seems to toughen the exterior or outer crust of many baked goods and/or impede browning. A good oven—any new oven, in fact—has a naturally convective interior by design, and that, with proper calibration, should ensure even and equitable air flow, whether the range you have is commercial or domestic. Domestic models, in their attempt to look and act more commercial, are improving. They are prettier, come in colors, and feature options like a convection warming oven. Commercial ranges, in their attempt to be more domestic, are evolving. Overall, the difference in a great-quality double oven—gas or electric, domestic or restaurant grade—is more narrow than it has ever been. Don't debate if you need two ovens or one; if you can fit in two, get them. The first time you host a dinner and want to serve bread *and* a pie, you will bless the two ovens.

Bakers really require the extra space and enjoy the sense of ease that a double oven provides.

loaves, large & small

There's no other way to say it: Bread is beautiful. It calls for modest ingredients; responds to care, time, and a modicum of baking expertise; and yields something that nurtures, nourishes, and inspires beyond its simple beginnings. All baking has spirit, but bread is truly soul food.

For all its grandeur, bread is four simple things: flour, water, yeast, and salt. Sometimes, you add sugar or butter, oil, honey, raisins, or chunks of cheese. Sometimes, you mix the dough with yeast, and it rises, it falls, and then you shape and bake it. Other times, you create sourdough or "sponge"-based doughs for breads that take longer rises and often have more interesting crumbs, incredible crusts, and a fragrance that will bring anyone to the kitchen with just one whiff.

One needs to let go of the notion that inexperience in bread baking equals difficulty. Instead, expect an awesome adventure with the same rises and falls as bread itself. You can have lofty loaves or ones that are flatter and denser but still fresh and wholesome—each one gently pushing you on your way to better breads.

A great tip to remember is that you can stop and restart the yeast-bread process along the way simply by covering the dough and tucking it into the fridge to retard the rise. Beyond that, there are handy things to assist and give the home baker options, such as faster-rising yeast, oversized mixers with newly designed dough hooks, and bread machines.

What *is* the myth concerning bread's mystery? It is largely about two things: how yeast works and how bread rises. Read all about yeast and flour in "Ingredients," beginning on the following page. All the skinny on bread will not only help you produce the best loaves ever, but the information will also apply to small breads and buns, pizza, and sweet yeast breads in the chapters that follow.

How does bread really become bread? Flour and water are worked until gluten (the latent elasticity in flour) is developed and you have dough with body. Yeast induces fermentation, or rise, which expands the dough, creating volume and structure. Once baked, the structure is set, and you have bread. Each of the simple elements has its role in creating this magic.

Ingredients

Water

Unless otherwise stated, water temperature should be warm: 100°F to 110°F. Cold water inhibits yeast, and water that is too hot might kill it.

If you have spring water on hand, it is preferable to tap water. Spring water generally does not contain bleach or fluorides and other chemicals used in tap water that might interfere with yeast activity. Moreover, spring water tastes better. That said, tap water is fine to use if that is your only source.

Yeast

• **Rapid-Rise Yeast** All yeast-based bread recipes in this book, unless otherwise stated, call for rapid-rise dry yeast (also known as quick-rise yeast, instant yeast, and bread machine yeast). Rapid-rise yeast is a new generation of yeast that is valued for its heartiness and consistent performance. It is especially resilient in that it can tolerate poor handling, which includes changes in temperature, using cold or hot water, and having too much fat or sugar in the recipe. These are all things that can impede otherwise great bread and that active dry yeast or fresh yeast might balk at.

Rapid-rise yeast comes in packets, usually packed in threes, or in 4-ounce jars; sometimes you can find it in vacuum "bricks" of about

1 pound. Once opened, you must refrigerate dry yeast, tightly sealed in a jar or container until you need it again. It lasts about three to four months in the fridge. You do not have to freeze it. *Fleischmann's* and *Red Star* (available in the U.S.) and *Eagle, Fermipan, Lallemand,* and *Saf* (available in Canada) each offer a version of rapid-rise yeast. Their products are available in the baking aisle of supermarkets; you can also find them at baking-supply Web sites (see "Source Guide," page 316), which supply commercial versions of their yeast products.

Although rapid-rise yeast manufacturers customarily advise bakers to mix their yeast with the flour called for in a recipe, I prefer to "waken" the yeast by mixing it with the water called for in a recipe. There are a few reasons for this. Yeast naturally wakes up best with direct contact with water. It will indeed "wake up" once a dough is moistened by adding water to the flour, salt, and yeast mix. Yeast most clearly dissolves, swells, and becomes fully activated when it is in direct contact with warm water. However, once instant yeast is hydrated, it does not particularly foam or bubble as active dry yeast does. Not to worry.

Secondly, yeast prefers a bit of warmth, and warm water provides exactly that.

I also believe how you handle yeast should be consistent, whether you are making sourdough bread or traditional loaves. The consistency of the yeast/water marriage, especially in a home kitchen, makes sense and just seems "right." Will your bread be fine if you add yeast to the flour? Certainly—the new yeast has been tested in a variety of ways, and they all work.

Though rapid-rise yeast recipes only need one rising, I still give my recipes two risings for end results that have a better crumb and texture and a longer shelf life.

How Yeast Works

When mixed with water and flour, dry yeast munches on the sugars present in the flour-water alliance (which, in turn, is the dough) and, in that fusion, creates carbon dioxide gas, which leavens (rises) the bread. Once baked, the taste of the gas is gone, but the structural transformation remains. It is sort of like a helium-filled balloon, wherein the helium disappears, but magically, you are left with the balloon structure. Now, if perchance you leave yeast to snack away too long during the rise, the yeast will turn on itself. The result is bread that either does not rise or has a telltale characteristic beery odor or simply smells too yeasty. In any case, if in doubt, a slight underrise is better than an overrise because you will get more rise in the oven anyway. If you are called away just as you put a dough up to rise, it is best to cover and refrigerate the dough and allow it a cool rise. A cool rise will delay the process and offer a window of time to tend to things outside the kitchen as well as to the bread without undue consequences to either!

• **Active Dry Yeast** This yeast is an older variety that needs warm water and a pinch of sugar to get it going (water to rehydrate it, sugar to start feeding it before the flour does), and if you provide these things, the yeast should "prove" active and healthy by bubbling or foaming. Active dry yeast is what most bakers up until the 1980s depended on, and recipes, remarkably (considering that the new yeasts are so much better), still call for it. If you prefer, you can use active dry yeast for my recipes, but follow the directions on the package to proof and allow doughs made with it a little more rising time than those using rapid-rise yeast. Overall, active dry yeast is a less vital yeast that needs a bit more care in handling and more time in the rise, as well as being less tolerant of such things as rich, buttery doughs or changes in temperatures than is rapid-rise yeast.

As with rapid-rise yeast, active dry yeast comes in packets, each measuring about 2¼ teaspoons of dry yeast. Alternatively, dry yeast comes in jars of about 4 ounces.

I prefer using the jars because measuring yeast by teaspoon amounts produces consistent results and also does not relegate you to dealing with whole or half packets that don't get fully used.

• **Fresh Yeast,** if you can find it, makes superlative bread. Some recipes in this book call for it—just to give you that opportunity to learn about it and simply inhale the subtle difference in scent that fresh yeast offers in baked bread. If you find fresh yeast (*Fleischmann's* still offers it in foil-wrapped chunks just under 1 ounce, in the dairy case), crumble it into the water in a recipe. It needs to be dissolved but not proofed because it does not bubble or foam on contact with water. Unlike rapid-rise yeast, which is generally sure to be

active, fresh yeast might not be active, but you don't know that until a bread doesn't rise.

Handling Yeast

What does yeast love? It thrives on your attention: Be alert to expiration dates on the package, use warm water (100°F to 110°F) in yeasted recipes, and protect it from direct contact with fats, such as oil or butter and sugar or other sweeteners. Yeast is keen about a bit of warm water and then the judicious addition of other ingredients, as called for in the recipe. My best tip is this trick of the trade: Mix the yeast with the warm water called for in the recipe; then cover it with 1 cup flour from the recipe to create a "shield" of flour that will protect it from the onslaught of other ingredients that might impede the yeast's performance. Stir this flour into the yeast and water and then proceed, knowing you have given your yeast a fair start and some flour "coverage."

Bread Flour

Most of the recipes in this chapter call for unbleached white bread flour (or use regular bread flour, if that is all you can find). Some recipes may call for both bread and all-purpose flour. The big benefit of bread flour is its high protein content, which leads to gluten development (the structure) in bread, and, in the end, supplies that satisfying chew of hearty baked breads.

How much flour should you add? This is a frequent question from new bakers. Start with about half of the flour in any recipe and increase it as the dough gets mixed. You might need a touch extra or a little less; the weather, the flour, and your handling will determine how much you ultimately need. The texture of the dough versus the measurement of the flour has the final say in how much flour you need.

I call for measuring-spoon amounts of yeast in my recipes instead of envelopes of yeast. Measuring yeast is more convenient and more in keeping with good baking procedures.

Mixing and Kneading

Start yeast bread recipes by mixing water and yeast together with a hand whisk to blend the two. This is best done in the mixer bowl of an electric stand mixer. If you do a lot of bread baking, I suggest investing in a 6-quart mixer, which gives you ample room to comfortably create breads without the dough being too large for the bowl's capacity. Then, using a wooden spoon, whisk, or spatula, add the other ingredients and most of the flour called for in the recipe. The dough will become heavier, and, at that point, you will need to attach a dough hook for a stand mixer or knead by hand.

Kneading is an over-and-fold motion, using either a dough hook or the heels of your hands to gently manipulate the dough and promote gluten development. You don't want to tear the dough or overdo kneading; you simply slowly maneuver the dough in a repeated motion. You want to transform dough into a resilient mass that has an elasticity to it. Do this slowly and observe the dough changing. In fact, resting the dough greatly changes its nature, and gluten still develops.

A bread machine's dough cycle is another option for mixing and kneading as well as rising. For bread machine application, in my recipes, mix everything called for in the recipe in the order given but hold back a good third of the flour until you see how much you will ultimately need. As the dough blade manipulates the dough, dust in more flour until the dough forms a ball and is being manipulated with some ease in the bread pan. Once it gets to that point, you can then close the machine and let it continue on its own until it signals you that the first rise is over. Then gently remove the bread onto a lightly floured work surface, gently deflate it, and proceed.

Rising

If you are using a stand mixer, this is the greatest tip you will ever discover regarding how to allow bread to rise: Instead of the traditional method of removing the bread to another greased bowl, laying moist kitchen towels on it, and covering it with plastic wrap, do this: Remove the dough hook; spray the dough with nonstick cooking spray (this prevents drying out or any skin or crust from forming as it rises) and cover the entire mixer and bowl with a tent formed from a large plastic bag (large clear trash bags are fine; see "Source Guide," page 316). This forms a "home proofer" (which, in the baking industry, is actually a walk-in-sauna rising room for breads) that is nicely humid and free from drafts. It saves you from messing

Kneading is an over-and-fold motion, using either a dough hook or the heels of your hands to gently manipulate the dough and promote gluten development.

with extra work bowls or dealing with sticky, floury tea towels or the possibility of the dough drying out because it rose beyond the borders of the tea-towel-and-plastic-wrap approach. (See photo, below left.)

Pan Preparation

The most common bread pan is a 9- x 5-inch loaf-pan. If you can find a large 12- x 5-inch loafpan, available from mail-order suppliers or commercial bakeware companies, that is about the handiest size to be had. It allows you to make one big loaf instead of two smaller ones. Alternatively, you can make almost any bread free-form by shaping the dough into one or two large balls, letting the dough rise on the baking sheet, and baking as is. The result is an attractive rustic-style bread. If you are baking a free-form loaf at a very high temperature, stack two baking sheets to prevent the bread's bottom from scorching while the rest of the bread browns.

Many of these recipes for free-form loaves call for a baking sheet lined with parchment paper. Sometimes I call for stacking two baking sheets together. This is because some breads brown on the bottom faster than they do on top, and *double sheeting* is a procedure that protects the bottom crust and allows the bread to brown all over without risking scorching.

Storage

Bread stores best at room temperature in a sealed zip-top plastic bag, in a bread box designed for bread storage, or in the freezer. Storing it in the fridge only hardens and stales bread.

Double sheeting is my procedure of stacking baking sheets to protect the bottom crust and allow the bread to brown all over without risking scorching.

Classic White Bread

Makes 2 medium loaves or 1 large round loaf

A fine white bread is art. Purity of crumb is its hallmark—all at once old-fashioned and yet as contemporary as tomorrow. This milk-enriched variation offers a nice boost of calcium.

This feathery white bread is grandma-style wonderful. It's the perfect grilled cheese sandwich bread, bread and butter bread, and toasting bread. Fresh yeast makes this superb, but regular rapid-rise yeast is fine. You could glaze this bread with an egg wash and top it with poppy seeds.

Hot-Air Rising

Some bread recipes in this book call for reducing the oven temperature once the bread goes in the oven. This is done because some breads profit from the boost they get from hotter temperatures to start them off, allowing them increased "oven spring." Reducing temperatures stabilizes and finishes baking the breads. Another plus in starting with a hotter oven is that the higher temperature compensates for the heat loss that occurs once you open the oven to put your breads inside to bake. When it is all about height, you want to do everything you can to lift up the bread and help its structure but not bake it so hot that it sets the outer crust and keeps the bread from expanding.

1	cup warm water (100°F to 110°F)
2	tablespoons rapid-rise yeast or 1.5 ounces fresh yeast, crumbled
1½	cups warm milk (100°F to 110°F)
2	tablespoons honey
1	tablespoon sugar
¼	cup unsalted butter, melted
2½	teaspoons salt
5	to 7 cups bread flour

Finishing Touches

Melted butter

Flour, for dusting

Generously spray two 9- x 5-inch loafpans with nonstick cooking spray. Line a large baking sheet with parchment paper. (Free-form bread can be baked on two stacked baking sheets, with the top sheet lined with parchment paper.)

In a mixer bowl, hand-whisk water and yeast together and let stand 2 to 3 minutes to dissolve yeast. Briskly whisk in milk, honey, sugar, butter, and salt and blend well. Add 3 to 4 cups of flour and mix to form a soft mass. Then attach dough hook and knead on lowest speed 6 to 8 minutes, adding more flour as necessary to form a soft, bouncy dough.

Remove dough hook from machine and spray dough with nonstick cooking spray. Cover entire mixer and bowl with a large clear plastic bag. Let dough rise 45 to 90 minutes until almost doubled.

Turn out dough onto a lightly floured work surface and gently deflate. For loaves, divide dough in half. Press each portion into a flattened oval, roll up into a snug log, and then place it in a prepared loafpan. Place loafpans on prepared baking sheet. Spray dough lightly with nonstick cooking spray and cover loosely with plastic wrap. Let rise 45 to 60 minutes until dough is quite puffy and has almost doubled.

Alternatively, for one large free-form loaf, shape dough into a large round ball and place on prepared baking sheets. Spray dough lightly with nonstick cooking spray and cover loosely with plastic wrap and let rise as for loaves.

Preheat oven to 375°F. Brush bread with melted butter or, for a more rustic look, brush lightly with melted butter and then dust on some flour. Place bread in oven (loafpans should be on prepared baking sheet) and immediately reduce oven temperature to 350°F.

Bake until nicely browned, 40 to 45 minutes. Let loaves cool in pans 10 minutes before turning out onto wire racks to cool completely. A free-form loaf can be cooled directly on baking sheets.

Caesar Salad Bread

Makes 1 large loaf

This is a dynamite, crusty bread with a cheesy, garlicky filling that bubbles up into the crust.

Olive oil, for pan

1/3 cup panko or semolina

Dough

1½ cups warm water (100°F to 110°F)

2 tablespoons rapid-rise yeast

¼ cup extra virgin olive oil

4 teaspoons sugar

2½ teaspoons salt

1 tablespoon seasoned salt

1 teaspoon dried Italian seasoning

1 teaspoon garlic powder

5 to 6 cups bread flour

Filling

½ cup mayonnaise

3 tablespoons extra virgin olive oil

1 tablespoon lemon juice

1 cup shredded Parmesan cheese

1 cup shredded mozzarella cheese

1 tablespoon crushed garlic

2 tablespoons minced fresh parsley

Finishing Touches

1 large egg

Pinch each sugar and salt

Parmesan and mozzarella cheese, garlic powder, salt, and pepper, as required, for dusting

Olive oil, for drizzling

This bread's filling oozes a bit, creating zesty pools of crisp cheese and spice. Do not worry about the filling coming out; that is supposed to happen with this bread so that you can be visually as well as fragrantly beguiled to try it.

Line a baking sheet with parchment paper. Drizzle olive oil in a 10-inch springform pan or round cakepan. Dust on panko or semolina and place pan on prepared baking sheet.

For Dough, hand-whisk water and yeast together in a mixer bowl and let stand 2 to 3 minutes to dissolve yeast. Briskly whisk in oil, sugar, salt, seasoned salt, Italian seasoning, garlic powder, and 3 to 4 cups flour. Mix and then knead with a dough hook on lowest speed of mixer 5 to 8 minutes, dusting in more flour as necessary to form a soft dough.

Remove dough hook and spray dough lightly with nonstick cooking spray. Cover entire mixer and bowl with a large clear plastic bag. Let dough rise 45 to 60 minutes until almost doubled.

Meanwhile, for the Filling, in bowl of a food processor, add mayonnaise, olive oil, lemon juice, Parmesan and mozzarella cheeses, garlic, and parsley and process 1 to 2 minutes. Set aside.

Turn out dough onto a lightly floured work surface and gently deflate. Pat or roll out into a large round about ½ inch thick. If dough retracts, let it rest a minute. Spread on filling and roll up dough snugly. Coil it up in prepared pan and pinch ends together.

Whisk egg and pinch of sugar and salt in a small bowl. Brush egg wash over dough; dust on Parmesan and mozzarella cheeses, garlic powder, salt, and pepper and drizzle with additional olive oil. Cover loosely with plastic wrap and let rise until dough is almost at top of pan, 45 to 60 minutes.

Preheat oven to 375°F. Bake 20 minutes and then reduce oven temperature to 350°F and continue baking until nicely browned and cheese is melted, another 20 to 30 minutes. Cool slightly before cutting into slices.

Handy Panko

Panko is the name for Japanese breadcrumbs. It is used in this recipe and in some other applications, such as crisping pizza bottoms. These fine slivers of dried white bread are commonly used in tempura, but they do double duty here to add texture and crispness to this bread, a marvelous spin on Caesar Salad. Panko is available in Asian food stores and specialty food markets. Some manufacturers bill it as an "extra crispy" coating.

Cinnamon Toast Bread

Makes 2 small loaves

This recipe makes two loaves that are gently fragrant with cinnamon and feathery of grain. Serve this superb bread warm or toasted with butter for a teatime treat.

If you have a hankering for a nutty addition to this cinnamon-scented bread, mix ground toasted walnuts into the dough along with the raisins and currants. This bread makes fine French toast and is perfect in a bread pudding.

Plumping Fruit

Plumping raisins, currants, and other dried fruits is a basic preliminary step in baking. If you don't reconstitute the fruit, you might end up with stubborn, dry nuggets of raisins in an otherwise soft and lovely bread. Refer to page 18 for my technique.

$\frac{1}{3}$ cup warm water (100°F to 110°F)
$4\frac{3}{4}$ teaspoons rapid-rise yeast
4 to 5 cups all-purpose flour
1 cup warm buttermilk*
$\frac{1}{4}$ cup unsalted butter, softened
$\frac{1}{3}$ cup sugar
1 large egg
$1\frac{1}{4}$ teaspoons salt
2 teaspoons ground cinnamon
$\frac{1}{2}$ cup raisins, plumped and dried

$\frac{1}{2}$ cup currants, plumped and dried

Finishing Touches

1 large egg
Pinch each sugar and salt
Milk, optional

Cinnamon-Sugar Topping

$\frac{1}{3}$ cup sugar
2 teaspoons ground cinnamon

*You can otherwise stir 1 teaspoon lemon juice into 1 cup milk and let stand 1 minute.

Spray two 8- x 4-inch loafpans with nonstick cooking spray and place on a large baking sheet lined with parchment paper.

In a mixer bowl, hand-whisk water and yeast together and let stand 2 to 3 minutes to dissolve yeast. Add 1 cup flour and then stir in buttermilk, butter, sugar, egg, salt, cinnamon, and most of remaining flour. Mix ingredients and then attach dough hook and knead on lowest speed of mixer about 6 to 8 minutes, adding more flour as necessary to make a soft dough. Stop machine after 5 minutes and add raisins and currants. Knead again, also dusting in more flour (since fruit and nuts will loosen dough again) to achieve a soft dough, another 4 to 6 minutes.

Remove dough hook from machine. Spray dough lightly with nonstick cooking spray and cover entire mixer and bowl with a large clear plastic bag. Let dough rise 1½ hours. Turn out dough onto a lightly floured work surface and gently deflate. Shape into two loaves and place in prepared pans.

Cover loosely with plastic wrap and let rise 45 to 70 minutes or until almost doubled. Whisk egg and pinch of sugar and salt in a small bowl and brush on bread. Alternatively, brush with milk.

Preheat oven to 350°F.

In a small bowl, mix Cinnamon-Sugar Topping ingredients and sprinkle evenly over breads.

Place pans on prepared baking sheet. Bake until done, about 35 to 45 minutes. Let cool in pans 10 minutes before turning out onto wire racks to cool completely.

Birdseed Bread

Makes 2 medium loaves; pictured on page 28

Here, you'll find the comfort of good carbs in a bread that is lofty with a soft grain and has an inviting wholesome fragrance. One of my testers makes this bread at least twice a week. This is one of my favorite "healthy" breads that pleases mainstream bakers who are resistant to multigrain baking. Contrary to popular belief, some breads made with multigrains and seeds, such as this one, rise fairly fast, so watch the rise and make sure this special bread doesn't overproof.

2	cups warm water (100°F to 110°F)	¼	cup dark rye flour
5	teaspoons rapid-rise yeast	1	cup whole wheat flour
3	tablespoons canola or vegetable oil	½	cup chopped sunflower seeds
1	tablespoon fresh lemon juice	2	tablespoons cracked wheat
2	tablespoons honey	2	tablespoons ground flax seeds
2	tablespoons brown sugar	2	tablespoons sesame seeds
1	tablespoon baker's caramel, optional (see note at right)	3	to 4 cups bread flour
1	tablespoon salt		

Finishing Touches

Sunflower seeds, cracked wheat for dusting top of bread

Spray interior of the large bowl of an electric mixer with nonstick cooking spray in order to keep dough from sticking. Spray two 9- x 5-inch loafpans with nonstick cooking spray and place on a large baking sheet lined with parchment paper; set aside.

In a mixer bowl, hand-whisk water and yeast together and let stand 2 to 3 minutes to dissolve yeast. Briskly whisk in oil, lemon juice, honey, brown sugar, baker's caramel (if using), salt, rye flour, whole wheat flour, sunflower seeds, cracked wheat, flax seeds, and sesame seeds. Stir well to blend. Fold in 2 cups bread flour and blend with a wooden spoon a few minutes. Attach dough hook and knead on lowest speed of mixer 8 to 10 minutes, adding remaining bread flour as necessary to make a sticky but cohesive dough.

Remove dough hook and shape dough into a ball in bowl. Spray dough lightly with nonstick cooking spray. Cover entire mixer and bowl with a large clear plastic bag and let dough rise 45 to 60 minutes until almost doubled. Turn out dough onto a lightly floured work surface and gently deflate. Let dough rest, lightly covered with a tea towel or plastic bag, 15 minutes. Divide dough in half and shape each into an oval. Sprinkle a sheet of parchment paper with sunflower seeds and cracked wheat. Firmly roll each dough in sunflower seeds and cracked wheat to coat top.

Place dough in prepared loafpans on baking sheet. Cover loosely with plastic wrap. Let breads rise 45 to 90 minutes until almost doubled in size.

Preheat oven to 375°F. Place bread in oven; immediately reduce oven temperature to 350°F. Bake until breads are nicely browned all over and seem crusty to the touch, about 35 to 40 minutes. Cool in pans on baking sheet.

Baker's Caramel

Baker's caramel—used in Birdseed Bread, Old-World Dark Rye (page 40), and a few other recipes in this book—is simply burnt sugar. See "Source Guide" (page 316) for ordering information or substitute kitchen bouquet, a similarly dark liquid that is used as a gravy browner. A little baker's caramel goes a long way to deepen the color of a rustic bread or a loaf of rye.

Hot Buttered Popcorn Bread

Makes 2 medium loaves or 1 large round loaf

This exceptional bread smells like movie-theatre popcorn and toasts like brioche. The popcorn flour comes from ground popped corn. Little flecks of popcorn hulls add roughage and a slight nuttiness.

The final butter basting makes this bread irresistible.

5 cups popcorn (⅓ cup unpopped kernels)	5 to 6 cups bread flour
1¼ cups warm water (100°F to 110°F)	**Finishing Touches**
3¾ teaspoons rapid-rise yeast	1 large egg
2 tablespoons sugar	Pinch each sugar and salt
¼ cup vegetable oil	Cornmeal
1 tablespoon real or artificial butter extract, optional	2 to 4 tablespoons salted butter, melted
2¼ teaspoons salt	

Spray two 9- x 5-inch loafpans with nonstick cooking spray and place on a large baking sheet lined with parchment paper. Alternatively, you can bake this bread in one big round free-form loaf on stacked baking sheets lined with parchment paper.

For popcorn, pop the corn. Pulverize it in batches in a food processor or mini chopper until you have about 2½ cups (**photos 1 and 2**). It is very lightweight and will fly around!

In a mixer bowl, hand-whisk water and yeast together and let stand 2 to 3 minutes to dissolve yeast. Briskly whisk in sugar, oil, butter extract (if using), and salt. Blend well. Add ground popcorn and 3 cups bread flour and mix. Knead with dough hook on lowest speed of mixer 6 to 8 minutes, adding more flour as necessary to form a soft, bouncy dough.

Remove dough hook, spray dough with nonstick cooking spray, and cover entire mixer and bowl with a large clear plastic bag. Let rise 60 to 90 minutes or until almost doubled.

Turn out dough onto a lightly floured work surface and gently deflate. Divide dough in half and form into two loaves; place in prepared pans or form a ball and place directly on baking sheets for a free-form loaf.

Whisk egg and pinch of sugar and salt in a small bowl. Brush loaves with egg wash. Cover loosely with plastic wrap and let rise until almost doubled, 45 to 60 minutes.

Preheat oven to 375°F. Brush bread again with egg wash and dust on some cornmeal.

Place bread in oven; immediately reduce oven temperature to 350°F. Bake until golden brown, 35 to 45 minutes.

As soon as bread comes out of oven, liberally brush with melted butter (**photo 3**). Let cool in pans 10 minutes before turning out onto wire racks to cool completely. Free-form loaf can cool directly on baking sheets.

Mr. O'Brien's Potato Bread with Chives

Makes 2 medium loaves or 1 free-form loaf

This bread has a tender but crackly crust and a moist interior. It begs to be paired with soup or a crock of butter and makes a banquet if you serve it with an omelet for supper or brunch.

1¼ cups warm water (100°F to 110°F)
5 teaspoons rapid-rise yeast
4 to 6 cups bread flour
1 cup warm mashed potatoes*
¼ cup warm milk
2 tablespoons unsalted butter, melted

1 tablespoon sugar
1 tablespoon salt
½ cup minced fresh chives or finely diced green scallions

Finishing Touch

Flour, for dusting

*Leftover seasoned mashed potatoes are fine.

Stack two baking sheets together and line top sheet with parchment paper to bake free-form or prepare two 9- x 5-inch loafpans by spraying with nonstick cooking spray and placing on a parchment paper–lined baking sheet.

In a mixer bowl, hand-whisk water and yeast together and let stand 2 to 3 minutes to dissolve yeast. Add 1 cup flour; then whisk in potatoes, milk, butter, sugar, and salt and blend well. Fold in almost all remaining flour. Mix ingredients and then knead with dough hook on lowest speed of mixer 8 to 10 minutes, adding flour as necessary to make a soft, bouncy dough. Dough should be slightly sticky but more or less cleaning sides of bowl. Midway through kneading, add chives or diced scallions.

Remove dough hook from machine, spray dough with nonstick cooking spray, and cover entire mixer and bowl with a large clear plastic bag. Let dough rise about 30 to 40 minutes until puffy but not quite doubled. Turn out dough onto a well-floured work surface and gently deflate. Divide in half and shape into small loaves for loafpans or make one large ball for a free-form loaf. Place on prepared baking sheets. Spray dough lightly with nonstick cooking spray, cover loosely with plastic wrap, and let rise 30 to 50 minutes until almost doubled. Dust loaves with flour.

Preheat oven to 350°F. Bake until just golden, about 30 to 35 minutes (45 minutes or so for larger loaf). Cool in pans 10 minutes before turning out onto a wire rack to cool completely. Free-form loaf can cool directly on baking sheets.

Spuds make this hearth-style white bread extra moist with good keeping qualities. Keep some bits of potato peel intact for the extra fiber as well as the slight freckles they give the crumb. The potatoes also help the fermentation. The shower of minced chives in the dough offers both seasonal and Irish green to delight the eye and palate.

Chive Talk

Chives are an ideal flavor and color addition in this jaunty bread. If chives are not an option, use finely minced scallions. When you use chives, you can be generous in measuring but use a more conservative amount of minced scallions, since their flavor is far more pronounced. Because breads generally are a neutral foundation, you can always import flavor in the way of fresh herbs or spices.

Old-World Dark Rye

Makes 3 medium loaves or 2 large loaves

If you are going to make only one rye bread, this should be it.

The secret ingredient in this great bread is *altus*. Altus is simply soaked leftover rye bread. A "sour" is the term for the starter you use when making rye bread, and it ensures you have authentic bakery-style rye that is positively rye-redolent. This version is similar to Russian black bread; to convert it to a light rye bread, omit the baker's caramel, coffee, and cocoa powder.

Old-World Rye Bread

There are two camps of rye-bread making: basic straight doughs (which, while easy and quick, lack real rye flavor and oomph) and the more authentic sourdough-based rye breads. But here's another rye to add to your repertoire: It is a deeply flavored, moist rye bread made with a rye-and-onion starter as well as soaked leftover rye bread. This technique is not unfamiliar to old-school bakers who used leftover stale rye bread in the dough. What began as a ruse of economy makes darn good bread, extending not only the dough but also the flavor and crumb. Use leftover rye bread of your own or purchase a loaf to get a head start. Many old-school Jewish bakeries use this technique, but it is often attributed to Michael London of the Rock Hill Bakehouse in New York.

24-Hour-Ahead Onion-Rye Sour

1   tablespoon caraway seeds
2   medium onions, chopped
3½ cups hot water
1   tablespoon rapid-rise yeast
2   cups stoneground rye flour

Rye Dough

All of the rye sour starter (3 cups)
6   slices old rye bread, chopped
1   tablespoon rapid-rise yeast
1   tablespoon salt
½   teaspoon malt powder
1   tablespoon brown sugar
1   tablespoon caraway seeds
1   tablespoon baker's caramel
2½ teaspoons cocoa powder
½   teaspoon fine instant coffee granules
5   to 7 cups bread flour

Finishing Touch

1   egg white whisked with 2 tablespoons water

For the Onion-Rye Sour, a day before, place caraway seeds in a small zip-top plastic bag. Run a rolling pin over them to crush slightly. Place onions in a cheesecloth bag; add caraway seeds to bag, tie, and set aside.

Hand-whisk hot water, yeast, and rye flour together in a large bowl to make a thick batter. Then swish onion bag in the sour, pushing it into the rye mixture. Cover the whole thing with plastic wrap and let froth and mature overnight.

The next day, remove onion bag, scraping off sour and mixing it with rest of sour mixture. Discard onion bag. Measure 3 cups starter for dough.

For altus, soak rye bread pieces in water (just enough to make rye bread mushy). Squeeze out water and set aside 1½ cups soaked bread.

Hand-whisk rye sour, yeast, salt, malt powder, brown sugar, caraway seeds, soaked rye bread, baker's caramel, cocoa powder, and instant coffee in large bowl of an electric mixer. Add 3 cups bread flour to make a soft batter. Knead with dough hook on lowest speed of mixer bowl 8 to 12 minutes, adding more flour as necessary to make a dense dough. (You might have to add a fair bit more bread flour.) Once dough is elastic and no longer too tacky, form into a ball (in work bowl). Remove dough hook and spray dough lightly with nonstick cooking spray; cover entire mixer and bowl with a large clear plastic bag. Let rise 30 minutes. Turn out dough onto a lightly floured work surface and gently deflate. Stack two baking sheets together and line top sheet with parchment paper.

Form dough into three medium oblong loaves or two large loaves. Place on prepared baking sheets. Cover loosely with plastic wrap and let rise 1½ to 2½ hours until 50% to 75% increased in volume.

Brush breads with egg white and water mixture.

Preheat oven to 425°F. Bake breads until deeply brown and hard and crusty to the touch, about 30 to 35 minutes, spritzing every so often with water.

Cool bread directly on baking sheets.

Greek Restaurant Whole Wheat Bread

Makes 1 large loaf

Add a touch of white flour to mostly whole wheat and include a judicious use of olive oil and some honey, and what have you? A heavenly, rustic whole wheat bread. Mop up your Greek salad with it or smear halved garlic cloves on a thick slice, drizzle on olive oil, and lightly grill. Then add some feta slabs and partially melt. Top with sliced tomatoes, minced kalamata olives, salt, pepper, and a dusting of oregano.

2	cups warm water (100°F to 110°F)
2	tablespoons rapid-rise yeast
1	cup white bread flour
2½	teaspoons salt
3	tablespoons honey
5	tablespoons olive oil

4	to 5 cups stoneground whole wheat flour, all-purpose or bread flour, or mixed, preferably organic

Finishing Touch

Whole wheat flour, for dusting

Stack two baking sheets together and line top sheet with parchment paper; set aside.

In a mixer bowl, hand-whisk water and yeast together and let stand 2 to 3 minutes to dissolve yeast. Stir in white bread flour. Then mix in salt, honey, oil, and half of whole wheat flour. Attach dough hook and begin kneading on lowest speed of mixer 8 to 10 minutes, adding additional whole wheat flour, as necessary, to form a soft but firm, somewhat tacky dough.

Shape dough into a rounded mass in mixing bowl. Spray inside of bowl and dough lightly with nonstick cooking spray. Cover entire mixer and bowl with a large clear plastic bag. Let rise about 45 to 90 minutes until almost doubled. Turn out dough onto a lightly floured work surface and gently deflate. Shape dough into an oval and place on prepared baking sheets. Spray dough lightly with nonstick cooking spray and dust with whole wheat flour.

Cover loosely with plastic wrap and let rise 45 to 70 minutes until dough is quite puffy.

Preheat oven to 375°F. Bake bread 15 minutes; then reduce oven temperature to 350°F and bake until it is well browned, another 20 to 30 minutes. Cool on baking sheets.

For the fullest flavor, use organic whole wheat flour for this recipe, if you have it, as well as Greek honey, Greek olive oil, and Greek sea salt.

Sharp Stuff for Nice Slices

A good bread knife should be at least 8 inches long and have a stainless-steel serrated blade. *Cutco*'s extra long slicing knife, while not a true bread knife, is one of the best for the job. Wood-handled serrated bread knives from *LamsonSharp* are attractive when cutting bread at the table. They also keep their sharp edges for sawing into fresh bread.

An ivory-handled bread knife from *Staffordshire* or other old English manufacturers is a real treat. A bread cutting board or tray is also handy for serving warm bread at the table.

Traditional Moist and Feathery Challah

Makes 2 medium loaves or 1 large loaf

The result here is a high-and-mighty crowning glory sort of challah. It is perfect when fresh and still warm and is great for sandwiches, toast, and French toast.

> **The egg wash used here features an added egg yolk for an especially deep golden glaze.**

Egg-Wash Glop? A Rescue in a Pinch

Ever notice how egg wash is somewhat sinewy, as the egg white strands never seem to quite blend with the yolks? You know how it is: You dip, brush, and still leave a trail of somewhat less-than-homogenous egg wash on the bread or on the counter? Professional bakers add a pinch of sugar or salt—or both—and then whisk the eggs. The result is an egg wash that has less "pull" to it and is a smooth liquid that easily lacquers your bread before baking.

2	cups warm water (100°F to 110°F)	2	egg yolks
2	tablespoons rapid-rise yeast		
6	to 8 cups bread flour		**Finishing Touches**
½	cup sugar	1	large egg
3½	teaspoons salt	1	egg yolk
⅓	cup vegetable oil		Pinch each sugar and salt
3	large eggs		Sesame seeds

Generously spray two 9- x 5-inch loafpans or one 12- x 5-inch loafpan with nonstick cooking spray. You can also bake one or both breads free-form, as braided challahs, on a baking sheet. Prepare a large baking sheet by lining with parchment paper.

In a mixer bowl, hand-whisk water and yeast together and let stand 2 to 3 minutes to dissolve yeast. Add 2 cups flour; briskly whisk in sugar, salt, oil, eggs, yolks, and most of remaining flour. Mix ingredients and then knead with dough hook on lowest speed of mixer 8 to 10 minutes, adding more flour as necessary to form a smooth, resilient dough or a soft, satiny, elastic bread dough.

Remove dough hook from machine; spray dough with nonstick cooking spray and cover entire mixer and bowl with a large clear plastic bag. Let dough rise 45 to 90 minutes until almost doubled.

Turn out dough onto a lightly floured work surface and gently deflate. Divide in half (for two breads, or leave as one portion for one large bread). Divide each portion into thirds and form into three balls. Place side by side in prepared loafpans. Repeat with remaining portion of dough or, alternatively, make three strands of each portion of dough and then braid, using three strands to make a braided dough.

Spray loaves with nonstick cooking spray. Place loafpan(s) on prepared baking sheet and cover loosely with plastic wrap. Let rise until doubled or dough is puffy and has almost reached just above top of the pan, 45 to 90 minutes.

Whisk egg and egg yolk in a small mixing bowl, adding sugar and salt to make a smooth egg wash that is well blended. Brush egg wash on bread as thoroughly and generously as possible; then sprinkle on sesame seeds. Preheat oven to 350°F.

Bake until well browned, about 40 to 45 minutes. If top of bread starts browning too quickly (and bread interior is not done), cover loosely with foil to protect top crust. Cool in pan 10 minutes before turning out to cool completely. Free-form loaves can cool directly on baking sheet.

BLT Bread

Makes 2 medium loaves or 1 large round loaf

This is otherwise known as perfect-for-summer-tomato-sandwiches bread. Add a smidgen of mayonnaise, lettuce, salt, and pepper or go all out with bacon, pancetta, or slices of sharp Cheddar or cream Havarti.

1   cup warm water (100°F to 110°F)
5   teaspoons rapid-rise yeast
5   teaspoons sugar
2¼ teaspoons salt
¼   cup vegetable oil or melted unsalted butter
½   cup warm milk (100°F to 110°F)

1   large egg
2   cups all-purpose flour
2   to 3 cups bread flour, or more

Finishing Touches

Melted butter
Semolina or cornmeal

Spray two 9- x 5-inch loafpans generously with nonstick cooking spray and place on a baking sheet lined with parchment paper. For a large free-form loaf, stack two baking sheets together and line top sheet with parchment paper.

In a mixer bowl, hand-whisk water and yeast together and let stand 2 to 3 minutes to dissolve yeast. Briskly whisk in sugar, salt, oil, milk, egg, and most of both flours and mix until blended. Attach dough hook and knead on lowest speed of mixer 8 to 10 minutes, adding more flour as necessary to form a soft, bouncy dough.

Remove dough hook and lightly spray dough with nonstick cooking spray. Cover entire mixer and bowl with a large clear plastic bag. Let dough rise 45 to 60 minutes or until almost doubled.

Turn out dough onto a lightly floured work surface and gently deflate. Divide dough in half, shape into oblong loaves, and place in two prepared 9- x 5-inch loafpans. Brush tops with melted butter. Alternatively, shape dough into a large round ball. Place dough on prepared baking sheets. Brush top with melted butter and dust with semolina or cornmeal.

Cover dough loosely with plastic wrap. Let rise 45 to 90 minutes until very puffy and doubled in size.

Preheat oven to 400°F. Place bread in oven and immediately reduce oven temperature to 350°F.

Bake 35 to 45 minutes or until well browned. Let loaves cool in pan 10 minutes before turning out onto wire racks to cool completely. For one loaf, let bread cool directly on baking sheets.

Chunky Cheese Bread

Makes 2 loaves

Bold to say but I believe true: This recipe alone is worth the price of the book. Years ago, with staring and expectant students, dough, and too much time on my hands as a baking instructor, I invented "instant" chunky cheese bread in hopes of keeping my students' attention via their appetites—it worked. Once the bread came out of the oven, the students all fought over the loaf.

1½ cups warm water (100°F to 110°F)
2 tablespoons rapid-rise yeast
¼ cup sugar
2½ teaspoons salt
1½ teaspoons dry mustard
2 large eggs
¼ cup vegetable oil
2 tablespoons unsalted butter, softened
5 to 6 cups bread flour

Chunky Cheese Part

2 cups shredded Cheddar cheese
2 scant cups cubed Cheddar cheese
2 tablespoons olive oil or melted butter
1 teaspoon seasoned salt or garlic salt
Sesame seeds

The seasoned salt can be your own favorite brand. It adds an extra zippy flavor that marries well to the melting cheese. *Keen's* is the dry mustard I recommend using in this recipe.

Generously grease two 8- x 4-inch or two 9- x 5-inch loafpans. (This is important to prevent bread from sticking to pan.)

In a mixer bowl, hand-whisk water and yeast together and let stand 2 to 3 minutes to dissolve yeast. Briskly whisk in sugar, salt, mustard, eggs, oil, butter, and half of bread flour and mix. Begin kneading with dough hook on lowest speed 5 to 8 minutes, adding more flour as necessary to make a soft, elastic dough. Form into a ball in mixing bowl, spray lightly with nonstick cooking spray, and cover entire mixer and bowl with a large clear plastic bag. Let dough rise 30 minutes.

Turn out dough onto a lightly floured work surface and gently deflate. **Divide** dough in half. Press each half into an oval and distribute 1 cup shredded cheese over each. Press in cheese and roll up each section into a jellyroll.

Using a dough cutter or sharp knife, cut each jellyroll into thick slices and then in half—basically into odd-sized chunks of dough. Arrange chunks of dough in loafpans. Scatter cubed Cheddar cheese over chunks of dough, drizzle with oil or butter, and scatter on seasoned salt or garlic salt (any gourmet herb mix will also do) and sesame seeds.

Place loaves on a baking sheet and cover loosely with plastic wrap. Let rise 30 to 45 minutes until quite puffy.

Preheat oven to 350°F. Bake until well browned and sizzling and cheese is melted, about 35 to 40 minutes. Cool in pan 10 minutes before removing and serving. Serve warm or as a sandwich base for *Black Forest* ham or turkey; you can also make an omelet sandwich, but be sure to toast bread first.

Pain Pesto

Makes 1 large loaf

This pesto bread is so marvelous and simple that you should run, not walk, to make it. It is zesty, pretty, flavorful, and addictive.

1¼ cups warm water (100°F to 110°F)

1 tablespoon rapid-rise yeast

4 cups, approximately, bread flour

⅓ cup extra virgin olive oil

5 teaspoons sugar

2¾ teaspoons salt

1 (10-ounce) jar of prepared pesto (about 1 generous cup)

Finishing Touches

Touch of olive oil

Dusting of salt, pepper, freshly grated Parmesan cheese, and minced fresh parsley

Stack two large baking sheets together and line top sheet with parchment paper.

In a mixer bowl, hand-whisk water and yeast together and let stand 2 to 3 minutes to dissolve yeast. Add 1 cup flour and stir briefly. Then stir in oil, sugar, salt, and most of remaining flour. Mix ingredients and then attach dough hook and knead on lowest speed 6 to 8 minutes until smooth and elastic, adding more flour as required.

Remove dough hook from machine and spray dough with nonstick cooking spray. Cover entire mixer and dough with a large clear plastic bag. Let rise 45 to 90 minutes or until almost doubled.

Gently deflate dough on a lightly floured work surface. Let rest 10 minutes and then roll out to a 20- x 20-inch shape. If dough resists, let it rest a few minutes and then roll out gently. Drizzle some additional olive oil on dough and then smear on pesto all over dough's surface. Roll up jelly-roll style. Shape into an "S" shape on prepared baking sheets.

Drizzle oil on top and dust with salt, pepper, Parmesan cheese, and minced parsley. Cover loosely with plastic wrap and let rise until puffy, about 45 to 60 minutes.

Preheat oven to 350°F. Press bread down slightly before it goes into oven. Bake until it is well browned, about 35 to 45 minutes. Cool to warm on baking sheets before cutting.

This bread is perfect served with brunch or an Italian-style supper—or simply with fresh cheeses, salad, and bowls of exotic olives. As a variation, you can make this with black olive tapenade or sun-dried tomato pesto.

Sourdough Starters

In very simple terms, a *starter* is exactly that—a mixture (flour, water, and yeast) that "starts off" a bread. It is best to use organic flour or unbleached flour in a starter, for together with spring water, this sort of slurry invites the most interesting wild yeasts present in the air. Sourdough starters are also called "pre-ferments." This pre-ferment gets added to a bread dough to assist the real rise that will occur once bread making is underway.

Books have been written solely on starters and sourdough bread, for it is indeed a genre of baking that can captivate you for a lifetime.

Why do we use starters? Because they initially kick-start the bread's rise and infuse it with special character that will be evident in the baked bread, especially in the taste of its crumb and the crackle of its crust. Starters promote consistent, long rises, which, in turn, promote a more complex nuance of flavor and a superb crust. Sourdough breads are also known for their big, moist crumb structures with holes and an overall rustic nature. Breads made with starters also stale at a slower rate due to the more developed character of the dough.

We also use starters because they are an especially merited dimension in bread making and a salute to our past. In the days before commercial dry yeast was available, sourdough starters, the bread legends of the frontier, were the leaveners of homesteaders, cowboys, and chuck wagon cooks. Sourdough starters have a legacy and a romance about them.

Starters can use commercial dry yeast (or not) or both airborne yeast and commercial dry yeast. Starters referred to as "mature" have been fed with flour and water over a lengthy period of time, allowing the yeast to multiply and strengthen the starter. Generally, if your starter is more mature, you get a yeast that is more vital, and the flavor notes in your resulting bread will be more complex.

The basic rule of sourdough starters is this: If it bubbles and froths, you are looking at something lively and destined to create a wonderful bread. If your starter or sponge is a little quiet, feed it. If it still doesn't respond, add a pinch of rapid-rise yeast to it. Once it is fed and bubbly, then use it. If you are not ready to use it, then put it to "sleep" or let it be dormant in the fridge. The fridge is where you should store sourdough. Adding warmth, more flour, and water is how you encourage it to be lively again. If your starter looks green or blackish and otherwise murky, that's normal—throw off the murk, feed the remaining starter, and proceed. The only time not to use a starter is when it has a pinkish hue around it, which is indicative of unwelcome bacteria. Throw out the starter immediately. You will have to create a new starter from scratch.

Sponge Starters

A lesser-known but really great starter is a sponge starter, sometimes referred to as a *poolish*. Sponge starters are less complex than true sourdough starters that have been built up and matured over days (even months). Sponge starters (also a blend of flour, water, and a touch of yeast) are mixed and left to sit for a brief time period, anywhere from one to sixteen hours. They are a boon if you are new to sourdough baking or simply want some of the attributes of sourdough bread but happen to be short on time or simply don't have a mature sourdough starter on hand.

Sponge starters (which look spongy and pudding-like) offer the same wonderful qualities to bread as other sourdough starters, such as tangy flavor, better conservation, crackling crusts and nice browning, and finer but still wonderful "holes" throughout. A sponge-starter bread is great when you want something less complex than true sourdough bread but more interesting than a straight white bread. Try your hand at a sponge-based bread with Outstanding French Country Bread on page 48. And flip to the Index (page 318) for a complete listing of my sourdough starter recipes.

24-Hour Sourdough Starter

Makes about 2 cups starter

This starter is a day-ahead sort of affair, allowing you some of the nice properties of sourdough starter without too much planning. It does not yield a mature starter with all of those rustic, acidic components, but it does offer a boost to any bread you add it to and helps with flavor and crumb. If you keep feeding it, it will become a mature starter, and that is always a good thing for any bread baker to have on hand. Sometimes I use this starter in the Artisanal Black Olive Bread on page 49 or in other breads requiring a sponge, where I simply use a warmed-up cup of this starter to replace a sponge starter. It is also good in any pizza dough recipe, adding a rustic crust to the finished product.

2 cups warm water (100°F to 110°F)	2 cups, approximately, all-purpose flour
	1/8 teaspoon rapid-rise yeast

In a ceramic or nonreactive bowl, whisk together water, flour, and yeast to make a gloppy or puddinglike batter. Cover loosely with plastic wrap and let sit at room temperature. Over the next 24 hours, it should foam and froth and then sink or deflate. If it deflates before the 24 hours pass, add 1 cup each of water and flour and stir well. After 24 hours, spoon it into a clean container with a snug cover and refrigerate indefinitely.

To revive the starter for a recipe, measure out what you need and allow starter to again froth and bubble, loosely covered. If it doesn't "wake up," then feed it with 1 cup flour (all-purpose or bread flour) and water. Then, once it is active and frothy, measure out what you need for the recipe. Return unused starter to its container and the fridge.

Pure spring water and organic flour create the best starters. Without the chlorides found in tap water, pure water and organic flour contain nothing that could interfere with the yeast activity you want to encourage in your starter.

Outstanding French Country Bread

Makes 2 medium loaves or 1 large loaf

My book would be incomplete without this recipe. It takes little planning and yet offers a rustic sourdough taste as well as a lot of sourdough character in the crust and crumb. This bread is good fresh or days old, toasted or not toasted. It rarely stales (providing you store it properly). This bread also freezes like a dream.

Atomize for Crisper Crusts

Nothing beats a commercial bread oven, or better yet, an outdoor bread oven, to create that wonderful crust that is so prized among bread bakers and fans. Atomizing, or spraying water into your home oven, is another way to go. The steam created assists in inducing a thin, crisp, and crackling crust, so have your mister ready. (Just don't spray the oven lightbulb.)

The Shortcomings of Slashing Too Late

Knowing just when to slash a rustic loaf before baking can be tricky and takes some experience. The best results come when using a sharp blade to slash. Breads are slashed to allow full expansion, or oven spring, when they go into a hot oven; however, if the bread dough has risen too much, it will deflate when you slash it. It might still recover with the oven heat to help it spring back. But if not, the bread will be fine, just not as big and expansive as you planned.

Sponge Starter (8 to 16 hours ahead)

1½ cups water
¼ teaspoon rapid-rise yeast
1½ cups, approximately, bread flour or organic white bread flour

Dough

All of Sponge Starter

1½ cups warm water (100°F to 110°F)
½ teaspoon rapid-rise yeast
2 tablespoons extra virgin olive oil
2¾ teaspoons salt
1 tablespoon sugar
4 to 6 cups bread flour

For Sponge Starter, in a small bowl, stir together water and yeast and let yeast dissolve by briskly whisking.

With a whisk or wooden spoon, stir in bread flour to make a thick mixture. It should be like a gloppy pudding. Cover bowl loosely with plastic wrap (leaving a small air space); let stand at room temperature 8 to 16 hours.

Stack two baking sheets together and line top sheet with two sheets of parchment paper. If your oven and baking sheet cannot accommodate two breads, prepare another set of sheets to bake second bread.

To make the bread, stir down starter to deflate it. Spoon it into mixer bowl. Hand-whisk in 1½ cups warm water, yeast, oil, salt, sugar, and most of flour. Stir to make a messy mass and then loosely cover bowl and let stand 15 minutes. Attach dough hook and knead on lowest speed of mixer until dough is smooth and resilient but not tough and bouncy. Remove dough hook and lightly spray dough with nonstick cooking spray. Cover entire mixer and bowl with a large clear plastic bag. Let rise 90 minutes to 2½ hours until dough has doubled.

Turn out dough onto a lightly floured work surface and gently deflate. Divide dough in half (or keep it as one large bread); form into two balls.

Gently place balls of dough, seam sides down, on prepared baking sheets. Spray dough with nonstick cooking spray. Cover baking sheets loosely with large clear plastic bag. Let dough rise until puffy (and 50% larger in volume).

Preheat oven to 475°F. Slash loaves with a sharp knife before baking. Spritz with water and dust with flour. (If dough deflates when you slash it, it rose too much but might recover with oven heat).

Atomize oven with a few squirts of water and place baking sheets on lowest oven rack. Spray oven interior every 5 minutes for the first 15 minutes. When 20 minutes remain, reduce heat to 425°F to finish baking. Loaf should be well browned after 25 to 35 minutes. Cool well on a wire rack before slicing. To store, keep in a loosely sealed plastic bag (which softens crust but keeps bread moist) or in a brown paper bag lightly sealed.

Artisanal Black Olive Bread

Makes 1 large free-form bread

This bread is beautifully rustic and European in looks and meant for a summer picnic basket. Use any combination of olives you like. I prefer a combination of pitted whole mild black olives as well as a few vinegary, spicy, tender-fleshed black olives that, regrettably, you will have to pit yourself. Take care not to overknead this dough; it is supposed to be slack and wet. Depending on the consistency of your starter, the flour you are using, and the season, you will need more or less flour. For a more rustic, tangy olive bread, use a more mature sourdough starter on another day, when you have thought ahead.

Sponge Starter (1 to 2 hours ahead)

1	cup all-purpose flour
1	cup, approximately, warm water (100°F to 110°F)
¼	teaspoon rapid-rise yeast

Dough

All of Sponge Starter
2   cups warm water (100°F to 110°F)
2   teaspoons rapid-rise yeast

2¾ teaspoons salt
1   tablespoon honey
3   to 4 cups, approximately, bread flour
3   to 4 cups black olives (variety of types), pitted

Finishing Touches

Flour
Olive oil, for drizzling

For Sponge Starter, in a medium bowl, hand-whisk flour, water, and yeast together to make a puddinglike mixture, about 2 minutes. If mixture is watery, add a bit more flour to make it puddinglike. Cover loosely with wax paper or parchment paper and let stand to ferment, 1 to 2 hours.
Line a large baking sheet with parchment paper and set aside.
Spoon Sponge Starter into a mixer bowl. To it, whisk in water, yeast, salt, honey, and most of bread flour, mixing to blend ingredients. Knead with dough hook on lowest speed of mixer 5 minutes; stop machine, cover dough loosely, and let rest 15 minutes. Resume kneading, adding more flour as necessary to form a soft, elastic dough. Dough will be a cohesive (not tough), resilient, soft dough.
Remove dough hook, spray dough lightly with nonstick cooking spray, and cover entire mixer and bowl with a large clear plastic bag. Let rise 1 to 3 hours or until dough has almost doubled.
Turn out dough onto a lightly floured work surface and gently deflate. Flatten dough into a large oval, about 12 x 10 inches. Press in olives all over dough. Fold over dough like a letter, in three folds, covering and pressing in olives, using a rolling pin to press them in. If olives pop out, coax them back in. Place bread on prepared baking sheet. Seal ends of bread, make three slash marks on top to expose olives a bit, and drizzle on olive oil.
Cover dough loosely with plastic wrap and let rise another 1 to 1½ hours until dough has almost doubled. Dust with flour.
Preheat oven to 400°F. Bake until browned, about 40 to 50 minutes. Drizzle very lightly with olive oil as it comes out of oven. Remove bread from oven and let cool on baking sheet at least 20 minutes before serving.

rolls, baby breads & buns

If the bread loaf is the bride of the table, then rolls, little breads, and buns are the wonderful maids of honor. Because they are smaller in stature, rolls and buns do not upstage a meal. Instead, they round it out.

Everything you need to know about the techniques of yeasted doughs—from ingredients to handling, rising, shaping, and baking—is covered in the previous chapter. What is important to know in addition to this general bread information is that you can take any bread recipe and relaunch it as a smaller bread, roll, or bun. You can even make a quartet of small loaves from a single bread recipe (which is lovely for dinner parties) and serve the loaves alongside pots of herb butter on their own little bread boards.

What is different about rolls or small breads? Two major things: Not only do they have a second rise in a shorter period of time, but they also bake quicker and cool faster. Because of these two attributes, small breads uniquely lend themselves to easy planning. This means you can add fresh rolls or buns to any meal, making rolls and smaller breads perfect for bakers in a hurry. Moreover, leftover rolls or buns freeze well, so consider making double batches exclusively so you'll have sandwich rolls on hand.

Remember the same basic counsel for these recipes as for large breads: Use warm water, unbleached bread flour, lively and active yeast, and classic techniques for mixing, kneading, rising, and forming.

You can bake most rolls free-form simply by shaping them and placing them, evenly spaced, on a baking sheet or in muffin pans. And finally, serve rolls warm, not hot. If you cut into them while they are hot, they will sink and deflate and also stale faster. Good things come to those who wait.

Italian Hard Rolls

Makes 12 rolls; also pictured on page 50

Enjoy these lean, crisp rolls that bake up rustic and satisfying. If you have sourdough starter on hand, you can substitute a cup of that instead of making this sponge.

Spritzing the rolls and the oven with water encourages a crisp baked crust.

2-Hour Sponge

1 cup warm water (100°F to 110°F)
2½ teaspoons rapid-rise yeast
1½ cups bread flour

Dough

1 cup warm water (100°F to 110°F)
1 tablespoon honey

3 tablespoons olive oil
2½ teaspoons salt
4 cups bread flour
All of the sponge (at left)

Finishing Touches

Flour, for dusting
Melted butter or olive oil

Line a large baking sheet with parchment paper. (These rolls also bake up nicely on a baking stone.)

For 2-Hour Sponge, mix ingredients in a mixer bowl just to combine to a puddinglike consistency. Cover loosely (not airtight) and let bubble and stand 2 hours, stirring down if sponge threatens to bubble over.

For Dough, add water, honey, olive oil, salt, and flour to sponge in mixer bowl and stir to combine. Attach dough hook and knead on lowest speed of mixer about 8 to 10 minutes, adding more flour as necessary to make a cohesive, elastic dough. Remove dough hook and spray dough with nonstick cooking spray. Cover entire mixer and bowl with a large clear plastic bag and let rise 45 to 90 minutes or until almost doubled.

Turn out dough onto a lightly floured work surface and gently deflate. Divide dough in 12 portions. Shape into oblong rolls.

Place rolls on prepared baking sheet. Spray lightly with nonstick cooking spray and cover baking sheet with plastic wrap. Let rise 20 to 30 minutes until puffy. Score rolls, leave them plain, or snip them with scissors for a decorative effect. Dust with flour, if desired.

Preheat oven to 400°F. Spray rolls lightly with water; spritz oven as well. Bake until done and rolls are brown all over, 25 to 28 minutes. For shiny rolls with a less crispy crust, paint with melted butter or olive oil before baking.

2511 Rolls

Makes 12 rolls

Why "2511 Rolls"? That is how many people downloaded this recipe in one hour on my Web site. A winner, for sure, by any count. The silky, soft dough bakes up into melt-in-your-mouth rolls that are the perfect size for sopping up turkey gravy. You can also bake these in a mini loafpan or muffin pan or put them in a round cakepan.

¼ cup warm water (100°F to 110°F)

2 tablespoons rapid-rise yeast

1¼ cups warm buttermilk

¼ cup unsalted softened butter, cut into small chunks

¼ cup sugar

2 teaspoons salt

5 to 6 cups all-purpose or bread flour

½ cup unsalted butter, melted

Generously spray a 12-cup muffin pan with nonstick cooking spray and place on a large baking sheet lined with parchment paper.

In a mixer bowl, hand-whisk water and yeast together and let stand 2 to 3 minutes to dissolve yeast. Briskly whisk in buttermilk, softened butter, sugar, salt, and most of flour. Knead with dough hook on lowest speed about 8 minutes, adding more flour as necessary to form a soft, smooth, and elastic dough. Remove dough hook and spray dough with nonstick cooking spray.

Cover entire mixer and bowl with a large clear plastic bag. Let rise until almost doubled, 45 to 60 minutes, or refrigerate overnight. If refrigerating, allow dough to warm to room temperature before proceeding.

Turn out dough onto a lightly floured work surface and gently deflate. Divide dough into 12 portions. Cut each portion into three chunks and dip chunks into melted butter. Alternatively, you can form the chunks into small balls. Place three chunks or balls into each well of a 12-cup muffin pan. Drizzle any leftover melted butter over rolls. Cover loosely with plastic wrap and allow to rise until doubled in bulk, 30 to 60 minutes.

Preheat oven to 375°F and bake 10 minutes. Then reduce oven temperature to 350°F and continue to bake until lightly browned (another 15 to 20 minutes). Cool in pan 10 minutes and then turn out to serve or cool completely.

These tender rolls are reminiscent of a French croissant in taste but with the velvety crumb of traditional white bread rolls.

Open-Hearth Cinnamon-Raisin-Buttermilk English Muffins

Makes 12 to 16 muffins

This recipe makes for wonderfully flavorful English muffins with a cinnamon-raisin spin. The longer you let your starter stand and ferment, the better, but even a "young" starter offers extra flavor to these authentic homestyle English muffins.

If you can find white whole wheat flour, it is ideal for this lightly wheaty muffin. Otherwise, regular whole wheat flour is fine. If you want to serve these muffins for breakfast, form them the night before, allow them to rise in the fridge overnight, and bake them the next morning. These English muffins freeze well, too.

Starter

2 cups water
½ teaspoon rapid-rise yeast
2 cups all-purpose flour
½ cup whole wheat flour

Dough

All of starter
¾ cup warm water (100°F to 110°F)
2 teaspoons rapid-rise yeast
¾ cup warm buttermilk
2 tablespoons honey
2 tablespoons sugar

1 tablespoon fresh lemon juice
2 cups white whole wheat flour
2½ teaspoons salt
¼ teaspoon baking soda
¼ cup stoneground cornmeal
3 cups, approximately, all-purpose flour or bread flour
1 cup raisins, plumped and dried (see page 18)
2 teaspoons ground cinnamon

Cornmeal, for skillet

For Starter, in a medium bowl, stir together water and yeast. Let stand a couple of minutes. Stir in flours to make a thick batter. Cover and let stand 2 to 12 hours.

For Dough, place starter in a mixer bowl and briskly whisk in warm water, yeast, buttermilk, honey, sugar, lemon juice, whole wheat flour, salt, baking soda, cornmeal, and half of all-purpose flour. Add only enough flour to make a sticky dough and mix with paddle attachment on lowest speed of mixer 2 to 3 minutes.

Leave paddle attached and spray dough, which should appear as a thick batter, with nonstick cooking spray. Cover entire mixer and bowl with a large clear plastic bag; let stand 20 minutes. Stir down batter and then mix with paddle again 3 to 5 minutes, still allowing for a very soft, wet dough and only adding enough flour to make dough barely a mass. Cover again and let rise until almost doubled in bulk, 30 to 60 minutes.

Stir down dough and spoon it out of bowl onto a lightly floured work surface. Gently knead in raisins and cinnamon. Let dough rest 10 minutes.

Clear work surface of flour and sprinkle it with cornmeal. Pat dough out to ¾-inch thickness. Cut into 3½-inch rounds using a cookie cutter. Place on a baking sheet, cover loosely with plastic wrap, and let rise until almost doubled, about 30 to 45 minutes.

Heat a cast-iron skillet to medium hot. Sprinkle skillet surface with cornmeal. Gently arrange English muffins, a few at a time, to fit. Bake until bottoms are browned, about 5 to 8 minutes. Turn, reducing heat if muffins are browning too quickly. Cool well and split with tines of a fork.

Crusty Rolls

Makes 12 rolls

Not lightweight but not too heavy, these rolls are perfect for a picnic. Make them big to hold cold cuts, or make them small to go with chilled salads.

Quick Sponge

1 cup warm water (100°F to 110°F)

2½ teaspoons rapid-rise yeast

1½ cups bread flour

Dough

1 cup warm water (100°F to 110°F)

1 tablespoon sugar

2 tablespoons canola or vegetable oil

4 cups bread flour

2¾ teaspoons salt

Finishing Touch

Flour, for dusting

Line a baking sheet with parchment paper (if baking rolls in a free-form style); alternatively, spray 12 mini loafpans generously with nonstick cooking spray.

For Quick Sponge, in a medium-sized bowl, hand-whisk water and yeast together and let stand 2 to 3 minutes to dissolve yeast. Fold in flour and mix to make a puddinglike, gloppy paste. Cover loosely with plastic wrap and let sit 1 hour.

For Dough, place Quick Sponge in a mixer bowl. Add water, sugar, oil, most of the 4 cups bread flour, and salt to sponge. Stir with a wooden spoon to make a mass. Let dough sit, uncovered, 10 minutes. Attach dough hook and knead on lowest speed of mixer to make a soft, elastic dough, about 8 to 10 minutes. Remove dough hook; spray dough with nonstick cooking spray and cover entire mixer and bowl with a large clear plastic bag. Let rise about 45 to 90 minutes.

Turn out dough onto a lightly floured work surface and gently deflate. Using a dough scraper or sharp knife, cut into 12 portions. Place portions of dough on prepared baking sheet with some space between them or place in mini loafpans on a baking sheet. Cover loosely with plastic wrap and let rise until puffy, about 30 minutes.

Preheat oven to 400°F. Mist rolls with water and dust with flour. Bake until beginning to turn medium brown, about 30 minutes.

Allow rolls to cool in mini loafpans 10 minutes before turning them out onto baking sheet to finish cooling. Free-form rolls can cool directly on baking sheet.

Everything Bagels

Makes 12 bagels

What else is as satisfying and fun as fresh bagels? Use fresh yeast for that unmistakable, authentic bagel-bakery scent; otherwise, rapid-rise yeast is perfect. These dynamite, crusty, huge bagels have a hefty overcoat of onions, poppy seeds, and sesame seeds, along with a touch of coarse salt.

Dough

2	cups warm water (100°F to 110°F)
¾	ounce fresh yeast or 1 tablespoon rapid-rise yeast
3	tablespoons sugar
2	teaspoons salt
2	teaspoons canola or vegetable oil
2	tablespoons cornmeal
5	to 6 cups bread flour

Kettle Water

About 6 quarts water	
¼	cup honey
1	tablespoon sugar
1	tablespoon salt

Finishing Touches

2	tablespoons poppy seeds
2	tablespoons sesame seeds
½	cup lightly sautéed chopped onions or dehydrated minced onion
1	tablespoon coarse kosher salt

Bagel dough needs to be slick and almost satiny-tough, so add as much flour as the dough can absorb. A bread machine is perfect for making batches of bagel dough and allowing you to add additional flour. A bread machine, because of its design and nonstick sides, helps the dough ingest the maximum flour needed for great bagel dough. However, your stand mixer with a dough hook is more similar to the revolving bagel mixers that bagel bakeries use.

Line two large baking sheets with parchment paper.

In a mixer bowl, hand-whisk water and yeast together and let stand 2 to 3 minutes to dissolve yeast (same approach for dry yeast). Briskly whisk in sugar, salt, oil, cornmeal, and most of flour and mix. Knead with dough hook on lowest speed about 8 to 12 minutes, adding enough flour (sometimes up to 2 cups) to make a slick, stiff dough. Remove dough hook and spray dough with nonstick cooking spray. Cover entire mixer and bowl with a large clear plastic bag. Let dough rise 45 to 60 minutes or until almost doubled.

Turn out dough onto a lightly floured work surface and gently deflate. Divide into 12 equal pieces, form each into a rope about 8 to 10 inches long, and then make a bagel or ring out of each. Place on prepared baking sheets. Spray lightly with nonstick cooking spray. Cover loosely with plastic wrap and let rise 15 to 20 minutes.

For Kettle Water, set 6 quarts water with honey, sugar, and salt to simmering.

Preheat oven to 400°F. Simmer bagels in batches of two to four bagels at a time, allowing 30 seconds per side. Place on prepared baking sheets; coat each bagel with seeds, onion, and some salt.

Bake until nicely browned, about 22 to 35 minutes, turning bagels at midpoint. Cool directly on baking sheets.

Bretzels

Makes 8 pretzels

Bretzels are similar to New York vendor or baseball-stadium hot pretzels. They are best hot out of the oven, but these are also scrumptious served at room temperature and doused with yellow mustard. Pack some in a picnic hamper along with pickled eggs, imported cheeses, and iced tea.

Bretzel Dough

1   cup warm water (100°F to 110°F)
1¾ teaspoons rapid-rise yeast
½   teaspoon salt
3   tablespoons sugar
1   teaspoon malt powder*
3   tablespoons vegetable oil
2½ to 3 cups bread flour

Kettle Water

About 6 quarts water
1   teaspoon baking soda
1   teaspoon salt
1   tablespoon sugar

Finishing Touches

Garlic powder
Coarse salt
Poppy seeds

Pretzel salt is coarse salt that is available at bulk or health-food stores or online. You can also use a bit of coarse sea salt.

*Malt powder adds a special flavor, but the bretzels are good without it. See "Source Guide" on page 316 for how to order.

Line a large baking sheet with parchment paper.

In a mixer bowl, hand-whisk water and yeast together and let stand 2 to 3 minutes to dissolve yeast. Briskly whisk in salt, sugar, malt, oil, and most of flour. Using dough hook, knead on lowest speed of mixer about 8 to 10 minutes, adding more flour as necessary to make a stiff dough.

Remove dough hook and spray dough with nonstick cooking spray. Cover entire mixer and bowl with a large clear plastic bag and let rise 40 minutes. Turn out dough onto a lightly floured work surface and gently deflate. Divide dough into eight portions. Shape into ropes and form each rope into a bretzel similar to how pretzels are configured.

Place on prepared baking sheet. Spray lightly with nonstick cooking spray. Cover loosely with plastic wrap and let rise 20 to 25 minutes.

Preheat oven to 425°F.

For Kettle Water, bring water to a boil and stir in baking soda, salt, and sugar. Drop in bretzels, a few at time, turning once, for a total of 10 to 20 seconds per side. Using a slotted ladle, remove each to prepared baking sheet and sprinkle with garlic, coarse salt, and poppy seeds.

Bake until browned, about 15 minutes. Cool directly on baking sheet.

Asiago-and-Cheddar Potato Rolls

Makes 12 to 16 rolls

These chewy, cheese-packed, moist rolls are great fresh, toasted, or used for sandwiches.

1½ cups warm water (100°F to 110°F)

2 tablespoons rapid-rise yeast

5 cups bread flour

2 tablespoons sugar

1 tablespoon salt

¼ cup unsalted butter, melted

1 teaspoon hot sauce

2 cups shredded unpeeled, washed red-skinned potatoes

2 cups shredded sharp Cheddar cheese

1 cup shredded Asiago cheese

Finishing Touches

2 tablespoons unsalted butter, melted

¼ cup cornmeal

½ cup, approximately, shredded Asiago cheese

Use Wisconsin Asiago cheese; it offers the right flavor and texture that these rolls need. Take care not to let your rolls overproof, or they'll deflate when you slash them. And be sure you use a sharp knife or razor blade to slash the top of each roll.

Line a large baking sheet with parchment paper.

In a mixer bowl, hand-whisk water and yeast together and let stand 2 to 3 minutes to dissolve yeast. Fold in 3 cups of flour and then stir in sugar, salt, butter, hot sauce, potatoes, and cheeses. Mix ingredients and then attach dough hook and knead on lowest speed 8 to 10 minutes, adding more flour as necessary to form a smooth but resilient dough. Remove dough hook and spray dough with nonstick cooking spray. Cover entire mixer and bowl with a large clear plastic bag. Let dough rise about 45 to 60 minutes until almost doubled.

Turn out dough onto a lightly floured work surface and gently deflate. Divide dough into 12 to 16 rolls and place on prepared baking sheet. Brush with melted butter and sprinkle tops lightly with cornmeal. Cover baking sheet loosely with plastic wrap and let rise 30 minutes.

Preheat oven to 400°F. Make a shallow slash on top of each roll. Bake 15 minutes; then reduce heat to 375°F, spray rolls with nonstick cooking spray, and sprinkle with ½ cup cheese. Bake another 10 minutes or until rolls are nicely browned.

Onion Knots

Makes 8 to 12 buns

This puffy egg-enriched dough bakes up into nicely browned deli-style buns with a crown of onions, salt, and poppy seeds. These are perfect fresh, split and toasted, or used for sandwiches. They also freeze well.

Though fresh onion makes a flavorful topping when it is sautéed, dehydrated minced onion sticks better to bread, is quick and easy to use, and offers a more subtle onion taste.

Dough

1¾ cups warm water (100°F to 110°F)

2 tablespoons rapid-rise yeast

5 to 7 cups bread flour

2 large eggs

⅓ cup vegetable oil

2½ teaspoons salt

⅓ cup sugar

Onion Topping

½ cup dehydrated minced onion

2 tablespoons canola or vegetable oil

4 teaspoons poppy seeds

1 tablespoon coarse salt, for sprinkling

Finishing Touches

2 large eggs

Pinch each sugar and salt

Line a large baking sheet with parchment paper.

In a mixer bowl, hand-whisk warm water and yeast together and let stand 2 to 3 minutes to dissolve yeast. Add 2 cups flour and then briskly stir in eggs, oil, salt, sugar, and most of remaining flour. Mix ingredients and then attach dough hook and knead on lowest speed 8 to 10 minutes, adding more flour as necessary to form a smooth but resilient dough.

Remove dough hook from machine and spray dough with nonstick cooking spray. Cover entire mixer and bowl with a large clear plastic bag. Let dough rise 45 to 60 minutes.

For Onion Topping, mix all ingredients in a small bowl and set aside.

For Egg Wash, whisk eggs and pinch of salt and sugar in a small bowl.

Turn out dough onto a lightly floured work surface and gently deflate.

Preheat oven to 400°F.

Divide dough into 8 to 12 portions. Flatten each portion with a rolling pin to an oval of about 6 to 8 inches. Place each portion on prepared baking sheet. Brush each with Egg Wash and then top with Onion Topping. Cover loosely with plastic wrap and let buns rise 15 to 30 minutes, just until slightly puffy.

Bake until evenly golden brown, about 18 to 24 minutes. Cool directly on baking sheet.

Real Butter Homestyle Crescent Rolls

Makes 10 to 12 rolls

If you like the taste and look of croissants but prefer *Pillsbury®* Doughboy easy with homemade great taste, these little crescent rolls are just the thing. The trick is a rich, buttery dough and an ingenious method of shaving thin sheets of butter off the block, using a cheese grater to create the butter "roll-in." It imitates the rolled French approach but uses Yankee expediency.

Dough

1 cup warm water (100°F to 110°F)
5½ teaspoons rapid-rise yeast
¾ cup warm milk
¼ cup unsalted butter
⅓ cup sugar
2½ teaspoons salt
2 cups all-purpose flour
2 to 4 cups bread flour

Butter Roll-In

1 cup cold unsalted butter*

Finishing Touches

1 large egg
Pinch each sugar and salt
1 tablespoon water
Sesame seeds, optional

The rolled-in butter shavings lead to many layers of flaky pockets in these *croissants de pâtissière*.

*Butter will be made into shavings, using a box grater.

Stack two large baking sheets together and line top sheet with parchment paper.

In a mixer bowl, hand-whisk warm water and yeast together and let stand 2 to 3 minutes to dissolve yeast. Briskly whisk in milk, butter, sugar, salt, and all-purpose flour. Add some of bread flour. Mix ingredients and then attach dough hook and knead 8 to 10 minutes on lowest speed of mixer, adding more flour as necessary to make a soft, bouncy dough. Remove dough hook and spray dough with nonstick cooking spray. Cover entire mixer and bowl with a large clear plastic bag. Let dough rise 45 to 60 minutes until almost doubled. Turn out dough onto a lightly floured work surface and gently deflate. Cover loosely with clear plastic bag and allow to rest 10 minutes.

Using a box grater, make shavings of the cold butter.

On a lightly floured work surface, roll out dough into a 12-inch circle. Using a pizza wheel, pastry cutter, or sharp knife, cut dough into 10 to 12 wedges. Arrange butter shavings all over dough.

Starting at outside edge, roll each section up into a snug crescent roll. Arrange rolls on prepared baking sheets, leaving 2 to 3 inches between them. Whisk egg, pinch of sugar and salt, and 1 tablespoon water in a small bowl. Brush rolls generously with egg wash. Sprinkle on sesame seeds, if desired.

Cover pan loosely with plastic wrap. Let rolls rise 30 to 45 minutes until almost doubled. Preheat oven to 375°F. Place rolls in oven, reduce oven temperature to 350°F, and bake rolls until browned, 25 to 30 minutes. Cool slightly on baking sheet before serving.

Old-Fashioned British Crumpets

Makes 14 to 18 crumpets

A crumpet is an English griddle bread—something between a pancake and an English muffin. When sampling a warm, fresh batch of these crumpets, most people agree that they're fabulous, needing only a drop of butter, some preserves, and a pot o' tea.

I wanted to call these 'Plop-Plop Fizz-Fizz Crumpets' because 'plop' goes the bubbly batter and 'fizz' goes the fragrant cooking. You can use a cast-iron griddle, an electric griddle, or a large skillet. Crumpet rings, much like English muffin rings, are entirely optional (you can even use lidless clean tuna cans). Most crumpet recipes call for baking soda, which is added near the end of the batter's rest time. Baking powder would make more sense in this context because it relies on heat and moisture for activation, but I stuck with tradition here.

1	cup warm water (100°F to 110°F)
2½	teaspoons yeast
1	cup warm milk (100°F to 110°F)
2	tablespoons unsalted butter
2	teaspoons salt
2	teaspoons sugar
½	teaspoon malt powder*, optional
3½	cups all-purpose flour
½	teaspoon baking soda
¼	cup warm water
	Unsalted butter, for griddle

*Available from *King Arthur Flour* or bagel bakeries. See "Source Guide" on page 316 for how to order.

In a mixer bowl, hand-whisk warm water and yeast together and let stand 2 to 3 minutes to dissolve yeast. Briskly whisk in warm milk, butter, salt, sugar, malt powder, and most of flour. Stir to encourage batter to become slightly elastic. Do not add too much flour. Mixture should be more batter than dough. Cover and let rest 45 minutes.

Dissolve baking soda in ¼ cup warm water. Stir dissolved soda into batter and cover. Allow to rise 20 to 30 minutes.

Preheat griddle to medium-low heat. Drop soup ladle–sized puddles of batter onto greased griddle. Reduce heat to low and cook until tops look dry, about 12 to 15 minutes. Usually these are not turned. Experiment as you like. Serve with whipped butter, honey, and preserves. Crumpets freeze well.

Buttermilk Submarine Sandwich Rolls

Makes 10 to 14 rolls

My three sons were addicted to inferior whole wheat rolls from a fast-food place. Yes, even a baker's boys stray. "I can make rolls like that," I said—and thankfully, the boys are back on the farm—eating homegrown, better whole wheat rolls from our own hearth. These are soft but the whole wheat flour makes them nicely nutritious and gently nutty in flavor.

½ cup warm water (100°F to 110°F)
2 tablespoons rapid-rise yeast
1½ cups warm buttermilk
¼ cup unsalted butter or oil
2 tablespoons sugar

2½ teaspoons salt
2 cups whole wheat flour, organic or regular
3 to 5 cups bread flour

Line two baking sheets with parchment paper.

In a mixer bowl, hand-whisk water and yeast together and let stand 2 to 3 minutes to dissolve yeast. Briskly whisk in buttermilk, butter or oil, sugar, salt, and whole wheat flour. Add 2 cups of white bread flour. Mix ingredients and then attach dough hook and knead 8 to 10 minutes on lowest speed of mixer, adding more flour as necessary to form a soft, bouncy dough.

Remove dough hook and spray dough with nonstick cooking spray. Cover entire mixer and bowl with a large clear plastic bag. Let dough rise 45 minutes. Turn out dough onto a lightly floured work surface and gently deflate. Cover loosely with plastic wrap and let rest 20 minutes.

Divide dough into 10 to 14 sections. Shape into oblong rolls. Arrange rolls on prepared baking sheets. Spray lightly with nonstick cooking spray and cover loosely with plastic wrap. Let rise approximately 30 minutes.

Preheat oven to 375°F. Bake rolls until browned, 20 to 25 minutes.

At my house, these rolls rarely have anything but turkey and lettuce put in them, but any filling would be perfect with such outstanding rolls.

Whiter Wheat, Well Worth Its Weight

White whole wheat flour is an alternative to regular whole wheat flour. The difference is in the taste. It is sweeter than regular whole wheat, but it offers all the nutrition of a whole wheat that includes the healthy bits of bran and germ. It can be used in many bread, roll, and pizza recipes. It is perfect for people who want a change or desire the nutrition of whole wheat without the aftertaste. It is also ideal for ladling more whole grains into kids, who somehow can always detect extra vitamins and protest! White whole wheat flour is available from *King Arthur Flour* and *Hodgson Mill.*

Whole Wheat-Honey-Walnut Buns

Makes 12 buns

Sweet and mellow, this dough is studded with the nutty goodness of walnuts. These buns are especially good served with honey butter.

Loafing Around

A mini loafpan is a specialty pan that is perfect to have on hand to make professional-looking mini loaves or rolls baked in a loaf shape. You can also use such a pan to make little quick breads or to bake up muffin batter to get little muffin loaves. *Wilton* offers a nice variety of petite loafpan sizes.

1½ cups warm water (100°F to 110°F)
2 tablespoons rapid-rise yeast
½ cup unsalted butter, melted
⅓ cup honey
2 teaspoons ground cinnamon
2 teaspoons salt

2 cups whole wheat flour
3½ to 4 cups bread flour
½ cup toasted chopped walnuts

Finishing Touches

Flour, for dusting
Cinnamon

Generously spray a connected 12-cavity mini loafpan with nonstick cooking spray. You can otherwise use two 6-cavity or three 4-cavity mini loafpans.

In a mixer bowl, hand-whisk water and yeast together and let stand 2 to 3 minutes to dissolve yeast. Briskly whisk in melted butter, honey, cinnamon, and salt. Fold in whole wheat flour and 1 cup bread flour. Knead with dough hook on lowest speed, adding more bread flour as needed until dough leaves sides of bowl. Dough should become soft but no longer sticky. You might need slightly more flour (add a small bit at a time). Knead about 5 minutes; then add walnuts and knead only until dough is again smooth and elastic, although nuts will peek out. Remove dough hook and spray dough with nonstick cooking spray. Cover entire mixer and bowl with a large clear plastic bag. Let dough rise 45 minutes.

Turn out dough onto a lightly floured work surface and gently deflate. Divide dough into 12 portions. Form into ovals and place in prepared pan. Spray lightly with nonstick cooking spray and cover loosely with plastic wrap.

Allow dough to rise about 40 minutes or until it is flush with top of loafpan. Dust with flour and cinnamon.

Preheat oven to 375°F. Place pan in oven and immediately reduce oven temperature to 350°F. Bake until tops are lightly browned, about 25 to 35 minutes. Cool in pan 10 minutes before turning out to cool completely.

Golden Corn Rolls

Makes 24 small or 12 large rolls

These great corn rolls are a cross between rich white bread and golden yellow corn bread.

2	cups milk
1	cup stoneground cornmeal
½	cup warm water (100°F to 110°F)
2	tablespoons rapid-rise yeast
5	cups, approximately, bread flour
½	cup unsalted butter, softened
½	cup sugar
3	large eggs

2½ teaspoons salt

Finishing Touches

1   large egg
Pinch each sugar and salt
Melted butter
Flour, for dusting

Line two large baking sheets with parchment paper.

In a small saucepan, heat milk and add cornmeal. Stir over medium heat and then reduce heat and cook until mixture thickens like porridge. Remove from heat and let cool to room temperature.

In a mixer bowl, hand-whisk water and yeast together and let stand 2 to 3 minutes to dissolve yeast. Add 1 cup flour and then add butter, sugar, eggs, salt, cooked cornmeal, and most of remaining flour. Let dough sit, covered, 15 minutes and then knead with dough hook on lowest speed 8 to 10 minutes, adding additional flour as necessary to make a soft dough.

Remove dough hook and spray dough with nonstick cooking spray. Cover entire mixer and bowl with a large clear plastic bag. Let rise 30 to 55 minutes until almost doubled.

Turn out dough onto a lightly floured work surface and gently deflate. Divide into 24 pieces to make small rolls, or make 1 dozen large rolls. Whisk egg and pinch of sugar and salt in a small bowl. Brush each roll with egg wash.

Place rolls on prepared baking sheets and spray with nonstick cooking spray. Cover loosely with plastic wrap and let rise about 40 to 60 minutes until almost doubled. Brush rolls with melted butter and dust with flour.

Preheat oven to 350°F. Bake until done and lightly browned, about 20 to 25 minutes.

These tender, golden, slightly sweet rolls are perfect to sop up gravy or use as the foundation for a cranberry turkey club sandwich the day after Thanksgiving. Of course, they are also wonderful toasted and buttered anytime. Make some little ones for the bread basket and some larger ones for sandwich rolls.

Bride's Boon Icebox Rolls

Makes 24 rolls

This recipe is for yesteryear's yeasted roll that rose in the icebox and yielded freshly baked puffy buns for supper the next day. Is it any wonder marriages endured?

¼ cup warm water (100°F to 110°F)
5¾ teaspoons rapid-rise yeast
6 cups bread flour
1 cup warm milk (100°F to 110°F)
1 cup half-and-half or light cream
½ cup unsalted butter, softened
2½ teaspoons salt

½ cup sugar
2 large eggs
1 tablespoon baking powder

Finishing Touch

Melted butter, for brushing

Line a large baking sheet with parchment paper.

In a mixer bowl, hand-whisk water and yeast together and let stand 2 to 3 minutes to dissolve yeast. Add 1 cup flour, milk, half-and-half, softened butter, salt, sugar, eggs, and baking powder and mix well. Add most of remaining flour and beat well until mixture is thick and doughlike. Cover and place in refrigerator.

The next day (up to 24 hours later), form dough into 24 rolls 1½ hours before ready to bake. Place on prepared baking sheet.

Preheat oven to 425°F. Brush each roll with some melted butter. Bake until golden brown, 15 to 20 minutes. Cool directly on baking sheet.

Old-Fashioned Yeasted Sweet Rolls

Makes 12 rolls

Not everyone likes things ultra sweet. Sometimes, a simple yeasted bun with strawberry jam and butter hits the spot. These make a wonderful offering for a coffee klatch or teatime gathering.

1½ cups warm water (100°F to 110°F)

2 tablespoons rapid-rise yeast

⅔ cup sugar

1 tablespoon pure vanilla extract

3 large eggs

⅓ cup unsalted butter, softened

2½ teaspoons salt

5 to 7 cups bread flour

Finishing Touches

1 large egg

Pinch each sugar and salt

Coarse or white sugar

Line a large baking sheet with parchment paper.

In a mixer bowl, hand-whisk water and yeast together and let stand 2 to 3 minutes to dissolve yeast. Whisk in sugar, vanilla, eggs, butter, and salt and blend well. Add 3 to 4 cups flour and mix. Knead with dough hook on lowest speed 6 to 8 minutes, adding more flour as necessary to make a soft, bouncy dough.

Remove dough hook and spray dough with nonstick cooking spray. Cover entire mixer and bowl with a large clear plastic bag. Let rise 45 to 60 minutes or until almost doubled.

Turn out dough onto a lightly floured work surface and gently deflate. Cut dough into 12 equal portions; shape each into a small round roll or bun.

Place rolls on prepared baking sheet, about 3 inches apart, and spray lightly with nonstick cooking spray. Cover loosely with plastic wrap and let rolls rise about 30 to 45 minutes until quite puffy and almost doubled.

Preheat oven to 375°F. Whisk egg and pinch of sugar and salt in a small bowl. Brush bread with egg wash and dust on some coarse or regular white sugar.

Place rolls in the oven, immediately reduce oven temperature to 350°F, and bake until nicely browned, 25 to 28 minutes. Cool rolls directly on baking sheet.

Bakers often opt for savory or slightly salted rolls or little breads as accompaniments for simple meals. Parker House and cloverleaf rolls are two examples of classic rolls of that variety. But sweet rolls were once a common treat in bakeries, cafés, and diners, as well as at home. They offered a respite from gooey cinnamon buns, but since they were slightly sweet, they were perfect with jam or preserves or simply enjoyed smeared with honey and butter alongside a pot of tea. Maybe they were borrowed from British teatime, where, to this day, sweet buns and rolls are still classic fare.

pizza & other flatbreads

Pizza dough is as versatile a dough as you can find. It is low in fat and easy to make. At the top of the list of its stellar qualities as a yeasted bread is the fact that it can thrive on barely a complete rise (for crisp pizzas), as well as a medium rise or a long rise (for thicker, chewier, heartier pizzas). In each case, you will be rewarded with a different crust—but an equally superlative pizza.

Pizza requires minimal—and yet unique—handling. Unlike bread dough, which often winds up as a loaf, pizza is a flatbread. It needs to rise, as bread does, but being a flatbread, it will not need as long of a rise, and a shorter or longer rise will yield different styles of pizzas and flatbreads, all of them good. Here, you'll discover my favorite versions of focaccia and fougasse, as well as several thick and chewy, cheesy, garlicky flatbreads.

Nothing is more authentic than pizza made at home with your regular oven and basic ingredients, tools, and equipment. Homemade pizza almost always outrivals the best from anywhere else. At the very least, it is going to be hotter and fresher! Follow my tips on the next pages and you can make exceptional pizzas of every possible description in your home oven. And what's more, they'll be crisper, zestier, and more flavorful. You just need some trade secrets and a wardrobe of recipes and ideas for variations. I believe the keys to success are using fresh ingredients and making small pizzas that are customized in order to create exotic fare versus just using the typical toppings. Pizzas can be symphonies of flavors, colors, textures, and tastes. Just remember—very little goes wrong in pizza making, and so much goes right.

Ingredients

Pizza dough can be made with all-purpose flour, bread flour, or a combination of the two. Pizza dough at its richest might feature a little sugar or honey, a touch of oil or shortening, some salt, and that is about it. It is a flatbread that really is a rustic throne to whatever you are garnishing it with. Rapid-rise yeast is ideal for pizza dough. You can use very little yeast for long- and slow-rise pizzas, or speed things up with more yeast for puffier, bready pizzas. Pizza edges can be plain, or you can crunch things up a bit by lining your pizza pan with olive oil and semolina, cornmeal, panko, or other breadcrumbs. You can also garnish the outer edges with sesame seeds for even more crunch and flavor. The key is to experiment with flavor and texture.

How to Make Pizza Dough

Methods

• **Bread Machine:** Add the recipe ingredients to the machine bread pan in the order given or per the machine instructions. Program on "Dough" cycle. Add a bit of flour or water if dough seems too slack or too dry. A soft, supple dough is easier to work with, so take care not to make a springy or heavy dough unless you want a bready pizza. Incidentally, a bread machine is a great pizza dough holding pen. If you want pizza dough ready and cannot be around to watch over it, make the dough with half the yeast called for in the recipe and use your bread machine. After six to eight hours, the dough will be perfect and ready to use.

• **Food Processor:** Place the liquid ingredients as well as yeast, salt, sugar, and 1 cup of the flour in the bowl of a large food processor and whiz to dissolve sugar and salt. Add remaining flour and process until a soft ball forms. Remove dough from the processor and allow to rest, covered with a tea towel, about 45 minutes.

• **Electric Mixer Using a Dough Hook:** Place water, other liquid ingredients, yeast, 1 cup of the flour, sugar, and salt in a mixer bowl; whisk briefly. Stir in remaining flour and then knead with a dough hook about 8 minutes to form a soft but not too sticky dough. Remove from the machine and allow to rest, covered with a tea towel, about 45 minutes.

• **By Hand:** Place water and yeast in a large bowl and whisk together briefly. Add sugar, salt, and oil and whisk; then stir in most of the flour and knead to form a soft but not too sticky dough. Knead 8 to 10 minutes. Remove dough from the bowl and allow it to rest, covered with a tea towel, about 45 minutes.

Never roll pizza dough. Simply cut off a hunk of dough, let it rest a few minutes, and gently stretch and coax it into shape.

Handling

Shorter kneads are best for pizza dough, and the slacker the dough, the more crisp and porous the finished pizza. In forming pizza, the best advice is to let it be. You never want to roll pizza dough; rather, cut off a hunk of dough, let it rest a few minutes, and gently stretch it into shape. If the dough retracts, give it a two- to three-minute respite. Stretch it again to fit your pan or simply to "pan it out" into a free-form pizza.

Baking Pizza

The only drawback when it comes to pizza is that home bakers have all-purpose ovens with large heating cavities, compared with a real pizza oven that features low headroom and an intense inferno to scorch and bake pizza to rustic perfection. There are baking stones (discussed below) and even home models of dedicated pizza ovens, but my recommendations are based on the typical ovens found in the home kitchen and easy-to-acquire tools and pans.

Oven Temperature

You might bake a pizza on the lower shelf or rack of your oven and, as the bottom browns, move it to an upper level to finish it off. A very hot oven (500°F) is best for pizza. It quickly bakes it on the top and the bottom. However, until you get used to the results of making pizza at home and know with certainty how hot is hot enough in your particular oven, rely on the oven temperatures given for each specific recipe. Baking on the upper or lower rack; using baking pans, stacked baking sheets, or baking stones; and preparing thin- or thick-crust pizzas with short or long rises are all variables that can affect the oven temperature.

Turning a Home Oven into a Pizza Oven

Here are a few ways to replicate a pizza oven in your home. Use a baking stone or tiles or try a stoneware assembly called a Hearth Kit (see "Source Guide" on page 316).

These vary in size, price, and performance, but all are rustic, heat-retentive surfaces that replicate an outdoor oven. It can be difficult to maneuver the stone or tiles once they are in the oven (they are hot and heavy!). You can arrange two layers of tiles—one layer of terra cotta tiles on the bottom rack and one on the upper—and this, while involving preparation, does indeed replicate a pizza oven. It is also nice to have tiles or a stoneware bottom to bake pies on.

Another trick is to bake the pizza on the upper rack and then slide it off (once it is set up a bit, it slides off easily) to a baking stone. Alternatively, make very thin pizzas that brown all over quite quickly on a baking sheet or in a cast-iron skillet.

As you can see, there are many roads to Rome when it comes to homemade pizza, and I generally use all of them—that is the fun of pizza!

Cast-Iron Skillets and Pizza Pans

Cast-iron skillets are about the best all-around pans for home pizza. They are convenient and they produce an amazing crust with little extra effort. Cast iron, aside from adding iron into everything cooked or baked on it, creates a rustic finish to pizzas.

Seasoned cast iron is the original and all-natural nonstick bakeware that offers great release, so crusts do not adhere to the bottom of the skillet. The skillets ensure perfectly round pizzas (if that is what you want). Having several sizes (10-, 9-, and 8-inch) means I can

make different varieties suiting different tastes and appetites. To prepare a seasoned cast-iron skillet, smear the bottom with a touch of olive oil or with oil and seasoned breadcrumbs. Place the pizza dough in the skillet and ease the edges of the dough to the sides of the skillet.

Some of the choices in pizza pans include anodized, black steel, or lightweight aluminum, as well as traditional or deep-dish.

The dual bonus with cast iron is that you can customize pizzas for each diner and conveniently use the skillet handle to take each pizza out of the oven. Pizzas also look nice served at the table in their baking skillets.

Anodized, a treated aluminum pan that attracts heat, is an excellent choice if you want a dark finish. Black steel makes for exceptional browning but is a little harder to maintain, since it must be seasoned and well dried to prevent rust. Commercial classic, lightweight, untreated aluminum pans are great for making thin and crisp pizzas. They are cheap and come in a large range of sizes.

Lastly, you can always bake pizzas in odd shapes and sizes on an olive oil–drizzled, parchment paper–lined rimmed baking sheet. Baking sheets are light and easy to handle and offer a lot of space to bake either a mammoth single pizza or a few small ones in rounds or ovals. They are also ideal when you want to pan out extra thin–crust pizzas.

Assembling and Garnishing Pizza

The key to pizza perfection is using fresh ingredients and making small custom pizzas. Follow my lead below.

1. Gently stretch the dough into pans or make some free-form pizzas, small or large.

2. Smear on some sauce and spices, such as garlic, salt, and pepper.

3. Add cheese and anything else you desire at this point. Loosely cover the pizzas with plastic wrap and let rise until ready for the oven.

4. Add some hot sauce after they come out of the oven.

In my test kitchen, we rarely serve pizza on plates. I serve pizza the way people serve seafood-boil suppers. The table is covered with parchment paper, a few pizza-cutting wheels, hot sauce, fresh herbs, and cheese. Everything is laid out, and then it is each person for himself. There are no dishes to clean up, and it feels more fun—like dining in a restaurant. In the end, pizza is not plate food anyway!

The Best Pizza Dough Ever

Makes 2 or 3 pizzas

1¾ cups warm water (100°F to 110°F)

2 teaspoons rapid-rise yeast

¼ cup semolina or 2 tablespoons cornmeal

2 teaspoons salt

1 tablespoon sugar or honey

3 tablespoons olive oil

2 cups all-purpose flour

3 to 4 cups bread flour

Olive oil, for drizzling

In a mixer bowl, hand-whisk water and yeast together and let stand 2 to 3 minutes to dissolve yeast. Briskly whisk in semolina, salt, sugar, oil, and all-purpose flour. Stir in enough bread flour to make a shaggy mass that is barely combined, about 2 minutes. Then cover loosely with plastic and let stand 30 minutes. Stir down dough and then knead with dough hook on lowest speed 6 to 8 minutes, dusting with additional flour as necessary to make a soft dough.

Remove dough hook, spray dough with nonstick cooking spray, and cover entire mixer and bowl with a large clear plastic bag. Let dough rise 45 to 60 minutes.

To make pizzas, gently deflate dough and divide into 2 or 3 large rounds, as required. You can place rounds in cast-iron skillets or on a parchment paper–lined baking sheet drizzled with olive oil. Stretch to fit pans, turning in edges to make a thick crust.

Once pizzas are formed, spray with nonstick cooking spray and then garnish as desired. Cover loosely with a large sheet of plastic wrap and let dough rise 90 minutes or until dough is very light and puffed up.

To bake, preheat oven to 475°F. Bake pizzas on upper rack until done and pizzas are browned all over, 12 to 20 minutes.

This recipe features two great methods from artisanal baking: resting the dough before it is thoroughly mixed and then allowing a long, slow second rise for a puffy, crisp pizza with nice holes inside. Topping the pizza before its second rise is one of my favorite tricks to better pizzas.

The Scent of Semolina

Semolina is a type of hard flour that comes from durum wheat. It can be very fine and powdery as a flour, but it is sometimes granular and similar to a fine cornmeal. It is good for giving a golden glow to a pizza dough; when dusted on the pan, it offers a nice crunch to pizza.

Classic Pizza Dough

Makes 3 (9-inch) pizzas

Every woman needs at least one little black dress and a perfect pizza dough. This dough is foolproof and is good for a variety of toppings.

1½ cups warm water (100°F to 110°F)

2½ teaspoons rapid-rise yeast

2 teaspoons sugar

1½ teaspoons salt

2 tablespoons olive oil

3 to 4 cups bread flour

Olive oil, for drizzling

Grease each of three 9-inch pizza pans with 1 tablespoon olive oil.

In a mixer bowl, hand-whisk water and yeast and let stand 2 to 3 minutes to dissolve yeast. Briskly whisk in sugar, salt, oil, and 2 cups flour and mix to make a soft mass. Knead with dough hook on lowest speed of mixer, dusting in additional flour as required to form a soft, elastic dough, about 5 to 8 minutes. Remove dough hook and spray dough with non-stick cooking spray. Cover entire mixer and bowl with a large clear plastic bag. Let dough rise until almost doubled, about 45 to 90 minutes.

Gently deflate dough. Press dough to fit prepared pans. If dough retracts, let it rest a few minutes and then gently coax it to fit pan. Drizzle a little olive oil on top of dough. Spread on tomato sauce and toppings of your choice.

Preheat oven to 425°F. Bake 15 minutes and then reduce oven temperature to 400°F. Bake another 15 to 20 minutes until cheese is melted and lightly browned.

Food-Court Pizza Dough

Makes 3 (12- to 14-inch) pizzas

Pan this dough out thick and give it a medium rise and a hot (not scorching) oven to get a food court–style pizza: thick, chewy, satisfying, and up for a hefty layer of cheese and pepperoni.

For quick suppers, I prepare this thin with an outer edge of sesame seeds and top it with Monterey Jack and fontina cheeses and herbs. When I serve it for crowds, family-style, or for kids, I pan it thick, smear it with sauce and mozzarella, and create a rolled border for added thickness as well as something to hold onto when eating a slice out of hand.

1 cup warm water (100°F to 110°F)

1½ teaspoons rapid-rise yeast

½ cup warm milk

3 tablespoons vegetable oil

4 teaspoons sugar

2 teaspoons salt

4 cups, approximately, bread flour

In a mixer bowl, hand-whisk water and yeast together and allow to stand 2 to 3 minutes to let yeast dissolve. Briskly whisk in milk, oil, sugar, salt, and most of bread flour. Using dough hook, knead on lowest speed of mixer 5 minutes to form a soft dough, adding more flour as required to help dough come together. Cover and let dough rest 20 minutes; then resume kneading on lowest speed of mixer and again adding only as much flour as required to permit dough to come together, another 3 to 4 minutes. **Remove** dough hook, cover entire mixer and bowl with a large clear plastic bag, and let dough rise until almost doubled in size, 1½ to 2 hours. Gently deflate dough and divide into portions to make the size pizza you want.

For thin, crisp pizzas, garnish as preferred, cover, and then allow a long

rise until dough is light and inflated. Preheat oven to 475°F. Bake on stacked parchment paper–lined baking sheets for 9 to 12 minutes.
For thick pizzas, pan out just under ½ inch thick, garnish, cover, and allow a short rise (30 to 45 minutes). Bake at 450°F on a parchment paper–lined single baking sheet 12 to 16 minutes.

Pizza Blanca

Makes 3 pizzas

Pizza Blanca Dough

2	cups warm water (100°F to 110°F)
2	teaspoons rapid-rise yeast
1½	cups all-purpose flour
3	tablespoons olive oil
4	teaspoons sugar
1¾	teaspoons salt
1½	cups or more bread flour
	Olive oil

Pizza Blanca Sauce

2	tablespoons butter
3	tablespoons all-purpose flour
1	cup milk
¼	teaspoon salt
⅛	teaspoon pepper
¼	teaspoon garlic powder
½	cup grated Parmesan or shredded Havarti cheese

Pizza Blanca Assembly Ingredients

12	cloves garlic, crushed
	Salt and pepper
	Large shavings of Parmesan cheese
	Minced fresh basil or oregano

Any pizza dough works with this recipe, but this rustic dough is created exclusively for this recipe. Garlic and fresh herbs make for a heady aroma here. A homemade and easy garlic béchamel is the crowning touch.

In a mixer bowl, hand-whisk water and yeast together and let stand 2 to 3 minutes to dissolve yeast. Add all-purpose flour and then briskly whisk in olive oil, sugar, and salt. Add most of bread flour and stir. Knead to make a soft, slack dough. Knead gently by hand or with a dough hook 5 to 8 minutes on lowest speed of mixer, dusting in more flour just to make dough hold together. Remove dough hook; spray dough with nonstick cooking spray. Cover entire mixer and bowl with a large clear plastic bag. Let dough rise 2 to 3 hours until puffy. Turn out dough onto a lightly floured work surface and gently deflate.

Line baking sheets with parchment paper; drizzle with oil. Divide dough into three portions; let rest 15 minutes. Stretch dough into three 9- to 12-inch rounds. Place on prepared baking sheets; cover loosely with plastic wrap and let dough rise.

To make Pizza Blanca Sauce, in a saucepan, melt butter and then stir in flour. Cook over medium heat 1 minute, stirring constantly. Slowly whisk in milk and cook, stirring until sauce thickens. Stir in salt, pepper, garlic, and cheese.

To assemble pizzas, smear crushed garlic on each. Dust with salt, pepper, freshly shaved cheese, and herbs. Drop dollops of sauce over surface, coating the top. Let pizzas rise a little or a lot (20 minutes to 1½ hours—the former for crisp and the latter for more bready). Preheat oven to 425°F to 450°F. **Bake** until cheese on top is sizzling and edges of pizzas are browned, about 10 to 15 minutes.

Cheesy Garlic Twisty Bread

Makes 24 small rolls

A pizza takeoff, these little rolls strike all the right notes: Made of a quick and light yeasted dough, each hides a chunk of cheese in its center and is dunked in a garlic-butter bath before being put in a small pan to rise. Once baked, the rolls—rife with herbs and garlic—are crusty outside and cheesy inside. A side of warm marinara for dipping is the final touch. Serve with a Caesar salad and Buffalo wings or alongside pizza, lasagna, or even broiled fish when you want something special to spruce up the meal.

In a pinch, you can start with leftover pizza dough or thawed frozen white bread dough. If you don't have panko, use regular breadcrumbs. The trick to this recipe is making a soft, light dough so that the rolls are light. Mozzarella is traditional, but Havarti or Monterey Jack actually melts better. These rolls are almost as good without the cheese.

Finishing Touches on Hot Pizza

The finishing touches are what separate home-baked pizza from what restaurants serve. Spritz extra virgin olive oil on the pizza as it comes out of the oven and then add some hot sauce and dust with finely minced fresh herbs for tons of cachet—and even more flavor and eye appeal.

Olive oil, for pan
⅓ cup panko or plain breadcrumbs

Dough

1 cup warm water (100°F to 110°F)
2½ teaspoons rapid-rise yeast
2 tablespoons olive oil
1¼ teaspoons salt
2 teaspoons sugar
3 to 4 cups bread flour

Garlic Dip

6 large cloves garlic, finely minced
¼ teaspoon salt
1 teaspoon garlic powder

¼ cup butter, melted
¼ cup olive oil
½ teaspoon dried Italian seasoning
¼ cup grated Parmesan cheese
24 chunks, each about ½ ounce, Monterey Jack, Havarti, or mozzarella cheese

Finishing Touches

3 to 4 tablespoons grated Parmesan cheese
½ cup finely shredded mozzarella
1 to 2 cups warmed marinara sauce

Line a baking sheet with parchment paper. Using a 13- x 9-inch pan or a 10-inch round cakepan or springform pan, drizzle olive oil to lightly cover bottom and dust on panko or other breadcrumbs. Place pan on prepared baking sheet.

In a mixer bowl, hand-whisk water and yeast together and let stand 2 to 3 minutes to dissolve yeast. Whisk in oil, salt, sugar, and most of bread flour. Mix ingredients and then knead with dough hook on lowest speed of mixer 8 to 10 minutes, dusting in more flour as necessary to make a very soft dough. Remove dough hook and spray dough with nonstick cooking spray. Cover entire mixer and bowl with a large clear plastic bag. Let dough rise 45 to 90 minutes or until almost doubled.

Meanwhile, prepare Garlic Dip. In a medium bowl, whisk minced garlic, salt, garlic powder, butter, oil, Italian seasoning, and Parmesan cheese.

Turn out dough onto a lightly floured work surface and gently deflate. Using a dough cutter or knife, cut dough into 24 portions. Tuck a chunk of cheese into each portion and then form into a taut ball. When all dough is prepared that way, dip each roll or ball into Garlic Dip. Line up in prepared pan. Top rolls with Parmesan and shredded mozzarella.

Cover rolls loosely with plastic wrap and let rise 45 to 60 minutes until almost doubled and very puffy. Preheat oven to 350°F. Bake until nicely browned on top and cheese is melted, 25 to 35 minutes. Pull apart bread to serve and offer marinara sauce on the side.

Pancetta Layered Bread

Makes 12 to 16 servings

A friend from Italy calls this *centi pelli* ("1000 skins") pizza, as there are many folds or stratas in this unique and rustic pizza bread.

Olive oil

Semolina, for dusting pan

Dough

1¾ cups warm water (100°F to 110°F)

1   tablespoon rapid-rise yeast

1   tablespoon sugar

2   large eggs

¼   cup olive oil

2   teaspoons salt

4½ to 5½ cups bread flour

Zesty Pancetta Filling

½   pound spicy salami, such as calabrese or pepperoni, thinly sliced

4   to 6 tablespoons olive oil

3   cloves garlic, minced

Salt and pepper to taste

2   teaspoons dried basil

2   cups grated Parmesan cheese

1   (6-ounce) jar artichoke hearts, coarsely chopped

1   cup black olives, pitted and minced

½   cup sun-dried tomatoes, minced

3   cups chopped cooked pancetta, drained

Finishing Touch

Semolina, for dusting

This bread would be lovely with a side salad of mâche lettuces and twin pestos of sun-dried tomatoes and artichokes. Serve with gazpacho and a jug of lemonade or sangría.

Line a 20- x 15-inch baking sheet with parchment paper. Smear olive oil on baking sheet and dust with semolina.

In a mixer bowl, hand-whisk water and yeast together and let stand 2 to 3 minutes to dissolve yeast. Briskly whisk in sugar, eggs, oil, and salt. Add flour and knead with dough hook on lowest speed 8 to 10 minutes, adding more flour as necessary to make a soft dough.

Remove dough hook and spray dough with nonstick cooking spray. Cover entire mixer and bowl with a large clear plastic bag. Let dough rise 30 minutes.

For Zesty Pancetta Filling, lightly sauté salami just to soften and cook slightly. Cool.

Turn out dough onto a lightly floured work surface and let rest 10 minutes. Then lightly roll out dough to a large rectangle, about 24 x 18 inches. Brush surface of dough with olive oil and then distribute minced garlic; dust with salt and generously with pepper. Dust on basil. Sprinkle on Parmesan cheese and then add artichokes, olives, sun-dried tomatoes, salami, and pancetta. Press ingredients into dough slightly.

Fold dough from top down into three or four folds, almost like you are folding a letter to mail. Gently lift dough onto prepared baking sheet. Using a rolling pin, press and roll dough out to fit to all corners of pan.

Smear top with olive oil; dust with semolina. Cover baking sheet loosely with large clear plastic bag, and let dough rise about 20 to 35 minutes.

Preheat oven to 350°F. Bake until top is golden brown, about 25 to 35 minutes. Cut or tear into large squares to serve.

Summery Tomato, Zesty Olive, and Onion Focaccia

Makes 2 breads

A local bakery puts out samples of its newest creations each week, and I am an avid fan. One day, it featured wonderful, puffy flatbread topped with fresh summer tomatoes, fat black olives, and slivered onions. Here is my own version.

Olive oil
Fine semolina, for dusting pan

Dough

1¼ cups warm water (100°F to 110°F)
1 tablespoon rapid-rise yeast
2 cups all-purpose flour
1 tablespoon sugar
1¾ teaspoons salt
¼ cup extra virgin olive oil
2 cups bread flour

Topping

6 to 8 medium to large ripe tomatoes, cut into thick slices and then quartered, or tons of cherry tomatoes, halved
2 cups pitted black olives, halved
1½ cups diced onions
Chopped fresh oregano, for dusting
Salt and pepper
Hot sauce
Fresh herbs

Prepare two 9-inch round cakepans with a smearing of olive oil and a dusting of semolina. Place on a parchment paper–lined baking sheet. You can also simply stretch these out gently to make free-form rounds and bake directly on prepared baking sheet.

In a mixer bowl, hand-whisk water and yeast together and let stand 2 to 3 minutes to dissolve yeast. Then add all-purpose flour and blend well. Add sugar, salt, and oil and mix well. Fold in bread flour. Knead with dough hook on lowest speed 5 to 8 minutes, adding more flour as necessary to make a soft, tacky dough. Remove dough hook, spray dough with nonstick cooking spray, and cover entire mixer and bowl with a large clear plastic bag. Let dough rise 60 to 90 minutes.

Turn out dough onto a lightly floured work surface and gently deflate. Divide in half and press each portion gently into prepared pans. Smear tops with oil and then garnish with tomatoes, olives, and onions and dust with oregano. Dust with salt and pepper.

Cover pans loosely with plastic wrap and let dough rise 45 to 60 minutes.

Preheat oven to 400°F.

Bake breads until golden or medium brown on top and tomatoes are softened, about 20 to 25 minutes. As breads come out of oven, drizzle on a bit more olive oil and some hot sauce and sprinkle with fresh herbs. Serve warm or at room temperature.

Double-Garlic Fougasse

Makes 1 large bread

A gourmet garlic experience, this is simply one of the zestiest, most addictive breads you will ever make. People literally tear into this while it is still hot. It is great served with salad, spaghetti, or on its own as a hearty snack. Fougasse is the flatbread of Provence, often slashed and stretched to resemble an ear of wheat.

1½ cups warm water (100°F to 110°F)	1 teaspoon, approximately, dried Italian seasoning
5 teaspoons rapid-rise yeast	4 to 6 cloves garlic, finely minced
1 tablespoon sugar	1 to 2 teaspoons garlic powder
2 teaspoons salt	½ cup, approximately, garlic-infused olive oil*
¼ cup olive oil	
4 to 5 cups bread flour	1 cup small hunks of Parmesan cheese, optional
Salt and pepper	

*Garlic oil makes this bread extra garlicky, but if you cannot find it, use extra virgin olive oil instead.

Line a large baking sheet with parchment paper.

In a mixer bowl, hand-whisk water and yeast together and let stand 2 to 3 minutes to dissolve yeast. Briskly whisk in sugar, salt, oil, and most of flour. Knead with dough hook on lowest speed of mixer 5 to 8 minutes, adding more flour as necessary to form a soft dough.

Remove dough hook from machine and spray dough with nonstick cooking spray. Cover entire mixer and bowl with a large clear plastic bag. Let dough rise 45 to 50 minutes. Meanwhile, assemble filling ingredients.

Turn out dough onto a lightly floured work surface and gently deflate. Pat out to a 12-inch round. Smear dough round with salt, pepper, Italian seasoning, minced garlic, garlic powder, 2 to 4 tablespoons garlic oil, and cheese (if using).

Roll up dough and let rest 5 minutes. Then roll dough flat again into a 10-inch round and repeat seasoning-oil treatment.

Let dough rest 10 minutes and then roll to a 12- to 15-inch round or oval (garlic and oil will leak out; this is fine).

Place dough on prepared baking sheet. Smear top with more salt, pepper, Italian seasoning, garlic, and oil. Make 3 deep cuts in dough going right through almost to baking sheet (**photo 1**). Stretch out these gashes somewhat to make 3 openings or ovals (**photo 2**).

Cover pan loosely with plastic wrap and let dough rise 30 minutes.

Preheat oven to 375°F. Bake bread 35 to 40 minutes until golden brown and crisp on the outside. Let cool slightly and serve.

Both fresh garlic and garlic powder dust this Mediterranean ode to garlic. If you can find fresh peeled garlic, which is increasingly available in specialty-food markets, invest in a full pound of it. It lasts for a year in the fridge or freezer and comes in handy for pizzas, vinaigrettes, or anything calling for fresh garlic.

Roasted Garlic and Potato Pizza à la Provence

Makes 8 to 10 appetizer servings or 6 to 8 main dish servings; also pictured on page 68

All this takes is pizza dough, mashed potatoes, onions, and bright slices of garden tomatoes. You have to make it to be convinced that potatoes on a pizza pie will bring raves. The garlic is pan-roasted with the onions and offers a special mellow garlic bouquet.

Olive oil
Cornmeal, optional

Dough

1½	cups warm water (100°F to 110°F)
5	teaspoons rapid-rise yeast
¼	cup olive oil
4	teaspoons honey
1	large egg
2½	teaspoons salt
4	to 6 cups bread flour

Topping

3	pounds onions, diced or thinly sliced
10	cloves garlic, peeled and minced
⅓	cup olive oil
2	to 3 cups mashed potatoes (leftovers are fine)

Finishing Touches

Salt and pepper
Chopped fresh thyme
Fresh minced chives

2	to 3 large tomatoes, sliced

Pizza on the House and Ready When You Are

One of two basic doughs and sauces are all you need to make a great pizza. After that, it is really a matter of technique. I often keep prepared dough on hand in oiled zip-top plastic bags in the fridge for last-minute pizzas. But you can also purchase dough from your local bakery, pizzeria, or supermarket. Or simply slap a premade *Boboli* round on the grill. If you have toppings prepped (or purchase pre-grated cheese and vegetables, meats, etc.), fresh, hot pizza can be made in less than 30 minutes.

Line a 21- x 15-inch baking pan with parchment paper. Drizzle on olive oil and dust with cornmeal (if using).

In a mixer bowl, hand-whisk water and yeast together and let stand 2 to 3 minutes to dissolve yeast. Then briskly whisk in oil, honey, egg, salt, and most of bread flour. Mix ingredients, attach dough hook, and knead on lowest speed 8 to 10 minutes, dusting in more flour as necessary to form a soft dough.

Remove dough hook from machine and spray dough with nonstick cooking spray. Cover entire mixer and bowl with a large clear plastic bag. Let dough rise 30 to 45 minutes or until almost doubled.

Meanwhile, in a large skillet, sauté onions and garlic slowly in olive oil over lowest heat possible. Sauté until caramelized and browned, 20 to 30 minutes. Cool well. Prepare mashed potatoes. Cool and reserve.

Turn out dough onto a lightly floured work surface and gently deflate. Pat out dough to fit pan. Drizzle on some olive oil and then smear on mashed potatoes. Top with caramelized onion and garlic; dust with salt, pepper, and a touch of thyme. Distribute chives on top of this. Top with sliced tomatoes.

Preheat oven to 350°F. Bake until golden brown on edges, 35 to 45 minutes. Sprinkle with additional fresh thyme.

Pepperoni Pizza Rolls

Makes 12 to 18 rolls

These rolls make a hefty lunchtime snack or midnight bite. Imagine cinnamon rolls—only done up savory-style with pepperoni and cheese. They are great hot or cold served with a salad and a tall glass of lemonade.

Dough

1½ cups warm water (100°F to 110°F)

5 teaspoons rapid-rise yeast

⅓ cup olive oil

2 tablespoons sugar

2½ teaspoons salt

4 to 5 cups bread flour

Filling

2 cups spaghetti sauce

2 cloves garlic, finely minced

3 tablespoons olive oil

Salt and pepper, for dusting

1 teaspoon dried Italian seasoning

1½ pounds shredded mozzarella cheese

8 to 12 ounces pepperoni, sliced

Finishing Touches

Olive oil

Freshly grated Parmesan cheese

Line a large baking sheet with parchment paper.

In a mixer bowl, hand-whisk water and yeast together and let stand 2 to 3 minutes to dissolve yeast. Briskly whisk in oil, sugar, salt, and most of flour. Mix ingredients and then knead with dough hook on lowest speed 8 to 10 minutes, adding more flour as necessary to make a soft, bouncy dough.

Remove dough hook and spray dough with nonstick cooking spray. Cover entire mixer and bowl with a large clear plastic bag. Let dough rise 45 minutes. Turn out dough onto a lightly floured work surface and gently deflate. Let stand another 20 minutes. Roll or press dough out into a 14- x 12-inch rectangle.

Smear on spaghetti sauce, garlic, and olive oil; dust with salt, pepper, and Italian seasoning. Scatter on cheese and pepperoni. Roll dough jellyroll style and place it on a baking sheet. Refrigerate or freeze 20 minutes and then cut into 1½ inch slices (chilling makes it easier to cut without it compressing dough).

Place slices (with some space between them) on prepared baking sheet. Brush tops with olive oil and dust with Parmesan cheese.

Cover baking sheet loosely with plastic wrap and let dough rise 20 to 35 minutes.

Preheat oven to 375°F. Bake until cheese is melted and bubbly and buns are golden, 20 to 25 minutes.

Deep-Dish Double-Crust Cheese Pizza

Makes 1 pizza, 6 to 8 servings

Two hands are what you need to hold up a piece of this double-crusted, cheese-filled Chicago-style pizza.

Olive oil
Seasoned breadcrumbs

Dough

½ cup warm water (100°F to 110°F)
5 teaspoons dry yeast
½ cup warm milk
2 tablespoons sugar
⅓ cup olive oil
2½ teaspoons salt
¼ cup cornmeal
1 cup all-purpose flour
5 to 6 cups bread flour

Sauce

2 cloves garlic, minced
2 tablespoons olive oil
1 28-ounce can Italian plum tomatoes
1 small onion, minced
1 small green bell pepper, chopped
1½ teaspoons dried oregano
1 teaspoon dried basil

½ teaspoon fennel seeds
½ teaspoon salt
¼ teaspoon pepper

Filling

2 cups shredded mozzarella cheese
1 cup shredded fontina or provolone cheese
¾ cup freshly grated Parmesan cheese
¼ teaspoon salt
¼ teaspoon pepper
1 teaspoon dried basil
¼ teaspoon dried oregano
2 cloves garlic, minced
Olive oil

Finishing Touches

Salt, pepper, garlic powder, and minced fresh herbs
Olive oil
Hot sauce

Drizzle bottom of a 10-inch springform pan with olive oil and sprinkle on seasoned breadcrumbs. Alternatively, you can use two 8-inch round cakepans. Stack two baking sheets together and line top sheet with parchment paper. Place pizza pan on baking sheet.

In a mixer bowl, hand-whisk water and yeast together and let stand 2 to 3 minutes to dissolve yeast. Briskly whisk in milk, sugar, oil, salt, cornmeal, all-purpose flour, and 5 cups bread flour and mix to make a soft mass. Knead with dough hook on lowest speed about 5 to 8 minutes, dusting in additional flour as required to form a soft, elastic dough. Remove dough hook and spray dough with nonstick cooking spray. Cover entire mixer and bowl with a large clear plastic bag. Let dough rise until almost doubled, about 45 to 60 minutes.

Meanwhile, for Sauce, sauté garlic in oil to soften. Add tomatoes, onion, green bell pepper, oregano, basil, fennel seeds, salt, and pepper. Simmer on low about 20 to 30 minutes, until sauce thickens. Cool thoroughly.

For Filling, toss together cheeses, salt, pepper, basil, oregano, garlic, and oil.

Turn out dough onto a lightly floured work surface and gently deflate. Cover loosely with plastic wrap, and let rest 15 minutes.

Press two-thirds of dough into a 12- to 14-inch circle. Line pan with dough, allowing for an overhang. Spoon in half of sauce and top with two-thirds of cheese filling; dust with some salt, pepper, garlic powder, and fresh herbs. Press out remaining dough. Press dough onto pizza, press overlap of bottom dough onto top, and pinch dough to seal. Brush with olive oil and season with more salt, pepper, garlic, and herbs. Smear on remaining sauce and top with remaining cheese filling. Add a bit more salt, pepper, garlic, and fresh herbs.

Preheat oven to 400°F. Bake 35 to 45 minutes until pizza is browned around edges and cheese is sizzling and golden. Let cool 10 minutes before cutting. Douse with hot sauce as it comes out of oven.

Garlic-Slathered Stretch Bread

Makes 2 flatbreads

No one remembers anything else about the meal when this bread is served. A simple white dough gets smeared with a garlicky paste that bubbles up in the oven and then gets crisp and bakes up into a golden wonder. This is one of those recipes that you will make once and then make once a week thereafter.

Olive oil

Dough

2   cups warm water (100°F to 110°F)

1¾ teaspoons rapid-rise yeast

1¾ teaspoons salt

4   teaspoons sugar

4   cups bread flour

Garlic Slather Topping

6   cloves garlic, finely minced

½   teaspoon salt

⅔   cup mayonnaise

1   cup grated Parmesan cheese

½   teaspoon dried Italian seasoning

⅓   cup extra virgin olive oil

2   cups shredded mozzarella cheese

Line a large baking sheet with parchment paper and drizzle with olive oil.
In a mixer bowl, hand-whisk water and yeast together and let stand 2 to 3 minutes to dissolve yeast. Briskly whisk in salt, sugar, and most of flour to make a soft dough. Knead with dough hook on lowest speed 5 to 8 minutes, adding more flour as necessary until dough is resilient but not tough. Remove dough hook and spray dough with nonstick cooking spray. Cover entire mixer and bowl with a large clear plastic bag. Let dough rise until doubled in size, 1½ to 3 hours.
Turn out dough onto a floured work surface; gently deflate. Cover dough loosely with plastic wrap and let rise. Meanwhile, make Garlic Slather Topping. Using a mortar and pestle, mash garlic with salt to a fine paste. Remove to a bowl. Fold in mayonnaise, Parmesan cheese, seasoning, and oil.
Divide dough in half. Stretch each to a long oval, about 18 x 6 inches. Place on prepared baking sheet, evenly spaced apart. Using back of a spoon, spread filling all over top of each bread. Top each with mozzarella cheese. Cover pan loosely with plastic wrap and let dough rise 1 to 1½ hours until puffy.
Preheat oven to 400°F. Bake until nicely golden on top and topping is sizzling, about 20 to 25 minutes.

Leftover bread can be sliced into sticks for dipping into marinara sauce or used as sandwich bread and pressed into a panini-style snack.

scones & biscuits

Scones and biscuits are particularly appealing for their flakiness and simplicity of taste, as well as for the fact that they create an oasis of pleasure when you enjoy them with a cup of tea or coffee. Both are incredibly fast and easy to bake, making them my first choice when hosting an impromptu visit from a friend.

As accustomed as we are to seeing scones in cafés throughout North America, they are undoubtedly British in heritage and are a wonderfully sweet example of how a baking concept can be adopted and adapted. Across the pond, scones are rather modest tidbits that are similar to soda bread and like our version of biscuits (whereas, in the UK, a biscuit is more likely to be a cookie). We New World bakers have made a big fuss over scones. In essence, we have taken the roots of this pastry into a new and inventive realm, keeping the things we like about scones and adding variations that only make them more enticing.

Scones can be rather glamorous, but, for all intents and purposes, they are essentially fat, large, and sweet biscuits. Scones rely solely on cold butter for that sought-after delicate, flaky texture. Biscuits are more often made with shortening. Scones can be filled with a myriad of good things, mostly sweet or nutty, and are just as often cut into wedges as presented in rounds or in drop form. Scones are served with coffee and tea or as a dessert, whereas biscuits, made in smaller batches, are served more as a side bread.

Both scones and biscuits retain a certain mystique and are closely tethered to heritage baking. People tend to bake scones from family recipes more than from books, since it is often a family member who holds the best and most treasured recipe in their files. Ah, but if only Grandma had thought to include the secret tricks!

Scones and biscuits are best made fresh and eaten the day they are baked—and who better than a home baker to offer that? Enjoy this mix of plump scones and biscuits on the following pages. They're bursting with fruit, cheese, nuts, chocolate, and more and will guarantee some great aromas in your kitchen.

Scones are easy to make—and biscuits even more so—but there are some key pointers to help you make the biggest, flakiest scones and biscuits ever. All ingredients being equal, the key is in the handling.

Ingredients

Scones and biscuits are simply mixed together from cream, milk, or buttermilk; butter and sometimes shortening; eggs; and, on occasion, salt and baking powder and/or baking soda. What is crucial is the freshness of the baking powder, so make sure yours is truly fresh.

Other ingredients—such as vanilla, chocolate chips, citrus zest, nuts, herbs, and cheese—are what dramatically change the flavor or even the texture of a scone, so be sure to use the best quality and handle all ingredients with care.

Mixing and Handling

Nothing makes shorter work of scones or biscuits than a generously sized (9- to 11-cup flour capacity) food processor that easily handles the step of cutting butter into flour. Then you can either finish the flaky gems in the machine or turn out the fat-flour mixture into a bowl and finish by hand.

For mixing these breads, nothing is better than a Danish dough whisk. It looks like a carpet beater but is, in fact, second to none as a tool that makes short work of combining the liquid (cream, buttermilk, egg) and fat-flour mixture that eventually becomes a scone or biscuit.

Scones and biscuits are all about three things: technique, technique, and technique. They are totally dependent on how you cut the fat into the flour and how you handle the dough. Proper or artful handling is where the flakiness of a scone or biscuit initiates its journey.

Cold butter and/or cold shortening and cold liquid render the best-textured scones and biscuits. Make sure then that the fat comes straight from the fridge and that the liquid ingredient is icy cold.

The first step in most scone or biscuit recipes instructs you to cut in the fat. What this means is to cut up the butter or shortening into small bits and then cut the bits into the flour until it resembles coarse meal. You can, as I mentioned, use a food processor or a pastry blender to do this. This can otherwise be done by gently sanding the flour and fat between your fingertips or by using two knives to cut through the fat and flour in a motion that resembles cutting meat on a plate. The resulting flour-coated grains are then just moistened with the liquid ingredient until they barely adhere.

Always retain some of the liquid rather than dumping it all in at once. You may actually need less liquid than the recipe calls for. Once the grains are moistened, gently knead the dough in the bowl into a shaggy mass by hand.

Turn out the shaggy dough onto a lightly floured work surface and gently knead no more than 8 to 10 times. Overworking the dough toughens the end product.

Use a cookie cutter dipped in flour to cut biscuits, making the cut in one clean punching motion. Do not twist as you remove the cookie cutter because this tends to make the biscuit topple sideways during baking. Biscuits can also be cut into squares with a sharp knife.

For fluffy layered biscuits, the dough should be rolled and cut between ½ inch to ¾ inch thick. Scones are typically cut and baked as wedges, but they can also be rounds.

Storage

Scones and biscuits freeze well stored in a zip-top plastic bag. Fresh ones are so fast and easy to make, though, that I recommend baking a fresh batch whenever you want to serve them. Toppings, such as finishing glazes or frostings, extend the shelf life of scones and biscuits while adding beauty.

Consider a large food processor your 'scone and biscuit' machine, since it does a great job of cutting fat into flour.

Blueberry-Blackberry Honey Butter-Glazed Scones

Makes 8 to 12 scones; also pictured on page 84

A double helping of berries makes these scones special. Almost any fruit would be delicious, but this mix of blue and black fruits is exceptional.

1	tablespoon fresh lemon juice
1	cup, approximately, whipping cream
3½	cups all-purpose flour
½	cup sugar
½	teaspoon salt
4	teaspoons baking powder
½	teaspoon baking soda
¾	cup unsalted butter, cut into chunks
1	large egg

2	teaspoons pure vanilla extract
½	to ¾ cup frozen blueberries
½	to ¾ cup frozen blackberries or raspberries

Finishing Touch

Milk or melted butter, for brushing

Glaze

⅓	cup honey
¼	cup unsalted butter

Put lemon juice in a 1-cup measuring cup, pour in whipping cream to 1-cup mark, and let stand a few minutes to make soured cream.

Preheat oven to 425°F. Stack two baking sheets together and line top sheet with parchment paper. Arrange oven rack to upper third position.

In a food processor, add flour, sugar, salt, baking powder, and baking soda and blend briefly. Add butter and pulse to make a coarse, grainy mixture. Turn out mixture into a large bowl and make a well in center. Add egg, vanilla, and enough soured cream to make a soft but firm dough. Gently fold in berries.

Knead briefly on a lightly floured work surface, adding more flour, if required, to make a firm dough. Pat out to 1-inch thickness. Cut into wedges or rounds and place on prepared baking sheets **(photo, at right)**. Brush each scone with milk or melted butter.

Bake until scones are nicely browned, about 16 to 19 minutes.

Meanwhile, for Glaze, heat honey and butter in a liquid measuring cup in a microwave until mixture is just simmering, about 1½ minutes at HIGH, stirring after 45 seconds.

Brush scones lightly with honey-butter glaze as they come out of oven. Let stand on baking sheets. Repeat with more honey-butter glaze, more generously, about 15 minutes later.

Fresh Scones 24-7

I love scones on day one. I still love them on day two and day three, but there is no ignoring the fact that they do start to dry out by then. The method of brushing them with a syrup of butter and honey once (as soon as they come out of the oven) and then again (about 15 minutes later) prolongs their freshness in a very sweet way, as evidenced in this recipe. The scones stay wonderfully moist and flavorful for a good four days, and the sweetened crust is irresistible. This is a trick you can anoint on any sweet scone.

My Best Flaky Buttermilk Scones

Makes 8 to 10 scones

The hefty quantity of butter used in these wonders makes them flaky and rich. You can substitute sour milk (milk with lemon juice added) or loose, plain yogurt for the buttermilk, and the scones will still do you proud.

The trick to these scones is shredding the cold butter, freezing it, and then mixing it in. It is an easy way to cut the butter into the dry ingredients, and it also results in extra high–rising pastrylike scones. If you have pastry flour on hand, you can substitute it for half of the all-purpose. I often add 2 teaspoons vanilla extract, but I like these scones with the pure taste of butter just as well.

4 cups all-purpose flour
½ cup sugar
½ teaspoon salt
2 teaspoons baking powder
½ teaspoon baking soda
1½ cups unsalted butter, cut into chunks or shredded and frozen

1 large egg
1¼ cups buttermilk

Finishing Touches

Milk or melted butter, for brushing
Sugar, for dusting

Preheat oven to 425°F. Stack two baking sheets together and line top sheet with parchment paper. Arrange oven rack to upper third position. **In a food processor bowl,** add flour, sugar, salt, baking powder, and baking soda and blend briefly. Add butter and pulse to make a coarse, grainy mixture. Turn out into a large bowl. Make a well in center; add egg and most of buttermilk and stir lightly with a fork to blend. Add remaining buttermilk if needed to make a soft shaggy dough.

Turn out mixture onto a lightly floured work surface and knead 8 to 10 times until mixture is just barely rollable. Pat or roll out to 1-inch thickness and cut into 3-inch wedges with a cookie cutter. To do this, cut a 4-inch circle and then cut it in half. This will give you nice wedges. Place wedges on prepared baking sheets. Brush tops with milk or melted butter and dust with sugar.

Bake until golden, about 12 to 15 minutes.

Mr. Darcy's Wheat Meal Scones

Makes 15 to 20 scones

Nothing beats these scones with their gentle spice, pure buttery taste, and lush scattering of currants and raisins. I call these "Mr. Darcy" scones because of their immutable British heritage and wonderful integrity of taste—and because Jane Austen would have approved.

½ cup uncooked regular oats
2⅔ cups all-purpose flour
⅔ cup whole wheat flour
⅓ cup firmly packed brown sugar
5 tablespoons white sugar
1 teaspoon salt
1 teaspoon baking powder
1 teaspoon baking soda
¼ teaspoon ground cloves
½ teaspoon ground cinnamon
¾ cup unsalted butter, cut into chunks

1 large egg
½ to ¾ cup buttermilk
½ cup dark raisins, plumped and dried (see page 18)
½ cup currants, plumped and dried (see page 18)

Finishing Touches

Milk, cream, or melted butter, for brushing
Coarse or regular sugar

These scones have a certain refinement, which is balanced by the different flours and modest use of spice. Use a food processor to pulverize the oats for these amazingly rustic wheat-and-oat scones.

Preheat oven to 375°F. Stack two baking sheets together and line top sheet with parchment paper. Arrange oven rack to upper third position. **In a food processor,** grind oats until fine. Add flours, brown sugar, white sugar, salt, baking powder, baking soda, cloves, and cinnamon and blend dry ingredients briefly. Add butter and pulse to make a coarse, grainy mixture.

Turn out mixture into a large bowl. Make a well in center and add egg and most of buttermilk; mix with a fork. Add remaining buttermilk if needed to make a stiff dough. Gently fold in raisins and currants. Knead on a lightly floured work surface a few times to get dough to hold together. Roll or press out to 1-inch thickness. Using a plain or preferably fluted 3-inch cutter, cut dough into rounds. Place on prepared baking sheets. Brush with milk, cream, or butter and dust with sugar. **Bake** until lightly browned around edges, 15 to 20 minutes.

Carrot Cake Scones

Makes 12 large scones or 24 miniatures

My test kitchen is where I like to push the baking envelope by combining flavors and concepts in new ways. In this scone recipe, there are neat elements of classic carrot cake in quick-to-whip-up miniature scones that are elegant enough for guests but also "carrot-cakey" enough for a summer picnic or brown-bag lunch.

You can make these scones large, but since they are rich, minis are a good way to go, too. Place each miniature scone in a paper liner to serve on a tray.

3 cups all-purpose flour
⅔ cup sugar
½ teaspoon salt
1 tablespoon baking powder
½ teaspoon baking soda
1½ teaspoons ground cinnamon
1 tablespoon orange zest, finely minced
½ cup ground walnuts
½ cup unsalted butter, cut into chunks
1 cup buttermilk
1 large egg
1½ teaspoons pure vanilla extract
1 cup shredded carrots
½ cup golden raisins or minced, dried pineapple

Cream Cheese Glaze

½ cup or 4 ounces cream cheese, softened
1½ to 2 cups confectioners' sugar
1 tablespoon fresh lemon juice
1 teaspoon pure vanilla extract

Finishing Touches

¾ cup toasted coconut
Carrot shreds
Orange zest
Ground cinnamon

Preheat oven to 400°F. Stack two baking sheets together and line top sheet with parchment paper. Arrange oven rack to upper third position.
In a food processor, add flour, sugar, salt, baking powder, baking soda, cinnamon, orange zest, and walnuts and blend briefly. Add butter and pulse to make a coarse, grainy mixture. Turn out into a large bowl. Make a well in center and stir in buttermilk, egg, and vanilla. Stir with a fork to make a soft batter; then fold in carrots and raisins (**photo 1**). Let rest 5 minutes.
Pat or press out dough to ¾-inch thickness on a floured work surface. Cut into 3-inch rounds (**photo 2**). Place on prepared baking sheets.
Bake until lightly browned, about 15 to 20 minutes. Cool scones on a wire rack.
Meanwhile, to make Cream Cheese Glaze, place cream cheese, confectioners' sugar, lemon juice, and vanilla in food processor. Process to make a smooth glaze. When scones are completely cooled, spread generously with cream cheese glaze (**photo 3**). Top with toasted coconut, carrot shreds, orange zest, and cinnamon.

1

2

3

Double-Dutch Chocolate Scones

Makes 12 scones

Cocoa in the batter and huge chunks of white and semisweet chocolate make these scones rich and full of added dimension. A final smear of melted chocolate makes these pretty sinful and, at the very least, extravagant. I also stir in toffee bits or chopped-up toffee candy bar for Chocolate-Toffee Scones.

Let Them Eat Cakelike Scones

If you want a cakey rather than flaky scone, any of the scone recipes in this chapter can be made by using softened butter. Cream the sugar and softened butter together, add the egg and liquid, and then add the flour. This makes for delightful scones that will be more cake-like and tender instead of flaky.

3   cups all-purpose flour
¾   cup sugar
½   teaspoon salt
¾   cup cocoa powder
1   tablespoon baking powder
½   teaspoon baking soda
Pinch ground cinnamon
¾   cup unsalted butter, cut into chunks
1   large egg
2   tablespoons strong brewed coffee
2   teaspoons pure vanilla extract

1   cup whipping cream
½   cup coarsely chopped semisweet chocolate
½   cup white chocolate, coarsely chopped

Finishing Touches

1   cup chopped semisweet chocolate, melted and cooled slightly
1   cup chopped white chocolate, melted and cooled slightly

Preheat oven to 425°F. Stack two baking sheets together and line top sheet with parchment paper. Arrange oven rack to upper third position.
In a food processor, add flour, sugar, salt, cocoa, baking powder, baking soda, and cinnamon and blend briefly. Add chunks of butter and pulse to make a coarse, grainy mixture.
Remove mixture to a large bowl. Make a well in center and stir in egg, coffee, vanilla, and most of cream. Stir with a fork, adding remaining cream if needed to make a soft dough. Stir in ½ cup each semisweet and white chocolate and then remove dough to a lightly floured work surface. Knead gently to make a dough that holds together. Divide dough in half and pat or roll each portion into a 6-inch circle, about 1½ inches thick. Cut each into 6 wedges.
Place on prepared baking sheets and place in oven. Reduce oven temperature to 400°F and bake until dry to the touch (it is hard to see by the color of the crust, since chocolate scones are dark to begin with), about 18 to 22 minutes.
Smear melted semisweet chocolate on each scone and, once chocolate sets, drizzle with white chocolate. Let chocolate set.

Mandarin and Chocolate Chip Scones

Makes 14 to 20 scones, depending on size

Need a quick baked gift that impresses a crowd? These gorgeous, tender, buttery, and lofty scones are perfect. The buttery glaze is made with orange liqueur, but orange oil or juice is also just dandy.

4   cups all-purpose flour

1   cup sugar

¾   teaspoon salt

4   teaspoons baking powder

½   teaspoon baking soda

1   cup unsalted butter, cut into chunks

1   large egg

1½   teaspoons pure vanilla extract

Zest of 1 orange, finely minced

¾   cup buttermilk

1   cup semisweet chocolate chips

Finishing Touch

Melted butter or milk, for brushing

Glaze

2½   cups, approximately, confectioners' sugar

2   tablespoons unsalted butter, melted

½   teaspoon orange oil or 1 tablespoon orange liqueur, such as Grand Marnier

Milk, as required

Preheat oven to 425°F. Stack two baking sheets together and line top sheet with parchment paper. Arrange oven rack to upper third position.
In a food processor, add flour, sugar, salt, baking powder, and baking soda and blend briefly. Add butter and pulse to make a coarse, grainy mixture. Turn out mixture into a large bowl and make a well in center. Add egg, vanilla, orange zest, and most of buttermilk. Stir with a fork, adding remaining buttermilk if needed to make a soft dough. Stir in chocolate chips.
Knead gently on a lightly floured work surface. Pat to 1-inch thickness. Cut into 14 to 20 circles or wedges. Place on prepared baking sheets and brush scones with butter or milk. Place in oven and immediately reduce oven temperature to 400°F. Bake until scones are nicely browned, about 12 to 18 minutes.
Whisk Glaze ingredients together in a small bowl, adding enough milk to make a drippy glaze. Slather on warm baked scones. Let glaze set.

Baking-Class Cranberry Cream Scones

Makes 10 to 12 scones

I teach how to make these scones at all my Pies 'n' Scones baking classes, and they never fail to win kudos. This recipe is one of my favorites, similar to one featured at the New England Culinary Institute in Vermont. While a guest teacher there, I often prepped my class ingredients alongside the student bakers and made batches and batches of these scones for the Sunday brunch at the hotel associated with the school.

3 cups all-purpose flour

⅔ cup sugar

1 teaspoon salt

1 tablespoon baking powder

¾ cup unsalted butter, cut into chunks

2 large eggs

1 teaspoon pure vanilla extract

⅓ to ½ cup heavy whipping cream or whipping cream, or more, as required

1½ cups frozen cranberries, coarsely chopped

½ cup currants or raisins, plumped and dried (see page 18)

Finishing Touches

Whipping cream

Sugar, for sprinkling

Preheat oven to 425°F. Stack two baking sheets together and line top sheet with parchment paper. Arrange oven rack to upper third position. **In a food processor,** add flour, sugar, salt, and baking powder and blend briefly. Add butter and pulse to make a coarse, grainy mixture. Turn out mixture into a large bowl. Make a well in center and stir in eggs, vanilla, and cream to make a soft but firm dough (**photo 1**). Fold in cranberries and currants. Knead by hand briefly on a lightly floured work surface (**photo 2**) and then pat into a large round. Dough should be about 1 inch thick. Cut into 4-inch circles (**photo 3**); then cut these in half. Place on prepared baking sheets. Brush generously with cream and sprinkle on sugar (**photo 4**). **Bake** until scones are lightly browned around the edges, about 15 to 20 minutes.

Cinnamon Bun Scones

Makes 15 to 20 scones or 36 miniatures

Want the taste but not the fuss of a yeasted cinnamon bun? Then these morsels are for you. Great for freezing, these scones are small enough that you can eat two and still feel you have not overindulged. Cinnamon is on the outside; inside is a tender crumb scone that has a light vanilla-butter scent.

3	cups all-purpose flour
1	cup sugar
¾	teaspoon salt
4	teaspoons baking powder
¾	cup unsalted butter, cut into chunks
2	teaspoons pure vanilla extract
2	large eggs

¾ to 1 cup heavy whipping cream or whipping cream

Cinnamon Dip

4	tablespoons unsalted butter, melted
2	teaspoons ground cinnamon
2	to 3 cups confectioners' sugar

Whipping cream or milk, as required

Preheat oven to 425°F. Stack two baking sheets together and line top sheet with parchment paper. Arrange oven rack to upper third position.
In a food processor, add flour, sugar, salt, and baking powder and blend briefly. Add butter and pulse to make a coarse, grainy mixture.
Turn out mixture into a large bowl. Make a well in center and stir in vanilla, eggs, and whipping cream to make a soft dough. If it is stiff, add more cream.
Using an ice cream scoop, deposit 15 to 20 scones on prepared baking sheets, or use a smaller 2-tablespoon cookie scoop and deposit 3 dozen baby scones (**photo 1**).
Bake until scones are puffy and golden brown, about 22 to 25 minutes.
Meanwhile, for Cinnamon Dip, whisk together all ingredients until you have a thick but drippy glaze. Add more confectioners' sugar or cream as required.
Cool scones to warm and then dip into Cinnamon Dip (**photo 2**). Dip scones again once topping is set.

Giant Sweet Cheddar Biscuits

Makes 5 to 7 large biscuits

Neighborhood cafés offer unique items to enjoy with coffee. One of the coffeehouses I frequent offers these rather flat biscuits they call scones, which are actually golden and sweet and feature huge chunks of sharp Cheddar cheese in a flattened pillow of pastry. They are as unusual as they are scrumptious. These scones are not light and flaky; they are solid and so very good.

If you are in a hurry or want another shape for your biscuits, simply make the dough a bit wetter and pat all of the dough into a prepared 9-inch square pan or a 10-inch cast-iron skillet. You can also roll or pat this biscuit dough out to a 1-inch thickness in rectangular pans. Mark off squares, cutting halfway through the dough. Then brush with butter and bake.

2 cups all-purpose flour
¼ cup sugar
1 teaspoon salt
2 teaspoons baking powder
½ cup unsalted butter, cut into chunks
½ cup shredded medium or sharp Cheddar cheese

1 large egg
⅔ cup, approximately, milk
1 cup, generous, ½-inch chunks of sharp Cheddar cheese
Melted unsalted butter, for brushing
Flour, for dusting

Preheat oven to 425°F. Stack two baking sheets together and line top sheet with parchment paper. Arrange oven rack to upper third position.
In a food processor, add flour, sugar, salt, and baking powder and blend briefly. Add butter and pulse to make a coarse, grainy mixture. Turn out into a large bowl. In center of dry mix, stir in shredded Cheddar and toss; then add egg and most of milk to make a stiff dough. Add more milk if needed for dough. Fold in Cheddar cheese chunks.
On a lightly floured work surface, knead dough gently. Press to ¾-inch thickness. Cut into 3- or 4-inch squares. Dab with a little melted butter. Dust with a bit of flour and place on prepared baking sheets.
Bake until golden brown, about 17 to 22 minutes.

Classic Southern Buttermilk Biscuits

Makes 12 biscuits

If you have *White Lily* flour on hand, you can use it for both the flours called for below. Otherwise, use a combination of all-purpose and pastry flours for these heavenly, light biscuits.

1¾ cups all-purpose flour
¼ cup pastry flour or all-purpose flour
1 tablespoon sugar
½ teaspoon salt
4 teaspoons baking powder
½ teaspoon baking soda

¼ cup plus 2 tablespoons shortening, or mix of unsalted butter and shortening
⅔ to ¾ cup buttermilk
Melted butter, for brushing
Flour, for dusting

Preheat oven to 425°F. Stack two baking sheets together and line top sheet with parchment paper. Arrange oven rack to upper third position.
In a food processor, add flours, sugar, salt, baking powder, and baking soda and blend briefly. Add shortening (or butter and shortening mixture) and pulse to make a coarse, grainy mixture. Sprinkle buttermilk over flour mixture, stirring lightly with a fork until ingredients are evenly moistened; mix by hand. Turn out dough onto a lightly floured work surface and knead a few more times until you are able to gently roll dough or it holds together.
Pat or roll out to ½- to ¾-inch thickness and cut with a 2-inch cookie cutter. Brush tops liberally with melted butter. Dust with flour. Place on prepared baking sheets. Bake until lightly browned, about 12 to 14 minutes.

Secret Trick 1860 Baking Powder Biscuits

Makes 12 to 16 biscuits

Pioneer cooks relied on fresh buttermilk for very light biscuits. The acid in buttermilk makes for especially high-risin' biscuits. My trick is to augment the tenderness of these biscuits by using whipping cream instead of buttermilk and "souring" the whipping cream with lemon juice. The result is an incredibly tender and flavorful biscuit. To make these shortcake biscuits, increase the sugar to ⅓ cup and use 6 tablespoons butter.

1	tablespoon lemon juice
⅔ to ¾	cup whipping cream
2	cups all-purpose flour
1	tablespoon sugar
½	teaspoon salt
4½	teaspoons baking powder
½	teaspoon baking soda

3	tablespoons shortening
3	tablespoons unsalted butter, cut into chunks

Finishing Touch

Milk or melted butter, for brushing

In a measuring cup, stir lemon juice and whipping cream together and let stand a few minutes.
Preheat oven to 425°F. Stack two baking sheets together and line top sheet with parchment paper. Arrange oven rack to upper third position.
In a food processor, add flour, sugar, salt, baking powder, and baking soda and blend briefly. Add shortening and butter and pulse to make a coarse, grainy mixture. Turn out into a large bowl, drizzle soured cream over the mixture, and stir lightly with a fork to blend. Turn out onto a lightly floured work surface and knead 8 to 10 times until mixture is just rollable.
Pat or roll out to 1-inch thickness and cut into 2-inch disks with a cookie cutter. Place on prepared baking sheets. Brush tops with milk or melted butter. Bake until golden, about 12 to 15 minutes.

For tender bottoms on your biscuits, bake on parchment paper–lined baking sheets; for crusty bottoms, bake in a cast-iron skillet on the upper oven rack and reduce the oven temperature to 400°F.

Cheese, Jalapeño, and Tomato-Pesto Biscuits

Makes 8 large biscuits

Savory, zesty, and satisfying, these huge biscuits are almost a meal in themselves. Split and serve them sandwich-style with a folded omelet.

You can also make these savory biscuits small and offer them with salsa as a party starter.

2 cups all-purpose flour
½ cup cornmeal
1 tablespoon sugar
1 teaspoon salt
1 tablespoon dry mustard
4 teaspoons baking powder
½ teaspoon baking soda
⅛ teaspoon black pepper
½ cup unsalted butter, cut into chunks
¾ cup, approximately, buttermilk
1 large egg
¼ cup finely minced green onions

3 tablespoons finely minced fresh cilantro
½ cup fresh or canned corn kernels
2 cups shredded sharp white or orange Cheddar cheese
2 tablespoons minced jalapeño peppers
3 to 4 tablespoons sun-dried tomato pesto

Finishing Touch

Melted butter

Preheat oven to 425°F. Stack two baking sheets together and line top sheet with parchment paper. Arrange oven rack to upper third position.

In a food processor, add flour, cornmeal, sugar, salt, dry mustard, baking powder, baking soda, and black pepper and blend briefly. Add butter and pulse to make a coarse, grainy mixture. Turn out into a large bowl. Sprinkle buttermilk over mixture, add egg, and stir lightly with a fork to blend. Add onions, cilantro, corn, cheese, and peppers and drop in bits of pesto. Mix to make a soft dough, adding more buttermilk, if required, to hold mixture together.

Turn out dough onto a lightly floured work surface and knead 8 to 10 times until dough is just rollable. Roll out to 1-inch thickness and cut into 3½-inch circles with a cookie cutter. Place on prepared baking sheets. Brush tops with melted butter.

Place biscuits in oven, reduce oven temperature to 400°F, and bake until golden and cheese is leaking out and melting, 18 to 20 minutes. Brush again with melted butter as biscuits come out of oven.

Overnight Flaky Angel Biscuits

Makes about 30 biscuits

A combination of yeast and baking powder—but no kneading—makes these biscuits extra light. An overnight rise makes them ready to bake. Prepare the dough and refrigerate. Portions of dough can be baked (or fried) as required. One of our testers, who has a bed-and-breakfast in New England, calls these biscuits "reputation builders." I call them "legend makers." If you decide to freeze them (unbaked), increase the yeast to 5½ teaspoons.

5½	cups all-purpose flour		5	teaspoons rapid-rise yeast
3	tablespoons sugar		½	cup warm water (100°F to 110°F)
2½	teaspoons salt		2	cups warm buttermilk
8	teaspoons baking powder			
1	teaspoon baking soda			**Finishing Touches**
½	cup shortening or butter		1	large egg, beaten
¼	cup unsalted butter, cut into chunks			Melted butter or flour

In a large bowl, stir together flour, sugar, salt, baking powder, and baking soda and blend briefly. Cut in shortening and butter until crumbly and well distributed. In a small bowl, sprinkle yeast over warm water and stir briefly to dissolve yeast.

Add yeast to flour mixture and mix once; then add warm buttermilk and toss with a fork to blend and moisten, creating a soft dough. Cover bowl and refrigerate (at least overnight or up to 2 days).

To prepare a batch of fresh biscuits, preheat oven to 400°F. Stack two baking sheets together and line top sheet with parchment paper. Arrange oven rack to upper third position.

Divide dough into thirds. On a lightly floured work surface, roll out one-third of dough to 1-inch thickness. Cut into rounds, wedges, or squares with a biscuit cutter or knife. For angel-shaped biscuits, cut into 4-inch rounds. Cut each round in half (**photo 1**) and, using a bit of a beaten egg, place two halves with rounded parts touching to form angel "wings" on prepared baking sheets (**photo 2**).

Place all biscuits on prepared baking sheets and, if desired, brush with melted butter or sprinkle lightly with a touch of flour.

Bake until lightly browned on top, 12 to 15 minutes.

For a delicate 'fairy dust look,' sift a touch of flour on these biscuits just before baking.

the muffin shoppe

Big, bold, gourmet-style muffins look gorgeous and are totally tempting. Contemporary muffins are really mega cupcakes or mini coffee cakes in disguise—no wonder we love them! Once you unleash the potential, the flavors and taste combinations of muffins know no bounds. The fact that they come in a variety of shapes, sizes, and flavors only heightens the draw.

Muffins today are a far cry better than they were before the seventies, when they were quaint and small and you could easily toss one back at breakfast or have two muffins, buttered, with tea or a bowl of soup. Since the muffin craze started, muffins have never looked the same as their humble ancestors. Muffins became bigger, for one thing, and far richer inside, for another.

Technically, muffins are simply quick breads baked in muffin cups. What you need to know is quite simple: Use the best-quality ingredients. Use an ice-cream scoop to scoop muffin batter and generously fill the pans to get those wonderful muffin tops.

Overall, muffins are the "something" that always seems to hit the spot, regardless of taste and appetite, for you can make them as diversely flavored as you wish and in different sizes. The other great news is that muffins are low-tech, suiting any baker's skills and requiring little time, tools, or forethought to create something wonderful. Muffins are neat, compact, and portable eat-out-of-hand perfections. They are, like scones, the ideal on-the-run food. Add to that the notion that muffins are as decadent or as healthy as you want them to be, and you can appreciate why few people say no to this treat. They are as good at breakfast and brunch as they are midmorning, after school, or after dinner. When you don't know what to bake or serve to impromptu guests who appear just as the coffee is brewed, muffins are the answer.

Ingredients

Muffins are usually chock-full of good things, from grains and fresh eggs to buttermilk or sour cream to dried fruits, nuts, and chocolate. Make sure all ingredients are fresh and properly handled.

Oil or Butter?

Because muffins are so flavorful and adaptable, you can interchange oil and butter. Butter offers a rounded, wonderful flavor, as only a dairy fat can. When you cream softened butter with sugar, you incorporate air. This is the method used predominantly in this chapter for tender, cakelike results. But muffins made with oil are also easy to whip up (just stirring, no creaming), and they also produce a light texture. Plus, you save on fat and cholesterol. Oil-based muffins have also proven to conserve better.

Eggs

Take the chill off eggs before baking with them (cold eggs will lower the temperature of your muffin batter, and a sacrifice in height will be the result). Do this by dipping eggs in the shell in a bowl of hot water for 1 to 2 minutes.

Mixing

Today's muffins are rich, and with the amounts of sugar and fat they call for, you needn't worry too much about making muffins tough by overmixing. But do be sure to blend ingredients thoroughly.

To mix muffins by hand, use a wooden spoon or a Danish dough whisk (see page 25 for more on this great tool). If you use a mixer, use the paddle attachment, cream butter and sugar on medium speed, and then reduce to low speed to add dry ingredients.

My favorite muffin tip: Use a large ice-cream scoop to deposit gobs of batter into each muffin cup.

Handling

Use deep muffin pans and place them on parchment paper–lined baking sheets to prevent overly browned muffin bottoms. Bake on the upper rack at higher heat for peaked muffin caps; bake on the lower rack at lower heat for mushroom-capped muffins. For either style, load the muffin cups very full.

To deposit muffin batter, use a commercial-quality ice-cream scoop, also known as a disher. For smaller muffins, use a mini ice-cream scoop.

Let baked muffins set up in their pans briefly before removing them, or you could risk losing a muffin top while trying to unmold the muffin before it is totally set up. To ensure that muffins release easily, spray the muffin pan's top surface, as well as the bottom and sides, with nonstick spray before filling and baking.

Storage

To store muffins, wrap each loosely in wax paper; then leave them under a cake dome or in a cake box or store them in a plastic storage container with the lid on loosely. Otherwise, humidity can form and get into the muffins and prematurely stale them. Muffins freeze well wrapped in wax paper and then placed in zip-top freezer bags.

Blueberries-and-Cream Mall Muffins

Makes 24 small or 12 large muffins or two 8- x 4-inch loaves

Two types of acidic dairy ingredients, buttermilk and sour cream, make these muffins special. No mixer necessary for these gems—hands and a whisk are all you need. Want big tops like the muffins the mall offers? Use this recipe and pile on the batter!

2¼ cups sugar	1 tablespoon baking powder
½ cup vegetable oil	¼ teaspoon baking soda
½ cup unsalted butter, melted	½ teaspoon salt
4 large eggs	1 cup buttermilk
1 tablespoon pure vanilla extract	½ cup sour cream
½ teaspoon each pure lemon and orange extract, optional	2 cups semi-frozen blueberries
5 cups, approximately, all-purpose flour	**Finishing Touch**
	Sugar, for dusting tops

Preheat oven to 425°F. Arrange oven rack to middle position (which is the upper third of many ovens).

Generously spray a 12-cup large or standard muffin pan or a 24-cup small muffin pan with nonstick cooking spray and then line with paper muffin liners. Place pan on a parchment paper–lined baking sheet.

In a mixer bowl, blend sugar with oil and butter. Briskly add eggs, vanilla, and other extracts. Fold in 4 cups flour, baking powder, baking soda, and salt. Blend somewhat before next blending in buttermilk and sour cream. Batter should be quite thick; if not, add a touch more flour. Gently fold in berries with a spatula, trying not to break them apart.

Using a large ice-cream scoop, scoop a very large amount of batter into prepared muffin cups, loading them as full as you can. You need almost a scoop and a half of batter per cup. (See photo at left). Dust tops of muffins with a little sugar.

Bake 15 minutes at 425°F; then reduce oven temperature to 350°F and bake until muffins are golden brown and spring back when gently pressed with fingertips, about 12 to 16 more minutes. Let cool 5 minutes before removing from pan.

For two 8- x 4-inch loaves, bake at 350°F for 45 minutes or more, using same fingertip test for doneness.

Blue About Blueberries?

Ideally, fresh is always better, but in the case of blueberry muffins, semi-frozen berries are somewhat easier to handle. Fresh blueberries are fragile, and if you mix them too much in the batter, they can break open and release their juices, which will mix with the leaveners in the batter and cause the batter to turn greenish blue. (The taste is not affected, but they can look odd!) Keep in mind that using any frozen fruit will make the batter seem firmer, as a sudden temperature drop occurs when the frozen fruit is added to the batter. This does not affect the results but actually makes these batters easier to scoop.

Java Streusel Banana Muffins

Makes 8 to 12 muffins or one 9- x 5-inch loaf

This update of classic, moist breakfast or snack muffins features a coffee streusel swirl. You can omit the streusel for classic banana muffins. This batter also bakes up nicely as a large banana loaf. If you forgo the streusel layer, you can add some chopped walnuts to the batter instead. If you like really big peaked muffins, this recipe is the ticket.

Like so many banana-based recipes, you can vary this one in many ways: Ice with chocolate or lemon icing (for banana cupcakes), use ½ cup buttermilk or yogurt as the liquid, or garnish before baking with a coconut and macadamia nut streusel instead of walnuts and butterscotch chips. The possibilities are endless.

Java Streusel*

4	tablespoons unsalted butter
¼	cup firmly packed brown sugar
½	teaspoon instant coffee granules
¼	teaspoon ground cinnamon
⅓	cup chopped walnuts
⅓	cup butterscotch or chocolate chips

Muffin Batter

¾	cup unsalted butter, softened
1	cup firmly packed brown sugar
½	cup white sugar
2	large eggs
2	teaspoons pure vanilla extract
2½	cups all-purpose flour
2	teaspoons baking powder
½	teaspoon baking soda
½	teaspoon salt
¼	teaspoon ground cinnamon
½	cup mild coffee or orange juice or buttermilk
1	cup pureed very ripe banana (about 2 large)
⅓	cup semisweet chocolate chips, optional
½	cup diced firm banana, optional

*Omit Java Streusel if you prefer classic banana muffins.

Preheat oven to 375°F. Generously spray a large or standard 12-cup muffin pan with nonstick cooking spray and place on a parchment paper–lined baking sheet. Arrange oven rack to upper-third position.

For Java Streusel, place all ingredients in a food processor and pulse to make a coarse, grainy mixture.

For Muffin Batter, in a mixer bowl, cream butter with both sugars until well blended. Add eggs and vanilla and mix well. Fold in flour, baking powder, baking soda, salt, and cinnamon. While dry ingredients are blending into batter, add coffee and pureed banana. Fold in chocolate chips and diced banana, if desired. Blend batter well, scraping bottom and sides of bowl to ensure batter is evenly mixed.

Scoop some batter into each muffin cup, filling about half full; deposit some of streusel and finish with batter. Alternatively, you can scoop batter into muffin cups and top with streusel. (If you want huge muffins, scoop batter into eight muffin cups and load them really full.)

Bake 30 to 40 minutes until muffins are gently browned around edges and seem set when touched. Cool well before removing from pan.

For a 9- x 5-inch loaf, the loaf rises very high and looks as though it might overflow, but it doesn't. If loaf is browning too fast at 375°F, reduce oven temperature to 325°F and increase baking time. The usual time is 60 to 65 minutes.

Lemon-Yogurt-Poppy Seed Muffins

Makes 12 muffins

The classic combo of lemon and poppy seeds will delight you in these jaunty yogurt-laden muffins. You can also use buttermilk for these in lieu of yogurt. The lemon syrup keeps these fresh for days. As an option, bake this batter in a 9- x 5-inch loafpan for a quick-bread version.

Muffin Batter

¼ cup unsalted butter, softened
¼ cup shortening*
1½ cups sugar
2 large eggs
2 teaspoons pure vanilla extract
Juice of 1 lemon
Zest of 1 lemon, finely minced
1 teaspoon pure lemon extract
1 cup plain yogurt
2¼ to 2½ cups all-purpose flour

2½ teaspoons baking powder
½ teaspoon baking soda
¼ teaspoon salt
2 to 4 tablespoons poppy seeds

Lemon Syrup

¾ cup water
¼ cup lemon juice
1 teaspoon lemon extract
1 cup sugar

Almost any muffin will work as a quick bread. Just fill the desired-size loafpan about two-thirds full of batter and bake until the loaf is set.

*Or use all butter.

Preheat oven to 375°F. Arrange oven rack to middle position. Line a large 12-cup muffin pan with paper liners and place pan on a parchment paper–lined baking sheet.

In a mixer bowl, cream butter with shortening until smooth and creamy. Blend in sugar and then eggs, vanilla, lemon juice, zest, lemon extract, and yogurt. Blend well; then fold in flour, baking powder, baking soda, salt, and poppy seeds.

Using a large ice-cream scoop, scoop a generous amount of batter into prepared muffin cups. Make sure you load muffin cups full, but deposit one muffin first as a test—batter should stay in place. If it topples over, that means you should add a bit more flour to remaining batter.

Bake until nicely browned around edges and muffins are set, about 28 to 32 minutes.

For Lemon Syrup, simmer water, lemon juice, extract, and sugar over low heat 5 minutes. Cool well.

Brush baked poppy seed muffins 2 or 3 times with Lemon Syrup while they are still warm. Let cool 5 minutes before removing from pan.

Bake-Shop Sour Cream-Rhubarb-Peach Muffins

Makes 12 muffins

I've always preferred big muffins and something in the way of a finishing touch—a streusel, a lemon glaze, or, in this case, a rich cream cheese fondant.

Feel free to change the fruit, citrus zest, or extract in these muffins; replace some white sugar with brown sugar or throw in some oats—this is a wonderful foundation muffin for your collection. You can also use thick plain yogurt to replace the sour cream.

Muffin Batter

¾	cup unsalted butter, softened
1⅓	cups sugar
2	large eggs
1	tablespoon pure vanilla extract
¾	cup buttermilk
1	cup sour cream
3½	cups all-purpose flour
4	teaspoons baking powder
¼	teaspoon baking soda
½	teaspoon salt
¾	cup chopped rhubarb
¾	cup chopped peaches
1	teaspoon finely minced orange zest

Cream Cheese Fondant

3	cups confectioners' sugar
2	to 4 tablespoons, or as required, orange juice
4	tablespoons cream cheese, softened

Preheat oven to 375°F. Arrange oven rack to middle position. Line a 12-cup muffin pan with muffin liners and place it on a parchment paper–lined baking sheet.

In a mixer bowl, blend butter and sugar until light and fluffy. Blend in eggs, vanilla, buttermilk, and sour cream until smooth, 2 to 3 minutes. Fold in flour, baking powder, baking soda, and salt and, when almost mixed, fold in fruit and orange zest. Scrape bottom of bowl occasionally to ensure nothing gets stuck in well of mixing bowl.

Scoop muffin batter very generously into one muffin cup; batter should stay put. If not, add a little bit more flour to batter to stiffen it. (This can vary depending on if you have used fresh or frozen fruit or how ripe the fruit is.) Using a large ice-cream scoop, scoop a generous amount of batter into each muffin cup.

Bake until muffins are nicely browned around edges and spring back when gently pressed with fingertips, 30 to 35 minutes.

Meanwhile, make Cream Cheese Fondant. In a medium bowl, briskly whisk together confectioners' sugar, orange juice, and cream cheese to make a drippy glaze. If it needs more sugar or liquid, add either in very small amounts to get required consistency.

Smear muffins with glaze, using your finger or a flat metal spatula to skim away excess. Allow glaze to set.

Vanilla-Apple-Cranberry Muffins

Makes 16 large muffins

What a way to meet the sunrise! Bake a batch of these sumptuous sour cream muffins in the morning and save some to celebrate an Indian summer afternoon.

1 cup unsalted butter, softened
1¾ cups sugar
4 large eggs
2 teaspoons pure vanilla extract
4 cups all-purpose flour
4 teaspoons baking powder
½ teaspoon baking soda
½ teaspoon salt
¼ teaspoon ground cinnamon

1 cup sour cream
1½ cups diced tart apples
1½ cups coarsely chopped frozen cranberries
¼ cup milk or water, or as required

Finishing Touches

Sugar and ground cinnamon
Slivers of (unpeeled) red apple

Preheat oven to 425°F. Arrange oven rack to middle position.
Line 16 muffin cups with muffin liners or spray generously with nonstick cooking spray; place pans on a parchment paper–lined baking sheet.
In a mixer bowl, blend butter and sugar; then add eggs and vanilla and blend until smooth. Stir in flour, baking powder, baking soda, salt, and cinnamon and then add sour cream to make a smooth batter. Fold in fruit by hand. If batter is very stiff, add a few tablespoons of milk or water.
Using a large ice-cream scoop, scoop a generous amount of batter into each muffin cup.
Dust with a bit of sugar and cinnamon. Finish with a sliver of apple nestled in the top.
Place muffins in oven. Immediately reduce oven temperature to 400°F. Bake 20 to 22 minutes until muffins are nicely browned and spring back when gently pressed with fingertips. Cool 5 minutes before removing from pans.

Sticky Cashmere Muffins

Makes 14 to 24 muffins

These decadent, gooey-topped, and delicately crumbed muffins are really luscious little cakes anointed with a toffee sauce and crowned in a gorgeous cashmere "overcoat" of coffee-kissed glaze.

Don't be put off by the three parts of this recipe. You can make the batter while the dates and Sticky Toffee Sauce are simmering. Practice your most gracious smile—the compliments won't stop. My baking testers unanimously voted this the best recipe ever (for that week anyway!), with tasters begging for crumbs off the baking sheet. For company dinners, bake these muffins in little ramekins and forgo the icing-and-muffin approach.

1½ cups pitted dates
1½ cups water

Muffin Batter

½   cup unsalted butter, softened
1   cup firmly packed light brown sugar
¼   cup white sugar
2   teaspoons pure vanilla extract
3   large eggs
2½ cups all-purpose flour
2   teaspoons baking powder
¼   teaspoon salt

⅛   teaspoon baking soda

Sticky Toffee Sauce

½   cup unsalted butter
1½ cups firmly packed light brown sugar
1   cup whipping cream

Cashmere Glaze

2   cups confectioners' sugar
1   teaspoon pure vanilla extract
Strong coffee, as required, to get a glaze consistency

Preheat oven to 350°F. Line a baking sheet with parchment paper. Set two muffin pans on it side by side, with muffin pans lined with paper liners. Spray top of muffin pans with nonstick cooking spray.

In a medium saucepan, heat dates in water and cook over low heat until dates are softened and are total mush. Remove from heat; let cool.

In a mixer bowl, cream butter and both sugars until well blended. Stir in vanilla and eggs. Fold in flour, baking powder, salt, and baking soda to make a soft but well-blended batter. Fold in cooled date mixture.

Using an ice-cream scoop, scoop batter evenly into prepared muffin cups, filling each two-thirds full.

Bake until muffins spring back when gently pressed with fingertips, about 30 to 40 minutes.

Meanwhile, for Sticky Toffee Sauce, place butter, brown sugar, and whipping cream in a small saucepan. Simmer 20 to 30 minutes until thickened and sticky, stirring every few minutes. Cool to room temperature.

For Cashmere Glaze, whisk confectioners' sugar, vanilla, and coffee, a little at a time, to make a thick glaze.

Once muffins are cooled, remove a conical center portion from each. Spoon in Sticky Toffee Sauce. Top with muffin cutout and press lightly. Smear on Cashmere Glaze. Let set. (You can also simply dip muffins in toffee sauce. They won't look quite as nice, but the taste is amazing.)

Mexican Vanilla Muffins

Makes 24 small muffins or 14 to 16 large muffins

These muffins waft the most incredible aroma as they bake. The recipe makes tiny, not-too-sweet, pop-in-your-mouth mini muffins that are somewhere between a muffin and a cake in texture. The final product is a delectable little morsel that is totally luscious when served with a pot of Darjeeling.

Muffin Batter

¾ cup unsalted butter, softened
1½ cups sugar
Scrapings of a vanilla bean* (photo, at right)
2 large eggs
4 teaspoons pure vanilla extract
3 cups cake flour**
1 tablespoon baking powder
½ teaspoon salt
1 cup milk

Vanilla Syrup

½ cup water
½ cup sugar
2 tablespoons light corn syrup
1 tablespoon pure vanilla extract

*Or use 2 teaspoons vanilla bean paste.
**Stir flour before measuring it. Instead of cake flour, you can use 2¾ cups all-purpose flour and 1 tablespoon cornstarch.

Preheat oven to 350°F. Arrange oven rack to middle position. Line a baking sheet with parchment paper and generously spray a 24-cup mini muffin pan with nonstick cooking spray and/or paper liners or use 14 to 16 regular muffins cups. Place on prepared baking sheet.

In a mixer bowl, cream butter and sugar until well blended. If using vanilla bean, add scrapings of bean in with butter.

Blend in eggs and vanilla extract. Fold in dry ingredients and gradually add milk. Scrape down bowl often to make sure ingredients are evenly incorporated. Fold in vanilla bean paste, if using.

Using an ice-cream scoop, scoop batter into prepared muffin cups, filling each three-fourths full. Bake until light golden brown, 17 to 20 minutes for little muffins or 20 to 24 minutes for larger ones, or until muffins spring back when gently pressed with fingertips.

Meanwhile, for Vanilla Syrup, gently boil water, sugar, and corn syrup 5 minutes. Cool to almost room temperature and stir in vanilla.

Brush each muffin twice with Vanilla Syrup and let stand until syrup is absorbed.

Using Mexican vanilla makes these sublime, but any high-quality pure vanilla is fine. _Nielsen-Massey_ Tahitian vanilla—which features warm, round flavor notes—is available from bakery suppliers. Or see 'Source Guide' on page 316 to contact the company.

Pralines-and-Cream Pecan-Caramel Muffins

Makes 12 large muffins; also pictured on page 100

Cutting corners? You can omit the Cream Cheese Topping and just go with the muffin batter topped with streusel.

These are totally amazing, decadent golden cakes of a butterscotch-caramel bent. A pecan-studded brown-sugar batter features a ripple of caramel and a baked-in cheesecake topping that is crowned with a pecan crunch streusel.

Pecan Streusel Topping

1	cup finely chopped pecans
2	tablespoons white sugar
½	cup firmly packed brown sugar
3	tablespoons butterscotch or caramel chips, optional
2	tablespoons unsalted butter, cut into chunks

Cream Cheese Topping

6	ounces cream cheese
1	large egg
¼	cup sugar
1	teaspoon pure vanilla extract

Muffin Batter

½	cup unsalted butter, softened
1	cup firmly packed brown sugar
½	cup white sugar
1	large egg
2	teaspoons pure vanilla extract
1	cup buttermilk or plain yogurt
2	cups all-purpose flour
2	teaspoons baking powder
½	teaspoon baking soda
¼	teaspoon salt
⅓	cup very finely chopped pecans
12	squirts of butterscotch or caramel sundae topping, optional

Preheat oven to 375°F. Arrange oven rack to middle position. Line a 12-cup large muffin pan with paper liners and generously spray liners with nonstick cooking spray. Place pan on a parchment paper–lined baking sheet.

For Pecan Streusel Topping, in a food processor, grind nuts, both sugars, and butterscotch chips, if desired, to make a fine meal. Add butter and pulse to blend. Put mixture into a mixing bowl. (This is a fine, gravelly streusel.)

Without cleaning food processor bowl, blend Cream Cheese Topping ingredients well and then spoon out into another bowl.

For Muffin Batter, blend butter with both sugars in food processor until well blended; then add egg and vanilla and mix well. Add buttermilk, flour, baking powder, baking soda, salt, and nuts and blend well, making sure no unblended sugar or butter is stuck in bottom of bowl.

Scoop some batter into each muffin cup, filling about half full. Squirt on some sundae topping. Spoon on some Cream Cheese Topping and then carefully add streusel.

Bake 30 to 35 minutes until muffins seem firm to the touch when gently pressed with fingertips. Let cool 5 minutes before removing from pan.

Double-Chocolate Sour Cream Mall Muffins

Makes 9 to 11 large muffins

High-heat, high-rack baking gives these puffy umbrella-topped muffins an impressive appearance.

½ cup unsalted butter, softened
1¾ cups sugar
2 large eggs
1 cup sour cream
1 teaspoon pure vanilla extract
2¾ cups all-purpose flour
¼ cup cocoa powder
2 teaspoons baking powder

½ teaspoon baking soda
¼ teaspoon salt
1 cup miniature chocolate chips

Finishing Touches

Melted white or dark chocolate, for drizzling, optional
Confectioners' sugar

Preheat oven to 425°F. Arrange oven rack to second shelf from top. Line a 12-cup muffin pan with paper liners. Spray top of muffin pan and liners with nonstick cooking spray. Stack two baking sheets together and line top sheet with parchment paper. Place muffin pan on prepared baking sheets.

In a mixer bowl, cream butter and sugar and then add eggs. Blend in sour cream and vanilla.

In a separate bowl, stir together flour, cocoa, baking powder, baking soda, and salt. Blend gently into batter. Once partially blended, fold in chocolate chips. If batter seems too loose, add a few tablespoons of flour (no more than 4 tablespoons) to make batter a bit stiffer. If batter seems too thick, stir in a bit of milk (up to ¼ cup).

Using a large ice-cream scoop, scoop a generous amount of batter into each muffin cup.

Bake 15 minutes and then reduce oven temperature to 400°F and finish baking, about 12 to 14 more minutes until muffins spring back when gently pressed with fingertips.

Let cool 5 minutes before removing from pan. Drizzle with melted white or dark chocolate or dust with confectioners' sugar.

Upper-Deck Muffins

For taller-capped muffins, the upper-rack oven position is best, but it depends on what style and size oven you have. The upper rack might be right underneath the broiler in some ovens or right in the middle for others. When recipes say upper-third oven rack position, use your judgement. You want the muffins high up (but not under the broiler). This will greatly enable taller peaked caps on your homemade muffins. Of course, in a bakery, commercial ovens offer bakers a choice of heating the upper and lower (and sometimes middle) heating elements differently, and this keeps bakers from shuffling trays from rack to rack. At home, we use different oven positions to mimic this effect.

Fresh Blackberry Streusel-Topped Muffins

Makes 9 to 12 muffins

These luscious bites are really just like tiny coffee cakes in a muffin shape. You can substitute sour cream for the buttermilk.

Streusel Topping

½ cup finely chopped walnuts or shredded coconut

⅓ cup firmly packed brown or white sugar

1 tablespoon unsalted butter

¼ teaspoon ground cinnamon

Muffin Batter

½ cup unsalted butter, melted

1 cup white sugar

½ cup firmly packed light brown sugar

1 tablespoon finely minced orange zest

1 large egg

1 cup buttermilk

2 teaspoons pure vanilla extract

2½ to 2¾ cups all-purpose flour

2 teaspoons baking powder

½ teaspoon baking soda

⅛ teaspoon salt

⅛ teaspoon ground cinnamon

2 scant cups semi-frozen blackberries

Preheat oven to 400°F. Arrange oven rack to middle position. Line a 12-cup muffin pan with paper liners and place it on a parchment paper–lined baking sheet.

Prepare Streusel Topping by rubbing or crumbling ingredients together with fingers; set aside.

In a large bowl, whisk together melted butter, both sugars, orange zest, and egg. Do not overbeat. Mixture should be pasty. Add buttermilk and vanilla.

In a separate bowl, stir together flour, baking powder, baking soda, salt, and cinnamon. Gently fold into batter. Once partially blended, fold in fruit. The use of semi-frozen fruit will help "firm up" the batter. If batter seems too loose, add a few tablespoons of flour (no more than 4 tablespoons) to make batter a bit stiffer.

Using a large ice-cream scoop, scoop a generous amount of batter into each muffin cup. Sprinkle streusel topping evenly over each muffin.

Bake 15 minutes. Reduce oven temperature to 350°F and bake another 12 to 15 minutes. Muffins should spring back when gently pressed. Allow to cool 5 minutes before removing from pan.

Zucchini, Citrus, and Honey Muffins

Makes about 14 to 16 muffins

One of my most-requested recipes, this is still one of the tastiest ways to use up extra zucchini. You can also make this muffin recipe using half zucchini and half carrot. These muffins are moist and bursting with flavor.

Muffin Batter

½ cup canola oil

½ cup unsalted butter, melted

1½ cups sugar

2 tablespoons honey

3 large eggs

1 tablespoon pure vanilla extract

¼ teaspoon orange oil, optional*

1 tablespoon finely minced lemon zest

1 tablespoon finely minced orange zest

2½ teaspoons ground cinnamon

⅓ cup buttermilk

3 cups, or a bit more, all-purpose flour

2½ teaspoons baking powder

½ teaspoon baking soda

½ teaspoon salt

½ cup finely chopped dates, optional

¾ cup golden raisins, plumped and dried (see page 18)

½ cup well-drained crushed pineapple

2 cups washed unpeeled shredded zucchini

Orange-Lemon Glaze

2 cups confectioners' sugar

1 tablespoon fresh lemon juice

Orange juice concentrate or juice, as required, about 3 to 6 tablespoons

Most muffin batters do double duty as soft cookies. Deposit the muffin batter directly onto a lightly greased baking sheet and bake until set and muffins (aka soft cookies) spring back when gently pressed and edges are browned.

*For information about orange oil, see page 17.

Preheat oven to 375°F. Arrange oven rack to middle position. Line 14 to 16 muffin cups with paper liners and place muffin pans on a parchment paper–lined baking sheet.

In a mixer bowl, blend oil, butter, sugar, honey, eggs, vanilla extract, orange oil, citrus zest, cinnamon, and buttermilk until smooth. Fold in dry ingredients and blend slightly; then fold in dates, if using, and next 3 ingredients to make a smooth but lumpy batter.

Using a large ice-cream scoop, scoop a generous amount of batter into each muffin cup.

Bake until muffins spring back when gently pressed, about 25 to 32 minutes. Meanwhile, make Orange-Lemon Glaze by whisking together ingredients to make a gloppy glaze.

Once muffins have cooled about 15 minutes in pans, dip each in Orange-Lemon Glaze. Dip again and let glaze set.

Baker's Best Bran Muffins

Makes about 16 to 24 muffins, depending on size

I must have worked on this recipe a zillion times to perfect the classic bran muffin: moist, sweet, healthy, and able to be made ahead. The secret is a rest in the fridge so that the batter stiffens a bit and the bran gets absorbed, giving you a nice rounded top on these muffins once baked.

My testers adored these muffins. Raves in the test kitchen mean it will be a sure hit with home bakers. Find natural bran on the cereal aisle in many supermarkets and in the grains section of health-food stores.

2½ cups plus 2 tablespoons all-purpose flour
1 tablespoon baking powder
4½ teaspoons baking soda
2 teaspoons ground cinnamon
½ teaspoon salt
¾ cup vegetable oil
1¼ cups firmly packed light brown sugar
2 tablespoons honey
¼ cup molasses
2 tablespoons pure maple syrup
1 teaspoon pure vanilla extract
¾ teaspoon maple extract

3 large eggs, beaten
2 cups buttermilk
1 cup wheat germ*
1 cup natural bran (not the cereal)
½ cup dates, plumped and dried (see page 18), coarsely chopped
1 cup raisins, plumped and dried (see page 18)

Finishing Touches

Wheat germ, oat bran, sesame seeds or sunflower seeds, for garnishing

*You can substitute 1 cup oat bran for a wholesome but slightly more dense muffin.

Preheat oven to 400°F. Arrange oven rack to middle position. Line two 12-cup muffin pans with paper liners and place on a parchment paper–lined baking sheet.

In a medium bowl, using a wire whisk, blend together flour, baking powder, baking soda, cinnamon, and salt.

In a mixer bowl, whisk together oil, brown sugar, honey, molasses, maple syrup, and extracts. Then whisk in beaten eggs. Stir in buttermilk, wheat germ, and bran. Allow batter to rest 10 minutes.

Stir dry ingredients into batter and whisk to partially blend. Using a rubber spatula, stir in dates and raisins. Blend batter well, making sure bottom of bowl does not have undistributed ingredients.

Cover batter with plastic wrap and allow to rest in fridge overnight or for at least 1 hour before baking.

Using a large ice-cream scoop, scoop a generous amount of muffin batter into prepared muffin pans. Fill any empty muffin cups halfway with water (this allows muffins to bake evenly).

Sprinkle tops with additional wheat germ, oat bran, sesame seeds, or sunflower seeds as garnish. Bake 20 minutes; then reduce oven temperature to 375°F and bake until done, about another 10 to 12 minutes. Let cool 5 minutes before removing from pans.

Deep Dark Chocolate Chunk Muffins

Makes 9 to 12 muffins

Admittedly, these muffins have a lot going on: cream cheese, sour cream, and chocolate chunks. But they bake up into tender, deeply chocolaty morsels with somewhat crackly tops and chunks of semisweet chocolate sticking out of them. Dust with cocoa or drizzle with melted white chocolate as options.

½ cup unsalted butter, softened

4 ounces cream cheese, softened

⅔ cup white sugar

½ cup firmly packed brown sugar

2 large eggs

2 teaspoons pure vanilla extract

½ cup sour cream

½ cup milk

2½ cups all-purpose flour

½ cup cocoa powder, measured and then sifted

2½ teaspoons baking powder

½ teaspoon baking soda

¼ teaspoon salt

1 cup semisweet chocolate chunks or chips

Finishing Touch

Confectioners' sugar, optional

Preheat oven to 350°F. Arrange oven rack to middle position. Line a 12-cup muffin pan with paper liners and place it on a parchment paper–lined baking sheet.

In a mixer bowl, cream butter and then add cream cheese, creaming to blend with butter. Blend in both sugars. Add eggs and vanilla and blend well. Fold in sour cream and milk.

In a medium bowl, blend together dry ingredients. Then fold into batter and blend well, making sure no ingredients remain unblended in well of mixing bowl. Fold in chocolate chips by hand.

Using a large ice-cream scoop, scoop a generous amount of muffin batter into each muffin cup. Bake until muffins spring back when gently pressed, about 28 to 32 minutes. Let cool 5 minutes before removing from pan. When cooled, dust with confectioners' sugar, if desired.

These would also be great if you slice off their caps, crown the muffins with ice cream, replace the caps, and then drizzle with hot fudge sauce. Course...then they would not be muffins; they would be paradise.

Cappuccino Muffins

Makes 8 to 12 tart-shaped muffins

Top off these coffee-batter muffins with a cap of sweetened cream cheese. You can also use regular muffin pans for these, but the yield will be higher. For those with nut allergies, substitute graham cracker crumbs for the walnuts.

Muffin Pans

Many bakeware companies offer various styles of bakeware choices for making muffins or miniature quick breads. There are square-bottom 12-cup muffin pans that make any muffin look like it came from a downtown coffeehouse. To line a nonround muffin pan (including a mini loafpan) with muffin liners, spread out the muffin liners to fit the shape. The batter will fill the liners and keep them in place as the muffins bake. This makes neat, easy-to-remove muffins with less cleanup. To make specialty muffins, consider miniature tart pans, tiny metal molds, tuna cans (washed, of course!), or paper collars that bake up tall muffins.

Cappuccino Topping

8	ounces cream cheese, softened
3	tablespoons sugar
2	tablespoons all-purpose flour
1	large egg
1	teaspoon pure vanilla extract

Muffin Batter

$\frac{1}{2}$	cup unsalted butter, softened
1	cup sugar
2	large eggs
1	teaspoon pure vanilla extract
3	tablespoons finely ground instant coffee granules

1	cup buttermilk
$2\frac{1}{2}$	cups all-purpose flour
$\frac{1}{4}$	teaspoon salt
1	tablespoon baking powder
$\frac{1}{4}$	teaspoon baking soda
$\frac{1}{3}$	cup ground walnuts

Finishing Touches

Confectioners' sugar

Cocoa powder, ground cinnamon, or vanilla powder,* for dusting

*Vanilla powder is a vanilla-scented powder with a light brown hue that contributes color and flavor to baked goods.

Preheat oven to 350°F. Arrange oven rack to middle position. Line 8 to 12 (4-inch) tart pans with muffin liners and spread them out to cover bottom of tart pans. Generously spray any exposed surface (inner sides) with nonstick cooking spray and place tart pans on a parchment paper–lined baking sheet.

For Cappuccino Topping, place all ingredients in a food processor and blend until smooth, about 2 to 4 minutes; set aside.

For Muffin Batter, in a mixer bowl, cream butter and sugar until smooth. Add eggs, vanilla, and coffee granules, and blend well. Stir in buttermilk and then fold in remaining ingredients to make a thick but soft batter.

Using a large ice-cream scoop, generously scoop batter into prepared tart pans. Top each evenly with Cappuccino Topping. Bake until topping is set, 30 to 38 minutes.

Cool well and dust with confectioners' sugar; then dust with cocoa, cinnamon, or vanilla powder, if desired.

Marvelous Marble Cream Cheese-and-Chocolate Muffins

Makes 12 to 14 muffins

These are hardly muffins—this is *Dean & Deluca*–type food. I baked these chocolate wonders in miniature loafpans, and the results were miniature cakes that are what we bakers call sheer "eye candy."

Cream Cheese Topping

8	ounces cream cheese, softened
1	large egg
1/4	cup sugar
1/4	cup all-purpose flour
1/2	teaspoon pure vanilla extract
1	cup coarsely grated or finely minced semisweet chocolate chips

Muffin Batter

1 1/2	cups sugar
3/4	cup vegetable oil
2	large eggs
1	teaspoon pure vanilla extract
2	cups all-purpose flour
2 1/2	teaspoons baking powder
1/2	teaspoon baking soda
1/2	teaspoon salt
	Pinch ground cinnamon
3/4	cup cocoa powder
1	cup mild brewed coffee or cola

Use a chef's knife or a food processor to mince or grate chocolate chips for this recipe.

Preheat oven to 350°F. Line a large 12-cup muffin pan with paper liners and place on a parchment paper–lined baking sheet. If you have extra batter, use another muffin pan, filling up empty muffin cups with water.

For Cream Cheese Topping, put all topping ingredients except grated chocolate in a food processor and process until smooth.

For Muffin Batter, in a mixer bowl, blend sugar, oil, eggs, and vanilla. Fold in flour, baking powder, baking soda, salt, cinnamon, and cocoa. As you are blending, stir in coffee or cola. Blend until smooth (this is a loose batter).

Pour batter into prepared muffin cups. Top each with a portion of cream cheese topping and sprinkle on some grated chocolate. Using a knife, gently swirl topping into batter.

Bake until done and cream cheese topping seems set to the touch and edges of exposed muffins seem firm to the touch, about 25 to 30 minutes. Let cool 15 minutes before removing from pans.

the cookie jar

I could wax lyrical about each genre of recipes in this book and pronounce each and every category the quintessential symbol of great home baking. I could, indeed, but for the fact that I honestly, unequivocally feel that cookies are the real heartbeat of home baking.

Cookies are the sort of crowd-pleasing, always-welcome, modest sweet treats that few pastry chefs ever want to bother with in quite the same loving way that home bakers want to. This homeyness is a huge part of what makes cookies the queen of the heap of home baking. They are the best things to come out of home kitchens.

Cookies also have the home-court advantage for pleasing family and friends in a heartwarming way. Cookies are all about full cookie jars, bake sales, brown-bag lunches, after-school snacks, weekend desserts, baseball and hockey dugout sustenance, gifts for friends or teachers, and a surprise on Sunday night when you thought there was no dessert.

More than this, cookies are pretty easy—even making the most complex cookie is not rocket science. Unlike pies, breads, or scones, the "humble" cookie, even done poorly, can be rather good. Cookies are about good ones, great ones, and the most memorable ones. In a way, they are all good. It is the nature of the treats. I have discovered that the tiniest tweak of a recipe I know well or presumed I knew inside out can result in a cookie that is a bit chewier, crisper, darker, rounder, bulkier, or chunkier. So, yes, you can perfect, diversify, and modify your cookie creations, and they will most likely always be delicious.

Mindful baking, such as care in handling and choice ingredients, is the difference between average cookies and a "patent-that-recipe" reaction. Great cookies are the stuff of urban legend and friends begging for the recipe.

Ingredients

Unsalted butter, unbleached all-purpose flour, the best and purest vanilla extract, and proper measuring of these things are your first steps toward cookie success. Make sure whichever ingredients you add to the dough (nuts, chocolate, etc.) are of the same high quality. Butter should be at room temperature and ready for creaming.

Handling

Unless otherwise stated, use a mixer with a paddle attachment to blend cookie dough. Occasionally, some recipes call for a food processor. Make sure your processor has a bowl large enough to accommodate the recipe.

Equipment

Parchment Paper

Lining the baking sheet with parchment paper results in cookies with even rolled edges that look professional. Using a lightly greased baking sheet instead can result in cookies with ragged or thin edges. But the best news about using parchment paper is that cookies tend to not have burned bottoms. Oh yes, you will also enjoy the easier cleanup.

Doubled-Up Baking Sheets

The following is the best baking tip I have to share, and while I recommend it for just about everything you bake, it is especially important in cookie baking.

When baking cookies (particularly on the bottom rack of your oven), use two baking sheets stacked together. This method ensures that the bottom bunch of cookies will not burn, as the doubled-up baking sheets are insulated and heat dissipates more evenly.

A small scoop is ideal for depositing cookie dough quickly, easily, and consistently sized.

You can also do this for the top rack of cookies if you are detained a couple of minutes; the stacked sheets give you a little more leeway before cookie bottoms burn. Discover which works best for you—stacked sheets on the top and bottom rack, or single baking sheets. Mostly, the richer the recipe (more sugar and butter), the more I advise you to use doubled-up baking sheets regardless of which rack you use. Overall, doubled-up sheets allow the bottom and edges of your cookies to stay golden, while the tops of the cookies finish browning.

Mini Ice-Cream Scoops

If you are scooping a lot of cookies, a small ice-cream scoop (also called a cookie scoop) is perfect for depositing cookie dough quickly, easily, and uniformly. Restaurant- and kitchen-supply stores have many sizes. You can deposit any drop cookie dough this way; then freeze cookie balls on baking sheets, bag them, and bake as needed.

Storage

Cookies are best fresh, but you can store them loosely wrapped in wax paper in a tin or in a glass cookie jar. Some cookies seem to do better if refrigerated. Crisp cookies don't fare well in plastic containers because humidity can build and cause cookies to soften. Covering a plate with a glass cake dome is another great way to store cookies. Oatmeal, shortbread, and filled cookies keep particularly well this way.

Triple-Threat Chocolate Fudge Cookies

Makes about 2½ dozen cookies

Mix up these crisp and chewy chocolate cookies that are bolstered by chunks of white chocolate and semisweet chocolate. Sometimes I find that rich chocolate cookies like these hold up better and taste more fudgy when chilled.

¾ cup unsalted butter, softened
6 tablespoons butter-flavored shortening
1 cup white sugar
⅔ cup firmly packed dark brown sugar
2 large eggs
2 teaspoons pure vanilla extract
2¼ cups all-purpose flour

⅔ cup cocoa powder, measured and then sifted
1 teaspoon baking soda
½ teaspoon salt
¼ cup half-and-half
1 cup semisweet chocolate chips or chunks
1 cup white chocolate chunks

Preheat oven to 350°F. Stack two baking sheets together and line top sheet with parchment paper.

In a mixer bowl, cream butter with shortening to blend, scraping down sides of bowl often. Add both sugars. Cream butter and sugars together until well blended. Stir in eggs and vanilla. If mixture seems curdled, stir in ¼ cup of the flour to bind dough.

In a medium bowl, stir together remaining flour, cocoa, baking soda, and salt. Mix into batter on low speed of mixer, scraping sides of bowl often. When almost blended, stir in half-and-half. Fold in chocolate chips and white chocolate chunks. Chill dough 10 minutes.

For each cookie, scoop about ¼ cup dough and place on prepared baking sheets, spacing 2 inches apart. Press dough down slightly with wet hands. Bake until cookies look just barely set (the middles will seem slightly wet), about 14 to 17 minutes.

Let cookies cool about 10 minutes on baking sheets before removing with a metal spatula. Let cool on wire racks. Store in refrigerator.

To Chill or Not to Chill

Some cookie doughs perform best when chilled before baking. A freshly made dough that seems too soft or greasy tends to melt and spread during baking because the fat in it is sometimes too warm from having just been mixed. Remember, too, that the heat of your mixer rotating the dough will heat it a bit. If you notice undue cookie spread or a yield of thin, raggedy-edged cookies, simply chilling the dough might be the solution.

Tender, Buttery Chocolate Chunk Cookies

Makes 3 to 4 dozen cookies, depending on size; also pictured in stack on previous page

I never get tired of perfecting one of my—and everyone else's—favorite cookies. These morsels are tender and wonderfully buttery tasting, with crisp edges, chewy centers, and gooey chocolate. If you want them doubly rich, with molten chocolate chunks studding the cookie landscape, use freshly chopped semisweet chocolate. Large cookies bake up into crinkly, dense, chewy cookies; smaller ones are more delicate and tender-crisp. This recipe quadruples nicely; I customarily freeze packets of dough and bake a dozen fresh cookies early in the day or just in time for after-school appetites.

1   cup unsalted butter, softened
1   cup firmly packed light brown sugar
½   cup white sugar
1½ teaspoons pure vanilla extract
2   large eggs

2   cups all-purpose flour
¾   teaspoon baking soda
¼   teaspoon salt
3   cups chocolate chips or coarsely chopped semisweet chocolate

Preheat oven to 350°F. Stack two baking sheets together and line top sheet with parchment paper.

In a mixer bowl, cream butter and both sugars until very smooth, about 3 to 4 minutes. Add vanilla and eggs and blend well. Fold in flour, baking soda, and salt and mix well, about 2 to 3 minutes. Fold in chocolate chips.

For each cookie, scoop 2 to 3 tablespoons of dough and place on prepared baking sheets, spacing 2 inches apart.

Bake 10 to 13 minutes for smaller cookies or 14 to 18 minutes for large ones. Cookies are done when they are just browned around the edges, are beginning to color on top, and seem dry to the touch. Let cool on baking sheets.

Cross-hatching chocolate chip cookies is one of my favorite tricks of the trade. When cookies come out of the oven, I score them in one direction with several little cuts using the side of a metal spatula, and then I cut across them, making a grid on the cookie surface, which exposes the melting chocolate. I started doing this a few years ago, and now my sons and their friends seem to prefer the cookies this way.

Kitchen Sink Cookies

Makes 2 to 3 dozen cookies

These cookies rock! They are funky, sticky, chewy, buttery, and crisp. The marshmallows and the cereal are part of their charm.

½   cup unsalted butter, softened
½   cup unsalted butter, melted and
    cooled
1½ cups firmly packed light brown
    sugar
¼   cup white sugar
1½ teaspoons pure vanilla extract
2   large eggs
2   cups all-purpose flour
1   teaspoon baking powder
¼   teaspoon baking soda

¼   teaspoon salt
1½ cups rolled oats
2   cups crisp rice cereal
1½ cups miniature marshmallows
½   cup butterscotch chips or toffee
    bits
1   cup semisweet chocolate chips
¾   cup chopped milk chocolate bars
1   cup sweetened shredded
    coconut, optional

This recipe takes both softened and melted butter for an optimally textured cookie.

Preheat oven to 350°F. Stack two baking sheets together and line top sheet with parchment paper.

In a mixer bowl, cream softened butter and melted butter with both sugars and vanilla. Add eggs, flour, baking powder, baking soda, and salt and blend well. Stir in oats, cereal, marshmallows, butterscotch chips, semisweet chocolate, milk chocolate, and coconut (if using) to make a well-blended cookie dough.

For each cookie, scoop 2 to 3 tablespoons of dough and place on prepared baking sheets, spacing 2 inches apart.

Bake 12 to 14 minutes until set all over. You should see crisp edges and some marshmallow leaking out. That is fine. Let cool on baking sheets.

Brittany Butter Cookies *(Galettes de Bretagne)*

Makes 2 to 3 dozen cookies

These are crumbly, buttery French cookies that are like shortbread. Similar fancy galettes available in imported-food stores are 6-inch disks of dense and buttery golden shortbread. They are also available as small, round cookies, like my recipe makes. They are a wonderful coffee cookie or gift cookie.

If you can find a better or more buttery cookie, let me know! These cookies are golden inside, with a burnished finish, thanks to the egg yolk glaze.

6	egg yolks
1¼	cups sugar
1	cup unsalted butter, softened
½	teaspoon pure vanilla extract
4	cups all-purpose flour

¼	teaspoon salt

Glaze

2	egg yolks
2	tablespoons water

Stack two baking sheets together and line top sheet with parchment paper. You will need to repeat this procedure for each batch.

In a mixer bowl, using whisk attachment, whisk egg yolks and sugar until thick and pale, 1 to 2 minutes. Slowly blend in softened butter and vanilla. Then gradually add flour and salt, blending until dough is thick and stiff. If it is still quite soft, add a bit more flour, a few tablespoons at a time. Knead dough gently and briefly on a lightly floured work surface. Then wrap dough well and refrigerate 45 to 60 minutes.

Preheat oven to 325°F. On a lightly floured work surface, roll dough to ¾-inch thickness (**photo 1**). Cut into 3-inch round cookies and place on prepared baking sheets (**photo 2**). Using tines of a fork, make a crisscross pattern on dough surface.

For Glaze, in a small bowl, whisk egg yolks with water. Brush each cookie generously with egg yolk glaze (**photo 3**). Bake until golden on top and browned around edges, 50 to 55 minutes. Let cool completely on baking sheets.

1

2

3

Mega-Butter Sugar Cookie Jam Sandwiches

Makes 14 sandwich cookies

These sandwich cookies are chunky when you bite into them, yet, with their buttery dough and jam layer, they are like pastry.

> I usually fill these sandwich cookies with jam, but I also use dulce de leche, buttercream icing, or chocolate-hazelnut spread on occasion.

1 cup butter, softened
1½ cups sugar
1 large egg
2 teaspoons pure vanilla extract
3 cups all-purpose flour
½ teaspoon baking powder
½ teaspoon salt

1 to 2 tablespoons whipping cream
Egg yolk and a bit of water, before baking

Finishing Touches

Raspberry and apricot jam
Confectioners' sugar, optional

Preheat oven to 350°F. Stack two baking sheets together and line top sheet with parchment paper.

In a mixer or food processor, cream butter and sugar into a pasty mixture. Add egg and vanilla and blend well. Fold in flour, baking powder, and salt to make a stiff dough, drizzling in cream as dough comes together. Cover and let rest 10 minutes.

On a lightly floured work surface, roll out dough to ¾-inch thickness. Cut into 3-inch rounds. Place cookies on prepared baking sheets and brush each with some egg yolk glaze.

Bake until done, about 25 to 35 minutes, and cookies begin to brown around edges and are golden brown all over. Let cool on baking sheets.

For each sandwich, smear jam on bottom of one cookie and then top with another cookie. Dust with confectioners' sugar, if desired.

Blueberry Hill Oatmeal Cookies

Makes 2 to 3 dozen cookies

Blueberries have joined the nutritionists' list of superfoods. Add them to this buttery brown sugar–based oatmeal cookie recipe and you will be rewarded with sprawls of blue in a crisp, coconut-laced cookie.

½	cup unsalted butter, melted	½	cup toasted coconut
½	cup firmly packed brown sugar	⅓	cup all-purpose flour
¼	cup white sugar	½	teaspoon baking powder
1	large egg	¼	teaspoon baking soda
2	teaspoons pure vanilla extract	⅛	teaspoon salt
¼	teaspoon lemon oil, optional	1	cup semi-frozen blueberries
2	cups rolled oats		

Preheat oven to 350°F. Stack two baking sheets together and line top sheet with parchment paper.

In a mixer bowl, blend butter and both sugars. Blend in egg, vanilla, and lemon oil (if using) and stir until mixture is smooth. Fold in oats and coconut and then add flour, baking powder, baking soda, and salt to make a nice dough. By hand, gently fold in blueberries.

Spoon out big mounds of dough (about 2 tablespoons full) on prepared baking sheets, spacing 3 inches apart.

Bake until done, about 14 minutes or until cookies begin to brown around edges.

Let cool on baking sheets 10 minutes before removing with a spatula. Let cool on a wire rack.

Oatmeal Options

Oatmeal comes in a few forms. Generally, quick oats are flat flakes that have been cut into slivers; they cook quickly. If you use quick oats in oatmeal cookies or scones, you get the oat taste with a more intense texture. If you use rolled oats, also called old-fashioned oats or "large flake oatmeal," you get a more discernable oatmeal taste in your cookie (or whatever you are baking) and a chewier texture. The two types are, to some extent, interchangeable, but I often use a combination for optimal taste and texture.

Strawberries and Cream Cookies

Makes 2 to 3 dozen cookies

This shortbread dough is enlivened with a splash of cream along with bits of dried strawberries.

¾ cup sugar

1 cup unsalted butter, softened

2 cups all-purpose flour

1 teaspoon pure vanilla extract

1 tablespoon whipping cream

¼ teaspoon salt

½ cup minced white chocolate

¾ cup dried strawberries, coarsely minced*

*Order dried strawberries online from nutsonline.com.

Preheat oven to 325°F. Stack two baking sheets together and line top sheet with parchment paper.

In a food processor, whiz sugar to finely pulverize, about 10 seconds.

In a mixer bowl, cream sugar and butter on low speed until well blended. Then add flour, vanilla, cream, and salt and blend well. When almost blended into a dough, add white chocolate and dried strawberries **(photo 1)**, mixing by hand to incorporate and make a firm dough.

Knead dough gently on a lightly floured work surface about 1 minute to make dough more firm and get it to hold together **(photo 2)**. Flatten dough into a disk, wrap well, and refrigerate 30 minutes.

Roll out gently about ½ inch thick and cut into small round cookies (about 2 inches in diameter).

Place on prepared baking sheets. Place in oven and immediately reduce oven temperature to 300°F. Bake until lightly browned around edges, about 40 to 50 minutes. Cool well before removing with a metal spatula.

About Cookie Spread

"Spread" is something professional bakers talk about when they refer to how a cookie spreads out on the baking sheet. If you want to avoid spread, work with chilled dough and do not press the cookie dough flat before baking.

Marcy's Legendary Chocolate Chip Cookies

Makes 7 to 10 jumbo cookies

I confess that I have never had the famous chocolate chip cookies from *Levain Bakery* of New York. I have only read the amazing accounts of these scone-sized chocolate chip phenoms. But I like the idea of monster cookies that create huge stirs, so here is my own version. I'd sooner break a cookie like this into big, gorgeous chunks than have two or three smaller cookies. It's just more fun.

These cookies have remarkable girth, amazing flavor, chewy centers, acres of chips, and a buttery, vanilla-kissed batter. You need two hands to hold one of these awesome cookies and three friends to share one with. I recommend double-strength vanilla (see 'Source Guide' on page 316). I would also use a mixture of chopped *Lindt* semisweet chocolate as well as regular good-quality chocolate chips. For the original *Levain Bakery* cookies, visit www.levainbakery.com for a taste of the cookies that New Yorkers devour before they get home!

1	cup unsalted butter, softened	2½ cups all-purpose flour
1½	cups firmly packed brown sugar	¾ teaspoon baking soda
¼	cup white sugar	½ teaspoon salt
1	tablespoon pure vanilla extract	2 cups semisweet chocolate chips
2	large eggs	1½ cups chopped semisweet
1	egg yolk	chocolate (preferably *Lindt*)

Preheat oven to 350°F. Stack two baking sheets together and line top sheet with parchment paper. Arrange oven rack to upper third position.

In a mixer bowl, cream butter with both sugars until well blended. Add vanilla, eggs, and egg yolk. Fold in flour, baking soda, salt, chocolate chips, and chopped chocolate and blend well to make a thick batter. If batter seems soft and greasy, add 2 to 4 tablespoons more flour. Dough should be soft but not too greasy or slack. You can also chill it 10 minutes if you think it has enough flour or let it stand 20 minutes. Either approach will help cookie dough "set up."

Scoop or form balls of 7 to 8 ounces of dough (yes, weigh it!) and place on prepared baking sheets about 2 to 3 inches apart. If you don't have a scale, use 1 cup of dough per cookie; each will measure 3 inches in diameter once placed on baking sheet. (Obviously, you can only bake a few of these at a time.)

Bake 20 to 24 minutes or until cookies are nicely browned on top and just set-up looking. Remove from oven and let cool on baking sheets 15 to 20 minutes before removing.

Mudslide Cookies

Makes 16 to 20 large cookies

These cookies, each masquerading as an extravagant brownie/torte, come in a few variations. What is constant is the huge amount of chocolate and the tiny amounts of butter and flour called for. They bake up into huge, luxurious chocolate clouds that feature just slightly crisp and crusty edges plus a melt-in-your-mouth soufflélike interior (well, maybe a touch firmer than that).

6	ounces unsweetened chocolate, coarsely chopped, melted
16	ounces semisweet chocolate, coarsely chopped, melted
$\frac{1}{3}$	cup unsalted butter, softened
$1\frac{3}{4}$	cups finely pulverized sugar
5	large eggs
$\frac{1}{2}$	cup all-purpose flour
$2\frac{1}{2}$	teaspoons baking powder
$\frac{1}{2}$	teaspoon salt
4	cups semisweet chocolate chips
$1\frac{1}{2}$	cups very finely chopped pecans or walnuts

Chocolate Trio Ganache

1	cup whipping cream
$\frac{3}{4}$	cup chopped semisweet chocolate
$\frac{1}{2}$	cup chopped milk chocolate
$\frac{1}{2}$	cup chopped white chocolate

Finishing Touches

Cocoa powder
Confectioners' sugar

Preheat oven to 350°F. Stack two baking sheets together and line top sheet with parchment paper.

Melt unsweetened chocolate and semisweet chocolate in top of a double boiler over very low heat, stirring to melt. Remove and let cool to room temperature.

In a mixer bowl, cream butter and sugar until well blended, 3 to 5 minutes on low speed. Add eggs, 1 at a time, and blend well after each addition. Fold in flour, baking powder, and salt and blend well. Fold in melted chocolate, chocolate chips, and nuts and blend well. Refrigerate dough 15 minutes.

For Chocolate Trio Ganache, bring cream to a simmer in a medium saucepan. Quickly whisk in three kinds of chopped chocolate, remove from heat, and stir to make a puddinglike mixture. Let cool and chill to make a spreadable glaze.

Using a large ice-cream scoop, deposit big mounds of dough on prepared baking sheets, about 3 to 4 inches apart. Bake 14 to 18 minutes or until cookies seem puffy, set up, and dry to the touch. (You might have to break off a piece of one, cool it slightly, and sample it; it is hard to judge when chocolate goods are done.) Cool and then smear each cookie with ganache or dust with cocoa or confectioners' sugar.

Make these bites tiny, and they become cookie truffles. They are not cookies to be trifled with! They are special-event cookies that are worth every delectable bite. The luxurious ganache topping is optional—these rich, wonderful cookies don't need more glitz, but the topping does give them added 'wow' appeal. What I like in my version is the coating of a tri-chocolate ganache. Use premium chocolate for these cookies (I use *Scharffen Berger*) and serve them fresh or semi-cold with espresso or cold milk.

White Chocolate-Macadamia Nut Cookies

Makes 3 to 4 dozen cookies, depending on size

These cookies are lightly sweet, buttery, crunchy, and crisp. Exotic macadamia nuts are perfectly paired with white chocolate, but pecans or peanuts would also be great.

Curdled Cookies?

After creaming the fat, sugar, and eggs, cookie dough often looks curdled. To remedy this, stir in a few tablespoons of the recipe's flour to bind the dough and then proceed as directed.

1	cup unsalted butter, softened	1	teaspoon baking soda
1	cup firmly packed brown sugar	½	teaspoon salt
½	cup white sugar	1	(12-ounce) package white chocolate chips
2	large eggs		
2	teaspoons pure vanilla extract	1½	cups chopped, toasted (if desired) macadamia nuts
2½	cups all-purpose flour		

Stack two baking sheets together and line top sheet with parchment paper. Arrange oven rack to upper third position.

In a mixer bowl, cream butter and both sugars until smooth. Blend in eggs and vanilla, scraping bottom of bowl often to make sure mixture is combined. Fold in flour, baking soda, and salt and mix well; then fold in white chocolate and nuts and blend another minute or two. If dough is too stiff to fold into, use fingers to knead the dough somewhat. Chill dough 20 minutes.

Preheat oven to 375°F.

For each cookie, spoon 2 to 3 tablespoons of dough onto prepared baking sheets, spacing 2 inches apart. Bake just until browned around edges, 9 to 13 minutes, turning baking sheets once to make sure baking is even. Let cool on baking sheets.

Hermit Cookies

Makes 12 to 18 large cookies

A picnic basket chock-full of these cookies and some icy milk brings raves. These are so old-fashioned and satisfying that they become almost cutting edge. Make them big and then break them in half to share. In a world of chocolate and caramel decadence, you might have forgotten how good a spice and raisin cookie can be—until now.

½ cup unsalted butter, softened
1   cup firmly packed light brown sugar
½ cup firmly packed dark brown sugar
1   tablespoon honey
2   large eggs
1   teaspoon pure vanilla extract
½ teaspoon pure orange extract
¼ teaspoon pure lemon extract
1¾ cups all-purpose flour

½ cup finely ground quick or rolled oats
¾ teaspoon baking powder
¼ teaspoon baking soda
¼ teaspoon salt
2   teaspoons ground cinnamon
½ teaspoon ground nutmeg
1½ cups raisins, plumped and dried (see page 18)
¾ cup dates, finely chopped
1   cup coarsely chopped pecans

Stack two baking sheets together and line top sheet with parchment paper. Spray parchment paper with nonstick cooking spray.

In a mixer bowl, cream butter and brown sugars until well blended. Add honey, eggs, and extracts and then fold in flour, oats, baking powder, baking soda, salt, cinnamon, and nutmeg. Blend well and fold in raisins, dates, and nuts to make a stiff batter. Chill dough 15 minutes.

Preheat oven to 350°F.

For each cookie, using wet hands, roll about ⅓ cup cookie dough in your palms, making it round. Press slightly on prepared baking sheets, spacing cookies 3 inches apart.

Bake 15 to 20 minutes until set and cookies are slightly flattened. Let cool on baking sheets.

Cold-Storage Facts for Cookies

Cookies retain their flavors best if stored in a tin in the fridge or in a cookie jar. You can also wrap cookie dough in wax paper or parchment paper and then place it in a freezer-proof bag. Cookie dough freezes well and lasts two to three months. Defrost dough in the fridge or on the counter; as soon as you can break off pieces to form drop cookies or roll the dough, you can use it for a new baking session.

I associate cookies like these with days gone by—when musicals seemed like real life, summer was endlessly long, and lemonade was actually made with real lemons.

Pumpkin Pocket Cookies

Makes 16 to 24 cookies

These gems are big, soft, and pillowy old-fashioned affairs.

Nicely spiced and gorgeous in color, these cookies are sort of like a mini pumpkin cake that you eat out of hand.

Store This!

Glass cookie jars display cookies visually—you see what you are getting. Search eBay and flea markets for antique or retro cookie jars and over-sized Mason jars. Keep large new Mason jars on hand for giving cookies as gifts. Tie each jar with a ribbon and include the recipe for the cookies.

2   tablespoons white sugar
1⅓ cups firmly packed brown sugar
½   cup unsalted butter, softened, or shortening
1   large egg
2   teaspoons pure vanilla extract
1   cup pumpkin puree
2   cups all-purpose flour
1   teaspoon baking powder
¼   teaspoon baking soda
⅛   teaspoon salt
1¼ teaspoons pumpkin pie spice
¼   teaspoon ground cinnamon
1   cup raisins, plumped and dried (see page 18), optional

Icing

3   cups confectioners' sugar
3   tablespoons cream cheese, softened
1   teaspoon pure vanilla extract
Water, as required, to make soft-icing consistency or glaze that holds

Preheat oven to 350°F. Stack two baking sheets together and line top sheet with parchment paper.

In a mixer bowl, cream both sugars and butter (or shortening) until fluffy. Add egg, vanilla, and pumpkin puree and blend well. Fold in flour, baking powder, baking soda, salt, pumpkin pie spice, and cinnamon and, when almost blended, fold in raisins (if using).

For each cookie, drop large gobs of dough about 2 to 3 inches apart on prepared baking sheets. Bake 15 to 17 minutes until cookies are firm. Cool well on wire racks before icing.

In a small bowl, whisk together Icing ingredients to make a smooth glaze. Smear or drizzle over almost totally cooled cookies and let set.

Deluxe Sticky Ooey-Gooey Peanut Butter Cookies

Makes about 12 to 16 large cookies

These huge, crisp-tender cookies house a center featuring an ooey-gooey peanutty filling. Make them big—the size enhances their marvelous texture and makes them total eye candy.

Cookie Dough

1/2	cup unsalted butter, softened
1/4	cup butter-flavored shortening (or use all butter)
1	cup peanut butter
1	cup white sugar
1/2	cup firmly packed dark brown sugar
2	large eggs
1	tablespoon pure vanilla extract
2½	cups all-purpose flour
1/2	teaspoon baking powder
1/4	teaspoon baking soda
1/8	teaspoon salt
1/2	cup miniature semisweet chocolate chips
1½	cups chopped peanut butter cup candies

Ooey-Gooey Filling

3/4	cup peanut butter
1/3	cup firmly packed dark brown sugar
1/2	cup sweetened condensed milk
2	tablespoons light corn syrup
1/4	cup confectioners' sugar
1/4	cup unsalted butter, softened

Vanilla: Seeing Double

Most cookies depend on sugar, butter, and vanilla as their main flavors. Vanilla extract is often very subtle. Most cookie recipes (including biscotti) can stand doubling up on this basic extract for enhanced flavor.

Preheat oven to 350°F. Stack two baking sheets together and line top sheet with parchment paper.

In a mixer bowl, cream butter and shortening together until well blended. Add peanut butter and sugars and blend well. Fold in eggs and vanilla.

Fold in flour, baking powder, baking soda, and salt to make a soft dough. Fold in chocolate chips and peanut butter cup candies.

For Ooey-Gooey Filling, in a food processor, blend all ingredients together 2 to 3 minutes to make a paste that holds together.

For each cookie, form a golf ball–size round of dough and gently press on prepared baking sheets. Deposit a large spoonful of filling onto each round of cookie dough, mostly in the center, and press lightly.

Bake until just set, about 12 to 15 minutes. Let cool on baking sheets at least 5 minutes before removing them to a wire rack to finish cooling.

Chocolate Ambivalence Cookies

Makes 28 to 32 sandwich cookies

These gourmet chocolate sandwich cookies are dipped in milk chocolate and semisweet chocolate. Wrap these cookies separately as gifts—they taste rich and are eye-catching—or just enjoy them as a secret indulgence.

1½ cups unsalted butter, softened
1¼ cups confectioners' sugar
1 tablespoon white sugar
½ teaspoon pure vanilla extract
2½ cups all-purpose flour
⅓ cup cocoa powder
¼ teaspoon baking powder
⅛ teaspoon baking soda
Pinch ground cinnamon
¼ teaspoon salt

Filling

8 ounces premium-quality white
  chocolate, melted

Melted Dipping Chocolate

4 ounces semisweet chocolate,
  melted
4 ounces milk chocolate, melted
Confectioners' sugar

In a mixer bowl, cream butter with both sugars. Add vanilla; then fold in flour, cocoa, baking powder, baking soda, cinnamon, and salt and blend well to make a soft dough. Pack onto parchment paper; wrap and chill about 30 to 45 minutes (or up to a few days).

Preheat oven to 350°F. Line a large baking sheet with parchment paper. **Roll out** chilled dough on a well-floured work surface to ¼-inch thickness. Cut into heart shapes of about 3 to 3½ inches. Arrange cookies on prepared baking sheet.

Bake until done, around 15 to 17 minutes, and let cool completely.

To assemble, smear melted white chocolate on one cookie and top with another cookie (undersides together). Repeat with all cookies. Let set. **Dip** half of each sandwich cookie in melted semisweet chocolate or smear tops with melted milk chocolate, using a small metal spatula. Or drizzle both types of melted chocolate on top or simply dust with confectioners' sugar. Let chocolate set and wrap each sandwich cookie separately.

Doubling Recipes

You can easily double or even quadruple cookie recipes and freeze the dough for bake-a-thons up to six months later. Freeze dough in large flattened disks or, if you are ambitious, in individual small rounds (use a miniature ice-cream scoop). Wrap disks in wax paper or parchment. For individual mounds of dough, freeze them on a baking sheet and then place them in a zip-top freezer bag and return to freezer.

Candy Bar Shortbread

Makes 2 to 3 dozen cookies

No one seems able to get enough of these rich shortbread cookies crowned with *Toblerone* chocolate.

1 cup unsalted butter, softened
⅔ cup sugar
2¼ cups all-purpose flour
Pinch salt

4 (3.52-ounce) *Toblerone* chocolate bars, coarsely chopped

Preheat oven to 325°F. Stack two baking sheets together and line top sheet with parchment paper.

In a mixer bowl, cream butter and sugar until blended. Add flour and salt and mix to make a stiff dough that does not quite hold together.

Pat dough into a 13- x 9-inch pan lined with parchment paper **(photo 1)** and set on prepared baking sheets or pat directly into a rectangle on baking sheets (about 14 x 10 inches). Bake until lightly golden, 25 to 40 minutes. Sprinkle chopped chocolate on hot uncut shortbread **(photo 2).** **Let set** about 5 minutes and smear chocolate around **(photo 3).** Cut into small squares and remove cookies to fridge or freezer to set up.

the biscotti
bakery

Ah, biscotti—the dippable, dunkable, intensely crunchy twice-baked Italian treats. They lend themselves to many variations, as you'll find on these pages. Traditional biscotti are a matter of a few simple but pure quality ingredients. In fact, many authentic Italian biscotti recipes do not even call for fat. If there is fat (butter or oil), it is in modest proportion, compared to a drop cookie, for example.

American-style biscotti are far richer, but no one seems to complain. Simple but often toothsome additions, such as nuts, dried fruit, extracts, chocolate, and spice, ensure that contemporary biscotti know no limits in gilding the lily. Since your biscotti are homemade and thrive on your personal touch, feel free to add whatever delights you, creating your own signature biscotti in the process. The thick batter is very accommodating—an affable host to pretty well anything you care to throw in. Plain biscotti can be gussied up with a slicked-on coat of melted chocolate and a dusting of chopped nuts or a sprinkle of confectioners' sugar.

These biscotti recipes are not fat-free (remember that egg yolks, while rich in iron, are also a fat), but biscotti can, in fact, be made without added fat. They will just be more brittle but still very good for dunking in coffee or tea. And when leaving out butter or oil, you also would be using less flour. The results are crisper but still tasty cookies. Moreover, any of these recipes calling for butter can alternatively be made with canola or vegetable oil without a noticeable difference in taste.

Biscotti are easily mixed by hand, especially if you are using melted butter or oil, but the easiest way is to use a stand mixer with the paddle attachment. A food processor is an option, but stir in extras like nuts and chocolate by hand so they will maintain their texture. Biscotti by nature are good keepers. You can display them for a week or more in a cookie jar. To assure baking success, check out the tips toward better biscotti on the following pages.

Ingredients

Use room-temperature large eggs and softened butter for well-blended biscotti dough.

My biscotti recipes all call for unbleached all-purpose flour by default. Unbleached all-purpose flour tends to behave exceptionally well in all cookie and biscotti baking and has no chemical aftertaste. But you can surely use regular all-purpose flour if you have it on hand.

Pure vanilla extract is the key component for most biscotti, tying in flavors and rounding out the simple tastes. Exceptional biscotti all start with pure vanilla extract (and I often feature more vanilla than you would expect). Nothing else replicates its natural, subtle bouquet. You can also use other extracts instead of—or in addition to—vanilla to change the flavor or give a multidimensional flavor to the batter.

How Much Flour to Add?

Biscotti dough is like a very thick paste. You might need to add a bit more flour to the dough, depending on the humidity of the day and your own handling of the dough, as well as what flour you use, how warm or fresh the eggs are, and what else you add (such as plumped raisins or ground nuts). How do you know? You will notice that the dough will be far too gloppy and will spread on the baking sheet rather than stay put. The dough should be soft enough that you can use a spatula to lift it but thick enough to stay in place on the baking sheet once you deposit it (see photos). If you do have a gloppy dough that spreads, fear not! It will just make for longer biscotti sticks.

Equipment

Baking Sheets and Parchment Paper

Large heavy-gauge rimmed baking sheets are ideal for biscotti. The heavy gauge reduces the chances of the

One recipe shaped on stacked large baking sheets = long, impressive biscotti.

One recipe shaped on two baking sheets = smaller, shorter biscotti.

biscotti burning and ensures even baking. And the large sheets are nice and roomy—allowing you to easily shape biscotti logs. Parchment paper makes for less work (no greasing the pan) and ensures that biscotti won't stick to your baking sheet or burn on the bottom. Parchment paper also enables you to lift the whole baked log off the pan and to cut the log into sticks on a cutting board.

Technique

One Log of Biscotti Dough or Two?

Use a spatula or wet hands to spread long ovals of biscotti dough on a baking sheet. A full recipe on a large baking sheet will yield long, large, impressive biscotti.

Alternatively, you can make two smaller mounds of dough and bake biscotti on two baking sheets. The result is shorter biscotti, which are equally appealing.

Which Baking Rack?

Bake biscotti in the upper third of your oven for the most even baking without the risk of browning the biscotti's undersides too much. This is important because after that first bake, biscotti get a second bake at a lower temperature to crisp them up.

When baking biscotti on the bottom rack of your oven, use two baking sheets stacked together. For the upper rack, the baking sheet can be single; the biscotti placed closer to the bottom are subject to more intense heat, so doubling up the baking sheets ensures they bake as evenly as the dough placed on the upper baking sheet.

How to Slice Biscotti

Use a long serrated bread knife and a gentle sawing motion to slice biscotti. If the biscotti log crumbles as you slice it, it needs more cooling time. Even chilling biscotti (or freezing, as stated on the next page) is a great way to ensure perfect, crumb-free slices. Cut biscotti logs on a cutting board and return slices to the baking sheet for the second baking.

The Second Baking

Biscotti do most of their crisping in the oven during their crucial and characteristic second bake, but they crisp up even more as they cool. Here's how you know when they've baked long enough: from experience, the time stated in the recipe, the slight browning of the biscotti, and actually tasting one that has cooled a bit. As your first batch of biscotti cools, you can easily see if the rest of the batch needs more baking.

It is better to underbake than to overbake. Remove biscotti from the oven as soon as they seem slightly colored and dry to the touch. As they cool, they will achieve their final crunchy texture.

For ultrathin biscotti that are easily sliced for the second bake, wrap partially baked biscotti logs (whole) overnight and freeze. Next day, slice the frozen logs as thin as you wish and bake the second requisite time to brown the biscotti. This is also a good tip if you are dealing with slicing biscotti that include whole nuts.

Cooling Biscotti

All biscotti can cool on the baking sheet, where they will continue to crisp up. Or you can cool biscotti on wire racks.

Use a gentle sawing motion with a serrated knife to slice biscotti.

Finishing Touches

All biscotti can be further adorned by finishing with a chocolate glaze. To glaze, melt white, semisweet, or milk chocolate. Using a flat, small icing knife, spread melted chocolate on one side of each cookie. Cool on a wire rack two to four hours until thoroughly dry. Alternatively, simply dip one end of each biscotti stick in the melted chocolate and let dry. Or double dip by dunking into dark chocolate, allowing to dry, and then taking a more shallow dip into white chocolate and allow to dry.

Storing Biscotti

Store biscotti in glass or ceramic cookie jars or wrap biscotti sticks in wax paper, twist ends to seal, and pack in storage containers. Biscotti, if kept dry, get harder and crisper. If packed in an environment that has some humidity, they will soften. You can also freeze baked biscotti, wrapped in wax paper and sealed in freezer bags, up to two months.

Due to their characteristic crisp and dry nature, a batch of biscotti makes a great choice when you want to mail a gift of cookies. Here's my best tip for mailing biscotti: Just skip the second baking because biscotti will naturally crisp up after a day or two in the mail.

Double-Fudge Biscotti

Makes 3 dozen biscotti

Anyone with a sweet tooth will find it very hard to pass on this sumptuous, fudgy edition of this crisp cookie.

1   cup unsalted butter, softened

1¾   cups sugar

3   large eggs

2   teaspoons pure vanilla extract

⅓   cup cocoa powder

2   teaspoons baking powder

¼   teaspoon baking soda

½   teaspoon salt

2½   cups, approximately, all-purpose flour

2   cups coarsely chopped semisweet chocolate or chocolate chips

1   cup coarsely chopped white chocolate

1   cup large pieces of white chocolate

Finishing Touches

4   ounces each semisweet and white chocolate, melted

Firming Up the Dough

Thick doughs, such as for biscotti, can be left to stand 10 to 15 minutes after mixing. This rest is a step that helps the dough firm up and become easier to handle; it also requires less flour overall. This recipe for Double-Fudge Biscotti employs this baker's trick of the trade. The extra time allows the flour to totally absorb the other ingredients and, consequently, to firm up the dough for better handling.

Preheat oven to 350°F. Line two small baking sheets or one large baking sheet with parchment paper.

In a mixer bowl, cream butter and sugar and then add eggs and vanilla. Fold in cocoa, baking powder, baking soda, salt, and flour to make a thick batter. Fold in chopped semisweet chocolate and chopped as well as pieces of white chocolate. Let dough stand a few minutes to thicken and firm up.

Spread dough into two logs on prepared baking sheets. (For larger biscotti, use one large sheet and spread out one large log of dough.)

Bake until set and biscotti logs are firm to the touch, about 35 to 45 minutes. Remove biscotti from oven and let cool 15 to 20 minutes. Reduce oven temperature to 325°F. Then, using a long serrated knife, slice logs on the diagonal into ½-inch-thick slices. Return biscotti to baking sheets; bake a second time to dry and crisp them, turning biscotti over once to ensure even baking and allowing 15 to 20 minutes per side. Let cool completely on baking sheets.

To finish biscotti, melt chocolate and drizzle, smear, or coat one end of each biscotto, as per your own taste, with semisweet and white chocolate. Let harden.

Dark and White Chocolate Chip-Almond Biscotti

Makes 1 to 2 dozen biscotti, depending on size; pictured on page 138

This classic-made irresistible version of biscotti has a double whammy of chocolate. These are crisp, sweet, and studded with white and dark chocolate.

¾ cup unsalted butter, softened

1¾ cups sugar

½ cup finely chopped almonds

½ cup ground hazelnuts

4 large eggs

1 tablespoon pure vanilla extract

1 tablespoon almond extract

3 cups all-purpose flour

2½ teaspoons baking powder

½ teaspoon baking soda

¼ teaspoon salt

⅛ teaspoon ground cinnamon

1 cup whole blanched almonds

1 cup semisweet chocolate chips

1 cup white chocolate chips or coarsely chopped white chocolate

Sheer Nuttiness

Whole nuts can make cutting biscotti difficult. To remedy this, you can freeze the whole logs of baked biscotti that contain whole nuts for one to two hours before cutting. When you cut semi-frozen biscotti logs, the nuts stay put and the logs tend to cut more easily than freshly baked, softer biscotti—and without crumbling.

Preheat oven to 350°F. Line two small baking sheets or one large baking sheet with parchment paper.

In a mixer bowl, cream butter and sugar until smooth. Stir in chopped almonds and ground hazelnuts. Blend in eggs, vanilla, and almond extract. Fold in flour, baking powder, baking soda, salt, and cinnamon and blend well. Fold in whole almonds and both types of chocolate chips.

Spread dough into two logs on prepared baking sheets. (For larger biscotti, use one large sheet and spread out one large log of dough.)

Bake until set and biscotti logs are firm to the touch and golden, about 40 minutes. If biscotti brown too quickly, reduce oven temperature to 325°F and bake a little longer.

Remove biscotti from oven and let cool 15 to 20 minutes. Reduce oven temperature to 300°F. Using a long serrated knife, slice logs on the diagonal into ½- to ¾-inch-thick slices.

Return biscotti to baking sheets and bake a second time to dry and crisp them, about 35 to 45 minutes, turning biscotti once during baking to ensure even baking. Let cool completely on baking sheets.

Blueberry Biscotti Bones

Makes about 14 biscotti

Drizzle these dunkable, funky cookies with melted white chocolate after they have cooled. These biscotti taste great with a mixture of fresh berries as well as plumped currants.

Form this biscotti dough into 'dog bone' shapes and bake them to a crunchy finish. These dense, crunchy sticks are studded with blueberries and scented with lemon and vanilla.

1 cup unsalted butter, softened
1¾ cups sugar
3 large eggs
2 teaspoons pure vanilla extract
½ teaspoon pure almond extract
¼ teaspoon lemon oil or ½ teaspoon pure lemon extract, optional
3 cups, approximately, all-purpose flour

2½ teaspoons baking powder
½ teaspoon salt
1 cup semi-frozen blueberries

Finishing Touches

1 large egg, whisked
Sugar, for dusting

Preheat oven to 325°F. Line one large baking sheet with parchment paper.
In a mixer bowl, cream butter and sugar. Add eggs, vanilla, and almond and lemon flavorings, blending well. Stir in flour, baking powder, and salt to make a thick dough. Gently fold in blueberries, using hands if necessary if dough is too stiff. If dough seems soft, add a bit more flour and chill dough 20 minutes before using.
Flour a work surface liberally. Divide dough into 14 sections and roll each into a "bone" about 6 to 8 inches long and 1 inch wide. Place on prepared baking sheet. Brush each cookie with beaten egg and then dust with sugar.
Bake until crisp and golden brown, about 30 to 40 minutes. Let cool completely on baking sheet.

Café Latte Caramel Biscotti

Makes 2 to 4 dozen biscotti, depending on size

Enjoy these mocha-vanilla biscotti showcasing a ribbon of sweet cream cheese "latte," swirls of melted caramel, and a hint of coffee.

Cream Cheese Latte

¾ cup (6 ounces) cream cheese, softened
1 large egg
¼ cup sugar
½ teaspoon pure vanilla extract

Biscotti Dough

¾ cup caramel or butterscotch chips
1 cup unsalted butter, melted
1½ cups sugar

3 large eggs
2 teaspoons pure vanilla extract
2 tablespoons warm brewed espresso or strong coffee
3 to 4 cups all-purpose flour
2 teaspoons baking powder
¾ teaspoon salt

Finishing Touches

Caramel chips
Freeze-dried instant coffee granules, for dusting

Preheat oven to 350°F. Line two baking sheets with parchment paper.
For Cream Cheese Latte, in a small bowl, blend cream cheese, egg, sugar, and vanilla and set aside.
For Biscotti Dough, place caramel chips in a bowl and microwave chips to melt; set aside. (If chips do not melt easily, add about 1 tablespoon softened unsalted butter to aid melting.)
In a mixer bowl, blend butter and sugar; then add eggs, vanilla, and brewed coffee. Stir in most of flour, baking powder, and salt and then blend in melted caramel chips. It does not have to be even; you are marbleizing dough with melted caramel chips. Add more flour if dough is not stiff.
Pat two logs of dough (about 8 x 4 or so) onto prepared baking sheets.
Spoon on cream cheese topping and, with fingers or a knife, deeply swirl topping somewhat into batter (**photo 1**). (These two textures are very different.) Sprinkle with more caramel chips and a dusting of coffee granules.
Bake until set and biscotti logs are firm to the touch, about 30 to 40 minutes. Remove biscotti from oven and let cool 15 to 20 minutes. Reduce oven temperature to 325°F. Using a long serrated knife, slice logs on the diagonal into ½-inch-thick slices. Return biscotti to baking sheets and bake a second time. Bake to dry and crisp them, turning once midway to ensure even baking, about 15 to 20 minutes per side. Let cool completely on baking sheets.

1

Apricot Sunrise Biscotti

Makes 2 to 3 dozen biscotti; also pictured on page 138

Some folks go ape for apricots. These biscotti feature California dried apricots and are laced with peach schnapps, apricot liqueur, or apricot nectar. You can use cut-up apricot leather instead of dried apricots.

Baking with liqueur is always interesting, and this method of dipping the baked biscotti into juice or liqueur and then dunking in sugar and baking again is one I favor. It makes something special into something spectacular.

½ cup unsalted butter, melted
1½ cups sugar
2 large eggs
1½ teaspoons pure vanilla extract
½ teaspoon orange oil or pure orange extract
3 to 4 cups all-purpose flour
1 tablespoon baking powder
½ cup peach schnapps, apricot liqueur, or apricot nectar
Zest of 1 orange, finely minced

¼ teaspoon salt
3 cups diced dried apricots, plumped and dried (see page 18)
½ cup minced golden raisins, plumped and dried (see page 18)

Finishing Touches

1 cup, or more, orange juice, peach schnapps, or apricot liqueur
1 cup, approximately, sugar

Preheat oven to 350°F. Line two small baking sheets or one large baking sheet with parchment paper.

In a mixer bowl, blend butter and sugar; add eggs, vanilla, and orange oil and blend well. Fold in flour, baking powder, liqueur, orange zest, and salt to make a thick batter. Fold in apricots and raisins and blend well.

Spread dough into two logs on prepared baking sheets. (For larger biscotti, use one large sheet and spread out one large log of dough.)

Bake until set and biscotti logs are firm to the touch, about 35 to 45 minutes. Remove biscotti from oven and let cool 15 to 20 minutes. Reduce oven temperature to 325°F. Using a long serrated knife, slice logs on the diagonal into ½- to ¾-inch-thick slices.

Dip each cookie, one side only, in orange juice or peach liqueur and then press into sugar. Place biscotti, sugar side down, on prepared baking sheets. Bake biscotti to dry and crisp them, about 20 to 30 minutes, turning once after 12 minutes. Let cool completely on baking sheets.

Rocky Road Biscotti

Makes 3 dozen biscotti

Think of these as brownies baked up into crisp chocolate sticks.

1 cup unsalted butter, softened	1 cup coarsely chopped white chocolate
1¾ cups sugar	1 cup miniature marshmallows
3 large eggs	1 cup coarsely chopped toffee bar or similar chocolate bar
2 teaspoons pure vanilla extract	1 cup chopped pecans
⅓ cup cocoa powder	1 cup coarsely broken pieces of white chocolate
½ teaspoon salt	
¼ teaspoon baking soda	**Finishing Touches**
2 teaspoons baking powder	4 ounces each dark and white chocolate
2½ cups, approximately, all-purpose flour	
2 cups coarsely chopped semisweet chocolate or chocolate chips	

> **Mix and match whatever you like here—this recipe makes chocolaty, chunky biscotti. The chocolate glaze slicks up what is already totally decadent.**

Preheat oven to 350°F. Line two small baking sheets or one large baking sheet with parchment paper.

In a mixer bowl, cream butter and sugar and then add eggs and vanilla. Fold in cocoa, salt, baking soda, baking powder, and enough flour to make a thick batter. Fold in chocolate chips, chopped white chocolate, marshmallows, chopped toffee bar, pecans, and white chocolate. Let dough stand a few minutes to thicken and firm up.

Spread dough into two logs on prepared baking sheets. (For larger biscotti, use one large sheet and spread out one large log of dough.)

Bake until set and biscotti logs are firm to the touch, about 35 to 45 minutes. Cool biscotti 15 to 20 minutes. Reduce oven temperature to 325°F.

Using a long serrated knife, slice logs on the diagonal into ½-inch-thick slices. Return biscotti to baking sheets and bake a second time to dry and crisp them, about 10 to 20 minutes, turning biscotti once at midway point to ensure even baking. Let cool on baking sheets.

Melt dark and white chocolate and drizzle, smear, or coat each biscotto with milk and white chocolate as per your own taste. Let harden.

Domenic's Saffron and Almond Biscotti

Makes 2 to 3 dozen biscotti, depending on size

Domenic is a graphic artist who shares my love for tango. Tango talk turned to baking talk, and Domenic shared his idea for a flavor of biscotti. These are as delicious to behold as they are to eat, and the fragrance of them baking is incredible.

A hefty pinch of saffron threads gives this biscotti a beautiful golden glow.

1   teaspoon saffron threads
1   tablespoon boiling water
1½ cups sugar
1   cup unsalted butter, melted
4   large eggs
2   teaspoons pure vanilla extract
1   tablespoon pure almond extract
½   teaspoon salt
2   teaspoons baking powder

½   cup ground almonds
3½ cups, approximately, all-purpose flour
2   cups whole almonds

Finishing Touches

1   egg yolk, whisked
⅓   cup sugar
½   cup slivered almonds

Preheat oven to 350°F. Line two small baking sheets or one large baking sheet with parchment paper.

In a small bowl, place saffron threads and mix with boiling water; let stand 5 minutes.

In a mixer bowl, blend sugar and butter well, about 3 minutes. Add eggs, saffron, vanilla, and almond extract and blend well, about 2 minutes. Fold in salt, baking powder, ground almonds, and almost all of flour. Mix until batter is thick and soft but holds together. Fold in whole almonds and add more flour if dough is not stiff.

Spread dough into two logs on prepared baking sheets. (For larger biscotti, use one large sheet and spread out one large log of dough.)

Brush top of each log with egg yolk, sprinkle on sugar, and press in slivered almonds.

Bake until set and biscotti logs are just browned and firm to the touch, about 40 to 45 minutes. Remove biscotti from oven and let cool 15 to 20 minutes. Reduce oven temperature to 325°F. Using a long serrated knife, slice logs on the diagonal into 1-inch-thick slices and return to baking sheets. Bake biscotti to dry and crisp them, about 15 to 20 minutes, turning biscotti once at midway point to ensure even baking. Let cool completely on baking sheets.

Tropical Spa Biscotti

Makes 2 to 3 dozen biscotti, depending on size

One bite of this uniquely tropical-flavored, coconutty cookie will transcend you to another place.

½ cup unsalted butter, melted
¼ cup vegetable oil
1½ cups sugar
3 large eggs
2 tablespoons rum or orange liqueur
2 teaspoons pure vanilla extract
¼ to ½ teaspoon lime oil
¼ teaspoon lemon oil
¾ teaspoon tangerine or orange oil
3½ cups all-purpose flour
2 teaspoons baking powder
½ teaspoon salt
Zest of 1 large orange, finely minced
Zest of 3 limes, finely minced

1 cup sweetened shredded coconut, toasted
½ cup macadamia nuts, chopped
1 cup cubed or diced pineapple from a 14-ounce can
1 cup chopped dried apricot
⅓ cup dried mango, diced
⅓ cup golden raisins
Sweetened shredded coconut, as required

Rum Topping, optional

1 cup rum or orange juice
1 to 2 cups sugar

The citrus oils are from *Boyajian*, but you can substitute citrus extracts. Dried mango is available in bulk food stores. The rum topping is optional, but if you choose to use it, reduce the sugar in the biscotti recipe by ¼ cup.

Preheat oven to 350°F. Line two small baking sheets or one large baking sheet with parchment paper.

In a mixer bowl, blend melted butter, oil, sugar, and eggs. Stir in rum, vanilla, and citrus oils. Mix well. Blend in flour, baking powder, and salt. Fold in citrus zest, toasted coconut, macadamia nuts, pineapple, and dried fruit to make a thick dough. Let dough stand 10 minutes.

Spread dough into two logs on prepared baking sheets. (For larger biscotti, use one large sheet and spread out one large log of dough.) It will be sticky. Top with shredded coconut, pressing in slightly.

Bake until biscotti logs seem set and dry, about 45 to 55 minutes. If logs are browning too quickly, reduce oven temperature to 325°F and lengthen baking time. Remove biscotti from oven and let cool 15 to 20 minutes. Reduce oven temperature to 325°F. Using a long serrated knife, slice biscotti into long diagonal slices.

For Rum Topping, before the second bake, place rum in a shallow dish and sugar on a baking sheet. Brush one side of each cookie liberally with rum or orange juice and then press lightly into sugar (parchment paper comes in very handy with this variation). Continue with second bake as directed below.

Return biscotti to baking sheets and bake a second time to dry and crisp them, about 20 to 35 minutes, turning once at midway point to ensure even baking. Allow cookies to dry and barely brown. Let cool completely on baking sheets.

French Chocolate-Mint Biscotti

Makes 2 to 3 dozen biscotti, depending on size

A slick of melted white chocolate makes these biscotti festive holiday food. Minced peppermint patties in the dough add to the glamour.

If you cannot find premium white chocolate (which melts well) or melt white chocolate easily (it is tricky, and you must do it slowly), use white chocolate confectioners' discs, which are available at culinary stores. They look like white chocolate but taste rather bland—however, they melt easily. You can also use dark chocolate for the special coating.

¾ cup unsalted butter, melted and still warm
½ cup cocoa powder, measured and then sifted
1½ cups sugar
4 large eggs
2 teaspoons pure vanilla extract
1 tablespoon double-strength brewed coffee or espresso
3 to 4 cups all-purpose flour
2 teaspoons baking powder

¼ teaspoon baking soda
¼ teaspoon salt
1 cup chocolate-covered peppermint patties, minced
½ cup semisweet chocolate, cut into coarse chunks

Finishing Touches

6 ounces white chocolate, melted
½ to 1 teaspoon pure mint extract

Preheat oven to 350°F. Line two small baking sheets or one large baking sheet with parchment paper.

In a mixer bowl, stir together melted butter and cocoa. Blend in sugar and then add eggs, vanilla, and coffee.

In a separate bowl, blend flour, baking powder, baking soda, and salt. Stir into wet batter and then fold in minced peppermint patties and semisweet chocolate.

Spread dough into two logs on prepared baking sheets. (For larger biscotti, use one large sheet and spread out one large log of dough.)

Bake until biscotti logs seem set, about 30 to 40 minutes. Remove biscotti from oven and let cool 15 to 20 minutes. Reduce oven temperature to 325°F. Using a long serrated knife, slice logs on the diagonal into ½- to ¾-inch-thick slices.

Return biscotti to baking sheets and bake a second time to dry and crisp them, about 15 to 20 minutes, turning once midway to ensure even baking. Since cookies are dark, it is difficult to judge when they are done. They should seem almost dry to the touch when ready. Let cool completely on baking sheets.

For coating, melt white chocolate slowly and then briskly whisk in mint extract very quickly so as to blend and flavor white chocolate without chocolate seizing up. You can spread or drizzle melted white chocolate onto one side of these baked cookies for a gourmet look.

Chianti and Parmesan Biscotti

Makes 2½ to 3½ dozen biscotti, depending on size

Like the crunch of biscotti but want a savory munchie instead? These crisp and tender bites are sort of like wine-and-cheese sticks eaten out of hand—perfect with a glass of wine or punch. If you use grated Parmesan cheese from the supermarket, it will likely be too salty, so either spring for imported Parmesan and grate it yourself or reduce the salt in this recipe by ¼ teaspoon.

½	cup light olive oil	2	cups freshly grated Parmesan cheese
3	large eggs		
1¼	teaspoons salt, or more to taste*	2	teaspoons baking powder
1	tablespoon sugar	¼	teaspoon baking soda
4	teaspoons cracked black pepper	2	to 2¼ cups all-purpose flour
2	tablespoons finely minced fresh parsley		
1	teaspoon garlic powder		
½	cup red wine, such as Chianti		

Finishing Touches

Light olive oil

Grated Parmesan cheese, for dusting

*Depending on how salty your Parmesan cheese is, you can add a touch more salt for more savory biscotti.

Preheat oven to 350°F. Stack two baking sheets together and line top sheet with parchment paper.

In a mixer bowl, blend oil, eggs, salt, sugar, pepper, parsley, and garlic powder. Blend in wine, cheese, baking powder, baking soda, and flour to make a stiff dough. Drizzle some oil on top baking sheet and dust on more Parmesan cheese.

Spread dough into a log about 10 inches long and 4 to 5 inches across and pat down to square off the dough neatly on prepared baking sheets.

Bake until set, about 35 to 45 minutes. Cool slightly on baking sheets. Wrap and refrigerate log 1 hour. Using a long serrated knife, slice log into ¼-inch-thick slices.

Preheat oven to 300°F. Return biscotti to baking sheets and bake a second time to crisp, about 20 minutes, turning once at midway point to ensure even baking.

Taste one biscotto after it cools. If it is crisp, biscotti are done. Otherwise, bake a little longer, 5 to 10 minutes. Let cool completely on baking sheets.

> These are a great cocktail party nibble or gift biscotti (with a bottle of Chianti, special olive oil, and a hunk of imported Parmesan). If you roll these like dog bones and slow-bake them, you get an entirely different presentation.

bars & squares

The most persuasive inspiration I had to become a professional baker was due to a square. This was no ordinary square, however, but rather one very special, consummately delectable morsel called an Apricot Square, which my mother raved about for years. Every social gathering in her day seemed to feature squares and dainty bars. What great biscuits were to the homesteaders in 1820, great squares were to the homemaker and baker in the fifties. It is odd how such a little thing could come to represent the pinnacle of good home baking. But my mother—who is still rather avant-garde and ahead of her time, regardless of the era—knew a good thing when she saw one. To her, and to many bakers in the know, a great square is the litmus test of a great baker.

Squares are both decadent and modest, small but satisfying. Since we also eat with our eyes, great-looking and great-tasting squares are a must. Take a tip from me—cut oversized bars and squares, and something modest becomes totally amazing.

Through the twentieth century until now, squares have come a long way. In the forties, they were the petite morsels served at women's luncheons. A woman could seal her reputation as a homemaker with a simple batch of great squares. In the sixties and seventies, squares seemed synonymous with three things: brownies, blondies, or health-wave granola bars. Muffins, cookies, and croissants often upstage squares, but the love of chocolate and the ever-aspiring coffeehouse trend seem to ensure that squares are here to stay. The new squares, however, are big, bold, decadent affairs.

What makes bars and squares ideal dessert finger food is that you can make hoards of them in a short time—unlike cookies or muffins, which require individual dispensing. This makes sense in the corner café but equally so on the home front. Moreover, squares are the perfect balance between cake and cookie, and their size easily accommodates small appetites (cut them dainty) or hearty ones (cut them large).

Ingredients

Ingredients for bars and squares, like with all other baking, should be the best of the best. For one thing, this is not the time to use shortening; you should always use butter. Everything else, from chocolate to raisins, is going to shine, so use the best-quality and purest ingredients, measure them properly, and handle with care.

Technique

General techniques of making good bars and squares vary little from recipe to recipe, but remember these essential tips.

This is the most crucial tip for producing superlative bars and squares: Always use the size pan called for in the recipe. Aside from using quality ingredients, this makes the most important difference in results.

Grease the pan well with nonstick cooking spray and evenly spread the dough in the pan, using a wet offset metal spatula to make the job easier.

Avoid overbaking, which results in tough squares, and underbaking, which causes doughy, uncooked squares. Observe baking times given in a recipe and check about 5 to 10 minutes early to see if they are set or almost done.

Cut squares when they are properly cooled or only slightly warm to avoid crumbling or ragged edges. The best trick here is to freeze or semifreeze squares before cutting them. This way, you get perfect portions.

Since most of these recipes freeze well and avoid the extra steps of rolling, cutting, or dropping the dough, it pays to make a batch each of two different varieties. Then wrap the squares well in plastic wrap or freezer bags and take out servings as you need them.

The beauty of bars and squares is that you can cut them into any dimensions you want or need. If you are serving one type of bar, larger portions make sense. For a variety of bars and squares to be served at a coffee klatch, cut them smaller so guests can sample the range.

Storage

Wrap bars and squares in wax paper and then place them on a cake plate with a dome cover. Bars and squares last well at room temperature if properly wrapped; or you can freeze them wrapped in wax paper and then packed in zip-top freezer bags or containers for up to two to three months. They also can be wrapped and refrigerated.

Vanilla Cheesecake-Stuffed Brownies

Makes about 10 large brownies

You can also add 2 ounces of melted chocolate to the cream cheese for a double-fudge cheesecake version of these deluxe bars. These freeze well—as most bars do—but they never seem to make it to the freezer!

Cheesecake Topping

8 ounces cream cheese, softened

¼ cup sugar

1 large egg

1 teaspoon pure vanilla extract

2 tablespoons all-purpose flour

Brownies

½ cup unsalted butter

7 ounces semisweet chocolate, coarsely chopped

1¼ cups sugar

1 teaspoon pure vanilla extract

3 large eggs

1 cup all-purpose flour

2 tablespoons cocoa powder

⅛ teaspoon baking soda

Pinch salt

Preheat oven to 350°F. Generously spray an 11- x 7-inch rectangular pan with nonstick cooking spray and place on a parchment paper–lined baking sheet.

For Cheesecake Topping, in a food processor or medium bowl, using a stiff wire whisk, blend cream cheese with sugar and then add egg, vanilla, and flour. Set aside.

For Brownies, melt butter and chocolate in a microwave-safe medium-size bowl in microwave 1½ to 2½ minutes and let cool to almost room temperature. Whisk in sugar, vanilla, and eggs until smooth. Fold in flour, cocoa, soda, and salt to make a smooth batter.

Pour or spoon batter into pan and place on prepared baking sheet. Add Cheesecake Topping in dollops on top of brownie batter. Using a butter knife, make deep swirls so that you get a contrast of batters (**photo 1**). (More contrast will appear after brownies are baked.)

Bake 35 to 40 minutes or until brownies seem just set. It is tricky to test these, but if they are just set to the touch and cheesecake part is not wet, then they are done. Cool in pan 1 hour and then refrigerate before cutting. These brownies are best kept refrigerated and are good served cold or warmed a bit. They also freeze well.

1

This is a blockbuster of a brownie, featuring a cheesecake filling swirling through a decadent fudge layer.

Caramel Swirl Hunks

Makes 16 to 24 brownies, depending on size; also pictured on page 152

These manly-sized squares are beefed up with chocolate chips and pools of dulce de leche.

2	cups unsalted butter, melted	1	teaspoon baking powder
3	cups firmly packed light brown sugar	½	teaspoon baking soda
⅓	cup white sugar	½	teaspoon salt
4	large eggs	1	cup semisweet chocolate chips or chopped chocolate
4	teaspoons pure vanilla extract	1	(13.4-ounce) can dulce de leche (or use half a batch of recipe below)
1	cup quick oats		
4	cups all-purpose flour		

Preheat oven to 350°F. Generously spray a 13- x 9-inch pan with nonstick cooking spray and place it on a parchment paper–lined baking sheet.

In a mixer bowl, blend butter and both sugars. Add eggs, vanilla, and oats and blend well. Fold in flour, baking powder, baking soda, and salt. Then fold in chocolate chips.

Spread batter in prepared pan. Top with dollops of dulce de leche and then swirl or smear dulce de leche into batter.

Bake 38 minutes or until batter is set (not wobbly and jiggly). If brownies seem browned around the edges but jiggly in the center, reduce oven temperature to 325°F and continue baking 10 to 15 minutes longer or until set.

Refrigerate or freeze 1 hour. Cut into large hunks or blocks.

Homemade Dulce de Leche

Makes about 2 cups

You can buy it ready-made, but dulce de leche, a Latin version of pure caramel, is easy to make at home. All you need is a can or two of condensed milk. This makes a double batch, but it seems to last in the fridge for quite a while and is great to keep on hand for recipes or for just warming and drizzling over ice cream.

2	(14-ounce) cans sweetened condensed milk

Spoon condensed milk in top of a double boiler. (I use a stainless-steel bowl set over simmering water.) Cook over low heat, stirring occasionally, 3 to 6 hours until milk turns deep amber in color. It does not take much pot watching. Once milk is a deep caramel color (or a bit lighter), it is done. Remove from stove; cool and then refrigerate. It will thicken a lot upon cooling. Store in the refrigerator 2 to 3 weeks.

Pecan Pie Bars

Makes 2 to 3 dozen bars, depending on size

When you have a hankering for pecans in a buttery crust, whip up these bars that satisfy like a pie and are good keepers at room temperature, in the fridge, or frozen. Cut them tiny, like little tasty gems, or bigger for traditional bars. Slow baking makes for an especially creamy and decadent filling.

Brown Sugar Shortbread Crust

2	cups all-purpose flour
1/3	cup white sugar
3	tablespoons light brown sugar
1/4	teaspoon baking powder
1/8	teaspoon salt
3/4	cup unsalted butter, cut into chunks

Pecan Pie Filling

1/2	cup unsalted butter, melted
1	cup firmly packed light brown sugar
1/2	cup light corn syrup
1	teaspoon pure vanilla extract
2	tablespoons whipping cream
2	large eggs
	Pinch salt
2	cups coarsely chopped pecans

Preheat oven to 350°F. Generously spray an 11- x 7-inch pan with non-stick cooking spray and place it on a parchment paper–lined baking sheet.

For Brown Sugar Shortbread Crust, in a food processor, blend flour, both sugars, baking powder, and salt together briefly. Add butter and pulse to break in butter until mixture just barely begins to hold together. Press into prepared pan and bake 20 minutes. Remove from oven. Reduce oven temperature to 325°F.

For Pecan Pie Filling, in a medium bowl, using a whisk, blend butter, brown sugar, corn syrup, vanilla, cream, eggs, and salt. Fold in pecans. Pour onto slightly cooled crust.

Bake 25 to 35 minutes or until filling is just set. Cool well or refrigerate before cutting into bars.

I have baked a lot of brownies, and after baking them, like, forever, I still learn something new with every batch. All brownies will dry out if overbaked, but most brownies are supposed to be dense—and it is better to underbake than overbake. If you underbake them, serve them ice-cold. The best advice for brownies is to hone in on one or two recipes you prefer and perfect them, especially nailing the proper bake time.

Mississippi Mud Bars

Makes 16 to 20 large or 32 small bars

These confections are best described as bars in the best old-fashioned sense of the word—when bars, piled on a plate, dominated the bake sale or commanded the attention of anyone coming into a diner looking for dessert. Tons of recipes with this name exist, but this is a definitive, perfected version.

Bars

- 2 cups sugar
- ¾ cup unsalted butter, cut into chunks
- 4 large eggs
- 2 teaspoons pure vanilla extract
- 1½ cups all-purpose flour
- ⅓ cup cocoa powder, measured and then sifted
- ¾ teaspoon baking powder
- Pinch baking soda
- ⅛ teaspoon salt
- ½ cup chopped walnuts, optional
- ½ cup semisweet chocolate chips
- 1½ cups sweetened shredded coconut, optional
- 1 (7-ounce) jar marshmallow creme

Mississippi Mud Icing

- 3 cups confectioners' sugar
- ½ cup unsalted butter, softened
- 1 teaspoon pure vanilla extract
- ½ cup cocoa powder, measured and then sifted
- ½ cup evaporated milk

Preheat oven to 350°F. Generously spray an 11- x 7-inch pan with non-stick cooking spray and place it on a parchment paper–lined baking sheet.
In a food processor, blend sugar and butter until pasty. Add eggs and vanilla; blend well. Fold in flour, cocoa, baking powder, baking soda, and salt and blend well. Fold in nuts, chocolate chips, and coconut and blend briefly. Spoon into prepared pan.
Bake until set and firm to the touch, 25 to 30 minutes. Spread marshmallow creme on hot cake and refrigerate, uncovered, 3 or more hours.
For Mississippi Mud Icing, blend all ingredients in a food processor until stiff and glossy. Using a metal spatula, dipped as required into hot water, spread icing on chilled uncut bars. Chill briefly to set icing. Cut into bars. These are messy. It is a good idea to serve them in splayed-out paper liners to hold all the gooey stuff and to keep chocolate from getting all over your hands.

These dark, delicious bars are topped with a sandbar of marshmallow topping and a nice paving of the best, shiniest chocolate icing you ever had.

Serendipity Deluxe Bars

Makes 24 to 36 bars, depending on size

This recipe starts with a shortbread base, follows with a silken chocolate filling, and ends with a chewy, nutty, oatmeal layer. During baking, the layers morph somehow, and the caramel and chocolate filling seem to reverse. These are good chilled or ice-cold—in bold bars or tiny bites on a sweets table. Just remember, the middle layer magically becomes your top layer after baking, via the heat of the oven. I suspect the reason why, but I would rather just enjoy the results and call it fortunate serendipity.

Shortbread Crust

2   cups all-purpose flour

½   cup sugar

¼   teaspoon salt

1   cup unsalted butter, cut into chunks

Chocolate Silk Truffle Layer

1   cup corn syrup

1¼ cups semisweet chocolate chips

1   cup sugar

4   large eggs

2   teaspoons pure vanilla extract

Caramel-Pecan-Oatmeal Layer

¾   cup unsalted butter, melted

¾   cup firmly packed brown sugar

¼   cup corn syrup

Pinch salt

½   cup finely chopped pecans

1   cup quick oats

Finishing Touch

White or dark chocolate, melted

> **Very hard to describe but very easy to eat! As one of my testers wrote, 'These are worth every one of the three layers.'**

Preheat oven to 350°F. Spray a 13- x 9-inch pan with nonstick cooking spray and line with parchment paper. Place pan on a parchment paper–lined baking sheet.

For Shortbread Crust, in a food processor, pulse flour, sugar, and salt. Add butter and pulse to create a mixture of coarse crumbs that barely stick together. Press firmly onto bottom of prepared pan. Bake 20 minutes or until lightly browned.

Meanwhile, in a large glass bowl, microwave corn syrup and chocolate chips until chocolate is almost melted, about 2 to 2½ minutes, stirring midway through so that chocolate melts evenly. Cool to room temperature. Then stir in sugar, eggs, and vanilla; mix well. Pour over hot crust; spread to evenly cover crust. Bake 27 minutes or until truffle layer is firm around edges and slightly soft in center.

For Caramel-Pecan-Oatmeal Layer, blend butter, brown sugar, corn syrup, and salt in a medium bowl. Stir in nuts and oats.

Once bars have baked, remove from oven and cool 10 minutes. Then carefully drop and spread on Caramel-Pecan-Oatmeal Layer.

Bake again, until set, 25 to 35 minutes. Bars will appear just set, and you will see a chocolate topping (not caramel—it will have disappeared).

Let stand 30 minutes and then refrigerate about 3 to 4 hours before cutting.

You can drizzle on white or dark chocolate as a finishing touch. These also freeze well but last about a week when refrigerated.

Metropolis Bars

Makes 36 to 60 bars, depending on size

These rich bars feature a cookie base, caramel, and a milk-chocolate coating. These bars contain no peanuts, making them perfect for kids and adults with nut allergies.

You can make these in a 13- x 9-inch pan for a slightly thinner cookie bottom and a thinner coating of caramel (but you will probably need to use more milk chocolate). These are best cut into bars and chilled. I prefer them with the thicker cookie bottom (so I use an 11- x 7-inch pan), but they are great either way. They have to be chilled to set, then warmed to cut and kept cool. In the test kitchen, we cut them into sticks, wrapped them in cellophane that we twisted at the ends, and froze them. Otherwise, they last about two weeks in the fridge.

Cookie Base

2¼ cups all-purpose flour
½ teaspoon baking powder
¼ teaspoon baking soda
¼ teaspoon salt
1 tablespoon corn syrup
⅓ cup white sugar
2 tablespoons firmly packed brown sugar
¾ cup unsalted butter, cut into chunks
2 tablespoons whipping cream or milk

1 teaspoon pure vanilla extract

Caramel Filling*

1 (14-ounce) can sweetened condensed milk
¼ cup unsalted butter
3 tablespoons corn syrup
½ cup firmly packed light brown sugar
3 (4- to 6-ounce) milk chocolate bars, such as *Cadbury Dairy Milk* or *Hershey's*

*Or 1 (13.4-ounce) can store-bought dulce de leche

Preheat oven to 350°F. Generously spray an 11- x 7-inch pan with non-stick cooking spray and place it on a parchment paper–lined baking sheet. **For Cookie Base,** in a food processor or large bowl, blend flour with baking powder, baking soda, salt, corn syrup, and both sugars. Add butter and pulse to break in butter until mixture resembles a fine meal. Turn out into baking pan and drizzle in cream and vanilla. Toss by hand to combine until you have a slightly damp, sandy mixture. Press or pat gently into pan. Place on prepared baking sheet and bake until edges are barely browned, 20 to 25 minutes. Remove from oven.

Meanwhile, to make Caramel Filling, in a medium saucepan, stir condensed milk, butter, corn syrup, and brown sugar over low heat. Simmer, stirring once in a while, 8 to 10 minutes, until mixture does not taste gritty (sugar dissolves), is thickened, and is about 245°F. Make sure, as best you can, the bottom does not burn. This is difficult, and if it occurs, do not stir the burnt part into the rest of the caramel. Shuffle saucepan somewhat off heat source and let mixture cook without combining scorched part (if it occurs) with nonscorched part. (If this occurs, it is usually 1 to 2 minutes before it is ready to remove anyway.)

Pour caramel over warm baked cookie bottom. Gently place chocolate bars on caramel. Using an offset spatula, gently coax chocolate over caramel to cover top. Just go slow and easy and you will find the chocolate enrobes the topping without removing the caramel. Alternatively, chop chocolate, sprinkle it over top, let it melt a bit, and then coat top. Refrigerate a few hours to let chocolate set. Remove from fridge, let warm up a bit, and then, using a very sharp knife, cut into "finger" bars.

Café Blueberry Squares

Makes 8 to 10 squares; pictured on page 152

I don't think anything is as pretty or as tasty as these big, bold blueberry bars that feature a brown sugar–oatmeal crust and berries as a tart, fruity counterpoint.

Crust and Topping

1½ cups all-purpose flour

1½ cups rolled oats

1 cup firmly packed brown sugar

½ teaspoon baking powder

¼ teaspoon salt

⅛ teaspoon ground cinnamon

1 cup unsalted butter, cut into chunks

Filling

3 cups blueberries or 2 cups blueberries and 1 cup raspberries

¾ cup sugar

2 tablespoons cornstarch

1 tablespoon lemon juice

Generously spray an 11- x 7-inch baking pan with nonstick cooking spray and place pan on a parchment paper–lined baking sheet.

For Crust and Topping, in a food processor, put flour, oats, brown sugar, baking powder, salt, and cinnamon and pulse to blend, about 20 seconds. Add butter and pulse to cut butter into dry ingredients until you have a crumbly mass, not dry but not sticking together.

For Filling, toss berries in a bowl with sugar, cornstarch, and lemon juice.

Spread or pat half of oatmeal mixture firmly into pan. Spread on blueberry mixture. Top as evenly as you can with remaining oatmeal mixture and press slightly. Chill 30 minutes.

Preheat oven to 350°F.

Bake 40 to 45 minutes until fruit starts to bubble; then reduce oven temperature to 325°F and bake until done, another 15 to 20 minutes or until fruit that bubbles is deeper in color and edges of squares are browned. Cool completely in pan before cutting or refrigerate 2 to 3 hours before cutting.

Brownie Fantasy Bars

Makes 20 or more bars, depending on size

These colossal bars are chock-full of good things. They are made from a swirly combination of blondie batter and a deep fudge-brownie batter. The dates, raisins, and marshmallows offer their own brand of chewiness in the finished bars, and the nuts somehow become extra buttery.

Each bite is an experience of caramel batter, fudge, and no end of goodies that all entice in different ways.

Batter One

¾ cup unsalted butter, melted
1½ cups firmly packed light brown sugar
2 large eggs
1½ teaspoons pure vanilla extract
1½ cups all-purpose flour
¼ teaspoon baking powder
¼ teaspoon salt

Batter Two

1 cup unsalted butter, melted
1 cup white sugar
¾ cup firmly packed brown sugar
3 large eggs
1 teaspoon pure vanilla extract
¾ cup cocoa powder
¼ teaspoon baking soda
¼ teaspoon salt

1 cup all-purpose flour
2 cups crisp rice cereal
1 cup miniature marshmallows
1 cup semisweet chocolate chips
1 cup coarsely chopped milk chocolate, such as *Jersey Milk* or *Hershey's* bars
½ cup raisins, plumped and dried (see page 18)
½ cup finely chopped dates
2 cups coarsely chopped chocolate cream-filled sandwich cookies
1 cup coarsely chopped walnuts or pecans

Finishing Touches

¼ cup each chocolate chips, butterscotch chips, and white chocolate chips

Preheat oven to 325°F. Generously spray a 13- x 9-inch pan with nonstick cooking spray and place it on a parchment paper–lined baking sheet. **Have** two large bowls ready. For Batter One, blend butter and brown sugar. Mix in eggs and vanilla and then fold in flour, baking powder, and salt to make a soft batter. Set aside.

For Batter Two, combine butter, both sugars, eggs, vanilla, cocoa, soda, salt, and flour and mix well. Then fold in cereal and next 7 ingredients, using a large spatula or wooden spoon to blend.

Spoon Batter Two into pan, using wet hands to spread batter in pan. Wash hands briefly. Spoon Batter One onto chocolate batter, using wet hands to deposit batter. Briefly mix batters to marbleize, using wet hands or a wooden spoon.

Bake until set or until spots of caramel batter seem set and slightly browned, about 45 minutes. Immediately sprinkle on three types of chips. Let set a minute and then smear with a knife as chips melt. Refrigerate 2 hours before cutting into bars. These freeze perfectly.

Grand Funk Granola Bars

Makes 12 large bars; also pictured on page 152

These gorgeous, big, and fairly nutritious but decadent bars had their debut in the sixties (along with some great music) and got updated for today.

½ cup unsalted butter, melted, or canola oil

½ cup honey

¼ cup firmly packed brown sugar

1 teaspoon pure vanilla extract

2 cups granola

2 cups miniature marshmallows

½ cup sweetened shredded coconut

½ cup chopped dates

¼ cup dried cherries or cranberries

⅓ cup raisins

¼ teaspoon ground cinnamon

¼ teaspoon salt

3 tablespoons all-purpose flour

2 cups crisp rice cereal

1 tablespoon sesame seeds

⅔ cup coarsely chopped pecans or almonds

Preheat oven to 350°F. Line a 9-inch square pan or, preferably, an 11- x 7-inch brownie pan with parchment paper and leave some over-hang. Place pan on a parchment paper–lined baking sheet.

In a large bowl, stir together butter, honey, brown sugar, and vanilla. Blend in granola, marshmallows, coconut, dates, cherries or cranberries, raisins, cinnamon, salt, flour, cereal, sesame seeds, and pecans. Spoon into prepared pan (**photo, at right**). Pat down lightly.

Bake on lower rack of oven 18 to 22 minutes or until top seems set. Refrigerate about 1 hour before cutting into bars. Turn out onto a board and cut with a sharp knife.

These are best stored individually wrapped in wax paper and frozen.

The Hunt for the Perfect Baking Pan

Pan size greatly affects the results of all baking—no more so than in the case of squares or bars. If you change the pan, you alter the bar. The very texture and crumb of a bar or square is modified simply by using a pan of one dimension or another. A half inch makes the difference between crisp, chewy, dense bars or cakey bars. It is often a matter of taste, but 11- x 7-inch or 11- x 8-inch pans make taller, bigger squares. The baking time might be a bit longer because you are baking a fuller and smaller pan, but often the results are nicer to look at. An 11- x 7-inch pan, which I call a brownie pan, can be hard to find. If you find one, especially a solid and heavy-weighted one (often available at such stores as *Sears* or *Wal-Mart*), buy a couple.

Bookstore Café Apricot Squares

Makes 12 to 16 squares, depending on size

These are the squares that inspired me to become a baker. A light tartlike pastry base hosts a tangy, bright apricot filling topped with more tart dough and a light shower of confectioners' sugar. You can roll out the top tart dough, but shredded frozen dough is prettier (and easier).

Bookstore cafés are just where you would expect to find such a lovely square.

Tart Pastry Crust

2¼ cups all-purpose flour
½ cup sugar
1 teaspoon baking powder
¼ teaspoon salt
¼ cup ground walnuts, optional
½ cup unsalted butter, softened
2 tablespoons shortening
2 large eggs
1 teaspoon pure vanilla extract
4 to 6 tablespoons whipping cream

Apricot Filling

¾ cup orange juice
2 tablespoons fresh lemon juice
4 cups dried apricots (preferably Californian)
⅓ cup sugar

Finishing Touch

Confectioners' sugar, for dusting

For Tart Pastry Crust, place flour, sugar, baking powder, salt, and nuts (if using) in a food processor. Add butter and shortening and pulse to make a mealy mixture. Add eggs, vanilla, and cream and pulse to form a soft dough.

Turn out pastry onto a lightly floured work surface and knead gently to form a firm but soft dough. Wrap in two equal sections. Refrigerate half of dough for an hour and place other half in freezer.

For Apricot Filling, place all ingredients in a small saucepan and simmer over low heat, tossing fruit to soften, about 8 to 12 minutes. Let cool about 15 minutes and then puree in food processor. Chill well.

Preheat oven to 350°F. Generously spray an 11- x 7-inch pan or a 9-inch square pan with nonstick cooking spray and place pan on a parchment paper–lined baking sheet.

Pat out refrigerated half of pastry dough in prepared pan. Bake about 10 to 12 minutes. Cool well.

Meanwhile, coarsely grate remaining frozen pastry dough on a box grater (**photo 1**). Spread Apricot Filling on baked pastry bottom (**photo 2**); then shower or disperse frozen grated pastry over apricot filling (**photo 3**).

Place pan on prepared baking sheet. Bake until top pastry is done, about 22 to 25 minutes. Cool completely in pan and then dust with confectioners' sugar.

King Congo Bars

Makes 12 large bars or 24 small ones

There are many versions of these blockbuster blondie-based bars. This one is *de ultresse:* big, bold, hunky bars that will wow your office buddies or knock the socks off the potluck group.

Sweetened shredded coconut adds a bit of extra sweetness and helps keep these bars moist and flavorful.

¾ cup unsalted butter, melted
2½ cups firmly packed brown sugar
3 large eggs
1 teaspoon pure vanilla extract
2¾ cups all-purpose flour
2 teaspoons baking powder
¼ teaspoon salt
1 cup semisweet chocolate chips

1 cup sweetened shredded coconut
½ cup white chocolate chips
½ cup chopped pecans
½ cup pitted, diced dates

Finishing Touch

1 cup semisweet chocolate chips

Preheat oven to 350°F. Generously spray a 13- x 9-inch pan with non-stick cooking spray and place it on a parchment paper–lined baking sheet.
In a mixer bowl, blend butter and brown sugar. Add eggs and vanilla and blend well. Fold in flour, baking powder, salt, chocolate chips, coconut, white chocolate chips, pecans, and dates. Spoon into prepared pan, using wet fingertips to spread, if necessary. Pat batter down. Place pan on prepared baking sheet.
Place in oven and immediately reduce oven temperature to 325°F. Bake 35 minutes until bars are set but still seem a bit soft. Sprinkle remaining chocolate chips on top and let sit; then, using a metal spatula, smear around to make a glaze.
Cool 20 minutes and then freeze 1 to 2 hours. Cut into bars and wrap each in cellophane.

Strawberry New York Cheesecake-Stuffed Blondies

Makes 16 to 20 squares, depending on size

Graham cracker crumbs, blondie batter, cheesecake, and a strawberry swirl are packed into these squares. Put the white chocolate chips in the blondie batter or sprinkle them on top after baking, as recommended here. The overall sensation is graham-flavored caramel bars with luscious cheesecake and a final sweet tang of strawberries.

Graham Layer

1½ cups graham cracker crumbs
⅓ cup firmly packed brown sugar
⅓ cup unsalted butter, melted

Cheesecake Layer

10 ounces cream cheese, softened
⅓ cup sugar
1 large egg
1 teaspoon pure vanilla extract
1 tablespoon fresh lemon juice
1 tablespoon all-purpose flour

Blondie Layer

¾ cup unsalted butter
1½ cups firmly packed light brown sugar
1 large egg
1½ cups all-purpose flour
⅛ teaspoon baking powder
¼ teaspoon salt
1 cup coarsely chopped pecans or walnuts, optional
⅔ cup strawberry jam
½ cup white chocolate chips

Preheat oven to 350°F. Generously spray sides and bottom of a jellyroll pan (for extra chewy blondies) or a 13- x 9-inch pan (for thicker blondies). Place pan on a parchment paper–lined baking sheet.

For Graham Layer, toss graham cracker crumbs, brown sugar, and butter in bottom of pan and press to cover pan bottom.

For Cheesecake Layer, place cream cheese and sugar in a food processor and blend briefly. Then add egg, vanilla, lemon juice, and flour and blend to make a smooth batter.

For Blondie Layer, in a medium saucepan over very gentle heat, melt butter and brown sugar together and cook until sugar dissolves somewhat (5 to 8 minutes). Spoon into a medium mixing bowl and let cool to room temperature. Then blend in egg, flour, baking powder, salt, and nuts. Spread batter evenly on graham crust, using a wet knife or spatula. Spread on half of strawberry jam. Then top with cream cheese batter and, using a metal spatula, swirl cream cheese batter deeply into blondie batter so that bottom crust, cheesecake batter, and blondie batter marbleize. Top with spoonfuls of remaining strawberry jam and swirl briefly.

Bake 25 to 28 minutes. Squares will seem set but might be slightly jiggly. Remove from oven; sprinkle on white chocolate chips and then smear after 10 minutes as chips melt. Cool 30 minutes on a wire rack. Chill bars in refrigerator. Cut into squares in pan.

quick breads
&
coffee cakes

Quick breads are so named because they are quicker than yeast-raised loaves. In fact, quick breads came about when "yeast powder" (the original name given to baking powder) of modern baking was invented around 1850. Serious bakers bemoaned the advent of baking powder, touting it as an evil that would see the demise of true yeasted loaves of bread. The reality is that an entirely new sort of baking was born via baking powder: quick breads.

Quick breads, as well as the broad spectrum of cakes called coffee cakes, tend to be sweet and tender but not overly rich. The coffee cakes and quick breads of yesteryear were decidedly plainer than the ones we now enjoy, their elevation in stature largely due to the coffeehouse movement. They are still (happily) quick and wonderfully moist, and because they are neither too high in fat nor too sweet, they are a perfect foil to hot beverages.

Lemon loaves, cranberry bread, and banana bread are at the forefront of the coffee klatch set, but there is no end to the possibilities. Almost any quick bread can be doubled into a Bundt or tube cake or made into miniature loaves or muffins. Most freeze well, making them wonderful hostess cakes or gift cakes.

Coffee cakes, like all quick breads, are easy to prepare and—as with all great baking—simply call for quality ingredients and mindful handling. What they all have in common is the hospitality they invoke, their ease of preparation, and the fact that they suit countless informal occasions.

Find on the following pages a nice mix of plain to fancy, fruit- or cream cheese–filled, chocolate and vanilla quick loaves and cakes for every day.

Italian Plum-Cream Cheese Coffee Cake

Makes 8 to 10 servings; also pictured on page 168

Plums bake up into a gorgeous deep scarlet color in this sunny cake. Freestone plums make the prep easy. The color of the stone fruit nestled in the cake batter makes this visually pretty, but the taste of tangy plums in a vanilla-kissed buttery cake is what sells it. In the spring, you can use fresh apricots instead.

Cake

½	cup unsalted butter, softened
3	tablespoons sugar
2	large eggs
1½	teaspoons pure vanilla extract
1¼	cups all-purpose flour
1	teaspoon baking powder
⅛	teaspoon salt

Filling

10	Italian plums, halved and pitted
4	ounces cream cheese, softened
½	cup sugar
¼	cup sour cream
¼	teaspoon pure lemon extract
¼	teaspoon pure almond extract
1	teaspoon pure vanilla extract

Preheat oven to 350°F. Generously spray a 9- or 10-inch springform pan or a fluted, deep tart pan with nonstick cooking spray and place pan on a parchment paper–lined baking sheet.

For Cake, in a food processor, cream butter and sugar until well blended. Add eggs and vanilla and blend until smooth. Fold in flour, baking powder, and salt to make a soft batter. Spread batter on bottom and sides of pan. (Batter will appear thin in pan.)

For Filling, prepare plums. Place them cut sides down on cake batter in pan (**photo 1**). Mix cream cheese and remaining ingredients in a small bowl with a whisk and spread over fruit in pan.

Bake until top is browned and appears set, about 45 to 50 minutes.

Cool well before serving.

Breakfast Café Cinnamon Crumb Cake

Makes 10 to 12 servings

This fragrant spice cake is easy but memorable. It can be made with oil or melted butter. Oil is quicker and butter is more flavorful, but either ingredient will yield a tender-crumbed cake. What makes this a snap is the fact that the topping is a crumb mixture that is also part of the batter. This recipe would also make fabulous mini loaves or muffins.

¾ cup unsalted butter, melted
2¼ cups all-purpose flour
1 cup firmly packed brown sugar
1 cup white sugar
¼ teaspoon salt
2 teaspoons ground cinnamon
¼ teaspoon ground nutmeg
1 cup chopped walnuts

1 teaspoon baking powder
1 teaspoon baking soda
1 large egg
1 teaspoon pure vanilla extract
1 cup buttermilk

Finishing Touch

Confectioners' sugar, for dusting

Preheat oven to 350°F. Generously spray a 9- or 10-inch springform pan or a 13- x 9-inch pan with nonstick cooking spray. Place pan on a parchment paper–lined baking sheet.

In a mixer bowl, blend butter, flour, both sugars, salt, 1 teaspoon cinnamon, and nutmeg. Remove ¾ cup of this mixture and add chopped nuts and remaining 1 teaspoon cinnamon to it. Set aside (this will be the crumb topping).

To remaining batter, add baking powder, baking soda, egg, vanilla, and buttermilk. Using a hand whisk, blend well.

Spoon batter into prepared pan. Sprinkle on reserved crumb topping. Bake until cake tests done and springs back when gently pressed with fingertips, about 40 to 45 minutes. Serve warm or at room temperature. Dust with confectioners' sugar.

French Lemon Loaf

Makes 8 servings

In France and in French pastry shops on this side of the Atlantic, little pound cakes are called *quatre-quatre* cakes. They usually come in lemon or chocolate flavors and are sometimes marbleized. While simple, they somehow retain that Gallic flair. French pound cakes are slightly finer grained and more delicate than their American counterpart. This lemon loaf is gorgeous and is perfect for any pot of tea you pair with it. The high egg content makes it particularly melt-in-your-mouth tender.

Cake

1⅓ cups sugar

Zest of 1 large lemon, finely minced

1¼ cups unsalted butter, softened

1   teaspoon pure lemon extract

6   large eggs

2   cups all-purpose flour

2   tablespoons milk

2¼ teaspoons baking powder

¼   teaspoon salt

Lemon Glaze

½   cup water

¼   cup lemon juice

½   cup sugar

1   teaspoon pure lemon extract

Preheat oven to 350°F. Stack two baking sheets together and line top sheet with parchment paper. Generously spray a 9- x 5-inch loafpan with nonstick cooking spray. Cut out pieces of parchment paper and line pan's inner sides and bottom with them. Place pan on prepared baking sheets.

In a mixer bowl, blend sugar and lemon zest 2 minutes (**photo 1**). Add butter and lemon extract. Beat until light and fluffy, about 3 to 5 minutes. Blend in eggs and add some of flour from recipe if mixture seems curdled. Add milk and fold in remaining flour, baking powder, and salt. Spoon batter into prepared pan.

Bake 1 hour and then reduce oven temperature to 325°F; bake another 10 to 20 minutes or until cake tests done or is peaked and cracked in center but set and dry to the touch. Remove cake and, after 10 minutes, unmold onto a wire rack set over a parchment paper–lined baking sheet.

Meanwhile, for Lemon Glaze, simmer water, lemon juice, and sugar in a saucepan 5 minutes. Cool to warm and then stir in lemon extract. Using a cake tester, skewer, or small paring knife, make small holes or slits in cake surface (**photo 2**).

Drizzle or spoon glaze over cake (**photo 3**). Recoup extra glaze and drizzle back onto cake.

I use one of my best flavor tricks in this loaf: To get the most citrusy bang for your buck, blend citrus zest with sugar before adding it to a batter.

Chic Chocolate Loaf

Makes 8 servings

Enjoy this tender chocolate tea bread infused with a chocolate syrup that keeps the cake moist. If you don't have chocolate extract for the syrup, use vanilla extract instead. You can also simply stipple the cake with melted semisweet chocolate after it cools.

Cake

1¼ cups unsalted butter, softened

1¼ cups sugar

3 ounces unsweetened chocolate, melted and cooled

1½ teaspoons pure vanilla extract

5 large eggs

2 cups all-purpose flour

¼ cup whipping cream

2 teaspoons baking powder

⅛ teaspoon baking soda

¼ teaspoon salt

Chocolate Syrup

¾ cup water

½ cup sugar

1 teaspoon pure chocolate extract

Preheat oven to 350°F. Line a baking sheet with parchment paper. Generously spray a 9- x 5-inch loafpan with nonstick cooking spray. Cut out pieces of parchment paper and line pan's inner sides and bottom with them. Place pan on prepared baking sheet.

In a mixer bowl, cream butter and sugar until light and fluffy, about 3 to 5 minutes. Blend in cooled chocolate and vanilla and then blend in eggs. Add some of flour from recipe if mixture seems curdled. Add whipping cream and fold in remaining flour, baking powder, baking soda, and salt. Spoon batter into pan **(photo, at right)**.

Bake 1 hour and then reduce oven temperature to 325°F; bake another 10 to 20 minutes or until cake tests done or is peaked and cracked in center but set and dry to the touch. Remove cake from oven. After 10 minutes, unmold onto a wire rack set over a parchment paper–lined baking sheet.

Meanwhile, for Chocolate Syrup, simmer water and sugar in a saucepan 5 minutes. Cool to warm; stir in chocolate extract. Using a cake tester, skewer, or small paring knife, make small holes or slits in cake surface.

Drizzle syrup over cake. Recoup extra syrup and drizzle back onto cake.

I often cut pieces of parchment paper and line loafpans (and other cakepans) with them. The parchment lining assures you that your bread or cake will come easily out of its pan.

Raspberry Ripple Cream Cheese Coffee Cake

Makes 8 to 12 servings

Elegant and easy, this moist streusel-topped coffee cake does triple duty as a breakfast sweet, a coffee- or tea-break snack, or a springtime dessert for a more elaborate meal.

Filling

1	(3-ounce) package cream cheese, softened
1	large egg
2	tablespoons sugar
½	teaspoon pure vanilla extract

Cake

2¼ cups all-purpose flour

¾ cup sugar

¾ cup unsalted butter, cut into chunks

2 teaspoons baking powder

½ teaspoon baking soda

⅛ teaspoon salt

½ teaspoon ground cinnamon

1 tablespoon finely minced orange zest

1 large egg

1 teaspoon pure vanilla extract

¾ cup buttermilk

1 cup raspberry preserves

Finishing Touch

Confectioners' sugar, for dusting

Preheat oven to 350°F. Generously spray a 9-inch tart or springform pan with nonstick cooking spray. Place pan on a parchment paper–lined baking sheet.

For Filling, in a food processor, blend cream cheese with egg, sugar, and vanilla; spoon mixture into a small bowl and set aside. Do not wash food processor bowl.

For Cake, combine flour and sugar in food processor. Cut in butter until mixture is a crumbly streusel. Set aside ½ cup streusel mixture for topping. Transfer remaining streusel mixture to a mixer bowl and stir in baking powder, baking soda, salt, cinnamon, and orange zest. Stir in egg, vanilla, and buttermilk to make a soft batter. Chill batter about 15 minutes for easier handling.

Spread or pat two-thirds of batter over bottom and up sides of prepared pan (flour hands to make this easier). Spread or disperse cream cheese filling and then raspberry preserves on top of batter. Spoon or dollop remaining batter over cream cheese–jam layer. Sprinkle on reserved streusel mixture.

Bake at 350°F for 35 minutes or until cake tests done. Cool well. Dust with confectioners' sugar.

Cranberry-Orange-Walnut Tea Bread with Sweet Orange Glaze

Makes 8 to 10 servings

This jaunty little loaf is moist and not too sweet. It features a classic combination of flavors. This recipe doubles well, making it ideal if you want to have one loaf on hand as a hostess cake and another to give as a gift.

Cake

⅓	cup unsalted butter, softened
1	cup sugar
	Zest of 1 small orange, finely minced
1	large egg
1	teaspoon pure vanilla extract
½	teaspoon pure orange extract
½	cup orange juice
½	cup buttermilk
2	cups all-purpose flour
2	teaspoons baking powder
½	teaspoon baking soda
¼	teaspoon salt
1	cup cranberries, half of them coarsely chopped
½	cup chopped walnuts

Sweet Orange Glaze

⅓	cup orange juice
1	teaspoon lemon juice
2	to 3 tablespoons sugar

You can also make this a blueberry bread with blueberries replacing the cranberries, or use minced dried apricots for an apricot loaf. An apricot-cranberry combination is also delectable.

Preheat oven to 350°F. Generously spray a 9- x 5-inch loafpan with non-stick cooking spray. Place pan on a parchment paper–lined baking sheet.

In a mixer bowl, cream butter and sugar. Blend in orange zest, egg, vanilla, and orange extract. Mix in orange juice and buttermilk. Fold in flour, baking powder, baking soda, and salt to make a thick batter. Fold in cranberries and nuts.

Spoon into prepared pan and bake about 55 to 60 minutes or until cake is lightly browned and springs back when gently pressed with fingertips. Cool well on a wire rack.

Meanwhile, in a small saucepan, gently simmer ingredients for Sweet Orange Glaze 5 minutes. Cool.

Using a cake tester, skewer, or small paring knife, make small holes or slits in cake surface. Slowly drizzle glaze over cake, recouping the extra glaze and repeating once or twice. Let cake stand about 20 minutes before cutting.

Old-Fashioned Fragrant Banana Bread

Makes 8 to 12 servings

This is the cake that launched a lifetime of baking happiness. Who doesn't start their baking career with a banana bread recipe and always return to yet another great banana bread recipe? Recipes with too much banana make a rubbery, dense loaf, but this one is perfect. I like this bread with raisins and chocolate chips (½ cup of each), but you can make it with nuts alone.

½ cup unsalted butter, softened	2 cups all-purpose flour
1 cup sugar	1 teaspoon baking powder
2 large eggs	½ teaspoon baking soda
1 cup mashed very ripe banana	¼ teaspoon salt
¼ cup sour cream	1 cup chopped walnuts
1 teaspoon pure vanilla extract	

Preheat oven to 350°F. Line a baking sheet with parchment paper. Generously spray a 9- x 5-inch loafpan with nonstick cooking spray and place pan on a parchment paper–lined baking sheet.

In a mixer bowl, cream butter and sugar until well blended. Add eggs, banana, sour cream, and vanilla. Fold in flour, baking powder, baking soda, and salt, scraping bowl often. Mix on low speed; then fold in walnuts.

Spoon batter into prepared pan. Bake until bread springs back when gently pressed with fingertips, 50 to 55 minutes. It may have a crack in the center. This is perfectly wonderful and common. If bread seems not quite done, reduce oven temperature to 325°F and bake 10 to 15 more minutes.

Cool in pan 20 minutes; then turn out and cool on a wire rack.

This sweet bread is tender and moist. It sits firmly, like a prim schoolmarmish loaf, but it wafts a banana-walnut fragrance that seduces when you cut the first slice.

Celtic Oatmeal-Coconut Crunch Tea Cake

Makes 8 to 10 servings

Regular oats shine in this round, buttery little cake that is mellow with brown sugar and topped with a pecan-coconut broiled topping. The topping forms a chewy oatmeal cookie of a frosting on the moist cake. It is a typical Irish tea cake that has become a regular in my kitchen ever since I first made it. The scent of it baking will bring crowds to your door.

Cake

1/4 cup boiling water

1 cup very hot milk

1 cup quick-cooking oats

1/2 cup unsalted butter, softened

1 1/4 cups firmly packed light brown sugar

2 large eggs

1 teaspoon pure vanilla extract

1 1/2 cups all-purpose flour

1 teaspoon baking powder

1/4 teaspoon baking soda

1/2 teaspoon ground cinnamon

Pinch ground nutmeg

1/8 teaspoon salt

Oatmeal-Crisp Broiled Topping

4 tablespoons unsalted butter, melted

1/2 cup firmly packed light brown sugar

1/4 cup half-and-half or whipping cream

1/2 cup sweetened shredded coconut

1/4 cup quick-cooking oats

1/2 cup chopped walnuts or pecans

Preheat oven to 350°F. Generously spray a 9-inch round cakepan with nonstick cooking spray. Place pan on a parchment paper–lined baking sheet.
In a medium bowl, stir boiling water, hot milk, and oats together and let stand 20 minutes.
In a mixer bowl, cream butter with brown sugar until smooth. Mix in eggs and vanilla and blend well. Fold in oat mixture and then flour, baking powder, baking soda, cinnamon, nutmeg, and salt. Blend to make a smooth batter, making sure no butter/sugar bits stick to bottom of mixing bowl. Spoon batter into prepared pan.
Bake 30 to 35 minutes or until cake springs back when gently pressed with fingertips. Remove cake from oven.
Meanwhile, while cake bakes, in a medium bowl, blend together all topping ingredients.
Set the oven on Broil. Spread topping on cake and place cake under broiler on second shelf for 3 to 5 minutes until topping begins to bubble, watching carefully so it does not burn. Cool well.

Ultra Sour Cream-Pecan Coffee Cake

Makes 12 to 16 servings

This is a sumptuous, golden, moist coffee cake to beat the band.

If you collect sour cream coffee cake recipes, you have to try this one. It is extra tall and grand; it features a vanilla-kissed spiced streusel and the mellow tang of two full cups of sour cream. It is mouthwatering tender and golden crumbed.

Vanilla-Pecan Streusel

1⅓ cups firmly packed brown sugar
¼ cup white sugar
2 tablespoons confectioners' sugar
1½ cups finely chopped pecans
1 tablespoon pure vanilla extract
¼ cup unsalted butter, cut into chunks
5 teaspoons ground cinnamon
½ teaspoon ground cloves
½ teaspoon ground allspice
⅛ teaspoon ground nutmeg

Cake

2 cups unsalted butter, softened
2½ cups sugar
2 tablespoons pure vanilla extract
4¼ cups all-purpose flour
6 large eggs
5 teaspoons baking powder
¾ teaspoon baking soda
½ teaspoon salt
2 cups sour cream

Finishing Touch

Confectioners' sugar, for dusting

Preheat oven to 350°F. Generously spray a 10-inch angel food cakepan with nonstick cooking spray and place pan on a parchment paper–lined baking sheet.

Cut out pieces of parchment paper to line inner sides of pan and a narrow piece of parchment to also line inner cone or pedestal centerpiece of pan. (You want to have an extra collar on the pan to support this high-rising coffee cake.)

For Vanilla-Pecan Streusel, place all ingredients in a food processor bowl and pulse to create a crumbly mixture. Set aside.

For Cake, in a large mixer bowl, cream butter, sugar, and vanilla until smooth. Blend in 1 cup flour. Scrape bowl. Add eggs, 1 at a time, and blend well. Fold in remaining flour, baking powder, baking soda, and salt and add to mixer on low speed until ingredients are almost totally blended, about 2 minutes; then add sour cream. Mix another 2 to 4 minutes.

Spoon one-third of batter into prepared pan. Smooth batter and carefully place half of Vanilla-Pecan Streusel on top. Top with another third of batter and then top with most of streusel. Cover with remaining batter and top with remaining streusel.

Bake until cake tests done, covering it lightly with foil after 50 minutes of baking to protect streusel from browning too much. Cake is done when it springs back when gently pressed with fingertips, about 75 to 90 minutes, or when a toothpick inserted into middle comes out clean. If cake appears underdone but is overbrowning on top, reduce oven temperature to 325°F and allow to finish baking. Let cake cool 1 hour in pan and then remove to a wire rack to finish cooling. Dust with confectioners' sugar before serving. This cake freezes well.

Best-Ever Little British Butter Cake with Raspberry Filling

Makes 10 to 12 servings

Ever want a trouble-free, breezy little cake that goes with anything? This cake is stellar stuff and has a nice British flair to it. It improves each day after baking and is wonderful plain, with a dusting of confectioners' sugar, or smeared with a thin layer of raspberry jam or whatever you want to slather on it. What's more, you just dump all of the cake's ingredients into a food processor.

Cake

⅔ cup unsalted butter, cut into chunks

1⅓ cups sugar

3 large eggs

2 teaspoons pure vanilla extract

1 cup warm milk

2 cups all-purpose flour

2½ teaspoons baking powder

½ teaspoon salt

½ cup raspberry jam

Glaze

1 cup, approximately, confectioners' sugar

1 teaspoon pure raspberry extract*

Cream or water, as required

*Use almond extract if you cannot find raspberry.

This is one of my favorite cakes of all time.

Preheat oven to 350°F. Generously spray a 9-inch round cakepan or a 9-inch springform pan with nonstick cooking spray and place pan on a parchment paper–lined baking sheet.

For Cake, in a food processor, pulse butter and sugar until well blended. Add eggs and vanilla and blend well. Stir in milk, flour, baking powder, and salt and blend 1 to 2 minutes, scraping down the bowl a few times, to make a soft batter. Spoon batter into pan.

Bake until just beginning to brown and firm to the touch, 45 to 55 minutes. Cool well before removing from pan and assembling. (You can serve it plain at this point, with just a dusting of confectioners' sugar, or with sweetened berries.)

Split cake in half horizontally. Place bottom half of cake on a cake platter. Spread raspberry jam on bottom of cake and then top with remaining half of cake.

For Glaze, whisk confectioners' sugar, raspberry extract, and enough cream or water to make a smearable glaze. Smear glaze carefully over cake and let set.

Friendship Sourdough Coffee Cake

Makes 10 to 14 servings

A taste of sourdough coffee cake from a local bakery taught me that not all sourdough starters are used for bread baking. The cake I tried was majestically statuesque, slightly coarse in texture, and resplendent with cinnamon and other fresh spices—just plainly, wonderfully different. Here is my version.

This cake, based on a sourdough starter, is easy. Plus, there is no milk involved. A one- to two-day-old starter is fine for this recipe, but a warmed-up, mature starter (if you have one in the fridge) would be even better. You can also use the starter on page 47.

Crumb Topping

¼ cup unsalted butter, cut into chunks
1 cup coarsely chopped walnuts or graham cracker crumbs
½ teaspoon ground cinnamon
⅓ cup all-purpose flour
½ cup firmly packed dark brown sugar
¼ cup confectioners' sugar

Sourdough Cake Batter

1 cup unsalted butter, softened
1 cup white sugar
1¼ cups firmly packed dark brown sugar
2 tablespoons molasses
4 large eggs
2 teaspoons pure vanilla extract
1½ cups sourdough starter, not too cold
¼ cup sour cream
3 cups all-purpose flour
2½ teaspoons baking powder
1 teaspoon baking soda
½ teaspoon salt
2½ teaspoons ground cinnamon
1 teaspoon pumpkin or apple pie spice

Preheat oven to 350°F. Generously spray a 13- x 9-inch pan with non-stick cooking spray. Place pan on a parchment paper–lined baking sheet.

For Crumb Topping, in a food processor, pulse all ingredients to make a coarse-crumbed mixture. Set aside.

For Sourdough Cake Batter, in a mixer bowl, cream butter with both sugars and molasses until fluffy. Add eggs and vanilla and blend well. Fold in sourdough starter, sour cream, and then flour, baking powder, baking soda, salt, cinnamon, and pumpkin pie spice. Blend well on low speed of mixer to make a smooth batter. If batter is very loose, stir in a few more tablespoons of flour.

Spoon batter into prepared pan. Top with Crumb Topping. Bake until cake springs back when gently pressed with fingertips and seems set, about 45 to 55 minutes.

City Bakery Apple-Raspberry Upside-Down Cake

Makes 8 to 10 servings

This simple butter cake is almost three inches high and a quaint seven inches round. The taste is unbelievable. Imagine a tangy but sweet fruit topping acting as a glistening ruby halo on a little butter cake. This one is truly unique—a lip-smacking cake you'll rave about days after it disappears.

Fruit Topping

1½ cups diced peeled apples	
1 cup fresh cranberries	
½ cup fresh raspberries	
½ cup sugar	
¼ cup cranberry or apple juice	
2 tablespoons cornstarch	

Cake

½ cup unsalted butter, softened

1 cup plus 2 tablespoons sugar
2 large eggs
2 teaspoons pure vanilla extract
½ cup buttermilk
2¼ cups all-purpose flour
2¼ teaspoons baking powder
¼ teaspoon baking soda
¼ teaspoon salt

Preheat oven to 350°F. Generously spray a 7-inch cakepan or an 8-inch springform pan with nonstick cooking spray and line bottom with a circle of parchment paper. Place pan on a parchment paper–lined baking sheet.

For Fruit Topping, toss all ingredients in a medium bowl and then spoon into prepared cakepan.

For Cake, in a mixer bowl, cream butter with sugar until well blended and fluffy. Add eggs, vanilla, and buttermilk and blend well. Fold in dry ingredients and blend well. Spoon batter over fruit in cakepan.

Bake until firm and cake springs back slightly when gently pressed with fingertips, 50 to 65 minutes. Cool 15 minutes and then invert cake onto a serving plate. Serve just warm or at room temperature.

Sticky Toffee Tea

Makes 1½ cups, approximately, blended tea mix; enough for 16 cups of tea

It's easy to brew up some of your own tea blends. Just try this black tea that is touched up with minced toffee bars. Mmmmmm!

1 cup leaf black tea, such as orange pekoe

1½ cups minced toffee bar or chocolate-coated toffee bar

Toss tea and minced candy together. Use about 1 tablespoon tea per 8 ounces boiling water. Brew as for tea, in a tea ball, steeping 5 to 10 minutes. Store tea blend in a jar in a cool, dry place.

Banana-Sour Cream-Toffee Chip Crumb Cake

Makes 10 to 12 servings

This cake has a mild banana taste with a tender crumb and wonderful toffee chip topping. It is nice and easy if made in a 13- x 9-inch pan but prettier baked in a 10-inch springform pan and cut into wedges.

Toffee Chip Topping

¼ cup confectioners' sugar
⅓ cup all-purpose flour
2 tablespoons unsalted butter, softened
¼ cup toffee bar bits, such as *Heath* or *Skor*

Cake

2¾ cups all-purpose flour
2½ teaspoons baking powder
½ teaspoon baking soda
½ teaspoon salt
¾ cup unsalted butter, softened
1½ cups sugar
3 large eggs
1½ teaspoons pure vanilla extract
½ cup mashed banana
1 cup sour cream

Finishing Touch

Confectioners' sugar, for dusting, optional

Preheat oven to 350°F. Generously spray a 10-inch springform pan or a 13- x 9-inch pan with nonstick cooking spray and place pan on a parchment paper–lined baking sheet.

For Toffee Chip Topping, in a small bowl, blend confectioners' sugar and flour. Using your fingertips, rub butter into flour mixture to make a mealy crumb mixture. Stir in toffee bits and set topping aside.

In a medium bowl, hand-whisk together flour, baking powder, baking soda, and salt.

In a mixer bowl, cream butter and sugar until fluffy, about 5 minutes. Add eggs and vanilla and blend well, scraping bottom of bowl occasionally to ensure there's no unmixed butter and sugar. Add banana, sour cream, and dry ingredients. Mix on low speed until thoroughly blended, about 2 to 4 minutes, scraping mixture on sides and bottom to ensure all batter is blended.

Spoon batter into prepared pan. Distribute topping over batter.

Bake until cake is done, springs back when gently pressed with fingertips, and seems set, about 45 to 50 minutes for a 13- x 9-inch pan or 55 to 70 minutes for a springform pan.

Let cool about 15 minutes before unmolding gently onto a serving plate. Dust with confectioners' sugar, if desired.

Golden Applesauce Pound Cake

Makes 12 to 14 servings

The aroma of this cake baking makes it difficult not to hang around the kitchen until the cake is done. A classically autumnal cake, it is moist, golden, and replete with apples, butter, and a gentle touch of spices.

2	cups golden raisins	1½	teaspoons ground cinnamon
1	cup unsalted butter, softened	¼	teaspoon salt
1¾	cups sugar		Pinch mace
5	large eggs	½	teaspoon freshly grated nutmeg
1½	teaspoons pure vanilla extract	¼	teaspoon ground allspice
2	teaspoons lemon zest, finely minced	¼	teaspoon ground ginger
3	cups all-purpose flour	1⅔	cups applesauce
1½	teaspoons baking soda		
½	teaspoon baking powder		**Finishing Touch**
			Confectioners' sugar, for dusting

Preheat oven to 350°F. Generously spray a 10-inch angel food cakepan or a 12-cup Bundt pan with nonstick cooking spray and place pan on a parchment paper–lined baking sheet.

Plump raisins (see page 18) and coarsely chop. Set aside.

In a mixer bowl, cream butter until light. Add sugar, blending well. Add eggs, 1 at a time, scraping bowl occasionally until they are all incorporated. Stir in vanilla and lemon zest. In another bowl, stir together dry ingredients; add to batter, alternating with applesauce, blending on low speed of mixer. Fold in chopped raisins.

Pour batter into prepared pan. Bake until cake tests done, about 60 to 65 minutes. Let cake cool well in pan before inverting. Dust with confectioners' sugar before serving.

Town Hall Mulled Apple Cider Tea

Makes 2 to 4 servings

Slightly spiced with cinnamon and orange, this tea is a heartwarming brew after you rake the leaves.

4	cups apple juice	Honey, to taste
¼	teaspoon pumpkin pie spice	
½	teaspoon ground cinnamon	**Finishing Touches**
1	cup cranberry juice, optional	Orange slices and cinnamon sticks, for serving
1	to 2 cups brewed orange pekoe tea, optional	

Warm up all ingredients for tea in a saucepan over medium heat and then keep warm in a thermos. Serve by the cupful and garnish each cup with an orange slice and a cinnamon stick.

pies, tarts & pastries

Pies and pastries, as with recipes in the sweet yeast baking chapter that follows, is a somewhat hybrid genre of baking. The emphasis is on all things light, delicate, buttery, and flaky.

Pies, tarts, and pastries from the home baker are a tad different than what you expect to find in bakeshops and patisseries. What I like best about homestyle pastries is their butter base and simple tastes, their lighter crumb, and their interesting roots, which are often country-baker oriented. Until you have something butter- and sugar-based that is more dough than crust and crumb, you forget how good something pure and simple can be.

The recipe collection here is a broad range of small and large pastries, things quite American as well as those best described as quasi-European. There are a few recipes that are not based on pie or tart dough, such as choux paste–based crullers, but, for the most part, the emphasis on technique is about all-purpose flaky pie dough (typically made with shortening) and, on occasion, tart dough (which is, by contrast, generally a richer dough made with butter and added sugar).

What binds the pastries in this chapter together is their buttery taste, their lightness of crumb, and the wonderful fillings that go in them. These pastries can accompany coffee or tea or serve as the dessert to a simple or extravagant meal. Remember to check out the "Holiday Baking" chapter for more outstanding, seasonal samples of pies and pastries, such as Classic Pumpkin Pie, White Chocolate Thanksgiving Pecan Pie, and Classic Linzertorte.

Ingredients

Think of the ingredients in pie dough as a culinary cast of characters. In this "cast," however, there are no supporting roles; each ingredient is a star, secondary to no other. In order of proportion, the cast includes: flour, fat, water, sugar, and salt.

Flour (and a Little Elf Called Gluten)

All-purpose flour produces the very best piecrusts. Because all-purpose flour has a low protein content, gluten development can be kept to a minimum. No discussion of pie is complete without saying a few words about gluten, an elastic protein that provides structure for baked goods. Gluten is the stuff bread bakers sing the praises of, for it is responsible for the wonderful chewiness in bread. This "elf" is activated in two ways: by contact with liquid (in this case, water) and by kneading dough. Several methods help avoid provoking the gluten elf while making pie dough, thereby reducing the problem of tough piecrust.

First, use all-purpose flour unless the recipe states otherwise. Avoid overworking the dough and make sure the liquid you use is ice-cold (gluten development is also inhibited by cold temperatures). Chill the dough before working with it. Lastly, you can add a small amount of an acidic ingredient, such as vinegar or lemon juice, because acid inhibits gluten development as well.

Fat: Lard, Shortening, Unsalted Butter

There are several options as far as the fat is concerned. When making pie dough, fat refers to either lard, shortening, or unsalted butter. For tarts, butter is the rule.

Lard produces the flakiest dough. Shortening works exceedingly well in the texture department; butter creates slightly less tender dough but offers incomparable flavor. Just the scent of a butter-based piecrust baking is magnetic. Added to that, nothing helps piecrust brown as well as butter does. In the past, my personal choice for fats was part shortening (for texture) and part butter (for taste). These days, inasmuch as piecrust is a backdrop to a pie's filling, I use all butter. If you use shortening, opt for the new generation without trans fat that is now on the market.

Liquid

Liquid, such as ice water, is used in pie and pastry dough to hold things together. Liquid is what enables the fat and flour fusion to become a viable structure, which is a dough that can be rolled out and maneuvered. It allows a tiny bit of the gluten to wake up in the dough and create hidden strands to give dough a cohesive structure.

The usual liquid component in pie dough is ice water. The colder the water used, the flakier the crust, as cold water serves the dual purpose of inhibiting gluten development and preventing the fat content in the dough from becoming too warm.

Depending on the pie's flavor, orange juice, apple cider, and ginger ale are all acceptable substitutions or additions, as long as they don't exceed the original amount of liquid called for in the recipe.

Handling Pie Dough

The important thing to remember about pie dough is to work with well-chilled dough. The fridge is your ally in pastry making. If dough gets warm and/or seems greasy or soft or if it is difficult to roll, simply chill it. If it gets warm and is already rolled and fitted into a pie or tart pan, chill it. Chilling ensures flakiness later on.

Use a nice, wide, heavy rolling pin. The pin will release the dough easily, and the dough will be less likely to absorb extra, unnecessary flour.

Work carefully with pie dough. Rushing is never a good idea in baking, but in pastry making, more than any other genre of baking, rushing sacrifices texture and appearance.

If you're baking on an excessively hot day, then be prepared to refrigerate your dough at various intervals for at least 20 minutes each time to keep it from becoming too warm.

Measure, Don't Wing It

It is crucial to properly measure ingredients. Cooks are fond of saying they never measure and things still come out well. Bakers know better; if you want to bake better, measure better. The best rule of thumb for flour is to stir the flour with a fork or to whisk it slightly before measuring it. This is not the same as sifting, but it does aerate the flour somewhat. Then I simply scoop the measuring cup into the flour canister and level off the top. Sifted flour measures under the amount needed;

flour that is packed measures over the amount needed. If you have a scale, the most important ingredients to weigh are the flour (which is 4.5 ounces per measured cup) and butter (which is 8 ounces solid fat per measured cup). For liquids, use a glass measuring cup with a pouring spout. Read the measurements at eye level, filling exactly to the line indicated.

Mixing the Dough

If you are making pie dough by hand, "cut" or "rub" the cold fat into the flour. This phrase means to simply break up the fat into small pieces and toss them with flour. Use your fingertips to do this. Otherwise, you can use a pastry blender to cut fat into flour. What you want to end up with is small bits of floured-coated butter or fat crumbs.

Evenly dispersing fat and flour results in a short crust—that is, a crust that is somewhat cookielike in texture. Uneven mixtures of fat and flour (some smaller pieces, some larger pieces) result in a long, flaky dough that looks slightly marbleized when you roll it out. This is fine. It is far better to err on the side of underblending or cutting in the fat than overworking it. Above all, do not squeeze the flour-fat pieces together. Keep the mixture dry and your touch gentle, almost reluctant. When properly made cold pie dough hits a hot oven, flaky crust results.

Next, make a well in the center of the work bowl and stir in the ice water or other appropriate liquid. Turn the bowl as you work, combing through the dough with lightly spread fingers, bringing the mixture into the center to blend. When the dough congregates in the center and is a rough mass, turn it out onto a lightly floured work surface.

Knead or work it very briefly and then pat it all around to smooth it somewhat, folding it over (rather than kneading it) to refine this mass into a flattened disk. Wrap it in plastic wrap and chill the dough thoroughly before using. Fresh dough is too elastic to work

The way I measure flour is to lightly stir it with a fork or whisk; then simply scoop the measuring cup into the flour and level off the top.

with and must have a short relaxation spell before being rolled out.

If you are making lots of pastry or are in a hurry or simply prefer it, this whole operation can be done quickly and easily in a food processor. Use the pulse feature to cut the fat into the flour. Add the ice water through the food chute and be careful not to overprocess the dough. Turn off the processor as soon as the dough forms a ball.

Rolling Out the Dough

There is a clear line between rolling out dough and stretching it to fit. To roll out dough, first dust your work surface with all-purpose flour. Place the dough in the center and roll it from the center of the dough outward. Turn the dough clockwise slightly and roll outward again, eventually creating a circle. Use the same pressure on the surface of the dough (do not press down as you get to the outer edge) and avoid rolling back and forth. Try to roll only once and then turn the dough again. Lift the dough if it sticks and lightly dust underneath it with additional flour if needed. When the dough is two inches wider than the perimeter of the pieplate you are using, fold the dough in half and then in half again and place the point of this triangle in the middle of the pieplate. Do not try to pick up the whole circle of dough to transport it. This may stretch or rip the dough and will cause it to retract during baking or have a tough texture.

If at any point the dough retracts as you are rolling it, the gluten content has been provoked. It is indeed salvageable, but you should replace the dough in the fridge to relax it again. If you must use dough scraps, reroll these only once, because additional handling toughens the dough.

30-Second Classic Pie Dough

Makes 2 double crusts or 4 single crusts

This food-processor recipe makes a classic pie dough that pastry chefs dote on. Use it with any filling or for any presentation. It makes a big, comfortable batch, which is a good bet for novices first learning to roll out dough. You can double this recipe and freeze the extra dough. Thirty seconds? I figure 15 to assemble the ingredients and 15 to whip this up. This dough can be made using all butter or with half butter and half shortening. It makes two dough disks; each disk makes one 8- to 10-inch double piecrust or two single (bottom) crusts. If you choose shortening, opt for the new generation without trans fat.

As Easy as Pie

Recipes for pie dough, officially known as shortcrust pastry, are based on the French formula for *pâte brisée*, meaning, literally, "broken dough." What this implies is that pie dough should break and flake apart easily. This flakiness is the hallmark of well-made dough and results when there is a perfect balance of flour to fat and liquid ingredients, as well as proper handling. Salt is used for flavor, and sugar is added for flavor and to assist the crust in browning. In some recipes, additional ingredients, such as whole eggs or yolks, are incorporated, giving the crust an added richness and an extra seal against wet fillings in desserts, such as in cream pies.

3	cups all-purpose flour	2	teaspoons fresh lemon juice
2	teaspoons sugar	4	to 8 tablespoons ice water
¾	teaspoon salt		
1	cup unsalted butter, cut into 16 chunks*		

*Or use half butter and half shortening, or use half or three-fourths butter and half or one-fourth lard. Butter is best for flavor; shortening or lard will lend more flakiness.

Place flour in a food processor. Add sugar and salt and process 20 seconds to combine. Stop machine. Add chunks of butter on top of flour mixture. Process by pulsing to break up butter into flour mixture until it looks crumbly.

Drizzle lemon juice and ice water on top and turn machine on for exactly 15 seconds until mixture more or less holds together.

Turn out dough onto a lightly floured work surface. Knead very gently for a few seconds to smooth out dough. Pat into two flattened disks and wrap well in plastic. Use each disk for a double-crust pie or to make two single pie bottoms, quiches, tarts, or free-form pies.

Chill dough at least 1 hour or overnight before using. This dough can be frozen up to 2 to 3 months if you want to use it later. This recipe doubles well if your food processor can handle 6 cups of flour.

Preheat oven to 400°F. Roll out dough on lightly floured work surface and place in a 9-inch piepan or other desired pan. Bake 15 to 20 minutes or until edges appear slightly browned, with another piepan weighing crust down (**photo, at far right**).

Sour Cream Pie Dough:

You can also use 2 to 3 tablespoons sour cream in place of the ice water in this dough for a richer and still flaky dough.

All-Butter, One-Egg Pie Dough

Makes 2 double crusts or 4 single crusts

This butter– and egg–enriched dough is a favorite. Sometimes an egg holds things together a bit better, so this piecrust is ideal for wetter fillings and easy for novice pie bakers.

3	cups all-purpose flour	1	large egg
2	teaspoons sugar	4	to 8 tablespoons ice water
¾	teaspoon salt	1	tablespoon fresh lemon juice
1	cup unsalted butter, cut into 16 chunks*		

*Or use half butter and half shortening.

Place flour in a food processor. Add sugar and salt and process 20 seconds to combine. Stop machine. Add chunks of butter on top of flour mixture. Process by pulsing to break up butter into flour mixture until it looks crumbly.

Add egg and drizzle ice water and lemon juice on top. Turn machine on for exactly 15 seconds until mixture more or less holds together.

Turn out dough onto a lightly floured work surface. Knead very gently for a few seconds to smooth out dough. Pat into two flattened disks and wrap well in plastic. Use each disk for a double-crust pie or to make two single pie bottoms, quiches, tarts, or free-form pies.

Chill dough at least 1 hour or overnight before using. This dough can be frozen up to 2 to 3 months if you want to use it later. This recipe doubles well if your food processor can handle 6 cups of flour.

Preheat oven to 400°F. Roll out dough on a lightly floured work surface and place in a 9-inch piepan or other desired pan. Bake 15 to 20 minutes or until edges appear slightly browned, with another piepan weighing crust down **(photo, at right)**.

What you are trying to achieve in pie dough is an explosion of moisture, which produces that hallmark flakiness. How? When you rub fat into flour, you are creating tons of little flour-coated fat granules. Once the dough hits the oven, the heat of the oven changes the moisture inherent in the fat, and that explodes, turns to steam, and pushes up the layers into flakiness.

Blind Baking

Blind baking means baking a pie shell without its filling or prebaking a pie shell. Most books say to use pie weights or dried beans to keep the dough from buckling. Instead, use another piepan or tart pan that is the same or very similar in dimension and press the pie or tart dough down using the empty pan as your weight. You can either spray the bottom of the empty piepan with nonstick cooking spray to ensure release or place a piece of parchment paper (cut in a round to fit) between the pie dough and the piepan that is weighing it down. This is far easier than fiddling with pie weights.

Rougemont Apple Pastry Cake

Makes 12 to 16 servings; also pictured on page 184

This is one of my favorite pastries of all time—one you will want to make again and again. Simply put, this cake, based on a pastry crust, will make you famous. The pastry crust lines a springform pan, and the filling is a mile high with apples. It is, as I always boast, worth the price of the book.

Rougemont, incidentally, is 'red mountain' in French and refers to the apple region just outside Montreal. Many apples from those orchards have met their destiny in this recipe. This dessert needs an overnight stay in the fridge before serving. If you have store-bought refrigerated or frozen pie dough on hand, using it is fine and will save you a step.

How Many Apples Are Enough?

Ever find you follow a recipe for pie or anything requiring a fruit filling only to find out your filling doesn't quite rise to the occasion? You want the filling to be almost flush with the top of your pan in any pastry or pie. To test out what is a sufficient amount of apples (or blueberries, peaches, etc.) for a specific recipe, prepare the fruit and place it in the empty piepan and see if you require more fruit. Then prep whatever extra you need. That way, the fruit is prepped and you can be confident that you will have enough filling.

Pastry Crust

2   cups all-purpose flour
1   tablespoon sugar
½   teaspoon salt
¾   cup unsalted butter, cut into chunks
4   to 6 tablespoons ice water or half-and-half

Apple Filling

10   to 12 large apples, cored, peeled, and cut into ¼-inch slices
¼   cup sugar
1   tablespoon cornstarch
1   teaspoon ground cinnamon

½   cup raisins, plumped and dried (see page 18)
1   tablespoon lemon juice

Vanilla Sauce

½   cup unsalted butter, melted
1   cup sugar
2   teaspoons pure vanilla extract
4   large eggs
2   tablespoons all-purpose flour
1   teaspoon ground cinnamon

Finishing Touches

Confectioners' sugar
Apricot jam, warmed

Line a baking sheet with parchment paper. Brush bottom and sides of a 10-inch springform pan with melted butter and place on baking sheet.
For Pastry Crust, place flour, sugar, and salt in a food processor. Add butter and pulse to make a grainy mixture. Add water and pulse to make a shaggy dough. On a lightly floured work surface, gather dough together, kneading a few moments to make a smooth dough. Wrap and chill dough at least 1 hour before rolling out.
Meanwhile, for Apple Filling, toss apples with sugar, cornstarch, cinnamon, raisins, and lemon juice.
Preheat oven to 350°F. Roll or press out dough evenly and fit on bottom and sides of prepared pan (dough should be between ⅛ to ¼ inch thick) **(photo 1)**. Fill with Apple Filling, pressing gently **(photo 2)**. For final layer of apples, arrange apples in concentric circles **(photo 3)**. Apples should come to top of pan. If they don't, prepare more to fill out the pan, tossing with 2 tablespoons sugar and a touch of cinnamon.
Cover pan lightly with aluminum foil.
Bake cake 60 to 75 minutes or until apples are soft, removing foil after 20 minutes. The top apples might seem dry and browned around their edges, but interior apples should begin to feel soft—use a skewer to test apples.
For Vanilla Sauce, in a small bowl, blend melted butter, sugar, vanilla, eggs, flour, and cinnamon. Pour this over hot pastry cake, trying to get sauce to drip into crevices. Bake another 20 minutes. Cool on a wire rack.
Refrigerate pastry cake at least 6 hours or preferably overnight. Dust with confectioners' sugar or brush with warmed apricot jam before serving.

French Cruller Doughnuts

Makes 12 to 15 cruller-style doughnuts, depending on size

This light doughnut is not fried and features a unique, slightly custardy interior. The secret is essentially a classic choux paste base that is baked and then dunked in a bath of luscious glaze—twice!

Choux Paste Doughnut Base

1	cup milk
1	cup water
3	tablespoons sugar
½	teaspoon salt
1	cup unsalted butter
2	cups all-purpose flour
2	teaspoons pure vanilla extract
8	large eggs

Creamy Vanilla Glaze

½	cup unsalted butter, melted
2½	to 3 cups confectioners' sugar
2	teaspoons pure vanilla extract
2	to 4 tablespoons hot water

Preheat oven to 400°F. Stack two baking sheets together and line top sheet with parchment paper. Have another baking sheet lined with parchment paper nearby.

For Choux Paste Doughnut Base, in a medium saucepan, stir milk, water, sugar, and salt together over medium heat. Stir in butter and allow it to melt. Increase heat and bring mixture to a rolling boil. Stir in flour all at once. Blend well with a wooden spoon, adding vanilla and beating briskly until mixture forms a ball that leaves sides of pan. Beat vigorously 1 to 2 minutes before removing from burner and turning out into a mixer bowl. Allow mixture to cool 5 minutes.

Using a wide whisk or a wooden spoon, add eggs, 1 at a time, until mixture is smooth and glossy. Spoon choux paste into a large pastry bag fitted with a ½-inch star tip. On prepared baking sheets, leaving some space between each pastry, make a 4-inch circle of batter with another circle on top (concentric circles) (**photo, at left**). If you don't have a pastry bag, use a soup spoon to spread out a ring of batter as best you can. It will be fine once it puffs.

Bake pastry 15 minutes; then reduce oven temperature to 375°F and bake another 15 to 20 minutes or until doughnuts are light in texture and medium brown all over. Cool slightly.

To make Creamy Vanilla Glaze, whisk everything together in a medium bowl to a thick glaze consistency, mixing in more confectioners' sugar or water, if needed, to achieve a gloppy, thick glaze. Dip each doughnut once, let excess drip off back into bowl, let set, and then glaze again. Let doughnuts set on a wire rack.

Pie Dough Apple Strudel

Makes 8 to 12 servings

This is one of those big, hunky apple pastries like you see and admire in bakery shop windows. Somehow, frozen apple slices offer a different apple experience and make preparation quick and easy.

Strudel Pie Dough

2	cups all-purpose flour
1	tablespoon sugar
½	teaspoon salt
½	cup unsalted butter, cut into chunks
¼	cup shortening
2	to 4 tablespoons ice water

Filling

6	cups frozen sliced apples
1¼ cups sugar	

1	teaspoon apple pie spice or ground cinnamon
1	tablespoon fresh lemon juice
½	cup golden raisins or pitted sour cherries

Finishing Touches

1	large egg

Pinch white sugar
Coarse sugar, for dusting
Confectioners' sugar, for dusting

Frozen apple slices are generally cut from Northern Spy apples and are cut thick, uniformly, and then frozen. The combination of the apple, the cut, and the freezing produces a starchy apple slice that bakes up flavorful and holds its shape. These fat, dense apple wedges fill up every possible gap so that each bite of strudel is solid apple.

For Strudel Pie Dough, place flour, sugar, and salt in a food processor. Add chunks of butter and shortening and pulse to make a grainy mixture. Add water and pulse to make a shaggy dough. On a lightly floured work surface, gather dough together, kneading a few moments to make a smooth dough. Wrap and chill at least 1 hour before rolling out.

For Filling, toss apples, sugar, pie spice, lemon juice, and raisins or cherries in a large bowl.

Preheat oven to 400°F. Stack two baking sheets together and line top sheet with parchment paper.

For strudel, divide dough in half. Roll out a section at a time on a lightly floured work surface to a rectangle of 16 to 18 inches x 14 inches. Place half of apple filling on one end of dough (the end nearest you), leaving a 2-inch border. Roll up gently, flattening ever so slightly. Place on prepared baking sheets. Repeat with remaining dough and filling. Whisk egg and pinch of white sugar in a small bowl. Make slits on top of strudel logs, brush with egg wash, and sprinkle with coarse sugar.

Bake until golden brown, 35 to 50 minutes, reducing oven temperature to 375°F after 20 minutes (filling will begin to bubble out of slits). Cool to room temperature before serving. Dust with confectioners' sugar.

Red Raspberry and Plum Pie

Makes 6 to 8 servings

Sweet red plums and fresh raspberries make this a resplendent pie for the Fourth of July. You can use a basic pie dough or this richer version enhanced with whipping cream.

Crimping Shouldn't Cramp Your Style

There are a variety of ways to properly crimp pie edges in a decorative fashion.

- The simplest way is to press fork tines all around the dough's edge or to press the dough into a zigzag edge by putting the thumb and index finger of one hand behind a section of dough and pressing the index finger of the other hand into the space between your finger and thumb.
- You can also make a "braid" of dough and, using egg wash or water as "glue," coil this braid on the outside edge of the pie.
- Alternatively, cut small leaves of dough and make a trail of leaves as your pie border.
- For classic latticework, simply cut pastry strips a half inch wide using either a pizza roller or a serrated pastry wheel. Allow a 1-inch overhang to extend on each end of the pie and use water or egg wash to hold the strips in place; then trim. These strips can also be interwoven on a flat surface and then transferred to the pie top by sliding a cardboard round underneath to lift the lattice. Once on the pie, this treatment has an interesting basketlike look.

Rich Pie Dough

2½ cups all-purpose flour
1 tablespoon sugar
¾ teaspoon salt
1 cup unsalted butter, cut into chunks
¼ cup whipping cream
2 to 4 tablespoons ice water, as required

Raspberry-Plum Filling

6 to 8 cups quartered small plums

2 cups raspberries
¾ cup sugar
2 teaspoons fresh lemon juice
1 tablespoon all-purpose flour
1 tablespoon cornstarch

Finishing Touches

Milk or cream, for brushing
White sugar, for dusting
Confectioners' sugar, for dusting

Generously spray a 9- or 10-inch quiche pan with a removable bottom with nonstick cooking spray (you can also use a large piepan or a tart pan, which is similar to a quiche pan but not as deep). Line a baking sheet with parchment paper.

For Rich Pie Dough, place flour, sugar, and salt in a food processor. Add chunks of butter and pulse to make a grainy mixture. Add cream and a little ice water, and pulse to make a shaggy dough. On a lightly floured work surface, gather dough together, kneading a few moments to make a smooth dough. Wrap and chill at least 1 hour before rolling out.

For Raspberry-Plum Filling, in a large bowl, gently toss plums with raspberries, sugar, lemon juice, flour, and cornstarch.

Preheat oven to 400°F. Divide dough in half. Roll pastry to fit pan bottom and sides. Mound plum filling in prepared pie shell. Roll remaining pastry to cover pie and press into place, sealing well. Make air slits, finish side borders, brush top with milk or cream, and dust with white sugar.

Place pan on prepared baking sheet and bake 15 minutes. Reduce oven temperature to 375°F and bake until juices begin to come through top and side surfaces and top is lightly browned. Remove from oven and allow to cool well on a wire rack.

Before serving, dust with a generous shower of confectioners' sugar.

Filo Pumpkin Tart

Makes 6 to 8 servings

Here, Greek pastry chef meets *The Pilgrim's Progress.* This is a cradle of golden filo pastry that swathes itself around a silken pumpkin pie filling. So quick and easy, so sinfully good—this could become an instant new tradition.

Filo Crust

¾ cup unsalted butter, melted
12 filo leaves

Pumpkin Filling

1½ cups canned pumpkin puree
½ cup firmly packed brown sugar
½ cup white sugar
3 large eggs

2 teaspoons pure vanilla extract
¾ cup whipping cream
1½ teaspoons pumpkin pie spice

Finishing Touches

Confectioners' sugar, for dusting
Ice cream
Custard sauce

Preheat oven to 375°F. Line a baking sheet with parchment paper.

Place a 9-inch pie or tart pan on prepared baking sheet. Smear a little melted butter on bottom of pan and drape a sheet of filo on top. Repeat with 7 more filo leaves, smearing each with butter before adding the next one.

For Pumpkin Filling, in a medium bowl, using a hand whisk, blend pumpkin with both sugars, eggs, vanilla, whipping cream, and pumpkin pie spice. Mix well and spoon into filo tart shell. Fold overlap of pastry inwards, crimping edges to make a thickened border. Butter 4 remaining filo leaves and stack them on top of each other. Roll up into a snug roll and arrange this on tart border to add a nice outer edge.

Bake 15 minutes and then reduce oven temperature to 350°F and continue baking until tart is done, about 20 to 25 more minutes.

Chill 1½ hours or overnight before serving. Dust edges of tart with confectioners' sugar before serving or serve with ice cream or custard sauce. Store in refrigerator.

Finishing Touches and Extra Tricks

• Bake all pies on a baking sheet lined with parchment paper. This takes care of any spillage and prevents the pie's bottom from burning as the upper crust finishes baking.

• To seal the upper crust of a pie to the bottom edge, brush the bottom edge with egg wash, milk, or water and press the two crusts together.

• Tops of pies should be glazed both to assist in browning and to develop that finished look. Use egg wash (one whole egg beaten with 2 tablespoons water or milk), a beaten egg white, or milk or cream brushed evenly over the top surface. Sprinkle a little sugar on top of the glaze for a homey, old-fashioned look.

• Once a pie is glazed, use a small paring knife or the tines of a fork to cut vents in the top crust. Insufficient air vents will force the hot filling to rise up and separate the two crusts.

• Bake a pie in a relatively hot oven (about 400°F) unless the recipe states otherwise. Bake pies on the lower third of the oven to ensure the bottom crust browns well. Fruit pies are done when the top is evenly golden brown and the juices are bubbling through the air vents.

Chocolate Extravagance Tarts

Makes 8 tarts

I see classic little tarts like these in almost every café I visit. They have buttery bottom crusts and a soufflélike chocolate filling that puffs up, cracks, and settles before being dusted with confectioners' sugar. These tarts always make a statement—they look like they are from a French pastry shop, but they are rather easy to make. Grated chocolate in the tart shells makes these unique. This recipe was the most popular chocolate pastry for half a decade on my Web site! It is now happily retired on this page.

These are luxury-sized four-inch tarts, but you can also make them smaller.

Tart Dough

1½ cups all-purpose flour
½ cup grated semisweet chocolate
½ cup confectioners' sugar
¼ teaspoon salt
¾ cup unsalted butter, cut into chunks
1 teaspoon pure vanilla extract

Chocolate Soufflé Filling

8 ounces semisweet chocolate
¼ cup espresso or strong coffee, warm
1 teaspoon pure vanilla extract
4 large eggs
⅓ cup sugar
Pinch salt

Finishing Touches

2 ounces white chocolate or dark chocolate, melted, for drizzling
Confectioners' sugar

In a food processor, place flour, grated chocolate, confectioners' sugar, and salt and blend briefly. Add butter and pulse to break butter into mixture and make a grainy mixture. Add vanilla and pulse briefly; then process to make a dough that just sticks together. (Add a touch of light cream or water to help it along, if needed.)

Remove pastry from processor and gently knead on a lightly floured work surface a couple of minutes to smooth out dough. Wrap and chill dough 10 minutes. Then divide dough into 8 equal portions and press out onto bottom and sides of ungreased 4-inch tart pans. Using a fork, prick bottoms. Place tart shells on a large baking sheet lined with parchment paper.

Preheat oven to 350°F. Bake tart shells until lightly colored, about 15 to 20 minutes. Cool well.

For Chocolate Soufflé Filling, melt chocolate and set aside to cool. Stir in warm espresso or coffee and vanilla.

Meanwhile, with a whisk attachment on an electric mixer, beat eggs with sugar and salt until very light and thick, about 5 to 8 minutes. Add some of egg mixture to melted chocolate and mix well. Then fold in remaining egg mixture to chocolate, blending gently but thoroughly. Spoon chocolate filling equally into baked tart shells.

Place filled tart shells on baking sheet. Bake until filling puffs and seems set, about 15 to 20 minutes. Cool well. Remove sides from pans to release tarts. Drizzle with melted chocolate or dust with confectioners' sugar.

French Chocolate Silk Pie

Makes 6 to 8 servings

This dark and velvety chocolate experience is luscious and smooth as silk. Old-fashioned chocolate silk pies called for melted chocolate, eggs, and butter, and the pies required no cooking or refrigeration. These days, we need things a bit safer (a baked filling ensures food safety) and a tad more decadent. This new spin on a great pie of old does the trick.

1   prebaked 9-inch pastry shell, see page 188
4   tablespoons unsalted butter
1   cup coarsely chopped semisweet chocolate
1   (14-ounce) can sweetened condensed milk
½   cup half-and-half or light cream
Pinch salt

2   large eggs
1   teaspoon pure vanilla extract
1   tablespoon all-purpose flour

Finishing Touches

Whipped cream
Chocolate shavings
Vanilla ice cream
Hot fudge sauce

Preheat oven to 350°F. Line a baking sheet with parchment paper and place baked pie shell on it.

In a saucepan, melt butter and chocolate together over low heat.

In a medium bowl, whisk condensed milk with warm chocolate-butter mixture. Stir in cream, salt, eggs, vanilla, and flour; whisk well.

Spoon filling into baked crust and bake 35 to 40 minutes until edges of pie are lightly golden brown. Serve warm or chilled.

Offer this with whipped cream and chocolate shavings, or vanilla ice cream and hot fudge sauce. Store pie in refrigerator.

Cookie-Crumb Crust

Makes 1 crumb crust

Cookie crusts are great for no-bake chilled pies as well as cheesecakes. Vary the crust per the filling. Check the "Say Cheesecake" chapter for additional crumb crust possibilities.

1½ cups cookie crumbs*
4   tablespoons unsalted butter, melted
3   to 4 tablespoons sugar

1   teaspoon pure vanilla extract, optional
Pinch ground cinnamon, optional

*This can be graham cracker crumbs, chocolate graham cracker crumbs, chocolate wafer crumbs, tea biscuit or vanilla wafer crumbs, or homemade cookie crumbs.

Toss all ingredients in a bowl to coat crumbs in butter and sugar. Press into a 9-inch piepan. Chill or bake as per recipe instructions.

Toffee Banana Cream Pie

Makes 8 to 10 servings

This is the most luxurious of all cream pies. It is as decadent as pie gets.

Whipped to Perfection

For stiff, stable whipped cream, sweeten it with confectioners' sugar. The cornstarch in it stabilizes whipped cream, whereas regular white sugar can cause it to weep or break down more easily.

1   prebaked 9-inch piecrust or a 9-inch graham cracker or vanilla wafer crust

Custard

1   cup sugar
½   cup all-purpose flour
⅛   teaspoon salt
2   cups milk
4   egg yolks
1   teaspoon pure vanilla extract
1   tablespoon unsalted butter

Banana Filling and Topping

1   (5.9-ounce) package vanilla or banana instant pudding, prepared per package instructions and chilled
2   cups whipping cream
2   tablespoons confectioners' sugar
1½   cups, approximately, miniature marshmallows, divided
2   to 3 ripe bananas, peeled and sliced into ½-inch slices
¼   cup toffee bits, optional
1   cup coarsely crushed vanilla wafers

Have 9-inch piecrust ready.

For Custard, combine sugar, flour, and salt in a small bowl and whisk to blend. In a heavy 3-quart saucepan, over low heat, stir half of milk with egg yolks and add flour mixture. Increase heat to medium and add rest of milk and vanilla, stirring constantly. Bring to a gentle boil and, when mixture begins to thicken, add butter, continuing to stir. Reduce heat and simmer until custard coats a spoon and is thick. Remove from heat, spoon into a bowl, smear top with the end of a stick of butter (this prevents a skin from forming), and press plastic wrap directly onto custard. Chill 1 hour.

Meanwhile, for Banana Filling and Topping, prepare pudding mix and chill. In a mixer bowl, whip cream with confectioners' sugar until stiff. Fold whipped cream into chilled pudding and chill 1 hour.

Remove chilled mixtures from fridge. Fold ½ cup miniature marshmallows into custard.

To assemble, spoon half of custard into piecrust. Place a layer of banana slices on piecrust and then top with some toffee bits and chopped wafers. Spoon rest of custard over banana layer and sprinkle with remaining toffee bits. Put down another layer of vanilla wafers and another layer of banana slices and then top with pudding–whipped cream mixture.

Refrigerate pie 1 to 3 hours or overnight.

Before serving, preheat oven to 400°F. Top pie with remaining 1 cup miniature marshmallows and bake on top oven rack just to brown marshmallows. Remove and serve at once. Store in refrigerator.

Diner Lemon Meringue Pie

Makes 6 to 8 servings

What pie repertoire is complete without this tart treat? This pie is lemony in a multidimensional way, which is what makes it extra special.

1   prebaked 9-inch piecrust or a
    9-inch graham cracker crust

Filling

1   cup sugar
6   tablespoons cornstarch
Pinch salt
2   cups water
5   egg yolks
3   tablespoons unsalted butter,
    softened

½   cup fresh lemon juice
Zest of 1 lemon, finely minced
½   teaspoon lemon oil, optional
¼   teaspoon citric acid, optional

Meringue

5   egg whites
¼   teaspoon cream of tartar
Pinch salt
½   cup sugar

Preheat oven to 350°F. Place prepared piecrust on a parchment paper–lined baking sheet.

For Filling, in a heavy 3-quart saucepan, combine sugar, cornstarch, salt, and water to blend over low heat. Add egg yolks, whisking all the while. Bring to a gentle bubble over medium-low heat and let thicken, about 4 to 5 minutes. Remove pan from heat; add butter, lemon juice, zest, and, if desired, oil and citric acid. Pour filling into piecrust.

To make Meringue, using whisk attachment, place egg whites in a mixer bowl. Gently whisk to foam the whites on low speed and then increase speed to medium; dust in cream of tartar, salt, and sugar. Beat until smooth and glossy, about 2 to 3 minutes.

Spread meringue on pie with a spoon or pipe it out of a pastry bag. Place pie in oven on upper shelf. Bake until meringue is golden and firm to the touch, about 12 to 15 minutes. Cool to room temperature before serving. Refrigerate up to a day ahead (to preserve filling, but it invariably compromises meringue). Store in refrigerator.

Pieplates as Pretty as You Please

Pieplates come in ceramic, graniteware, *Pyrex*, aluminum, stainless steel, nonstick, or nickel plate (usually European). I like old-fashioned graniteware pie tins, restaurant-quality aluminum, and ceramic. I find a pie will "sweat" in a glass pieplate, even though this material allows you to see if the bottom crust is browning; stainless looks good but is not conductive. The fluted sides of quiche or tart pans make a home pie seem professional. Either one is a good choice when you want a finished crust but lack expertise or a pie that is going to be for company. For more on pieplates, check out page 23.

French Strawberry Tart

Makes 8 servings

This delicacy can be made early in the day and refrigerated until ready to serve.

This chilled summer pie is another example of how a few simple elements combine elegantly. Prebaked pastry, a simple custard, fresh berries, and a slick of currant jelly make this special. Add 1½ cups of whipped cream to the pastry cream for a variation that makes for a lighter-textured filling.

Tart Dough

2   cups all-purpose flour
3   tablespoons sugar
½   teaspoon salt
½   cup plus 2 tablespoons unsalted butter, cut into chunks
3   to 6 tablespoons ice water or whipping cream
1   egg yolk

French Pastry Cream Filling

5   egg yolks
½   cup sugar
1   teaspoon pure vanilla extract
¼   teaspoon pure almond extract
2   cups milk
6   tablespoons all-purpose flour
1   teaspoon melted butter

Finishing Touches

1   pint fresh strawberries, washed and dried
1   cup red currant jelly or sieved apricot preserves, warmed

Mint leaves, for garnish

For Tart Dough, place flour, sugar, and salt in a food processor. Add butter and process to break fat into flour until you have a coarse, grainy mixture. Add water and egg yolk to make a soft dough. As soon as it holds together, remove to a lightly floured work surface and knead briefly to make a smooth dough. Wrap and refrigerate at least 1 hour before rolling out.

Preheat oven to 425°F. Line a baking sheet with parchment paper.

Roll out dough to ⅛-inch thickness. Line a quiche, pie, or tart pan with dough. Trim borders. Place a circle of parchment paper on inner surface of pastry. Place an empty piepan on top to hold pastry down (see photo, page 189). Place pie shell on prepared baking sheet and place in oven.

Immediately reduce oven temperature to 350°F and bake 25 to 30 minutes, removing top piepan and parchment paper for the last 10 to 12 minutes to dry out inner crust. Only bake long enough so that crust gets gently browned all over. Cool well before filling and assembling tart.

To make French Pastry Cream Filling, beat egg yolks and ¼ cup sugar until pale. Stir in vanilla, almond extract, and ½ cup milk. Sift in flour; blend well. In a medium saucepan, over low heat, heat remaining 1½ cups milk and remaining ¼ cup sugar to a boil. Remove from heat and gradually pour hot milk mixture into yolk mixture, whisking all the while. Return entire mixture to saucepan and simmer 1½ to 2 minutes until mixture thickens, whisking briskly. Remove from heat and pour into a bowl to cool.

Brush top of pastry cream with melted butter (this prevents a skin from forming) and cover with plastic wrap or wax paper directly onto surface of pastry cream. Refrigerate until thoroughly cool (or up to 3 days).

To assemble tart, whisk chilled pastry cream to loosen it. Spread pastry cream into pastry shell. Top with strawberries arranged in concentric circles. Brush with warmed jelly. Garnish with mint. Store in refrigerator.

Pink Lady Apple Crostata

Makes 6 to 8 servings

This pretty tart is easy because you don't have to crimp a pie border, the fruit filling is exposed in an inviting way, and it looks fancy but is really quite simple to make. Apple brandy, such as Calvados, adds a nice touch if you want to use it.

I created this recipe when two cases of wonderful Pink Lady apples arrived on my doorstep. It works well with Golden Delicious, too, but nothing beats the strawberry scent and taste of Pink Lady apples.

Sweet Dough Crust

2 cups all-purpose flour
1 tablespoon sugar
½ teaspoon salt
¾ cup unsalted butter, cut into small chunks
1 large egg
3 to 6 tablespoons ice water

Filling

5 to 7 large apples, peeled, cored, and cut into wedges

1 tablespoon apple brandy, optional
¾ cup sugar
¼ teaspoon ground cinnamon
Pinch ground cloves
2 tablespoons unsalted butter, cut into small pieces

Finishing Touches

1 large egg
1 tablespoon half-and-half
Sugar

For Sweet Dough Crust, in a food processor, mix flour, sugar, and salt. Add butter chunks and pulse to produce a coarse, crumbly mixture. Add egg and water. Pulse to make a shaggy dough. Turn out onto a lightly floured work surface and knead a few seconds. Form dough into a disk. Wrap well and chill 30 to 45 minutes.

Prepare apples. Toss apples in a large bowl with brandy, sugar, cinnamon, cloves, and small pieces of butter.

Preheat oven to 425°F. Stack two baking sheets together and line top sheet with parchment paper.

On a lightly floured work surface, roll dough to a 9- or 10-inch circle. Transfer to prepared baking sheets by folding in quarters and then unfolding on prepared baking sheets. Mound fruit in center or arrange wedges in concentric circles, leaving a small border to dot with butter. Fold border inward and press gently onto fruit—it doesn't matter if it forms creases. Whisk egg and half-and-half in a small bowl. Brush crust that is exposed with egg wash and sprinkle with sugar.

Bake until apples are oozing juices and caramelizing, about 25 to 35 minutes. Serve warm or at room temperature with vanilla ice cream.

Very Bumbleberry Pie

Makes 6 servings

Bumbleberry pie is a treat from Western Canada. There is no such thing as a bumbleberry, of course! This is a sweet mélange of different fruits (largely berries, such as strawberries, raspberries, and blueberries) and a touch of rhubarb. Try it once and you'll wish there really were bumbleberry bushes to plant immediately.

Pie dough for a double 9-inch pie, see page 188

Filling

½ cup ground fresh or frozen cranberries

2 apples or a pear and an apple, shredded (skins on)

2 cups fresh or frozen raspberries

2 cups fresh or frozen blueberries

1 cup chopped strawberries

1 cup finely diced rhubarb

1 cup sugar

2 tablespoons all-purpose flour

1 tablespoon cornstarch

Finishing Touches

Milk, for brushing

Sugar, for dusting

Preheat oven to 425°F. Line a baking sheet with parchment paper and place a 9-inch piepan on it. Roll out and place bottom pie dough in pan.
For Filling, in a large bowl, gently toss together fruit and rhubarb and then add sugar, flour, and cornstarch. Mound fruit into piecrust and top with remaining dough rolled out. Crimp sides.
Make air vents with a paring knife. Brush pie top and sides with milk and dust with sugar. Bake 20 minutes and then reduce oven temperature to 350°F and bake another 20 to 25 minutes or until you can see fruit juices bubbling out of vents in piecrust.
Let cool to warm on a wire rack. Serve warm with vanilla ice cream.

Good piecrusts are rarely upstaged by their fillings. To my mind, you should taste the crust and be wowed and then further seduced by a great filling.

sweet yeast baking

S weet yeast baking is a wonderful venue for baking, as it combines some of the attributes and appeal of bread baking with much of the appeal of pastry baking. Sweet yeast baking is for those who enjoy buttery, slightly sweet baked desserts with old-fashioned and often European roots. Of course, there are also Americanized treats, such as those you see in coffeehouses, and they are also included in this chapter.

The array of outstanding sweet yeast baked goods—from luscious cinnamon buns to buttery coffee cakes—is astounding because a sweet dough is one of the most versatile doughs for baking. A sweet dough does not have to be as rigorously kneaded as bread dough, for you want baked goods that are tender without being extremely chewy or crusty. Hence, the doughs for sweet baking are rich, which makes them supple to work with. Being richer, staling is also a rare occurrence, since richer doughs, once baked, last rather nicely—if they are not instantly devoured!

Most of the essentials on what you need to know about sweet yeast baking are found in "Loaves, Large & Small" on pages 30 to 33. The unique specific considerations about this genre of baking are offered here.

Ingredients and Special Handling

Unlike savory yeast bread recipes, many sweet yeast recipes call for milk; however, yeast tends to be sluggish if you try to hydrate it with cold or even warm milk, especially in comparison to how frisky yeast reacts when it is hydrated with water. This being the case, my recipes generally call for a bit of warm water to start the yeast off before adding milk and other rich products that can impede yeast, such as butter, sour cream, and sugar. Starting the yeast off with a bit of warm water, regardless of which ingredients follow, helps it get off to a strong start, which is something it will need because yeast has to work a bit harder in a sweet dough to leaven.

Speaking of yeast, rapid-rise yeast is extra resilient and perfectly designed to handle the demands of a sweet dough. Two particular brands that I highly recommend for sweet yeast baking include *Fermipan* and *Saf Gold,* but *Fleischmann's* and *Red Star* are fine, too.

Most savory yeast recipes call for bread flour, but sweet yeast baking can take a combination of bread and all-purpose flours or, for an exceptionally tender product, use only all-purpose flour. Doing so will result in a baked item with a touch less body or chewiness, but you will be rewarded with a slightly more pastrylike final result. It is really up to you, and I suggest you experiment. Just remember that if you are out of bread flour, you can make anything in this chapter with all-purpose flour.

Because sweet yeast dough is rich and that is a trial for yeast, help it out by using warm milk, softened butter, and eggs that have been dipped in hot water to take the chill off of them.

A cool rise, which works well for many breads, is also something you can do with a sweet yeast recipe—this is good to remember if you want to form cinnamon buns, refrigerate them overnight, and then bake them first thing in the morning. Nothing beats warm cinnamon buns.

Other than that, follow the recipes and remember some of the basics of general bread baking—and you are on your way.

Storage

Most sweet yeast recipes can stand up to three to four days covered in a cake dome or in an airtight wrap on the counter and still be fresh for eating. If you have leftovers, freeze them, covering them well

with plastic wrap and then with foil or place in an airtight container. Rewarm, unwrapped, in a low oven (325°F) or serve at room temperature. Sweet yeast baking is designed to be eaten within a few days of baking. You can, however, prepare the dough, let it half rise, and freeze the unbaked product up to a month. Defrost in the fridge overnight and then bake as required.

Because sweet yeast dough has rich ingredients that can hinder yeast, help it out by using warm milk and softened butter, and take the chill off of eggs with a dip in hot water.

Chewy Chocolate Sticks

Makes 12 pastry sticks

These sticks are not puffy in the way that yeasted sweets usually are. If you want them puffier and more bready, just let them rise longer before baking.

Dough

1¼ cups warm water (100°F to 110°F)
1 tablespoon rapid-rise yeast
2 large eggs
¾ cup sugar
1 teaspoon salt
½ cup unsalted butter, softened
2 teaspoons pure vanilla extract
⅓ cup dry milk powder
2 cups all-purpose flour
2 cups bread flour

Filling

1 cup sugar
4 tablespoons cocoa powder
½ teaspoon ground cinnamon
¼ cup unsalted butter, softened and cut into small pieces
1 cup raisins, plumped and dried (see page 18)
1 cup chocolate chips

Finishing Touches

Egg white, beaten
Sugar, for dusting

Stack two baking sheets together and line top sheet with parchment paper. You will need to repeat this procedure for each batch.

In a mixer bowl, hand-whisk water and yeast together and let stand 2 to 3 minutes to dissolve yeast. Briskly whisk in eggs, sugar, salt, butter, vanilla, milk powder, and most of flours and blend well. Attach dough hook and knead on lowest speed of mixer 8 to 10 minutes, adding remaining flour as necessary to form a soft dough.

Remove dough hook and spray dough with nonstick cooking spray. Cover entire mixer and bowl with a large clear plastic bag. Let dough rise 30 to 60 minutes or until almost doubled.

Turn out dough onto a lightly floured work surface and gently deflate. **Press** or roll out dough to a 20- x 10-inch rectangle. Blend sugar, cocoa, and cinnamon and scatter over dough. Dot with butter and sprinkle raisins and chocolate chips over dough (**photo 1**).

Roll up dough into a log; then flatten gently so it is a flattened log. Using a sharp knife or dough scraper, cut into 12 cylinders or logs and place on prepared baking sheets, stretching each a little bit and twisting (**photo 2**). Brush pastries with beaten egg white and dust with sugar. Cover loosely with plastic wrap and let sticks rise 30 to 40 minutes or until almost doubled.

Preheat oven to 350°F. Bake until well browned, about 25 to 30 minutes (**photo 3**). Let cool on baking sheets.

These are big twists with just enough sweetness and spice.

Yeasted Pumpkin Bread with Cinnamon-Pecan Swirl

Makes 3 loaves

Here's a lofty, pretty-hued bread with a treat tucked into the center. Enjoying this bread is a wonderful way to get some vitamin A into your daily diet. This bread is perfect for Thanksgiving or as a wonderful fall sweet bread to share with a friend over coffee.

If there are leftovers, use them to make bread pudding or French toast.

Dough

1	cup warm water (100°F to 110°F)
2	tablespoons rapid-rise yeast
1	cup pumpkin puree
¼	cup unsalted butter, softened
⅔	cup sugar
1	large egg
2	teaspoons salt
5	to 6½ cups bread flour

Filling

¼	cup unsalted butter, softened
¾	cup firmly packed brown sugar
2	teaspoons ground cinnamon
½	teaspoon pumpkin pie spice, optional
1	cup chopped pecans
1	cup currants, plumped and dried (see page 18)

Finishing Touches

1	large egg, beaten
	Sugar
	Ground cinnamon

In a mixer bowl, hand-whisk water and yeast together and let stand 2 to 3 minutes to dissolve yeast. Briskly whisk in pumpkin puree, butter, sugar, egg, and salt and blend. Add 4 cups bread flour and mix. Attach dough hook and knead on lowest speed of mixer 8 to 10 minutes, adding more flour as necessary to make a soft but elastic dough.

Remove dough hook and spray dough with nonstick cooking spray. Cover entire mixer and bowl with a large clear plastic bag. Let dough rise about 30 minutes or until almost doubled.

Meanwhile, for Filling, in a small bowl, blend together butter, brown sugar, and spices. Have pecans and currants nearby.

Turn out dough onto a lightly floured work surface and gently deflate. Divide into three portions. Press each into a 10-inch oval or circle. Scatter brown sugar mixture over surface of each piece and then scatter pecans and currants over each.

Spray three 8- x 4-inch loafpans with nonstick cooking spray. Roll up each oval or circle of dough into a snug jellyroll. Place each in a prepared loafpan. Place loafpans on a parchment paper–lined baking sheet and cover entire sheet loosely with plastic wrap.

Let dough rise 45 to 60 minutes or until almost doubled. Brush each loaf with beaten egg and sprinkle with sugar and cinnamon.

Preheat oven to 350°F. Bake on lower oven rack 30 to 35 minutes until lightly browned.

Granny-McIntosh Apple Buns

Makes 12 to 16 buns

These buns fly out of the kitchen, but they also stay fresh for a few days.

Dough

1½ cups warm water (100°F to 110°F)

5 teaspoons rapid-rise yeast

5 to 7 cups all-purpose flour

½ cup unsalted butter, softened

1 cup sugar

2 teaspoons pure vanilla extract

3 large eggs

1 teaspoon salt

Filling

6 to 8 McIntosh apples, peeled and thinly sliced

2 large unpeeled Granny Smith apples, shredded

1 cup unsalted butter, softened and cut into small pieces

½ generous cup sugar

1 teaspoon ground cinnamon

Finishing Touches

2 large eggs

Pinch sugar

Cinnamon Fondant

1½ cups confectioners' sugar

1 teaspoon pure vanilla extract

¼ to ¾ teaspoon ground cinnamon

Water, as required, to make a thick glaze

This slightly sweet dough gets panned out like a pizza; spread with softened butter and sugar; and treated to a dual bouquet of sliced and shredded apples, both tart and sweet.

Stack two large baking sheets together and line top sheet with parchment paper. You will need to repeat this procedure for each batch.

In a mixer bowl, hand-whisk water and yeast together and let stand 2 to 3 minutes to dissolve yeast. Add 1 cup flour and blend and then add butter, sugar, vanilla, eggs, salt, and then most of remaining flour. Mix and then knead with dough hook on lowest speed 5 to 8 minutes, adding more flour as necessary to make a soft dough.

Remove dough hook and spray dough with nonstick cooking spray. Cover entire mixer and bowl with a large clear plastic bag. Let dough rise about 40 to 50 minutes or until almost doubled.

Meanwhile, prepare apples and have other filling ingredients nearby. Whisk eggs and pinch of sugar in a small bowl for egg wash.

Turn out dough onto a lightly floured work surface and gently deflate. Roll out to a 22-inch circle. Deposit pieces of butter all over dough's surface. Scatter sliced apples over dough. Top with sugar and cinnamon and then scatter shredded apple on top. Cut into 12 to 16 wedges (this is messy, but it will be fine). Stretching each wedge slightly, roll up each wedge into a crescent, starting at wide end. If apples leak out, just stuff them back in.

Place on prepared baking sheets, brush each crescent bun with egg wash and cover loosely with plastic wrap. Let rise 30 to 45 minutes or until almost doubled.

Preheat oven to 350°F. Bake until golden brown, 35 to 45 minutes.

For Cinnamon Fondant, whisk ingredients in a small bowl until smooth and soft. Smear fondant on buns with a flat spatula, skimming away excess.

Homemade Franchise-Style Doughnuts

Makes 36 medium doughnuts; also pictured on page 204

You know the place that makes doughnuts that are served fresh and hot, and they sometimes give you one free as you gaze at a conveyor belt of doughnuts in various states of manufacture? Are these just like those? Almost.

> Grab a fryer or wok and a paper baker's hat and get ready to enjoy the most tender and delectable doughnuts at home.

Dough

¼ cup warm water (100°F to 110°F)
2 tablespoons rapid-rise yeast
1½ cups warm milk
⅔ cup sugar
1¼ teaspoons salt
2 large eggs
⅓ cup shortening
5 cups, approximately, all-purpose flour

Vegetable oil or shortening, for frying

Creamy Butter Glaze*

½ cup unsalted butter
2 cups confectioners' sugar
1½ teaspoons pure vanilla extract
4 to 6 tablespoons hot water
1 ounce semisweet chocolate, melted, optional

*Double the amount of glaze you make if you want just as many chocolate-covered doughnuts as vanilla. Divide glaze into two bowls.

In a mixer bowl, hand-whisk warm water and yeast together and let stand 2 to 3 minutes to dissolve yeast. Briskly whisk in milk, sugar, salt, and eggs and blend. Add shortening and most of flour and blend. Then knead with a dough hook on low speed only until smooth (it is not necessary to knead this dough a long time).

Remove dough hook and spray dough lightly with nonstick cooking spray. Cover entire mixer and bowl with a large clear plastic bag. Let dough rise 50 to 60 minutes or until almost doubled.

Turn out dough onto a lightly floured work surface and gently deflate. Roll to ½-inch thickness and, using a doughnut cutter, cut into doughnuts (**photo 1**). (Each doughnut should weigh just under 2 ounces of raw dough.) Cover doughnuts loosely with plastic wrap and let rise 20 to 40 minutes.

Heat vegetable oil or shortening in a fryer (or wok) to 350°F. Slide in doughnuts, a few at a time, and fry about 1 minute per side (**photo 2**). Remove from oil onto a wire rack set over parchment paper.

For Creamy Butter Glaze, melt butter and then whisk it in a medium bowl with confectioners' sugar, vanilla, and hot water. Smear doughnuts in glaze (**photo 3**). Let set and smear again.

For Chocolate Glaze, if desired, add 1 ounce melted chocolate to one entire recipe of Creamy Butter Glaze. Smear doughnuts in Chocolate Glaze.

Baker's Bubka with Crumb Topping

Makes 2 medium bubkas or 1 large bubka

Bubka is pure heaven to me because it strikes the right notes of sweet and bready. I often use a bread machine to make the dough, although I have to give the mixing a hand at first by using a rubber spatula to blend the dough.

> This bubka is relatively easy to make. It is not as complicated as true Danish bubka, with its rolled-in blocks of butter, but it is certainly richer and moister than a sweet dough.

Bread-Machine Labor Issues

Often, rich doughs—especially those exceeding four cups of flour—need assistance during the initial part of the dough cycle in many bread machines. To remedy this, using a rubber spatula, move flour from the sides or corners into the center and make sure the dough is being well mixed. Dust in additional flour as required to make a soft, bouncy ball.

Dough

1½	cups warm water (100°F to 110°F)
2	tablespoons rapid-rise yeast
3	large eggs
2	egg yolks
2	teaspoons pure vanilla extract
1	teaspoon pure almond extract
2	teaspoons lemon juice
¾	cup sugar
1	teaspoon salt
⅓	cup milk powder
3	cups all-purpose flour
¾	cup unsalted butter, softened
3	cups bread flour
1	large egg

Pinch sugar

Filling

4	tablespoons unsalted butter, softened
1	cup firmly packed brown sugar
½	cup chopped almond paste
2	tablespoons corn syrup
2	teaspoons ground cinnamon
¾	cup chopped almonds, optional

Crumb Topping

4	tablespoons unsalted butter, cut into chunks
½	scant cup confectioners' sugar
½	cup all-purpose flour

Sugar, for dusting

Generously spray two 9- x 5-inch loafpans with nonstick cooking spray. Stack two baking sheets and line top sheet with parchment paper. For an extra large bubka, use a 10-inch angel food cakepan sprayed with nonstick cooking spray. Place pans on prepared baking sheets.

In a mixer bowl, hand-whisk water and yeast together and let stand 2 to 3 minutes to dissolve yeast. Briskly whisk in eggs, egg yolks, vanilla, almond extract, lemon juice, sugar, salt, milk powder, and all-purpose flour. Then stir in softened butter and most of bread flour. Mix dough; then knead as it becomes a mass, with a dough hook or by hand, about 8 to 10 minutes until smooth and elastic, adding more bread flour as required.

Remove dough hook and cover entire mixer and bowl with a large clear plastic bag. Let dough rise about 45 to 90 minutes until puffy or almost doubled in size. This is also an ideal dough to refrigerate overnight and resume next day, allowing dough to warm up a bit before proceeding.

Whisk egg and pinch of sugar in a small bowl for egg wash.

For Filling, in a food processor, process butter, brown sugar, almond paste, corn syrup, cinnamon, and almonds to make a soft paste or filling.

For Crumb Topping, in a small bowl, mix butter, confectioners' sugar, and all-purpose flour together to make a crumbly topping. Set aside in refrigerator.

Turn out dough onto a lightly floured work surface and gently deflate. Divide dough in half. On a well-floured work surface, roll half of dough into a 16-inch square. Spread filling over dough. Roll up dough into a large jellyroll. Cut in half. Place both halves in one of prepared 9- x 5-inch pans, beside each other—it doesn't matter if they are a little squished. Brush with egg wash and dust with some sugar. Repeat with remaining dough and filling. Spray tops of both loaves with nonstick cooking spray. Place pans on prepared baking sheets and cover loosely with plastic wrap. Let rise until bubka is flush with or a touch over sides of pans, 45 to 75 minutes. Brush with egg wash. Sprinkle with Crumb Topping.

Preheat oven to 350°F. Bake 40 to 50 minutes (55 to 70 minutes for one large bubka) until bubka is medium brown. Cool in pan 15 minutes before removing to a wire rack or serving plate.

Yeasted Bakery-Style Sweet Buns

Makes 12 buns

These old-fashioned sweet rolls are great toasted and served with coffee or tea.

Dough

1½	cups warm water (100°F to 110°F)
2	tablespoons rapid-rise yeast
1	tablespoon pure vanilla extract
²⁄₃	cup sugar
3	large eggs
⅓	cup unsalted butter, softened
2½	teaspoons salt

5	to 7 cups bread flour
2	large eggs
Pinch sugar	

Butter Crumb Topping

½	cup unsalted butter, cut into small pieces
½	cup all-purpose flour
⅓	cup confectioners' sugar

Line a large baking sheet with parchment paper.

In a mixer bowl, hand-whisk water and yeast together and let stand 2 to 3 minutes to dissolve yeast. Briskly whisk in vanilla, sugar, eggs, softened butter, and salt and blend well. Add 3 to 4 cups bread flour and mix. Then knead with dough hook on lowest speed of mixer 6 to 8 minutes, adding more bread flour as necessary to form a soft, bouncy dough.

Remove dough hook and spray dough with nonstick cooking spray. Cover entire mixer and bowl with a large clear plastic bag. Let dough rise 30 to 60 minutes or until almost doubled.

Turn out dough onto a lightly floured work surface and gently deflate.

Cut dough into 12 equal portions. Shape each into a small round roll or bun. Place about 3 inches apart on prepared baking sheet. Whisk eggs and pinch of sugar in a small bowl. Brush each bun well with egg wash.

For Butter Crumb Topping, in a small bowl, rub ingredients together to form a crumbly mixture. Distribute carefully on top of each bun.

Cover buns loosely with plastic wrap and let rise about 30 to 45 minutes or until quite puffy and almost doubled.

Preheat oven to 350°F. Bake 28 to 35 minutes or until browned all over.

Sour Cream-Caramel-Cinnamon Buns

Makes 16 to 20 buns

There is really only one word for these buns: awesome. They can be made a day ahead and left for a slow, cool rise in the fridge. In fact, they have a better texture with a cool rise. These buns are delicate and feathery and also massive and gorgeous. You can bake up a pan of these buns and freeze another batch, unrisen and unbaked. When you're ready, let the frozen batch rise overnight in the fridge and bake them off the next morning.

Cinnamon buns are always decadent, but these are pretty well queenly. It is the combination of cinnamon, brown sugar, caramel, and butter that makes these buns almost sleazy good!

Dough

1/3	cup warm water (100°F to 110°F)
5	teaspoons rapid-rise yeast
3/4	cup warm milk
3	large eggs
3/4	cup unsalted butter, cut into small chunks
3/4	cup sugar
1 1/4	teaspoons salt
1	tablespoon pure vanilla extract
1/2	cup sour cream
1/4	teaspoon ground cinnamon
6	to 8 cups all-purpose flour

Filling

1	cup unsalted butter, softened
1 1/2	cups firmly packed brown sugar
2	teaspoons ground cinnamon
1	cup chopped pecans, optional
1	cup raisins, plumped and dried (see page 18)
1/2	cup caramel or butterscotch chips
1/3	cup caramel or butterscotch sundae topping

Caramel-Cinnamon Glaze

1 1/2	cups firmly packed brown sugar
1/2	cup unsalted butter, melted
1/4	cup corn syrup
1	teaspoon ground cinnamon

Baker's Fondant

2	cups confectioners' sugar
1	teaspoon pure vanilla extract
4	to 6 tablespoons water

Line a large baking sheet with parchment paper. Spray two 13- x 9-inch pans with nonstick cooking spray (you can also use three 9-inch cakepans).
In a mixer bowl, hand-whisk warm water and yeast and let stand 1 minute to dissolve yeast. Briskly whisk in milk, eggs, butter, sugar, salt, vanilla, sour cream, and cinnamon. As ingredients blend, fold in 4 to 5 cups flour and mix to make a soft dough. Then knead with dough hook on lowest speed 6 to 8 minutes, adding more flour as necessary to form a dough that is smooth and elastic but not tough. Remove dough hook and spray dough with nonstick cooking spray. Cover entire mixer and bowl with a large clear plastic bag. Let dough rise 45 to 60 minutes or until almost doubled.
Turn out dough onto a lightly floured work surface, gently deflate, and divide in half. Let dough rest 10 minutes. Then pat or roll out to a 16- to 18-inch square between 1/4 and 1/2 inch thick. Spread each half with equal amounts of Filling ingredients, smearing on softened butter and then sprinkling on brown sugar, cinnamon, nuts, raisins, and caramel chips. Drizzle with sundae topping.
For Caramel-Cinnamon Glaze, smear each pan with half of brown sugar. Drizzle with melted butter and corn syrup and sprinkle with cinnamon.
Roll up each portion of dough, starting with edge of dough closest to

you, into a snug jellyroll. Cut into ¾-inch-thick slices and arrange in
rows in prepared pans. Spray with nonstick cooking spray. Cover loosely
with plastic wrap and let rise 40 to 60 minutes or until almost doubled.
Preheat oven to 350°F. Bake about 30 to 35 minutes until buns are medium
brown. Invert buns onto a parchment paper–lined baking sheet or large
platter. Drizzle excess syrup from the bottoms of pans over tops of buns.
For Baker's Fondant, in a medium bowl, whisk together confectioners'
sugar, vanilla, and enough water to make a spreadable glaze. Pour or spread
fondant over buns. Serve buns warm or at room temperature.

Chelsea Morning Buns

Makes 20 buns

Well, of course that is a whimsical name, but it is based on something authentic and quite historical. English Chelsea buns are what we call cinnamon or sticky buns on this side of the pond. This version, however, makes buns that are a little smaller and more tender and buttery than American-style cinnamon buns.

Chelsea buns date back to the *Bun House* of Chelsea, England, as far back as the late seventeenth century. Talk about a baking legacy.

Dough

- ¼ cup warm water (100°F to 110°F)
- 4 teaspoons rapid-rise yeast
- 2 cups all-purpose flour
- ⅓ cup sugar
- 1 teaspoon salt
- Pinch ground cinnamon
- ½ teaspoon finely minced fresh lemon zest
- ½ cup unsalted butter, softened
- 2 large eggs
- 1 cup warm milk
- 2½ to 4 cups bread flour

Filling

- ½ cup unsalted butter, softened
- ½ cup firmly packed brown sugar
- 2 tablespoons white sugar
- 2 teaspoons ground cinnamon
- 3 tablespoons honey
- ½ cup raisins, plumped and dried (see page 18)
- ⅓ cup currants, plumped and dried (see page 18)

Glaze

- 1½ cups confectioners' sugar
- Milk, as required

Generously spray a 13- x 9-inch pan with nonstick cooking spray. Place pan on a parchment paper–lined baking sheet.

In a mixer bowl, hand-whisk water and yeast together and let stand 2 to 3 minutes to dissolve yeast. Then add all-purpose flour, sugar, salt, cinnamon, zest, butter, and eggs and stir. Add milk and most of bread flour and mix; then knead with dough hook on lowest speed of mixer, adding more flour as necessary to make a soft dough. Remove dough hook and spray dough with nonstick cooking spray. Cover entire mixer and bowl with a large clear plastic bag. Let dough rise about 35 to 45 minutes or until almost doubled.

Turn out dough onto a lightly floured work surface and gently deflate. Roll out to a 12- x 14-inch rectangle. Let dough rest 10 minutes and then flatten again with a rolling pin. Smear on softened butter and sprinkle with both sugars and cinnamon. Drizzle with honey and then scatter on raisins and currants.

Roll up dough into a jellyroll. Cut into 20 portions with a sharp knife or dough cutter. Place snugly in prepared pan. Cover loosely with plastic wrap and let rise 30 minutes.

In a small bowl, whisk together confectioners' sugar and enough milk to make a glaze that can be smeared or drizzled.

Preheat oven to 350°F. Bake until buns are golden brown, 30 to 40 minutes.

Let cool and turn buns over. Glaze buns.

Toronto Blueberry Buns

Makes 12 to 16 buns

These buns are large circles of dough that are filled and then folded in half for half-moon-shaped pastries. The scent (let alone the taste) of the fresh blueberry filling is so good that you might forget to save some for the buns and just eat the filling straight!

Dough

1	cup warm water (100°F to 110°F)
1	tablespoon rapid-rise yeast
4½ to 5	cups all-purpose flour
¾	cup sugar
3	large eggs
½	cup unsalted butter, softened
1¼	teaspoons salt
1½	teaspoons pure vanilla extract

Fresh Blueberry Filling

2	cups fresh or frozen blueberries
⅔	cup sugar
1	tablespoon fresh lemon juice
1	tablespoon cornstarch dissolved in 3 tablespoons water

Finishing Touches

1	large egg
Pinch sugar	
Regular or coarse sugar, for dusting	

Stack two baking sheets together and line top sheet with parchment paper. You will need to repeat this procedure for each batch.

In a mixer bowl, hand-whisk warm water and yeast together and let stand 2 to 3 minutes to dissolve yeast. Add 1 cup flour to mixture and then add sugar, eggs, butter, salt, vanilla, and most of remaining flour. Knead with dough hook on lowest speed 5 to 8 minutes, adding more flour as necessary to make a soft dough. Remove dough hook and spray dough with nonstick cooking spray. Cover entire mixer and bowl with a large clear plastic bag. Let dough rise about 70 to 90 minutes or until almost doubled.

Meanwhile, for Fresh Blueberry Filling, place blueberries, sugar, and lemon juice in a small saucepan and heat gently. Stir in cornstarch mixture and cook over medium heat, stirring berries and letting them just burst open, until mixture becomes like pie filling, about 3 to 4 minutes. Remove filling from heat, turn out into a bowl, cover with greased wax paper, and refrigerate until needed.

Turn out dough onto a lightly floured work surface and gently deflate. Divide in half and roll out to ½-inch thickness, allowing dough to rest a few minutes afterward so it does not retract too much. Cut dough into 5-inch circles.

Whisk egg and pinch of sugar in a small bowl. Place dough cutouts on prepared baking sheets. Brush edges of dough cutouts with egg wash; deposit blueberry filling in middle of each (**photo 1**). Seal; press edges with a fork. Brush again with egg wash (**photo 2**) and dust with regular or coarse sugar. Loosely cover with plastic wrap and let rise 30 to 60 minutes until almost doubled.

Preheat oven to 350°F. Bake buns until golden brown, 25 to 30 minutes.

A quaint place called the *Open Window Bakery* in Toronto offers buns bursting with fresh blueberries, for which they are legendary. Most sweet buns call for relatively lean doughs that use oil or vegetable shortening. For my version of blueberry buns, I prefer using butter. A simple egg wash and a dusting of sugar are the perfect finishing touches.

White and Dark Chocolate Bread

Makes 2 medium loaves

This bread is a chocolate and bread lover's nirvana. A little Montreal bakery called *Olive & Gourmando* inspired me to create my own version of the lovely chocolate bread for which they are renowned. Chef Dyan Solomon prefers *Valrhona* cocoa powder and a unique chocolate fudge filling of butter, cocoa, and brown sugar swirled in. My wonderful, sumptuous bread is sharply bittersweet with cocoa, moist and chewy, and replete with a sweet chocolate swirl and nuggets of bittersweet chocolate chunks nestled in the filling. Two days of cool rises (but little hands-on work) result in two plump chocolaty loaves that the best and toniest bakery in New York City would love to offer.

> For the holidays, I make this bread and add kirsch-soaked sour dry cherries. This tasty treat is perfect fresh or toasted (in a toaster oven), with espresso, tea, or slathered with cinnamon butter for breakfast.

Chocolate Bread Dough

1¾ cups warm water (100°F to 110°F)
5 teaspoons rapid-rise yeast
½ cup sugar
1 teaspoon salt
⅔ cup *Valrhona* cocoa or other bitter European-style cocoa
4 to 5 cups bread flour

Chocolate Fudge Filling

¼ cup unsalted butter, softened
1 cup firmly packed brown sugar
⅓ cup white sugar
½ cup cocoa powder
¾ cup coarsely chopped bittersweet chocolate
¼ cup coarsely chopped milk chocolate or white chocolate

Finishing Touches

Sugar
Cocoa powder
Ground cinnamon

Spray inside of a large zip-top plastic bag with nonstick cooking spray.

For Chocolate Bread Dough, in a mixer bowl, hand-whisk water and yeast together and let stand 2 to 3 minutes to dissolve yeast. Briskly whisk in sugar, salt, cocoa, and 3 cups flour to make a batter. Knead with dough hook on lowest speed 5 to 8 minutes, adding more flour as necessary to make a soft but sticky dough.

Turn out dough onto a lightly floured work surface and gently deflate. Shape dough into a round, put in a zip-top plastic bag, and refrigerate overnight or at least 8 hours. Periodically check bread, and if you see it rising, open bag, gently deflate dough, and then reseal bag.

For Chocolate Fudge Filling, place butter, both sugars, and cocoa in a food processor and process a few minutes to make a pasty mixture. Place in a zip-top plastic bag and seal. Roll out (while in bag) to flatten. Refrigerate filling.

The next day, remove dough from bag and turn out onto a lightly floured work surface. Roll or press dough out to a 16- to 18-inch x 10-inch rectangle. Break filling into pieces, and spread pieces over surface of dough. Sprinkle chopped chocolates over filling.

Spray two 8- x 4½-inch loafpans with nonstick cooking spray.

Roll up dough snugly as a jellyroll, starting at short side. Once it is a log, cut it in half and place each half in one of prepared loafpans, pressing in slightly. Insert each loafpan into a large plastic bag; seal and refrigerate overnight.

The next day, take loafpans out and place on a large baking sheet lined with parchment paper. Spray tops with nonstick cooking spray. Sprinkle each loaf with sugar and a touch of cocoa and cinnamon. Cover them loosely with plastic wrap and allow loaves to rise until puffy and much larger, 2 to 4 hours. They will just reach tops of loafpans.

Preheat oven to 350°F. Place breads on lower rack of oven and bake until done and breads sound hollow when tapped, about 35 to 45 minutes.

Cool 20 minutes before removing to a wire rack to cool completely.

cake creations

More than any other type of baking, cakes are about celebration. They are meant to be special and cause oohs and aahs the minute they are presented. Cakes usher in birthdays, anniversaries, rites of passage, and holidays. No matter the occasion, they are synonymous with loving effort and an unabashed feeling of indulgence. Cakes are also simply happy food—they immediately bring smiles! They are not about diets and restraint. Cakes are meant to be big and impressive—the main event of special occasions. If you don't have cake, you don't have the same feeling about an occasion, for a cake is the exclamation mark of the event at hand. Even bringing out the cake provides the pacing, energy, and drama of the occasion.

The cakes in this chapter are not geared towards coffee klatch moments, although they can perform just fine in that regard. These are more grand finales, much like cheesecakes. These cakes are a delight to make, for they demand, in the nicest of ways, the sheer pleasure of your unadulterated devotion to detail and finishing touches, as well as that special energy that comes when you know that what you are baking will bring such pleasure.

Like all great baking, lavish or modest, cakes start with a foundation of superb ingredients: butter, pure vanilla extract, unbleached all-purpose flour, and the best of whatever else is called for, be it coconut, walnuts, chocolate, or unique ingredients.

Nothing makes a statement like the perfect cake matched to an occasion. The meal might be spectacular and the company sublime, but *cake* has the last word. It is the opportunity for a baker to be creative and shine. Cakes are, in a phrase, memory food. No wonder people often say, "That takes the cake!" The recipes in this chapter certainly do.

Ingredients and Handling

It is good practice to take the chill off of eggs before using them so as not to impose a really cold ingredient on the batter. A colder batter never gets as much height, since it has to work that much more to leaven itself, despite the leaveners in the cake.

Do make sure your baking powder—the main leavener used in cakes—is as fresh as can be.

When measuring flour in cake baking, be precise. Cakes are delicate and rely on accuracy. Stir the flour in your flour canister and then scoop and level off the flour in the measuring cup.

Most recipes begin by creaming softened butter and sugar together. This is best done with the paddle attachment of your stand mixer and always on low speed of the mixer. Once the butter and sugar are well blended, add the eggs and vanilla and continue as the recipe states. Always check the well of the mixer bowl to ensure no unblended ingredients accumulate at the bottom. I recommend using shortening or nonstick cooking spray to grease your pans, not butter. (Butter tends to burn.)

Storage

A glass cake dome is your best bet for storage. It presents and stores the cake nicely. Plastic cake storage containers are also available. You want a sealed container that holds a cake without squishing it and allows for some air flow (so the cake does not get gummy) but prevents the cake from drying out.

Classic American Chocolate Layer Cake

Makes 12 to 14 servings, or 24 regular or 48 small cupcakes

This cake is velvety crumbed, moist, and higher than you can imagine. If you always liked the convenience of a cake mix but wanted a from-scratch layer cake to boast about, this is the recipe.

A tender yellow cake is the foundation of many celebratory moments that take candles or icing or both. It is also the real cake behind the name 'chocolate layer cake.' This cake works well as a sheet cake, a layer cake with chocolate or white icing, or as the most amazing cupcakes.

Cake

1	cup unsalted butter, softened
2	cups sugar, pulverized
3	large eggs
2½	teaspoons pure vanilla extract
3	cups all-purpose flour
4	teaspoons baking powder
¼	teaspoon salt
1½	cups warm milk

Chocolate Frosting

4	cups confectioners' sugar
¼	cup cocoa powder
¾	cup unsalted butter, softened
1	cup semisweet chocolate chips, melted
Milk, as required	

Preheat oven to 350°F. Generously spray two 9-inch round cakepans with nonstick cooking spray and place pans on a large parchment paper–lined baking sheet.

In a mixer bowl or large food processor, blend butter and sugar until fluffy and thoroughly combined. Then add eggs and vanilla and blend well. Add flour, baking powder, and salt, drizzling in milk as mixture blends to make a smooth batter. Spoon batter into prepared cakepans.

Bake until cakes spring back when gently pressed with fingertips, 35 to 40 minutes. Cool slightly. Unmold cakes from pans, cool on wire racks, and then gently wrap in wax paper or plastic wrap. Chill in freezer 30 minutes or wrap and refrigerate until you are ready to frost.

For Chocolate Frosting, place confectioners' sugar and cocoa in a mixer bowl and whisk by hand. Add butter and chocolate chips and mix on low speed so that sugar doesn't fly out of bowl. Add a bit of milk, as required, and increase speed to high; whip to make a fluffy frosting. Spread Chocolate Frosting between layers and then on sides and top of cake. You can also frost this cake with Butter–Cream Cheese Frosting, page 240, or Pastry Chef Buttercream, page 249.

Easy Devil's Food Cake

Makes 8 to 12 servings

This low-slung, moist chocolate cake is a classic. You can frost it with chocolate icing or with this spectacular, glossy Sour Cream Frosting.

Cake

4   ounces unsweetened chocolate, coarsely chopped
¼   cup cocoa powder
1¼ cups boiling water
1   cup unsalted butter, softened
1   cup firmly packed dark brown sugar
⅔   cup white sugar
3   large eggs
1½ teaspoons pure vanilla extract
½   cup sour cream

1½ cups all-purpose flour
1   teaspoon baking soda
¼   teaspoon salt

Sour Cream Frosting

3   (1-ounce) squares unsweetened chocolate
½   cup unsalted butter, softened
3   to 4 cups confectioners' sugar
½   cup sour cream
1   teaspoon pure vanilla extract

This recipe makes a devilishly dark cake that is sublime as a chocolate layer cake and perfect as a birthday cake or as dark chocolate cupcakes.

Preheat oven to 350°F. Generously spray two 9-inch round cakepans or one 13- x 9-inch pan with nonstick cooking spray. Place pans on a large parchment paper–lined baking sheet.

Place chopped chocolate and cocoa in a medium-size bowl and cover with boiling water. Stir to melt chocolate and then cool.

In a mixer bowl, cream butter and both sugars until fluffy and well combined. Blend in eggs, vanilla, and then sour cream. Blend in cooled melted chocolate and then fold in flour, baking soda, and salt.

Spoon batter into prepared pans. Bake until cakes spring back when gently pressed with fingertips, 30 to 35 minutes. Cool well before frosting.

For Sour Cream Frosting, melt chocolate squares in microwave; stir and cool. In a mixer bowl, cream butter, confectioners' sugar, and sour cream until smooth. Mix in melted chocolate and vanilla to blend. Spread Sour Cream Frosting between layers and then on sides and top of cake. Store cake in refrigerator.

Stacked Crêpe Cake

Makes 8 to 10 servings

A seasoned crêpe pan or a small nonstick skillet is a must for this dessert. It is an easy but elegant, extravagant, trendy little cake that is much like a concept cake that many bakeries, especially the renowned *Lady M* in New York City, are making famous. Make your crêpes as thin and crisp as you can without burning them. Thicker crêpes make this more of a torte (softer and more cakey), but it is sumptuous regardless. This cake cuts best when well chilled.

This buttery stack of crêpes, all sandwiched together with layers of *crème légère*, takes classic French pastry elements and spins them into a luscious crêpes-and-cream concoction extraordinaire.

Crêpe Batter

2	cups all-purpose flour
1/8	teaspoon baking powder
1/4	teaspoon salt
1/3	cup sugar
2	cups milk
4	large eggs
1/3	cup unsalted butter, melted
1/2	teaspoon pure orange extract, optional
1	tablespoon pure vanilla extract
	Butter, for greasing pan

Custard Filling

1/2	cup all-purpose flour
1/2	cup white sugar
1/8	teaspoon salt
4	egg yolks
2	cups milk
2	teaspoons pure vanilla extract
1	tablespoon unsalted butter
2	cups whipping cream
2	to 3 tablespoons confectioners' sugar

Finishing Touch

Confectioners' sugar

For Crêpe Batter, place flour, baking powder, salt, and sugar in a food processor and blend briefly. Add milk, eggs, butter, and extracts and whiz to blend into a thin batter, about 15 seconds. Let batter rest 15 minutes. **Heat** a 10- or 11-inch nonstick skillet or special crêpe pan and dab in a little butter. Smear on 1/4 cup crêpe batter to coat pan.

Cook until bottom browns and then turn over once to cook other side until it, too, is nicely browned. Stack crêpes with parchment paper between each one to prevent sticking. Finish making crêpes, using all of batter. You might have extra to snack on with maple syrup, but this recipe allows for an imperfect practice crêpe or two. You should have 10 to 14 crêpes.

If you are not serving cake that day, you can chill crêpes overnight, covered, and assemble cake the next day.

For Custard Filling, you will be making a custard first, to which you will later add whipped cream.

To make Custard Filling, in a medium bowl, whisk together flour, sugar, salt, egg yolks, and 1/3 cup milk. In a medium saucepan, bring remaining 1²/₃ cups milk to a gentle boil. Whisk in egg yolk mixture, stirring all the while until mixture thickens and begins to bubble gently. Remove from heat and let cool 5 minutes before stirring in vanilla and butter. Spray surface of custard with nonstick cooking spray. Cool to almost room temperature; cover with plastic wrap (this will prevent skin from forming on top of custard). Refrigerate until needed.

To assemble cake, have crêpes nearby. Cut out a piece of parchment paper to line bottom of a 9- or 10-inch springform pan. Using springform pan bottom, trim crêpes and place each on a sheet of wax paper until all are trimmed. Replace pan bottom in cakepan.

Whip whipping cream with confectioners' sugar until stiff peaks form. In a large bowl, mix ⅓ of whipped cream into custard and then gently fold rest of whipped cream into custard. Place 1 crêpe on bottom of springform pan. Smear on ¼ to ⅓ cup filling. Place a crêpe on top, pressing lightly, and continue filling and stacking crêpes, pressing lightly each time you add a crêpe until filling is used up. Chill 2 to 4 hours or overnight.

To serve, unmold cake and sift confectioners' sugar over top.

Supermarket Yellow Cake for Strawberry Shortcake

Makes 6 to 8 servings

Whew—a long recipe name but a shorter-than-shortcake recipe to make. You know those tender, light yellow cake layers they sell in the supermarket to top with berries and whipped cream for shortcake? This recipe makes that sort of cake. It has cake-mix texture but homemade, from-scratch taste.

½   cup unsalted butter, softened
1   cup sugar, finely pulverized*
1   large egg
1½ teaspoons pure vanilla extract
1½ cups all-purpose flour
2   teaspoons baking powder
¼   teaspoon salt

1   cup warm milk

Finishing Touches

Confectioners' sugar, for dusting
Whipped cream
Fresh berries, diced or whole

*Pulse sugar in a food processor 1 to 2 minutes.

Preheat oven to 350°F. Generously spray a 9-inch round cakepan with nonstick cooking spray and line with a circle of parchment paper. Put pan on a large parchment paper–lined baking sheet.

In a mixer bowl (or use a food processor), cream butter and sugar until fluffy. Add egg and vanilla and blend well.

Fold in flour, baking powder, and salt. Drizzle in milk, blending well and ensuring that nothing is stuck in bottom of mixer.

Pour into prepared cakepan. Bake 35 to 40 minutes or until cake tests done when gently pressed with fingertips. Let cool 15 minutes. Remove from pan and place cake on a serving plate.

Dust with confectioners' sugar and serve with whipped cream and fresh diced strawberries, or ice cream and any mix of berries.

Pure vanilla extract can be costly, especially when vanilla prices rise worldwide. If you find a lesser brand of pure vanilla, you can, in fact, fortify it somewhat. To do this, add one or two cut-up vanilla beans to an inexpensive vanilla extract. The extra beans strengthen the infusion and make for a far more boldly flavored vanilla—perfect for all of your baking. Vanilla beans are available in gourmet shops and many grocery stores.

Sticky Date Toffee Cake with Hot Toffee Sauce

Makes 8 to 10 servings

This is the Aussie answer to tiramisù. It is a hot trend Down Under—and now here. Forget that it has dates (you won't notice in the least); you will only notice that this is a delightful cake with a pronounced toffee flavor and an exceptionally moist texture. This is a sweet treat that tastes like a sticky toffee pudding but cuts like a cake.

Cake

1½ cups pitted dates
1½ cups water
4 teaspoons pure vanilla extract
1 teaspoon baking soda
½ cup unsalted butter, softened
1 cup firmly packed light brown sugar
¼ cup white sugar
2 teaspoons finely minced orange zest

3 large eggs
2 cups all-purpose flour
1½ teaspoons baking powder
¼ teaspoon salt

Hot Toffee Sauce

¾ cup firmly packed light brown sugar
1 cup whipping cream
½ cup unsalted butter, softened
½ teaspoon pure vanilla extract

Preheat oven to 350°F. Line a baking sheet with parchment paper. Generously spray a 9-inch springform pan with nonstick cooking spray and line bottom with a circle of parchment paper. Place pan on prepared baking sheet.

In a medium saucepan, simmer dates in water and vanilla until they are softened and almost mushy. Remove from heat and stir in baking soda (mixture will foam a bit). Let cool well.

In a mixer bowl, cream butter with both sugars and orange zest until fluffy. Blend in eggs and then fold in flour, baking powder, and salt. Blend well. Add dates. Spoon batter into prepared pan and bake until just set, 35 to 40 minutes.

Meanwhile, make Hot Toffee Sauce. Bring brown sugar, cream, and butter to a simmer and let simmer 5 minutes to thicken. Stir in vanilla.

When cake is done, poke holes all over it with a skewer and then drizzle sauce onto warm cake and allow it to be partially absorbed. Serve warm or at room temperature. Refrigerate leftovers and microwave portions when serving. This cake is also good with crème anglaise.

cake creations   227

Jamaican Banana Layer Cake

Makes 12 to 16 servings

This is one of my career-starter cakes, a specialty layer cake I created for a restaurant where I once worked. I discovered not everyone likes cheesecake, carrot cake, or solid chocolate cake. This moist, fragrant, luscious banana cake is a tropical symphony, and it keeps well.

Dark rum is my preference in this cake, but any type of rum will taste great, actually.

1½ cups heavy cream, soured*
1 tablespoon lemon juice
1 cup unsalted butter, softened
2 cups sugar
4 large eggs
2 teaspoons pure vanilla extract
1 tablespoon strong coffee or rum
1 cup pureed banana
3½ cups all-purpose flour
4 teaspoons baking powder
½ teaspoon baking soda
½ teaspoon salt
⅛ teaspoon ground cinnamon
1 cup sweetened shredded coconut
½ cup finely chopped macadamia nuts

½ cup semisweet chocolate chips

Jamaican Frosting

4 tablespoons cream cheese, softened
¾ cup unsalted butter, softened
3 to 4 cups confectioners' sugar
1 tablespoon rum
4 to 6 tablespoons, or as required, strong coffee

Finishing Touches

2 to 3 bananas, thinly sliced
Toasted coconut
Toasted chopped macadamia nuts

*To sour the cream, in a small bowl, stir cream with lemon juice and let stand until cream curdles.

Preheat oven to 350°F. Generously spray three 9-inch round cakepans with nonstick cooking spray. Place on parchment paper–lined baking sheets.

In a large mixer bowl, cream butter with sugar until pasty. Add eggs, vanilla, coffee or rum, and then pureed banana. Fold in soured cream and then fold in flour, baking powder, baking soda, salt, and cinnamon. Blend well, scraping bottom of bowl often to ensure ingredients are properly blended.

Spoon batter evenly into prepared pans. Sprinkle coconut, nuts, and chocolate chips over batter in each pan.

Bake 30 to 35 minutes until cakes spring back when gently pressed with fingertips. Cool 10 minutes. Invert layers onto a large sheet of parchment paper on a work surface and transfer to freezer to chill 30 minutes.

For Jamaican Frosting, place all ingredients in a mixer bowl or food processor and blend, adding enough coffee as required to make a spreadable frosting.

To assemble cake, place 1 cake layer on a serving platter, smear on some frosting, and then add a layer of sliced bananas. Repeat with second layer, using remaining sliced bananas. Add final cake layer and frost top and sides of cake. Garnish top and sides with toasted coconut and macadamia nuts. Chill slightly before serving.

Irish Whiskey Apple Cake

Makes 12 to 14 servings

You can coat the inner sides of your baking pan with finely ground rolled oats to create a crunchy crust.

Apple Filling

5	cups apples, cored, pared, and sliced*
1/3	cup golden raisins, plumped, dried (see page 18), and minced
2	tablespoons fresh lemon juice
1/4	cup sugar
2	teaspoons ground cinnamon

Cake

2	cups sugar
1	cup unsalted butter, softened
2	teaspoons finely grated lemon zest

4	large eggs
1½	teaspoons pure vanilla extract
1	tablespoon fresh lemon juice
1/4	cup apple juice
1/4	cup favorite Irish whiskey
3	cups all-purpose flour
1	tablespoon baking powder
½	teaspoon salt

Finishing Touch

2	tablespoons sugar mixed with 1 teaspoon ground cinnamon

*I recommend Golden Delicious and Cortland apples, not Granny Smith, for this dessert.

Preheat oven to 350°F. Generously spray a 9- or 10-inch angel food cakepan or tube pan with nonstick cooking spray. Line a baking sheet with parchment paper and place pan on it.

Toss apples with raisins, lemon juice, sugar, and cinnamon. Set aside.

In a mixer bowl, cream sugar with butter and lemon zest until smooth. Add eggs, vanilla, lemon juice, apple juice, and whiskey. Fold in flour, baking powder, and salt to make a smooth batter. Stir apple mixture into batter and then spoon batter into prepared pan. Dust with sugar-cinnamon mixture.

Bake until cake springs back when gently pressed with fingertips, about 75 to 90 minutes. Cool well before unmolding to a serving plate and cutting.

Caramel-Chocolate Cookie-Stuffed Sour Cream Deluxe Cake

Makes 12 to 16 servings

Every once in a while, you need to make a huge, decadent coffee cake like this one that keeps well, is homey but elegant, and is just fraught with good things.

This cake is stuffed full of cookie-bar chunks, hunks of milk chocolate, dark chocolate chips, and swirls of amber dulce de leche. This is a big, bold, masterful cake.

Sinking Chips Cause Cake Slips

Ever notice how sometimes things like chocolate chips sink in a cake? To prevent that, you can use smaller chips or chill the cake batter before panning it and then dispersing the chips into the batter. You can also sprinkle in the chips rather than folding them in, strategically distributing them all over the batter and not in any one place.

1	cup unsalted butter, softened
2	cups sugar
5	large eggs
1	tablespoon pure vanilla extract
1	cup sour cream
4	cups all-purpose flour
4	teaspoons baking powder
½	teaspoon baking soda
½	teaspoon salt
3	cups coarsely chopped *Twix* candy bars (6 to 8 packages)
1	cup coarsely chopped milk chocolate bar
½	cup semisweet chocolate chips
1	cup chopped pecans, optional
¾	cup dulce de leche or thick caramel sundae topping
⅓	cup chocolate syrup

Finishing Touches

½	cup, approximately, melted semisweet chocolate chips
	Confectioners' sugar, for dusting, optional

Preheat oven to 350°F. Generously spray a 10-inch angel food cakepan with nonstick cooking spray. Place pan on a parchment paper–lined baking sheet.

In a mixer, cream butter and sugar until light and fluffy and well blended. Add eggs, vanilla, and sour cream and mix well. Fold in flour, baking powder, baking soda, and salt and blend, making sure nothing is stuck in well of mixing bowl. Fold in about one-third each of chopped candy bars, chocolate chips, and pecans (if using).

Spoon two-thirds of batter into prepared pan and add dollops of dulce de leche or caramel sundae topping and some chocolate syrup as you are spooning in batter. Deposit on another third each of candy bar pieces, chocolate chips, and pecans. Top with remaining third of batter and top this with remaining dulce de leche and chocolate syrup and remaining candy bar pieces, chocolate chips, and pecans. (Exact amounts are not that important; you are trying to layer cake batter with chunky ingredients and caramel and chocolate syrups. It doesn't have to be exact.) Swirl batter with a knife, making sure chunkier pieces, such as candy bar pieces (on top), are somewhat covered with batter so they bake into top surface of cake.

Bake until cake springs back when gently pressed with fingertips, about 75 to 85 minutes. Cool well and then unmold cake onto a serving plate. Drizzle with melted chocolate. Chill cake 20 minutes or so and then dust with confectioners' sugar, if desired.

Baking with Fluted Tube Pans

Here are some things you need to know for Bundt cake–baking success:

Many a Bundt pan is labeled as nonstick. This means it is only sort of nonstick; the pan still needs treatment before baking and some TLC afterwards.

As for treating the pan, remember this: Use shortening or nonstick cooking spray, NOT butter. While butter wins in the taste department, it has a low burning point, which means it will burn faster, result in a browned cake bottom, and possibly create a greasy scum that sticks (invisibly, for the most part) on the pan.

Like most nonstick cookware, darker surfaces brown cakes faster. The remedy? Place pans on baking sheets lined with parchment paper. This helps cakes bake evenly, and the bottoms will not get scorched.

No matter what pan is labeled nonstick (except for the new silicone ones), they are not 100% nonstick. They may start out being 100% nonstick, but over time and with frequent baking, an invisible grease scum will coat the pan's surface. This buildup compromises the nonstick attributes. The best way to treat these pans is to thoroughly coat them with shortening. Cakes that have tons of neat things in them (lots of chocolate, gooey bits) will be more problematic, but again, shortening should help.

Lastly, make sure you really clean the Bundt pan well after each use. That means scalding hot water, soap, and soft cleaning pads—no steel wool.

Like most nonstick bakeware, darker surfaces brown cakes quickly. Remedy? Place pans on baking sheets lined with parchment paper. This helps cakes bake evenly, and the bottoms will not get scorched.

Chocolate Chip-Sour Cream Marble Cake

Makes 12 to 18 servings

This tender-crumbed, lusciously flavored butter cake slices like velvet.

Baker's Chocolate Paste

Hot water, as required

3 tablespoons cocoa powder

Cake Batter

1 cup unsalted butter, softened

2 cups sugar

4 large eggs

2½ teaspoons pure vanilla extract

1½ cups sour cream

3 cups all-purpose flour

2¾ teaspoons baking powder

¼ teaspoon baking soda

½ teaspoon salt

⅓ cup miniature chocolate chips
(or minced regular ones)

Finishing Touches

½ cup melted semisweet chocolate chips

Confectioners' sugar, for dusting

Preheat oven to 350°F. Generously grease a 12-cup Bundt pan with shortening. Place pan on a parchment paper–lined baking sheet.
In a small bowl, whisk hot water into cocoa to make a smooth paste (photo, at right).
In a mixer bowl, cream butter and sugar until light and fluffy. Blend in eggs and then vanilla and sour cream, scraping bottom of bowl every so often to make sure it is evenly combined. Fold in flour, baking powder, baking soda, and salt and blend well. Remove one-third of batter to another bowl and blend this with chocolate paste.
Spoon half of vanilla batter, then chocolate batter, and then dollops of remaining vanilla batter into prepared Bundt pan. Add miniature chips and swirl gently to distribute. Bake 65 to 75 minutes or until cake is browned and springs back when gently pressed with fingertips. If cake appears to be browning quickly yet does not seem done, reduce oven temperature to 325°F and bake a little longer. Let cake cool in pan 15 minutes and then invert onto a serving plate.
Drizzle with melted chocolate or simply dust with confectioners' sugar before serving.

Baker's chocolate paste is a quick trick from pastry chefs who use cocoa and hot water (or melted butter) instead of a square of melted chocolate. It is a neat, speedy trick for home bakers, too.

Lemon-Yogurt Cheesecake Bundt

Makes 12 to 14 servings

This is a meltingly tender, wonderfully tangy cake with a depth of lemony notes that perks up any palate.

Cake

1	cup light olive oil or vegetable oil
½	cup unsalted butter, melted
2	cups white sugar
	Zest of 1 lemon, finely minced
4	large eggs
2	cups plain yogurt
2	tablespoons fresh lemon juice
2	teaspoons pure vanilla extract
4	cups all-purpose flour
4	teaspoons baking powder
½	teaspoon baking soda
½	teaspoon salt

Lime Syrup

¾	cup water
½	cup lime juice
1½	cups sugar
¼	teaspoon lime oil

Lemon-Lime Cream Cheese Glaze

2	cups confectioners' sugar
4	ounces cream cheese, softened
2	to 3 tablespoons lemon and lime juice, mixed

Finishing Touches

Lemon and lime zest
Confectioners' sugar, for dusting

Preheat oven to 350°F. Generously spray a 9- or 10-inch fluted tube pan (not with a removable bottom) with nonstick cooking spray. Line a baking sheet with parchment paper and place pan on it.

In a mixer bowl, beat oil, butter, sugar, and lemon zest together until well blended, about 3 to 5 minutes. Add eggs, yogurt, juice, and vanilla; blend well, about 2 minutes. Fold in flour, baking powder, baking soda, and salt and blend well, making sure no uncombined ingredients cling to bottom of mixing bowl. Spoon batter into prepared pan.

Bake until cake is set and tests done with a cake skewer that comes out clean, about 60 to 80 minutes. Cake will have fine cracks on the surface. If cake is brown on top but doesn't seem done inside, reduce oven temperature to 325°F and let bake at lower temperature until done. Cool in pan 15 minutes before unmolding onto a serving platter.

Meanwhile, for Lime Syrup, in a small saucepan, bring all ingredients to a boil. Let simmer 5 minutes. Cool. Poke holes all over cake with a cake skewer. Drizzle some of syrup over cake. Let set. Repeat several times over a 30-minute period.

For Lemon-Lime Cream Cheese Glaze, blend all ingredients in a medium bowl with a whisk or in a food processor to make a drippy glaze. Put glaze in a measuring cup with a pouring spout and drizzle over cake. Garnish with citrus zest and edible fresh flowers or dust with confectioners' sugar.

Dark Fudge Bundt Cake

Makes 12 to 14 servings

This moist, tall cake is perfect when you want a deep, dark chocolate cake that is free of fuss and doesn't require icing or glaze, just a dusting of confectioners' sugar. This is a pass-this-recipe-down-and-around keeper.

Cake

1¾ cups white sugar

1   cup firmly packed brown sugar

1   cup unsalted butter, melted

3   large eggs

2   teaspoons pure vanilla extract

3¼ cups all-purpose flour

¾   cup cocoa powder

2   teaspoons baking powder

1½ teaspoons baking soda

½   teaspoon salt

1¾ cups warm coffee or flat cola

Finishing Touches

¾   cup semisweet chocolate chips

Confectioners' sugar

Preheat oven to 350°F. Generously grease a 12-cup Bundt pan or 9- or 10-inch fluted tube pan with shortening and place pan on a parchment paper–lined baking sheet.

In a mixer bowl, by hand or in a food processor, combine white sugar, brown sugar, and butter. Add eggs and vanilla; beat 1 minute until smooth. Add flour, cocoa, baking powder, baking soda, and salt. Stir briefly and then drizzle in coffee or cola, stirring at the same time to make a smooth batter.

Spoon batter into prepared pan. Bake 60 to 72 minutes or until top springs back when pressed with fingertips. (Bundt cakes often take longer to bake than tube-pan cakes do.)

To finish cake, sprinkle chocolate chips on top of cake as soon as it comes out of oven and allow to sit on cake to melt. Use a butter knife to swirl melted chocolate in a decorative fashion. As cake comes to room temperature, give it a gentle shake to loosen it from bottom of pan—but do not remove it from pan. Place cake in fridge to firm up chocolate. Once chocolate is well set, place a plate on top of pan and invert cake onto plate. (If any of melted chocolate gets on the plate when you do this—just smear it back on top of cake with a butter knife or metal spatula). When chocolate is cooled and set, dust with confectioners' sugar.

When working with chocolate, remember that coffee tends to enhance or sharpen chocolate's flavor. This recipe is a good example. Adding vanilla extract melds chocolate with coffee and mellows it; whereas adding almond or orange extract or a mint component, for example, adds yet another dimension of 'chocolate aura.'

Finnegan's Chocolate Cream Cake

Makes 12 to 16 servings

Here's an easy cake that slices like "buttah," is as moist as fresh bread, and tastes like fudge laced with Irish cream. As far as cakes go, this would be the pot o' gold. You can literally dump the entire list of cake ingredients into a food processor and then pour the batter into the pan—and you would still have success.

Cake

1	cup unsalted butter, softened
2	cups white sugar
1	cup firmly packed light brown sugar
3	large eggs
2	teaspoons pure vanilla extract
3	cups all-purpose flour
¾	cup cocoa powder
2½	teaspoons baking powder
¾	teaspoon baking soda
½	teaspoon salt
1⅓	cups brewed warm coffee
⅓	cup Irish cream liqueur or milk

Chocolate Cream Glaze

¾	cup whipping cream
1	cup semisweet chocolate chips
¼	cup Irish cream liqueur or strong coffee

Finishing Touch

Confectioners' sugar

Preheat oven to 350°F. Generously grease a 12-cup Bundt pan or a 10-inch tube pan with shortening. Place pan on a parchment paper–lined baking sheet.

In a mixer bowl, cream butter with both sugars. Then add eggs and vanilla. Blend on low speed 1 minute until smooth. Add flour, cocoa, baking powder, baking soda, and salt. Stir briefly; then drizzle in coffee and Irish cream, stirring at the same time to make a smooth, somewhat loose batter.

Spoon batter into prepared pan. Bake 55 to 65 minutes or until cake springs back when gently pressed with fingertips. (Bundt cakes take longer to bake than tube pan cakes do.) Cool cake well and then invert onto a serving platter.

For Chocolate Cream Glaze, bring whipping cream to a boil in a small saucepan. Add chocolate chips, reduce temperature to low, and whisk to blend and melt chocolate. Add Irish cream. Remove from heat after 1 to 2 minutes and stir until smooth. Let cool to room temperature before using. If you cannot glaze cake right away, refrigerate glaze and gently rewarm and then drizzle over cake.

Place cake in fridge to firm up chocolate after glazing. Once chocolate is set, dust with confectioners' sugar.

Black-and-White Cookie Ripple Coffee Cake

Makes 12 to 16 servings

The inner sandwich cookies melt slightly and become a fudgy ripple in this cake, while the top cookies remain slightly crunchy.

Cake

1	cup unsalted butter, softened
2	cups sugar
6	large eggs
1	tablespoon pure vanilla extract
1¾	cups buttermilk
4	cups all-purpose flour
4	teaspoons baking powder
¼	teaspoon baking soda
½	teaspoon salt
30	chocolate sandwich cookies, coarsely chopped

Glaze

1½	cups confectioners' sugar
2	to 6 tablespoons water, as required
½	teaspoon pure vanilla extract

Preheat oven to 350°F. Line a baking sheet with parchment paper and set aside. Generously spray a 9-inch tube pan with nonstick cooking spray and place pan on prepared baking sheet.

In a mixer bowl, cream softened butter and sugar on medium speed until well blended. Add eggs, 2 at a time, and blend on medium speed until blended, scraping bowl often to make sure no butter or sugar sticks to bottom. Add vanilla and buttermilk and blend well. Fold in flour, baking powder, baking soda, and salt and blend until batter is smooth, about 2 to 4 minutes.

Pour two-thirds of batter into prepared pan. Sprinkle two-thirds of cookie pieces over batter, putting more on perimeter than directly in middle area (cookie pieces are less likely to sink when dispersed this way). Top with remaining batter and top batter evenly with remaining cookie pieces.

Bake 45 minutes and then reduce oven temperature to 325°F. Finish baking until cake tests done with a cake skewer that almost comes out clean, another 15 to 20 minutes. Cool 10 minutes in pan before turning cake out onto a serving plate.

For Glaze, in a small bowl, whisk together confectioners' sugar, water, and vanilla to make a drizzly glaze. Drizzle glaze over top of cake with a fork or whisk. Let glaze set.

The chocolate sandwich cookie love affair continues with this riveting, tall, golden, moist coffee cake featuring chopped cookies as the streusel, all finished with a stippling of vanilla glaze.

Hummingbird Carrot Cake

Makes 14 to 20 servings

This fabulous, moist, flavorful cake predates the '70s version of carrot cake. It is an all-season, winning dessert that freezes like a charm. Nothing beats this cake for flavor. If you want it as a sheet cake, use a 13- x 9-inch pan and divide the frosting ingredients in half. Like most carrot cakes, this is easily mixed by hand.

Cake

3	cups all-purpose flour
2	cups sugar
2½	teaspoons baking powder
½	teaspoon baking soda
1	teaspoon ground cinnamon
½	teaspoon salt
3	large eggs
1½	cups vegetable oil
2	teaspoons pure vanilla extract
1	(8-ounce) can crushed pineapple, undrained
2	cups chopped pecans
2	cups finely chopped banana
¾	cup grated carrot

Cream Cheese Frosting

2	(8-ounce) packages cream cheese, softened
1	cup unsalted butter, softened
4	cups, approximately, confectioners' sugar
2	teaspoons pure vanilla extract

Finishing Touches

Ground pecans
Ground cinnamon

Preheat oven to 350°F. Generously spray three 9-inch round cakepans with nonstick cooking spray. Place pans on parchment paper–lined baking sheets.

In a large bowl, combine flour, sugar, baking powder, baking soda, cinnamon, and salt and blend briefly. Add eggs and oil; stir until dry ingredients are moistened. Stir in vanilla, pineapple, pecans, chopped banana, and carrot; blend well.

Spoon batter into prepared pans. Bake 25 to 30 minutes. Let cool in pans 20 minutes before unmolding onto wire racks to cool.

For Cream Cheese Frosting, mix all ingredients together until blended. Spread frosting between layers and then on sides and top of cake. Garnish with ground pecans and a light dusting of cinnamon.

Vintage Southern Tea Room Caramel Cake

Makes 12 to 16 servings

Imagine a golden-crumbed cake that is moist but not too heavy (nor too light) and finished with a retro brown sugar frosting. It tastes like penuche fudge soaked into a glorious yellow cake. One bite and you are in *Pleasantville.* This is good as a layer cake and works just as well as a homey 13- x 9-inch sheet cake if you prefer cutting hunks of caramel-soaked cake instead of wedges of layer cake. Either way, this is totally amazing.

Cake

2½ cups all-purpose flour
2   cups sugar
2   tablespoons cornstarch
1   tablespoon baking powder
⅛ teaspoon baking soda
½ teaspoon salt
1   cup unsalted butter, cut into chunks
3   large eggs
1   egg yolk
2½ teaspoons pure vanilla extract
1   teaspoon butter extract, optional
1⅓ cups warm buttermilk

Brown Sugar Frosting

1   cup unsalted butter
2   cups firmly packed light brown sugar
1   teaspoon baking soda
2   teaspoons corn syrup
Pinch salt
1   teaspoon pure vanilla extract

> **You don't see cakes like this around anymore, and they were once the star attractions of tea rooms, county fairs, and diners. Even chocoholics crave more of this cake after just one bite.**

Preheat oven to 350°F. Generously spray two 9-inch round cakepans with nonstick cooking spray and place pans on a large, parchment paper–lined baking sheet.

In a mixer bowl, place flour, sugar, cornstarch, baking powder, baking soda, and salt and blend ingredients. Add butter and blend to break up butter into dry ingredients to get a grainy mixture. Blend in eggs, egg yolk, vanilla, butter extract, and buttermilk to make a batter, scraping sides and bottom of bowl occasionally to ensure batter is evenly blended.

Spoon batter into prepared pans. Bake until cakes spring back when gently pressed with fingertips, 30 to 35 minutes.

Cool in pans 15 minutes before unmolding onto a wire rack to cool.

For Brown Sugar Frosting, place butter, brown sugar, baking soda, corn syrup, salt, and vanilla in a 3-quart saucepan. Cook over low heat until mixture thickens and reaches soft ball stage (234°F). If you don't have a thermometer, cook mixture 20 to 30 minutes until a bit of mixture seems to hold together like soft taffy when dropped on a cold plate. You can increase heat to make it cook faster, but slow and steady makes for better results.

Remove frosting from heat and let it cool and thicken. You can whip half the frosting with a mixer on medium speed 2 minutes and then on high 1 minute to lighten. Use this to frost two layers of cake together; it will spread like frosting. Pour remaining slightly warm frosting over top layer of cake and let it drip down. This cake freezes well.

Italian Cream Wedding Cake

Makes 10 to 14 servings; also pictured on page 220

For years, I heard about a cake with this name, and home bakers sent e-mails galore asking for the recipe. I researched, baked, taste-tested, and finally created a definitive Italian Cream Cake, which is great party fare or terrific as a special wedding cake. It also keeps well and serves a crowd. If you are really rushed, you can use instant vanilla pudding instead of making the pastry cream.

You can also offer this special-occasion cake with raspberries or lemon sorbet on the side.

Pastry Cream Filling

6	egg yolks
½	cup sugar
¼	cup all-purpose flour
2	tablespoons cornstarch
2	cups milk
1½	teaspoons pure vanilla extract

Cake Batter

½	cup unsalted butter, softened
½	cup shortening or unsalted butter
1½	cups sugar, divided
5	large eggs, separated
2	teaspoons pure vanilla extract
¼	teaspoon pure almond extract
½	teaspoon pure lemon extract
½	teaspoon pure orange extract
¾	cup buttermilk
2	cups all-purpose flour

2	teaspoons baking powder
¼	teaspoon baking soda
⅛	teaspoon salt
½	cup toasted shredded coconut
½	cup toasted pecans, finely chopped

Butter–Cream Cheese Frosting

¼	cup unsalted butter, softened
¾	cup cream cheese, softened
2	cups confectioners' sugar
1½	teaspoons pure vanilla extract
1	teaspoon fresh lemon juice
Milk, as necessary	

Finishing Touches

Chopped toasted pecans
Toasted shredded coconut
White chocolate shavings or curls

Make Pastry Cream Filling a few hours ahead or up to 3 days ahead. For pastry cream, mix egg yolks and sugar in a mixer with whisk attachment 6 minutes on high speed. In a small bowl, whisk flour and cornstarch together.

Pour milk and vanilla into a 3-quart heavy saucepan and heat to simmering.

Slowly add half of hot milk to egg yolk mixture, whisking all the while so as not to cook eggs. Pour egg mixture back into milk mixture in pot. Whisk briskly, increase heat, slowly add flour mixture, and cook until mixture thickens, about 2 to 3 minutes. Remove from heat and let cool.

Place pastry cream in a bowl; spray top lightly with nonstick cooking spray and then cover with plastic wrap. Refrigerate 2 to 3 hours or overnight.

Preheat oven to 350°F. Generously spray two 9-inch round cakepans with nonstick cooking spray. Place pans on a parchment paper–lined baking sheet.

For Cake Batter, in a mixer bowl, cream butter and shortening until well blended and fluffy. Add 1¼ cups sugar and mix well. Blend egg yolks into butter mixture, scraping down bowl every so often (if mixture seems curdled, add some of flour called for in Cake Batter recipe). Fold in vanilla,

almond, lemon, and orange extracts. Blend in buttermilk and then fold in remaining flour, baking powder, baking soda, and salt. Lastly, add coconut and nuts.

Place egg whites in a clean mixer bowl, and, using whisk attachment, whip egg whites on low speed of mixer until frothy. Increase speed and slowly dust in remaining ¼ cup sugar. Increase speed and whip until whites are stiff and glossy, about 3 to 4 minutes. Fold one-third of egg whites into cake batter. Then carefully fold in remaining whites so as to incorporate whites but not deflate batter.

Spoon batter into prepared pans. Bake until cakes spring back when gently pressed with fingertips, 25 to 30 minutes. Cool cake layers well, and, once cooled, cover loosely with wax paper while making frosting.

For Butter–Cream Cheese Frosting, cream butter and cream cheese in a mixer with paddle attachment until smooth. Add confectioners' sugar, vanilla, lemon juice, and as much milk as is required to get a smooth and spreadable consistency. Whip on medium speed 3 minutes.

To assemble, cut each cake in half horizontally. Whisk or mix chilled pastry cream with a spoon to loosen it. Place 1 cake layer on a serving platter and cover with one-third of Pastry Cream Filling. Sandwich remaining layers the same way, leaving top layer plain.

Frost cake sides and then top with Butter–Cream Cheese Frosting. Dust top with a fine mixture of pecans, coconut, and white chocolate shavings or curls. Chill 1 hour before serving (or up to 3 days).

La Diva Chocolate Cake

Makes 8 to 12 servings

A dual ganache treatment of both milk chocolate and then dark chocolate offers an unbelievable assault on the taste buds. This cake is great an hour after baking or five days later. You can also freeze it for two to three months. Why is it called a "diva" when it's so amenable? Good girls finish last—great cakes are real divas.

Every gal should have one perfect chocolate cake in her repertoire. And this one is perfect. It is easy, moist, and sturdy, and it cuts like smooth, chocolaty velvet.

Cake

2	cups all-purpose flour
½	cup cocoa powder
1½	teaspoons baking powder
¾	teaspoon baking soda
⅛	teaspoon salt
1	cup chopped semisweet chocolate
½	cup unsalted butter
1	cup boiling water
2	cups sugar
3	large eggs
2	teaspoons pure vanilla extract
½	cup sour cream
½	cup grated semisweet chocolate

Milk Chocolate Ganache

⅔	cup whipping cream
6	ounces milk chocolate, coarsely chopped

Dark Chocolate Ganache

¾	cup whipping cream
1¼	cups semisweet chocolate, chopped
2	tablespoons unsalted butter, cut into bits

Finishing Touches

Confectioners' sugar
Chocolate curls

Preheat oven to 350°F. Line a baking sheet with parchment paper. Generously spray a 10-inch springform pan with nonstick cooking spray and place pan on baking sheet.

For Cake, in a large bowl, hand-whisk flour, cocoa, baking powder, baking soda, and salt together. In a medium bowl, place chopped chocolate and butter and cover with boiling water, whisking to blend and melt chocolate. In a mixer bowl, on low speed, blend sugar, eggs, and vanilla very well until light, about 3 minutes. Fold in sour cream and then dry ingredients, melted chocolate, and grated chocolate. Blend well, scraping bowl often to ensure evenly blended batter, about 2 to 4 minutes. Spoon batter into prepared pan. Bake until cake springs back when gently pressed with fingertips, about 55 to 65 minutes. Cool in pan 15 minutes before unmolding. Wrap and freeze 1 hour before garnishing cake.

To make Milk Chocolate Ganache, in a small saucepan, bring cream to just simmering. Quickly stir in chopped milk chocolate and stir until it melts, turning off heat as you do so. Mix well and chill until very firm. Then whip in a mixer on high speed to fluff.

For Dark Chocolate Ganache, in a small saucepan, bring cream to just simmering. Quickly stir in chopped chocolate and continue stirring until it melts, turning off heat as you do so. Mix well. When it is thick, stir in butter to blend in. Let cool to room temperature. Chill until it can be poured over cake as a thick glaze.

To assemble and garnish cake, invert cake onto a serving platter. Spread Milk Chocolate Ganache on top of cake. Chill cake 20 to 30 minutes. Then pour Dark Chocolate Ganache over top of cake. Chill briefly and then garnish with confectioners' sugar, chocolate curls, or a pesticide-free red rose.

Fallen Soufflé Chocolate Torte

Makes 6 to 8 servings

Do not overbake this cake. It is meant to be a crusty-topped, soft, low-slung cake.

Cake

8	ounces semisweet chocolate
1	cup unsalted butter
8	egg whites
⅛	teaspoon salt
¾	cup sugar, divided
6	egg yolks

Finishing Touches

2	tablespoons cocoa powder
	Raspberries, pureed
2	cups whipped cream
	Melted semisweet chocolate, for drizzling

Digging into this cake is the closest you will come to eating a truffle with a fork.

Preheat oven to 325°F. Line bottom of a 9-inch springform pan with parchment paper and generously spray parchment and inner sides of pan with nonstick cooking spray.

In a double boiler set over low heat, melt 8 ounces chocolate and butter. Set aside to cool.

In a mixer bowl, using whisk attachment on low speed, whisk egg whites with salt until they foam a bit. Then increase to high speed and dust in ¼ cup sugar until fluffy and stiff. Transfer to a large bowl.

In mixer bowl, whisk egg yolks and remaining ½ cup sugar until very pale. Stir in melted chocolate–butter mixture. Fold in some egg whites to lighten chocolate and whisk very thoroughly. Gently fold in remaining egg whites in batches, showing more restraint and calmness so as to have a light, chocolaty batter.

Spoon batter into prepared pan. Bake about 35 to 45 minutes until barely set and still a bit wobbly. If you test cake at this point with a toothpick, it will come out with bits of batter on it—that is fine. Take cake out and, after 15 minutes, unmold onto a serving plate.

When cool, dust generously with cocoa or serve each piece with some raspberry puree and a dollop of whipped cream. You can also drizzle on warm melted semisweet chocolate.

Classic Dark Chocolate Layer Cake

Makes 12 to 14 servings

This is one of those big, fat layer cakes that stands tall, cuts clean, and is ultra impressive.

Cake

1	cup unsalted butter, softened
2	cups sugar
3	large eggs
2	teaspoons pure vanilla extract
2½	cups all-purpose flour
¾	cup cocoa powder
2¼	teaspoons baking powder
1	teaspoon baking soda
½	teaspoon salt
1	cup buttermilk
¾	cup sour cream

Icing

½	cup semisweet chocolate chips, melted and cooled
¾	cup unsalted butter, softened
1	teaspoon pure vanilla extract
¾	cup cocoa powder, measured and then sifted
3	to 4 cups confectioners' sugar, measured and then sifted
½	cup half-and-half or water

Finishing Touch

Chocolate shavings or curls

Preheat oven to 350°F. Generously spray two 9-inch round cakepans with nonstick cooking spray and line with parchment paper circles. Place pans on a parchment paper–lined baking sheet.

In a mixer bowl, cream butter and sugar until light and fluffy. Add eggs and vanilla and blend well. In a separate bowl, whisk together flour, cocoa, baking powder, baking soda, and salt. Fold dry ingredients into wet and mix, adding buttermilk and sour cream as mixture blends. Blend on low speed about 3 minutes, scraping sides and bottom once to incorporate all ingredients. Pour batter into prepared pans.

Bake on middle oven rack, 35 to 40 minutes, until cakes barely spring back when gently pressed with fingertips. Let cool in pan.

For Icing, in a mixer bowl, on low speed, blend melted chocolate with butter. Add vanilla, cocoa, and half of confectioners' sugar. Add remaining confectioners' sugar and mix slowly. Once sugar is more or less blended in, whip on high speed, using whisk attachment, adding a bit of half-and-half or water to get a light, fluffy consistency. If not using icing right away, rewhip before using. Add additional warm water (1 tablespoon at a time) to get correct consistency.

To frost cake, semi-freeze layers first, 20 to 45 minutes, for easier handling. Turn flatter side (the bottom) of 1 layer down. Ice that layer. Top it with other layer, with bottom of cake facing up. Press down lightly and finish icing sides and top of cake. Add chocolate shavings or curls.

I could tell you that chocolate is known to contain beneficial antioxidants that allay health concerns, but chocolate is first and foremost the most lavish, flavorful ingredient you can work with. It transforms everyday baking into extravagances. Chocolate, whether you are a quiet fan or an ardent follower, is incredibly satisfying, delivering more taste per bite than almost any other flavor. Whether you make a modest chocolate treat or an extravagant one, anything with chocolate in it exponentially ups the feeling of the occasion. Brown sugar and cinnamon are lovely, but chocolate tells you to prepare for something special!

Chocolate Curls

A quick and easy way to make chocolate shavings or curls is to shave the edge of a chocolate bar with a vegetable peeler.

Chocolate-Zucchini Cake with Chocolate-Orange Glaze

Makes 12 to 14 servings

Try this excellent cake that is moist with zucchini, mellow with chocolate, and gently spiked with a touch of orange. It helped make my cake-baker reputation in many of the cafés where I used to supply desserts.

Cake

½   cup unsalted butter, softened
½   cup vegetable oil
2   cups sugar
4   large eggs
3   ounces semisweet chocolate, melted
2   teaspoons pure vanilla extract
Zest of a small orange, finely minced
½   cup milk
2   cups shredded zucchini
2½ cups all-purpose flour
2½ teaspoons baking powder
1   teaspoon baking soda
¼   teaspoon salt
1   teaspoon ground cinnamon

Chocolate-Orange Glaze

3   ounces semisweet chocolate, melted
1   to 2 tablespoons unsalted butter
¼   teaspoon orange extract

Finishing Touches

Cocoa powder
Confectioners' sugar, for dusting

Preheat oven to 350°F. Generously grease a 12-cup Bundt pan or 10-inch angel food cakepan with shortening; place on a parchment paper–lined baking sheet.

In a mixer bowl, cream butter and oil with sugar until well blended. Add eggs, 1 at a time, and then melted chocolate, vanilla, orange zest, and milk. Stir in shredded zucchini. Fold in flour, baking powder, baking soda, salt, and cinnamon and blend until batter is thoroughly combined. Spoon batter into prepared pan.

Bake approximately 1 hour or until cake springs back when gently pressed with fingertips. Let cake cool in pan 15 minutes and then invert onto a serving plate.

For Chocolate-Orange Glaze, melt chocolate with butter in a saucepan over medium-low heat. Add extract. Stir to make a soft glaze and then drizzle over cake. You can also frost with a favorite icing or simply dust with cocoa or confectioners' sugar.

Sweet Cream Chocolate Cake

Makes 12 to 14 servings

Not all cakes need buttermilk or sour cream. Some tender chocolate cakes—like this one—have a sweet-cream base and are so good and old-fashioned in the best of ways.

Cake

4	ounces unsweetened chocolate
¾	cup unsalted butter, softened
1½	cups sugar
3	large eggs
2	egg yolks
2	teaspoons pure vanilla extract
1	teaspoon chocolate extract or 1 tablespoon strong coffee
1	cup whipping cream
½	cup ice water
2	cups all-purpose flour
¼	cup cocoa powder
2	teaspoons baking powder
½	teaspoon baking soda
½	teaspoon salt

Icing

½	cup semisweet chocolate chips, melted and cooled
¾	cup unsalted butter, softened
1	teaspoon pure vanilla extract
¾	cup cocoa powder, measured and then sifted
3	to 4 cups confectioners' sugar, measured and then sifted
½	cup half-and-half or water

Make this a layer cake by spooning the batter into two greased 9-inch round cakepans lined with parchment paper. Bake at 350°F for 35 to 38 minutes; then frost as directed below.

Preheat oven to 325°F. Generously spray a 13- x 9-inch pan or a 10-inch springform pan with nonstick cooking spray; place pan on a parchment paper–lined baking sheet.

Melt chocolate and allow to cool. Meanwhile, in a mixer bowl, cream butter and sugar until light and well blended. Fold in eggs, yolks, vanilla, and chocolate extract or strong coffee. Blend well, 2 to 3 minutes, scraping bowl often to ensure nothing is stuck in well of mixer bowl. Blend in melted chocolate and then fold in whipping cream, water, flour, cocoa, baking powder, baking soda, and salt. Blend well on low speed of mixer to make a soft, smooth batter, about 2 to 4 minutes.

Pour batter into prepared pan. Bake until cake springs back when gently pressed with fingertips, about 65 to 75 minutes. Let cake cool in pan on a wire rack.

For Icing, in a mixer bowl, on low speed, blend melted chocolate chips with butter. Add vanilla, cocoa, and half of confectioners' sugar. Add remaining confectioners' sugar and mix slowly. Once sugar is more or less blended in, whip on high speed, using whisk attachment, adding a bit of half-and-half or water to get a light, fluffy consistency. If not using icing right away, rewhip before using. Add additional warm water (1 tablespoon at a time) to get correct consistency. Frost top of cake if baked in 13- x 9-inch pan. If baked in springform pan, unmold cake and frost top and sides.

To frost as a layer cake, semi-freeze layers first, 20 to 45 minutes, for easier handling. Turn flatter side (the bottom) of 1 layer down. Frost that layer. Top it with other layer, with bottom of cake facing up. Press down lightly and finish frosting cake.

Chocolate Mousse Cake

Makes 12 to 20 servings

This is a triumph—a real clip-and-save recipe you will enjoy for special occasions and holidays or when you are asked to "bring the dessert." A rich chocolate mousse is sandwiched between layers of moist chocolate cake—all topped with a slick ganache glaze. A combo of chocolate shavings and confectioners' sugar would do nicely as a finale, or you could use just a slight shower of cocoa. Then trim with a red rose, and you're good to go. This is good enough for a wedding reception. The best part is it is as easy as pie to make. It is simply cake, a foolproof mousse, and glaze. But wow!

What Is Ganache?

There are glazes, icings, frostings, and toppings, but ganache is in a class by itself. It is essentially chocolate and whipping cream melted together. As it chills, the mixture goes from being a glaze to a stiff chocolate mixture that is the center of truffles. You can also whip chilled ganache with some unsalted butter to make a fluffy frosting that is rich and doesn't have the telltale grit of confectioners' buttercream. Pastry chefs adore ganache, and it is easy enough to make that it should be in every home baker's repertoire. Just remember that warming it up restores its pourable glazelike nature, and chilling it makes it whippable. Even as a glaze, it is also richer and more dimensional in flavor than simple melted chocolate.

Cake

2½ cups all-purpose flour
2   cups sugar
1   cup cocoa powder, measured and then sifted
1½ teaspoons baking powder
1½ teaspoons baking soda
½   teaspoon salt
1¼ cups unsalted butter, melted
1½ cups warm flat cola
3   large eggs
2   teaspoons pure vanilla extract
¼   teaspoon ground cinnamon

Chocolate Cream Mousse Filling

2   cups semisweet chocolate chips

⅓   cup boiling water
3   cups whipping cream
Confectioners' sugar

Glossy Chocolate Ganache

¾   cup heavy whipping cream
1   cup coarsely chopped Swiss semisweet chocolate
½   cup coarsely chopped milk chocolate

Finishing Touches

Chocolate shavings
Confectioners' sugar
Cocoa powder, for dusting

Preheat oven to 350°F. Generously spray a 9- or 10-inch springform pan with nonstick cooking spray. Place pan on a parchment paper–lined baking sheet.

In a mixer bowl, blend flour, sugar, cocoa, baking powder, baking soda, and salt together and then add remaining cake ingredients in the well, using a whisk and blending, until batter is smooth (it will be a somewhat thin batter).

Bake until cake springs back when gently pressed with fingertips, 45 to 60 minutes. Unmold cake from pan; chill in freezer 30 minutes or wrap and refrigerate until needed.

For Chocolate Cream Mousse Filling, place chocolate chips in a food processor and grind 1 to 2 minutes until almost finely ground—but not too fine. Continue processing while adding boiling water to melt chocolate until smooth, 1 to 2 minutes.

In a mixer bowl, whip whipping cream with confectioners' sugar until stiff. Fold about one-third of whipping cream briskly into melted chocolate. Then fold remaining whipping cream, in dollops, gently into chocolate. Chill 1 to 3 hours or overnight.

To make Glossy Chocolate Ganache, heat cream in a small saucepan. When it begins to bubble gently, add chocolates and stir well. Remove from heat as chocolate melts and continue stirring until ganache is smooth.

Pour ganache into a measuring cup with a pouring spout and set aside.

To assemble cake, using a large serrated bread knife, split cake into 3 layers. Assemble cake so that bottom (the flat side) becomes the top and the top is now the bottom. If top is very uneven, trim top of cake to make it more level.

Whip Chocolate Cream Mousse Filling lightly with a whisk and spread half on first layer. Cover with other cake layer and then spread on remaining mousse. Press top layer down gently but firmly. Place cake on a wire rack set over a large platter.

Pour ganache on top of cake (pour right onto the center), allowing excess to drip down cake sides. Chill cake briefly and then recoup any excess ganache and repeat process. Chill cake well before serving and garnish, if desired, with chocolate shavings and confectioners' sugar, or a dusting of cocoa and a pesticide-free red rose in the center.

Pastry Chef Buttercream
Makes 2 to 3 cups

Pastry chefs rely on a fondant-based buttercream as their mainstay frosting. Ask your neighborhood baker or pastry chef for fondant or see the note below to source out soft white fondant, which is the base of this icing. This recipe results in that fluffy, smooth, silky frosting that everyone loves and associates with store-bought cupcakes. It holds its shape and rewhips into the perfect consistency.

1 pound white fondant*	¼ teaspoon or more of other pure extracts, to taste, optional
1½ cups unsalted butter, softened	Food coloring, optional
½ cup shortening	
1 to 2 teaspoons pure vanilla extract	

*Soft white fondant is available from specialty pastry and baking suppliers, or wholesale or online retailers. See also our "Source Guide" on page 316.

In a mixer bowl, using paddle attachment, blend fondant with butter and shortening on low speed, about 3 to 4 minutes to blend well.

Switch to whisk attachment on mixer and whip on high speed to increase volume, about 5 to 7 minutes. Stop machine and add vanilla and, if desired, other extracts and food coloring and whip on medium speed another minute to combine. (Buttercream can be frozen up to 2 months or refrigerated up to 1 week.)

To rewhip before using, allow buttercream to warm up about 30 minutes and rewhip to fluff, about 2 to 3 minutes.

Use an offset spatula or the back of a spoon to smear deep swirls of frosting onto a layer cake. Always frost the top last.

Oh-So-Coconutty Cupcakes

Makes 12 cupcakes

These little cakes are coconutty to the nth degree. They include coconut milk, shredded coconut, and coconut extract in the batter plus a buttery frosting that's also anointed with coconut.

Coconut milk comes in a 12-ounce can. You must refrigerate it thoroughly so that it thickens to a consistency of somewhat solid fat. Shake the can first and then refrigerate it for a night or two before you make these cupcakes.

Cupcakes

1½ cups sugar

¾ cup unsalted butter, softened

3 large eggs

2 teaspoons pure vanilla extract

1 teaspoon pure coconut extract

¼ teaspoon pure almond extract

2½ cups all-purpose flour

2 teaspoons baking powder

¼ teaspoon baking soda

½ teaspoon salt

¾ cup chilled coconut milk

½ cup sweetened shredded coconut

Coconut Frosting

½ cup unsalted butter, softened

3 to 4 cups confectioners' sugar

Milk or water, as required (3 to 6 tablespoons)

1 teaspoon pure vanilla extract

1 teaspoon pure coconut extract

¼ teaspoon pure almond extract

Food coloring, if desired, to tint icing

Finishing Touch

Sweetened shredded coconut, for garnish, optional

Preheat oven to 375°F. Line a baking sheet with parchment paper. Line a muffin pan with paper liners and place pan on prepared baking sheet. Spray top of cupcake pan with nonstick cooking spray.

In a food processor, finely pulverize sugar 1 to 2 minutes. Add butter and process to blend butter and sugar well. Add eggs and extracts and process to blend. Fold in flour, baking powder, baking soda, and salt and pulse to blend a bit. Add chilled coconut milk. Blend well. Fold coconut in briefly.

Using an ice-cream scoop, deposit batter into prepared pan, filling almost full. Place on upper rack of oven, immediately reduce oven temperature to 350°F and bake 30 to 35 minutes or until cupcakes are golden and spring back when gently pressed with fingertips. Cool well.

Meanwhile, whip Coconut Frosting ingredients in food processor or a mixer until light and fluffy, adding food coloring, if desired. Smear frosting on cupcakes or pipe with a pastry bag using a star tip. Sprinkle coconut onto frosted cupcakes, if desired.

say
cheesecake

I began my baking career with mammoth muffins, mile-high carrot cakes, and showstopping cheesecakes. My cheesecakes were gorgeous, statuesque, flamboyant affairs. They weren't just cakes; they were creations and events. More succinctly, they were concept cakes. My cheesecakes did more than their share to establish my reputation as a baking professional. When *Bon Appétit* magazine requested my *Oreo* Cheesecake recipe for their famed R.S.V.P. column, I knew cheesecakes were in my destiny and were certainly my calling. I have never lost interest in creating (or eating) a new cheesecake.

What is it about cheesecake that immediately inspires glamour? Is it the decadence of a cake that is simply pure, rich cream cheese sweetened just so, kissed with vanilla, and lofty as a cloud? Or is it the notion of something smooth and creamy set in a buttery crust and crowned with crimson strawberries shimmering under a halo of apricot glaze? Cheesecake, even a modest one, has sheer glam appeal, being a silken concoction that unapologetically pulls out all the stops.

Most bakers will claim to have the best cheesecake, for no other recipe, save chocolate chip cookies, can account for such disproportionate culinary ego. Long after a cordon bleu meal fades to Cheshire cat–like memory, the taste of a superb cheesecake seems forever recorded on one's taste buds. "Wow, that was a great meal," people will say, "but, oh, *that cheesecake!*"

Three components separate the quality of cheesecakes: the recipe, the technique, and finally, the visual appeal of finishing touches. The recipes in this chapter showcase my most decadent creations.

Ingredients

The basic premise is to start with the best ingredients. Most cheesecakes are designed to feed a crowd, and being so rich, a little cheesecake goes a long way. This is why cheesecakes are incomparable celebration and party cakes, which means it is all the more important to use the crème de la crème of ingredients.

Cheesecakes can be made successfully with ricotta cheese, cottage cheese, low-fat cream cheese, and tofu, but for that truly classic texture we associate with this queenly dessert, pure cream cheese is a must.

Now that you've invested in the cheese, consider other ingredients. Unless otherwise specified, use large eggs. Extra large eggs won't give you more of a good thing but rather offset a presumably perfect balance of liquid to solid and eggs.

As for sugar, granulated white sugar is generally called for, although honey or brown sugar does wondrous things for maple or pumpkin cheesecake. And in some of my recipes, I use sweetened condensed milk, which adds a dairy sweetness and helps achieve an incredibly smooth texture.

These three ingredients—cream cheese, eggs, and sugar—appear in almost all cheesecakes. Everything else, including the crust, is a variable. Additions of sour cream, whipping cream, flour, cornstarch, preserves, nuts, and liqueurs are all happily subject to each recipe or baker's creative intervention. Cheesecake is so amicable when it comes to flavor additions that it is an ideal cake to change thematically via flavors and ingredients. There are bold and lavish cakes that pull out all the stops, but there are also some recipes that are pure and simple. And cheesecake, even in that humbler guise, is still a charmer.

Equipment

Special cakes demand special pans, and cheesecake is a perfect example. Springform pans allow the chilled cake to be properly unmolded for serving without marring the cake's surface or gouging out its sides. Almost any new pan performs well; it is when pans get bent or their spring mechanism wears out that you have to watch for leakage. The best rule of thumb is to find high-sided pans (3 inches or higher) that allow you to pile on the batter and not worry about overflow surprises. See page 22 in "Baking Secrets" for my recommended list of springform pan sizes for the home baker.

This is quite a conundrum in cheesecakes: Does one grease or not grease the pan? Logic dictates that a greased pan would help when unmolding the baked cake. Experience tells me that the cake rises higher if you allow the delicate batter to cling to ungreased sides. I tend to make large cheesecakes that reach the top of the pan, so I appreciate having some release that greased sides offer; therefore, I opt to spray my cheesecake pan's inner sides with nonstick spray.

To remove a baked, chilled cheesecake from its pan, run a flexible metal icing spatula that has been dipped in hot water along the inner sides of the pan. This loosens the cake from the sides of the pan and helps you unmold it.

One of my signature cheesecake techniques is packing the crust only on the bottom of the pan. This creates a thick, crunchy base that can stand up to the most decadent of fillings.

Preparing the Batter

A great cheesecake begins with proper mixing of the batter. One absolute must is to have all ingredients at room temperature. This allows for the proper incorporation of eggs and will result in the best texture and maximum cake volume. Properly creaming the cheese with the sugar and eggs is another essential step. First, the sugar is blended into the softened cream cheese until smooth. Once that is done, the eggs are added and thoroughly blended in, making sure nothing is stuck on the sides of the bowl. The batter should be as homogenous as possible, and this is achieved by slowly, consistently blending, not whipping the cheese. A stand mixer becomes a virtual necessity, but hand mixers, as well as large food processors, do an admirable job. Using low speed on the mixer prevents too much air from being incorporated into the batter, which can cause irreconcilable rifts in your finished product.

Baking Cheesecake

The recipes in this chapter use a variety of oven temperatures and two baking approaches—with a water bath and without. Cakes baked without a water bath are generally better baked at a lower temperature for a longer time, since there is no steam in the oven to help the cake bake through while keeping it moist. Cakes baked with a water bath tend to be creamier, almost like a mousse that is set up once it is chilled. I offer recipes using both methods and advise that if you prefer the results of one method or another, most of these recipes, unless otherwise stated, can be baked with or without a water bath. Make sure your pan is snug and that there is no leakage of batter or water from the water bath into the cake. If you are at all worried, a good rule of thumb is to wrap the outside of the pan in foil (see page 22).

A roasting pan or any pan that houses the springform pan in a water bath that reaches halfway up the sides of the springform pan is fine. Place the roasting pan with the water in it in the oven, and then position the cheesecake in place.

Cooling Cheesecake

My basic counsel is to cool your cheesecakes step-by-step, with no quick hot-to-cold changes in environment. Most of the recipes in this chapter cool for an hour or so in the oven after baking; then they further cool to room temperature on the counter before being refrigerated for the time given in each specific recipe. Refrigeration for 12 to 24 hours is ideal, for a cheesecake must be thoroughly "set" and chilled before serving.

Finishing Touches

All that is needed now are your inspirational touches to finish your triumph. Finishing touches are that extra bit of charm that make cheesecake unbeatable.

Nut-crunch topping finishes off pumpkin or pecan cheesecakes nicely, and a dark chocolate glaze makes a marble cheesecake a visual delight. Fresh fruit artfully arranged and glazed with apricot preserves always draws immediate attention. The way the cake tastes is the final test, but its visual impact is prime, especially when it holds court on a dessert trolley or party buffet.

Finishing touches are that extra bit of charm that make cheesecake unbeatable.

Storage

Cheesecakes can be served cold from the fridge or left out at room temperature for an hour before serving. Leftover cheesecake should be kept refrigerated, loosely covered, with the exposed cut edges covered with pieces of wax paper, cut to fit, so that the creamy cake does not absorb the odors of other foods in the fridge.

Most cheesecakes freeze well, but it is best to freeze them without their finishing touches. Save those adornments and apply them an hour before serving the cake.

Vanilla Crumb Crust

Makes 1 crust for a 9-inch cheesecake

This is a perfect crust for many types of cheesecakes. There's no need to prebake it.

1¾ cups vanilla wafer crumbs

⅓ cup firmly packed brown sugar

⅓ cup unsalted butter, melted

Mix ingredients together and press into bottom of a 9-inch springform pan sprayed lightly with nonstick cooking spray. Add desired cheesecake filling for a 9-inch springform pan and bake according to recipe directions.

Chocolate Crumb Crust

Makes 1 crust for a 9-inch cheesecake

Sometimes you need a chocolate cookie crust for a chocolate-oriented cheesecake. Chocolate wafer cookies, chocolate sandwich cookies, or chocolate shortbread are all good cookie choices for this crust.

1½ cups chocolate cookie crumbs

¼ cup finely ground white chocolate

3 tablespoons unsalted butter, melted

Mix ingredients together and press into bottom of a 9-inch springform pan sprayed lightly with nonstick cooking spray. Add desired cheesecake filling for a 9-inch springform pan and bake according to recipe directions. I particularly like using this crust as an option for Chocolate Eruption Cheesecake, page 264.

Chocolate Chip Cookie Dough Cheesecake

Makes 10 servings

This cake rocks. Use homemade cookie dough or use the store-bought option for a shortcut. This makes a creamy cheesecake with chunks of semi-firm dough throughout and chunks that are slightly set and cakey on top.

Crust

1½ cups shortbread cookie crumbs
¼ cup unsalted butter, melted
1 tablespoon sugar
Pinch ground cinnamon

Cheesecake

1 (18-ounce) package refrigerated chocolate chip cookie dough or the dough for Tender, Buttery Chocolate Chunk Cookies, well chilled, page 122

2 pounds cream cheese, softened
1 (14-ounce) can sweetened condensed milk
¼ cup sugar
Tiniest pinch salt
3 large eggs
2 teaspoons pure vanilla extract
2 tablespoons all-purpose flour
⅓ cup whipping cream
⅓ cup miniature semisweet chocolate chips

Preheat oven to 350°F. Line a baking sheet with parchment paper. Toss Crust ingredients in bottom of an ungreased 9- or 10-inch springform pan and press into pan bottom.

Cut up cookie dough into chunks (about 1 inch or less) and set aside **(photo 1)**.

In a mixer bowl, blend cream cheese with condensed milk, sugar, salt, eggs, vanilla, flour, and whipping cream, blending until smooth, about 4 to 6 minutes.

Turn out half of batter into prepared pan. Scatter on most of chocolate chips and half of chunks of cookie dough. Top with remaining batter, more cookie dough chunks, and remaining chocolate chips.

Place pan on prepared baking sheet. Place in oven and bake until just set, reducing oven temperature to 325°F around midpoint and baking a total of 35 to 45 minutes. Turn off oven, open oven door, and let cool in oven 1 hour. Refrigerate cheesecake several hours or overnight.

This is easy, fast, and a slice of heaven.

Chocolate Cheesecake Supremo

Makes 12 to 20 servings

What else do you call a cheesecake that is part cheesecake, part torte, and all decadence? The secret to this recipe is using one whole pound of the finest chocolate possible and having all the ingredients around the same temperature. This makes a beautiful, high-standing cake. Instead of cookie crumbs, use leftover chocolate cake pieces as the bottom crust for this luscious dessert.

Cheesecake Crack-Up

The issue here is how to avoid the greatest of all cheesecake evils: cracks—hairline, San Andreas, and otherwise. There are two methods of prevention.

• Method No. 1 subscribes to the notion of gradually cooling the cake. First, the oven heat is turned off and the cake "rests" in the oven with the door ajar for an hour. Then, it either rests some more at room temperature or is placed in a refrigerator. Gradually cooling the cake should help the cake resist cracking, since the changes in temperature occur slowly. I prefer this method.

• Cheesecakes baked in a water bath (Method No. 2) seem to fare better overall. They have a remarkably extra creamy texture from the gentle cooking and tend to set without cracking more often than cakes that are not baked in a water bath.

Crust

1½ cups chocolate cookie crumbs or
   leftover chocolate cake pieces
¼ cup unsalted butter, melted
2 tablespoons white sugar
2 tablespoons brown sugar

Cheesecake

1 pound semisweet chocolate
¼ cup unsalted butter
1½ pounds cream cheese, softened
1½ cups sugar
6 large eggs
2 teaspoons pure vanilla extract
1 teaspoon pure chocolate extract
¼ cup all-purpose flour
Pinch salt
½ cup whipping cream or sour
   cream

Finishing Touches

1 cup white chocolate, melted
¾ cup milk chocolate, melted, for
   drizzling
Cocoa powder, for dusting
Milk or Dark Chocolate Ganache,
   page 242

Preheat oven to 325°F. Line a baking sheet with parchment paper.

For Crust, in bottom of a 9-inch springform pan, toss cookie crumbs with melted butter and both sugars and press firmly into pan bottom. Place pan on prepared baking sheet.

For Cheesecake, melt semisweet chocolate and butter in a heavy saucepan over low heat; let cool.

In a mixer bowl, beat cream cheese with sugar until smooth. Add eggs, vanilla and chocolate extracts, flour, salt, and whipping cream; blend well. Fold in and blend the cooled chocolate. Pour filling into prepared pan.

Bake until just set, 55 to 75 minutes. Turn off oven, open oven door, and let cool in oven 1 hour before refrigerating 6 hours or overnight. To garnish, drizzle on melted white or milk chocolate, or dust with cocoa, or coat with ganache.

Cheesecake Truffle Bombs

Makes 24 to 32 servings

Cheesecake, chocolate, and a special technique make these a one-of-a-kind sensation. These frozen mini bites of New York–style cheesecake enrobed in a thick trufflelike coating are alone worth the price of the book. Bet you can't eat just one.

Cheesecake Batter

1	pound cream cheese, softened
¾	cup sugar
3	large eggs
2	teaspoons pure vanilla extract
⅓	cup whipping cream
Tiniest pinch salt	

Dipping Chocolates

12	ounces milk chocolate, melted
10	ounces each semisweet chocolate and white chocolate, melted, optional

Preheat oven to 350°F. Line a baking sheet with parchment paper. Line an 8- or 9-inch square pan with parchment paper or aluminum foil and spray with nonstick cooking spray. Place pan on prepared baking sheet.

In a food processor, whiz together Cheesecake Batter ingredients until smooth. Pour batter into pan. Bake until set, about 30 minutes. Cake should be firm to the touch but not dried out or curling in at the sides. Cool well in fridge. Cut into 24 to 32 small squares or scoop out portions of cheesecake using a mini ice-cream scoop. Place squares or scoops on a parchment paper–lined baking sheet and freeze 1 to 2 hours.

Meanwhile, melt Dipping Chocolates separately (your choice of one to three types).

To finish Cheesecake Truffle Bombs, using a fork to assist, dip and turn each frozen cheesecake portion in chocolate (**photo 1**). Let set on parchment paper–lined baking sheet and dip in or drizzle with another type of chocolate, if desired. Freeze briefly to set and then place in confectionary paper holders, if desired. Seal truffle bombs in a zip-top freezer bag and freeze up to 2 months. Serve frozen or thaw slightly and serve chilled.

I prefer to first dip these decadent frozen cheesecake bites in melted milk chocolate bars. I don't recommend chocolate chips for this recipe.

Double-Cream Cheesecake with Sour Cherry Glaze

Makes 12 to 20 servings; also pictured on page 252

If I had to choose one cheesecake to take to the proverbial desert island, this would be it. I have made many cheese-cakes—all good, all special. This one, however, is a heady delight. For one, the glaze on this beauty is a simple cherry topping made of pure, sour cherry juice (canned pure juice or juice drained off from sour cherries in the can) that is sweetened just a tad and thickened with cornstarch. The vibrant look and taste is the perfect foil of sweet and sour atop creamy and sweet. This cake stands firm and tall but is creamy and cuts into perfect slices.

Double Devon Cream

We all know half-and-half, whipping cream, light cream, and every cream in between, but there is another baker's secret. It is canned *Double Devon Cream,* also known as "thick cream." It is found in cans near the evaporated milk section in your supermarket or, often times, in Latin food stores, or online. From England, the cream is a whopping 48% butterfat and has the consistency of sour cream. It adds an incredible, luscious smoothness to cheesecake, and, being a canned dairy ingredient, is handy when the cheesecake urge strikes. The Double-Cream Cheesecake is a perfect recipe to showcase double cream, but almost any cheesecake recipe would do well with it used in place of whipping cream or sour cream. You can also reserve a can, chilled, to serve with fresh scones.

Graham Crust

1½ cups graham cracker crumbs
5 tablespoons unsalted butter
⅓ cup firmly packed brown sugar
Pinch ground cinnamon

Cheesecake Batter

2 pounds cream cheese, softened
1⅓ cups sugar
5 large eggs
2 teaspoons pure vanilla extract
1 tablespoon fresh lemon juice
¼ teaspoon pure almond extract

1 (10-ounce) can *Nestlé* double cream*
¼ cup all-purpose flour

Sour Cream Topping

1½ cups sour cream
2 tablespoons confectioners' sugar

Sour Cherry Glaze

1 cup sour cherry juice
¼ cup sugar
2 tablespoons cornstarch

*You can use *Double Devon Cream* (see text at left), found online, or use a blend of ¾ cup sour cream with ¾ cup whipped cream folded in.

Preheat oven to 325°F. Line a baking sheet with parchment paper.

For Graham Crust, toss graham crumbs, butter, brown sugar, and cinnamon together in bottom of a 9-inch springform pan and press firmly into pan bottom. Place on prepared baking sheet.

For Cheesecake Batter, in a mixer bowl, blend cream cheese with sugar until well blended. Add eggs and next 5 ingredients and blend well, still on low speed, about 5 minutes until totally smooth. Pour into springform pan and place in oven. Bake until just set, about 60 to 75 minutes.

Increase oven temperature to 350°F. Stir together sour cream and confectioners' sugar and spoon gently over top of baked cheesecake. Bake 8 minutes to just set sour cream topping. Turn off oven, open oven door, and let cool in oven 1 hour before refrigerating 8 hours or preferably overnight.

Make Sour Cherry Glaze about an hour before serving. In a small saucepan, heat cherry juice and sugar, reserving 2 tablespoons of juice in a small teacup. Stir cornstarch into reserved cherry juice while remaining juice comes to a gentle boil (just barely boiling). Whisk in cornstarch mixture and stir over medium-low heat, reducing heat to low as it thickens. This takes 1 to 2 minutes. Cool and then spread Sour Cherry Glaze on cheesecake. Let set. Unmold cheesecake onto a serving plate.

This is, without contest, an absolutely quintessential cheesecake—the type you sneak a small slice of every other day when you are not wowing guests with it.

Lemon Meringue Cheesecake

Makes 16 to 20 servings

This lemony cheesecake has an ingenious "meringue-type topping" of marshmallow creme. Chill the baked cake, slather on the marshmallow, briefly broil to brown the "meringue," and then serve. Offer some whipped lemon curd on the side. See the "Source Guide" for ordering superlative lemon extract and oil.

> My testers fell in love with this refreshing, creamy cake, giving it a 5-star thumbs-up and absolute raves.

Cheesecakes Make the Cut

Final frontier: cutting the cheesecake. Again, one has a choice of two noble alternatives. The first is to cut the cake with a long knife (not serrated) dipped first in hot water and cleaned before each subsequent cut. The second method is to cut the cake using unwaxed dental floss flexed tautly across the cake. Cuts are made by simply lowering the dental floss through the cake and pulling away the floss, much like using a wire to cut through potter's clay. Either method yields perfect, cleanly executed cake slices.

Crust

- 1½ cups crushed shortbread cookies (about 22 cookies)
- 6 tablespoons unsalted butter, melted
- 2 tablespoons sugar
- ½ teaspoon pure vanilla extract

Cheesecake Filling

- 2½ pounds cream cheese, softened
- 1¼ cups sugar
- ¼ cup all-purpose flour
- 1 (14-ounce) can sweetened condensed milk
- 5 large eggs
- 2 egg yolks
- ⅓ cup whipping cream
- 1 tablespoon pure vanilla extract
- 2 tablespoons fresh lemon juice
- 2 teaspoons pure lemon extract
- ½ teaspoon lemon oil, optional
- Zest of 1 lemon, finely minced

Finishing Touches

Store-bought lemon curd
- 1 (7-ounce) jar marshmallow creme
Raspberries
Mint leaves

Preheat oven to 325°F. For Crust, mix all ingredients and press into bottom of a 10-inch springform pan. Wrap outside of pan with foil to ensure no leakage of batter into water or water into cake. Set a roasting pan filled halfway with water in the oven.

For Cheesecake Filling, in a mixer bowl, blend cream cheese with sugar and flour. Add condensed milk and blend well. Then add eggs, egg yolks, whipping cream, vanilla, lemon juice, lemon extract, lemon oil, and zest and blend well on low speed, making sure no cream cheese is stuck at the bottom well of mixing bowl.

Spoon filling into prepared springform pan. Place cheesecake gently in water bath. Bake 45 to 60 minutes or until cheesecake is just set. Turn off oven, open oven door, and let cool in oven at least 1 hour. Refrigerate cheesecake overnight.

To garnish cheesecake, the next day or once cake is well-chilled at least 8 hours and 1½ hours before you want to serve it, unmold cake and cover with half of lemon curd. Then add marshmallow creme in dollops.

Preheat oven to 425°F and position oven rack to upper third position. Place cake in oven briefly to brown top (you can also use Broil setting but watch it carefully).

Serve cake, offering remaining lemon curd, whisked so that it is smooth. Garnish with fresh raspberries and a few mint leaves.

Rose Petals and White Chocolate Cheesecake

Makes 8 to 12 servings

This is an elegant little cheesecake made all the more glamourous because of its white chocolate cachet. I suppose this heart-shaped dessert would make a great Valentine's Day treat, but it is beautiful anytime—proof positive that fresh flowers and baking are a natural pair. The rose petals simply garnish the serving plate, but, oh, what a nice effect! Be sure to use rose petals grown without pesticides and gently rinse the petals in advance.

Filo Crust

1/3 cup unsalted butter, melted

16 sheets of filo dough

Cheesecake Filling

1½ pounds cream cheese, softened

1 cup sugar

3 large eggs

1½ teaspoons pure vanilla extract

1/8 teaspoon pure almond extract

1/4 teaspoon each orange and lemon oil

1/4 cup whipping cream

2 tablespoons sour cream

1/3 cup finely minced white chocolate

Finishing Touches

Confectioners' sugar

White chocolate and semisweet chocolate, melted

Make sure your white chocolate is a brand that melts easily. I recommend *Valrhona*, *Callebaut*, or *Lindt*. You can also use a regular round springform pan for this cake. Don't worry about patching the filo sheets all over it. It works out perfectly in the end, no matter how messy it might seem.

Preheat oven to 350°F. Line a baking sheet with parchment paper. Generously brush melted butter all over interior of a 9-inch heart-shaped springform pan.

Lay 12 sheets of filo on a work surface and brush 1 sheet at a time with melted butter. Drape each sheet of buttered filo into pan, (a few on the bottom, and then patch the sides as best you can). Bottom should have a few layers, and sides (patch pieces with some overlap) should be at least four layers thick. Leave any overlap hanging for now.

For Cheesecake Filling, in a food processor, blend cream cheese with sugar and then add eggs, extracts, and oils and blend until smooth. Add whipping cream and sour cream. Gently stir in white chocolate by hand.

Turn batter out into prepared pan. Drape overlap of filo onto center of cake.

Cut out four filo hearts to fit pan. Paint each with melted butter and drape on top of cake to fit. Gently crimp side or edges by hand.

Place cake on prepared baking sheet. Bake about 30 minutes and then increase oven temperature to 375°F or 400°F to assist browning the filo pastry and bake about 5 to 12 more minutes.

Remove cake from oven. Cool to room temperature. Chill at least 4 hours. Dust with confectioners' sugar before unveiling or drizzle with a mix of melted white and dark chocolate. Garnish with rose petals on a serving platter.

Chocolate Eruption Cheesecake

Makes 16 to 20 servings

I was once asked in my village-baker travels to create the recipe for a cheesecake that apparently was a restaurant rage in some cities. My Chocolate Eruption Cheesecake that evolved can be made in a few ways, but these elements are constant: caramel swirls, chocolate chunks, white chocolate, pieces of turtle-bar chocolates or similar pecan and caramel candy, and chocolate curls on top. I took my version up a level by adding hunks of homemade chocolate brownies. You can do the same or use store-bought brownies or a brownie mix. This is a dense, rich, gorgeous cheesecake that will be the talk of any party. It feeds a crowd and is the stuff of instant legend.

I suppose this sounds like an X-rated dessert, and it is if you are counting calories.

Bottom Crust

1 batch prepared brownies, recipe page 265, or 1 Chocolate Crumb Crust, page 256

Filling

2½ pounds cream cheese, softened
½ cup sugar
1 (14-ounce) can sweetened condensed milk
5 large eggs
⅓ cup whipping cream
2 tablespoons all-purpose flour
1 tablespoon pure vanilla extract
Pinch salt
1½ cups coarsely chopped white chocolate

1 cup semisweet chocolate chips or coarsely chopped chocolate
2 cups coarsely chopped chocolate caramel bars, such as *Snickers* or *Turtles* candy
1 cup coarsely cut chunks of brownie, homemade or prepared from a mix
½ cup dulce de leche or caramel sundae topping

Finishing Touches

¼ cup each, melted white, milk, and semisweet chocolate
Chocolate curls or shavings
Confectioners' sugar

Prepare brownies as first step and let cool. A brownie mix is fine, or a chocolate crumb crust or the brownie recipe that follows.

Preheat oven to 325°F. Line a baking sheet with parchment paper. Spray a 10-inch springform pan with nonstick cooking spray. Line bottom and sides of pan with pieces of parchment paper, cut to fit, allowing side pieces to extend a bit over top of pan (to make a collar). Arrange pieces of brownies to line bottom of pan.

For Filling, in a mixer bowl, blend cream cheese with sugar until smooth. Add condensed milk and blend in eggs, cream, flour, vanilla, and pinch of salt until smooth, about 5 minutes on lowest speed, scraping bottom of mixing bowl often to make sure batter does not stick in well of bowl.

Remove one-third of batter and mix with chopped white chocolate. Pour over brownies in springform pan. Fold remaining filling ingredients, except dulce de leche or caramel topping, into cheesecake batter. Mix gently by hand so as not to break up brownie chunks too much. Pour half of batter into pan (on top of white chocolate cheesecake batter) and then drop dollops of half the dulce de leche or caramel topping all over. Top with remaining batter and then remaining dulce de leche or caramel topping. Swirl batter with a knife very briefly. Pan will be very full.

Place cheesecake on prepared baking sheet and bake until set, about 45 to 55 minutes. Turn off oven, open oven door, and let cool in oven 1 hour and then in fridge overnight. Remove from pan and unmold onto a serving plate.

Before serving, drizzle melted white, milk, and semisweet chocolate over cheesecake, allowing them to drip down sides. On top of melted chocolate, garnish with chocolate curls or shavings and dust with confectioners' sugar.

Brownies for Chocolate Eruption Cheesecake

Makes 2 to 3 dozen brownies

Here's a perfect batch of brownies designed for this unique cheesecake.

1½ cups unsalted butter, melted

1½ cups white sugar

1½ cups firmly packed brown sugar

1½ teaspoons pure vanilla extract

4 large eggs

1½ cups all-purpose flour

1 cup cocoa powder

¼ teaspoon baking soda

¼ teaspoon salt

Preheat oven to 350°F. Line a baking sheet with parchment paper. Generously spray a 13- x 9-inch pan with nonstick cooking spray and line bottom with parchment paper.

In a food processor, blend melted butter with both sugars and then add vanilla and eggs. Stir in flour, cocoa, baking soda, and salt and process to make a smooth batter. Spoon into prepared pan.

Place pan on prepared baking sheet and bake until done and just set, 25 to 30 minutes. Cool and then place brownies (in pan) in freezer for 1 hour before cutting. To cut, unmold brownies and peel off parchment paper. Cut slab of brownies in half across the middle and then cut one half into strips or pieces to use for bottom of cheesecake. Chop remaining brownies for use in cheesecake filling. (There might be a little left over for nibbling.)

Shortbread Cookies 'n' Cream Cheesecake

Makes 16 to 24 servings

Here is a luscious, creamy cheesecake that uses any sort of shortbread cookies, homemade or store-bought. The result of combining cheesecake batter with chunks of shortbread is a luxurious, creamy cake that offers a dash of elegance and flair. It is good for a weekend dessert or a special occasion. This cheesecake can also be baked in a 13- x 9-inch pan, chilled, and cut into thin slices.

Crust

1½ cups shortbread or butter cookie crumbs*
2   tablespoons white sugar
3   tablespoons brown sugar
Pinch salt
6   tablespoons unsalted butter, melted

Cheesecake

2½ pounds cream cheese, softened
1   cup sugar
½   cup all-purpose flour
1   tablespoon pure vanilla extract
Tiny pinch salt
1   (14-ounce) can sweetened condensed milk
6   large eggs
½   cup whipping cream
2   cups coarsely chopped shortbread cookies

Finishing Touches

Melted white chocolate
Confectioners' sugar, for dusting

*This can be store-bought shortbread or homemade, page 279, or Danish butter cookies in a tin.

Preheat oven to 350°F. Line a baking sheet with parchment paper. Spray a 9- or 10-inch springform pan with nonstick cooking spray and place on prepared baking sheet.

For Crust, place cookie crumbs, white sugar, brown sugar, and salt in bottom of springform pan and mix with a fork to blend. Drizzle in melted butter and blend; then press into pan bottom.

In a mixer bowl, beat cream cheese with sugar and flour until smooth. Make sure nothing sticks to well of bowl. Add vanilla, salt, condensed milk, eggs, and whipping cream, blending well. Spoon half of batter into pan. Add most of chopped shortbread cookies to pan and swirl around. Add remaining batter and make sure cookies are distributed throughout, reserving a couple tablespoons of chopped cookies for the top (so some peek through as cake bakes).

Bake until cake is just set, 45 to 50 minutes. Turn off oven, open oven door, and let cool in oven 1 hour. Refrigerate 8 hours or up to 3 days, loosely covered.

Garnish with a stippling of melted white chocolate or dust with confectioners' sugar.

Chocolate Marshmallow Sundae Cheesecake

Makes 8 servings

In the States, chocolate-coated marshmallows on a cookie base are called *Mallomars*. In Canada, these adored cookies are called *Whippets*. This cheesecake marries the concept of that cookie to cake in a sublime and gooey mess of creamy cheese filling, milk chocolate, and graham biscuits. The cookies create an instant bottom crust that manages to coat the bottom, but some cookies float up and become part of the filling. if you double this recipe, you can make a knockout big version using a 10-inch springform pan.

Bottom Crust

8   or less *Mallomars* or *Whippet* cookies

Cheesecake

1½ pounds cream cheese, softened
1   cup sugar
3   large eggs
2   tablespoons all-purpose flour
1½ teaspoons pure vanilla extract
½   cup sour cream

Topping

6   to 8 *Mallomars* or *Whippet* cookies, for top

If you cannot find *Mallomars* or *Whippet* cookies, use a regular graham cracker crust and fold 2 cups quartered regular marshmallows and ½ cup coarsely chopped milk chocolate into the batter.

Preheat oven to 350°F. Line bottom of an 8-inch springform pan with a circle of parchment paper. Spray sides of pan with nonstick cooking spray. Put 8 or less cookies on pan bottom and cut some to fit, so that bottom is lined as snugly as possible. Place pan on a parchment paper–lined baking sheet.

In a food processor, beat cream cheese with sugar until smooth, scraping down bowl every so often. Add eggs, flour, vanilla, and sour cream and blend until smooth. Gently pour filling on top of cookie crust.

Bake 20 minutes or until cake is just barely set and then gently press 6 to 8 cookies to cover cake surface as a topping. Continue baking until cookies are melted and cake seems set, about 35 to 40 minutes. Turn off oven, open oven door, and let cool in oven 1 hour. Refrigerate at least 6 hours or up to 3 days before serving.

Crème Brûlée Cheesecake

Makes 16 to 18 servings

What works in a classic custard with a burnt sugar topping also works as a gourmet cheesecake. The burnt caramel in this case is not torched to a crackling finish. Instead, the silky-smooth burnt sugar caramel is poured on the chilled cheesecake and left to infuse it. Use my classic pie dough recipe on page 188 as the base for this luscious dessert.

The burnt sugar syrup penetrates the cheesecake, infusing the creamy interior to create an incredible taste sensation in this decadent concept cake.

Crust

1   (10-inch) circle of prepared pie dough

Crème Brûlée Topping

2   cups sugar
½   cup whipping cream
3   tablespoons unsalted butter

Cheesecake

2½ pounds cream cheese, softened
1⅓ cups sugar
½   cup sour cream
6   large eggs
¾   cup whipping cream
1   tablespoon pure vanilla extract
⅓   cup caramel chips, optional*

*Order caramel chips online or use butterscotch chips instead.

Preheat oven to 350°F. Line a baking sheet with parchment paper. For Crust, line bottom of a 10-inch springform pan with circle of pie dough; trim to fit. Prick pastry all over with a fork, place on prepared baking sheet, and bake until just browned, 20 to 25 minutes.

Meanwhile, for Crème Brûlée Topping, place sugar in a heavy-bottomed 2½-quart saucepan. Cook over medium heat, stirring occasionally, 15 minutes, until it reaches a dark amber color. Remove from heat and slowly add whipping cream. This will cool the mixture, but it will also foam and bubble up quite significantly, so take care. Once bubbling subsides, whisk butter thoroughly into caramel. Set aside to cool.

Wrap outside of springform pan with foil to ensure no leakage of batter into water or water into cake. Set a roasting pan filled halfway with water in the oven.

For Cheesecake, in a mixer bowl, blend cream cheese and sugar until smooth. Add sour cream, eggs, whipping cream, and vanilla and blend well until mixture is smooth and no bits of cream cheese remain. Fold in caramel chips, if using. Drizzle a few tablespoons of Crème Brûlée Topping onto bottom crust, spreading it thinly to coat crust. Pour cheesecake batter on top.

Place cheesecake gently in water bath and bake 55 to 60 minutes or until set. Carefully remove springform pan from water bath, place cheesecake on counter, and let cool to room temperature. Then refrigerate 6 hours or overnight.

To serve, make small slits with a paring knife or small holes with a wooden pick in top surface of cheesecake. Pour remaining Crème Brûlée Topping onto cake and let soak a few hours, or you can serve right away. (It is good either way.) Unmold to serve, conserving syrup and drizzling it onto cake.

Cinn-a-Bun Cheesecake

Makes 10 to 14 servings

This cheesecake is one of the best in my repertoire—it tastes like a sticky cinnamon bun in a creamy cheesecake package. If you can find cinnamon chips (much like chocolate chips), throw some in for extra cinnamon goodness.

Crust

1½ cups finely crushed cinnamon-raisin cookies or other spice cookies*

¼ cup unsalted butter, melted

2 tablespoons brown sugar

Filling

1½ pounds cream cheese, softened

1 cup sugar

½ cup sour cream or whipping cream

4 large eggs

2 teaspoons pure vanilla extract

¼ cup all-purpose flour

1 cup coarsely chopped cinnamon-raisin cookies or other spice cookies

1 cup raisins, plumped and dried (see page 18)

⅓ cup cinnamon chips, optional

¼ cup butterscotch or caramel sundae topping

1 teaspoon ground cinnamon mixed with ¼ cup sugar

Finishing Touch

Confectioners' sugar

This petite (8-inch) cheesecake delights with a gorgeous swirl of caramel, chunks of cinnamon-raisin cookies (store-bought or homemade), raisins, and cinnamon sugar.

*I use cinnamon-raisin *Coffee Breaks* cookies, but almost any sort of crisp spice cookies or graham crackers are fine.

Preheat oven to 325°F. Line a baking sheet with parchment paper.

For Crust, toss cookie crumbs, butter, and brown sugar together in bottom of an 8-inch springform pan. Press crust into bottom of pan and spray sides with nonstick cooking spray.

For Filling, in a mixer bowl, blend cream cheese, sugar, and sour cream until smooth, scraping bottom and sides of bowl to incorporate everything, about 3 to 4 minutes. Stir in eggs, vanilla, and flour and blend well 2 to 3 minutes.

Spoon one-third of filling into prepared pan and top with half each of chopped cookies, raisins, and cinnamon chips (if using). Drizzle on some butterscotch topping. Dust on some cinnamon sugar. Cover with another third of the cream cheese filling and then dust on more cookies, remaining raisins, more cinnamon chips, and more cinnamon sugar (you do not want to have raisins on top because they can scorch).

Add last bit of filling and finish top of cake with cookie crumbs, cinnamon chips, and a nice dusting of cinnamon sugar. You want to end up with a streusel-looking topping.

Bake 45 to 55 minutes. Turn off oven, open oven door, and let cool in oven 1 hour before removing to fridge. Chill cheesecake at least 6 hours or overnight before serving.

Dust with confectioners' sugar before serving.

Pumpkin-Butterscotch Swirl Cheesecake

Makes 14 to 20 servings

Spice, pumpkin, bourbon, and butterscotch. Who needs turkey? This is a sublimely spiced pumpkin cheesecake that is upgraded with a swirl of butterscotch or caramel. You can make your own or use a quality sundae topping or prepared dulce de leche. The Bourbon-Spiced Crème Anglaise is a crowning touch, but the cake shines with or without it.

Crust

1½ cups finely crushed gingersnaps
5   tablespoons brown sugar
5   tablespoons unsalted butter, melted
¼   teaspoon pumpkin pie spice
¼   teaspoon ground cinnamon

⅓   cup all-purpose flour
1¼ teaspoons ground cinnamon
1   teaspoon pumpkin pie spice
1   tablespoon pure vanilla extract
¾   cup whipping cream
½   cup caramel or butterscotch sundae topping

Cheesecake Batter

2½ pounds cream cheese, softened
¾   cup firmly packed light brown sugar
¾   cup white sugar
6   large eggs
1½ cups canned pumpkin puree

Finishing Touches

Bourbon-Spiced Crème Anglaise (at right)
Whipped cream
Toasted ground pecans and gingersnap crumbs, for dusting
Warm butterscotch or caramel sundae topping or dulce de leche

Preheat oven to 325°F. Line a baking sheet with parchment paper.

For Crust, combine gingersnap crumbs, brown sugar, butter, pumpkin pie spice, and cinnamon. Press into bottom of a 9- or 10-inch springform pan and place on prepared baking sheet.

For Cheesecake Batter, in a mixer bowl, blend cream cheese on low speed with both sugars until well blended. Add eggs and blend on low speed until smooth. Add pumpkin puree, flour, cinnamon, pumpkin pie spice, vanilla, and whipping cream, scraping sides and bottom of bowl often and blending until smooth. Swirl caramel topping into batter.

Pour batter into prepared pan. Bake until cake seems firm in center, 55 to 70 minutes. Turn off oven, open oven door, and let cool in oven until cake is almost at room temperature. Cover loosely with a sheet of wax paper and place in refrigerator to chill overnight.

Serve cake with Bourbon Spiced Crème Anglaise or with softly whipped cream and a dusting of ground toasted pecans mixed with crushed gingersnaps. Then add a final drizzle of sundae topping.

Bourbon-Spiced Crème Anglaise

Makes 2 cups sauce

This sauce is superb on Pumpkin-Butterscotch Swirl Cheesecake (at left) or with a dense chocolate torte, as well as with White Chocolate and Vanilla Bread Pudding (page 281).

2	cups whipping cream	1	teaspoon pure vanilla extract
¼	teaspoon ground cinnamon	2	tablespoons bourbon, optional
Pinch each ground nutmeg, cloves,		3	egg yolks
	and allspice	¼	cup sugar

Fill a large bowl with ice and water.

In a 2- or 3-quart heavy saucepan over medium heat, stir whipping cream with spices until gently simmering. Remove from heat. Stir in vanilla and bourbon.

In a medium bowl, beat egg yolks and sugar until pale and thick, about 2 minutes. Slowly drizzle in warm cream, whisking all the while. Return mixture to saucepan and cook over medium heat until sauce thickens, stirring gently, about 5 to 8 minutes. Place saucepan in prepared ice bath and stir sauce until cool.

Cover sauce with plastic wrap, pressing directly onto surface to prevent a skin from forming. Refrigerate until well chilled, about 2 hours. Serve chilled or warmed. Refrigerate up to 3 days.

> **Always use a heavy-bottomed saucepan when you are making a cooked custard sauce such as this. Stir the custard gently with undivided attention.**

holiday baking

What is nicest about the holidays, regardless of which one or which season, is that even the nonbaker, occasional baker, or cautious baker will give baking a shot. It is everyone-in-the-kitchen time. There is a simple, pure joy that comes with holiday baking—plus a very specific, heartwarming kind of energy.

What is more appreciated than holiday baking? Is anything cozier than being in a kitchen at holiday time, the counters overrun with ingredients, recipe cards, and baking books, along with computer-printout recipes scattered about, all just waiting for you to begin? Chances are, you have more time at the holidays to devote to baking. It is not something you are trying to fit in with everything else in your life; it is the focal point and priority.

Holiday baking in particular is the most rooted, bonding fare to be had. We remember how we gathered, who we were with, and what we shared at the table. Not surprisingly, we cherish making the same recipes to carry on that feeling, maintain our traditions, and recapture the unique warmth that doing those things brings.

Holiday baking covers a wide gamut of possibilities, from cookies to breads, cakes, pies, and pastries. It revs up your baking skills or makes you practice new ones. It is never just one sort of thing. Instead, it is variety baking at its finest hour—gift giving, hosting, and dessert sampling.

What you need to remember for this chapter is to have extra bakeware and ingredients on hand. Double up on vanilla, sugar, flour, and butter and have storage, wrapping, and packaging supplies ready. In fact, an extra fridge in the garage is my way to store blocks of butter, bushels of apples, and cases of eggs.

Include ingredients you might not indulge in at other times, such as specialty nuts, finer chocolate, double-strength pure vanilla extract, spirits, and whatever fine additives you can find—from almond paste to dulce de leche. Holiday time is the season to splurge with the more luxurious things.

Perfect Pecan Pie

Makes 8 to 10 servings; also pictured on page 272

What makes my pecan pie special is the use of my favorite brands of corn syrup and cane syrup, but you can use other brands and still have a great-tasting pie. For a Chocolate Pecan Pie, add ¾ cup chocolate chips to the filling.

Pecan Pie Pointers

Recipes for pecan pie are equally divided between those that call for chopped pecans and those that call for pecan halves. Pecan halves make the pie look incredibly inviting, but cutting neat wedges is a challenge. One solution is to freeze the baked pie, cut it into wedges with a serrated knife, and allow it to warm to room temperature.

Really good pecan pie is rare. Often, the nuts are small and indifferent, and the filling is too sweet or too skimpy. How do you make a better pecan pie? Go back to the roots: pure cane syrup and fresh Georgia pecans. Someone once said that good baking is a series of little things done right. This recipe proves it.

Pie Pastry*

1¾ cups all-purpose flour
2 teaspoons sugar
⅛ teaspoon salt
¼ cup unsalted butter, cut into chunks
2 tablespoons shortening or unsalted butter
4 to 5 tablespoons ice water

Filling

½ cup unsalted butter, melted
1½ cups firmly packed dark brown sugar
⅔ cup corn syrup, preferably *Tate & Lyle*
½ cup dark cane syrup, preferably *Steen's*, or molasses
6 large eggs, lightly beaten
2 teaspoons pure vanilla extract
2½ cups pecan halves

*Prebaking pastry is optional and depends on your crust texture preferences.

For Pie Pastry, mix flour with sugar and salt. Cut butter and shortening into dry ingredients to make a mealy mixture. Stir in water until dough can be gathered together in a mass. Knead gently on a lightly floured work surface to make a stiff dough. Wrap and chill 1 hour before rolling out.

Roll out pastry and place it in a 9- or 10-inch deep-dish tart pan with a removable bottom. Chill pastry 1 to 3 hours.

Preheat oven to 425°F. Bake pastry 15 minutes, if desired, with a piepan weighted down on it.

Reduce oven temperature to 325°F.

In a mixer bowl, blend melted butter with brown sugar, corn syrup, cane syrup, eggs, and vanilla. Stir in pecans. Pour filling into prepared pastry shell, gently turning over pecan halves to face right-side up. Place piepan on a baking sheet (in case of drips). Bake on lowest oven rack until just set, 55 to 70 minutes, reducing heat if necessary to ensure pie bakes through but does not bubble up.

Cool completely before serving. To slice evenly, freeze pie. Cut with a serrated knife and allow to warm to room temperature before serving.

White Chocolate Thanksgiving Pecan Pie

Makes 8 to 10 servings

Don't you find that sumptuous holiday desserts go up ten notches when you add white chocolate to them? Use the best quality chocolate you can find. This pie filling rises up, teeters a bit, and then slowly settles and sets. Use a 10-inch quiche pan with a removable bottom for this baby. Semi-freeze, cut, and then let the pie warm to room temperature for neat slices—and make sure you use a sharp, serrated knife to do the honors.

Prepared classic pie dough for a 10-inch bottom crust pie, page 188

Filling

4	ounces white chocolate
2	ounces semisweet chocolate
3/4	cup unsalted butter, melted and cooled
1	cup firmly packed light brown sugar
3/4	cup corn or cane syrup
4	large eggs, lightly whisked
2	teaspoons pure vanilla extract
2	tablespoons brandy, mild coffee, or cola
Pinch salt	
1	teaspoon lemon juice
1/2	teaspoon *Fiori di Sicilia** or pure orange extract, optional
3	tablespoons all-purpose flour
1 1/2	cups chopped pecans
1 1/2	cups small pecan halves

White chocolate adds a sophisticated flair to a heartwarming holiday. I love the 'oohs' of surprise I get each time this luxuriously revamped pecan pie is brought out.

*Fiori di Sicilia is a sublime citrus and vanilla essence. Find it online at kingarthurflour.com.

Preheat oven to 350°F. Line a baking sheet with parchment paper. Generously spray a 10-inch quiche pan with nonstick cooking spray and place on prepared baking sheet.

Roll pie dough out to a little less than 1/4 inch thick and line quiche pan with it. Press dough snugly into fluted edges. Place pan on prepared baking sheet. Set aside in fridge.

Melt both types of chocolate and let cool.

Meanwhile, in a food processor, cream butter and brown sugar together until well blended. Add corn or cane syrup, eggs, vanilla, brandy, salt, lemon juice, and extract (if using) and blend well. Fold in flour briefly. Turn mixture out into a large bowl. Whisk in both types of melted chocolate. Using a wooden spoon, fold in nuts. Spoon filling carefully into pan.

Place pie in oven, reduce oven temperature to 325°F, and bake until set, about 45 to 55 minutes. (Pie might rise up and threaten to overflow. Relax. If it seems to be on its way to doing this, reduce oven temperature to 300°F.) Cool pie to barely warm before serving.

Village Baker's Holiday Cranberry-Orange Bread

Makes 1 medium coffee cake

A stroll to the local French bakery inspired me to create this beautiful bread. Who could resist samples of tender chunks of sweet yeasted bread studded with chocolate and tart bits of cranberry? This is so good and so easy to make at home for the holidays, and it's perfect to serve to guests or for gift giving.

⅓ cup warm water (100°F to 110°F)

5 teaspoons rapid-rise yeast

4 to 5 cups all-purpose flour

¾ cup warm milk

¾ cup unsalted butter, softened

1 large egg

3 egg yolks

1 teaspoon salt

1⅓ cups sugar

1 teaspoon pure vanilla extract

½ teaspoon orange oil or pure orange extract

1½ cups coarsely chopped fresh or frozen cranberries

¾ cup miniature semisweet chocolate chips or regular chocolate chips, minced

Finishing Touches

1 large egg

Pinch each white sugar and salt

White sugar, for dusting

Confectioners' sugar, for dusting

Generously spray a 9-inch springform pan with nonstick cooking spray. Line a baking sheet with parchment paper and place pan on it.

In a mixer bowl, hand-whisk water and yeast together and let stand 2 to 3 minutes to dissolve yeast. Add 1 cup flour and then add warm milk, butter, egg, egg yolks, salt, sugar, vanilla, orange oil, and most of rest of flour. Mix ingredients and then, using dough hook, knead on low speed to make a soft dough, 8 to 10 minutes, adding more flour as required.

Remove dough hook, spray dough with nonstick cooking spray, and place a large clear plastic bag over entire mixer and bowl. Let dough rise 30 to 45 minutes or until almost doubled.

Turn out dough onto a lightly floured work surface and gently deflate. Press dough down into a flattened round and press cranberries and chocolate chips into dough, folding and incorporating as best you can—the shape doesn't matter at this stage.

Let dough rest 15 minutes and then cut into 12 portions. Shape each into a ball and arrange on one level in prepared pan. Whisk egg and pinch each of white sugar and salt. Brush dough with egg wash and dust with white sugar. Cover loosely with plastic wrap and let rise until puffy and almost doubled, about 45 to 60 minutes.

Preheat oven to 350°F. Bake bread until nicely browned, about 40 to 50 minutes.

Let cool and serve warm or at room temperature. If making this as a gift, leave it in the pan. Dust with confectioners' sugar, wrap in cellophane, and tie with ribbon.

Classic Roll-and-Cut Holiday Sugar Cookies

Makes 36 to 48 cookies, depending on size

Everyone needs a basic but delicious butter cookie that is easy to roll and perfect for decorating. This is a great one.

Cookies

2½ cups all-purpose flour
½ teaspoon baking powder
¼ teaspoon salt
1 cup unsalted butter, softened
¾ cup white sugar
¾ cup confectioners' sugar
1 large egg
2 teaspoons pure vanilla extract

Royal Icing

5 tablespoons meringue powder or
 2 pasteurized egg whites
6 tablespoons water
3½ to 4½ cups confectioners' sugar
Food coloring, as desired

For Cookies, in a bowl, blend flour, baking powder, and salt together. In a mixer bowl, cream butter, white sugar, and confectioners' sugar on medium speed until light and fluffy, about 30 seconds. Add egg and vanilla and mix until fully incorporated. Fold in flour mixture and continue blending until dough comes together, stopping and scraping down sides of bowl as needed. **Divide** dough in half, pat into disks, wrap in plastic wrap, and refrigerate until firm, at least 2 hours.

Stack two baking sheets together and line top sheet with parchment paper. You will need to repeat this procedure for each batch. Have another baking sheet ready, also lined with parchment paper.

Roll dough between lightly floured parchment or wax paper until about ⅓ inch thick. Transfer dough to prepared single baking sheet and refrigerate until firm, about 30 minutes. Cut into desired shapes using a cookie cutter; place them on prepared stacked baking sheets, leaving about 1 inch between cookies. (Gather dough scraps, pat into a disk, chill, and reroll one time.) Refrigerate cookies at least 30 minutes.

Preheat oven to 375°F. Bake cookies until bottoms are golden, about 10 to 15 minutes, depending on shape. Cool on baking sheets until firm enough to transfer to a wire rack to cool.

For Royal Icing, combine all ingredients except food coloring in bowl of a stand mixer fitted with paddle attachment. Mix slowly until stiff enough to form peaks. Icing should be pure white and thick but not fluffy and bubbly. If this happens, let frosting stand to settle, and then use a rubber spatula to vigorously beat and smooth out frosting. Alternatively, combine ingredients in a large bowl and beat with a hand mixer on low speed until frosting thickens to stiff peaks.

Add up to 1 tablespoon food coloring; mix with a rubber spatula until color is uniform. (Adding too much color reduces sheen and can break down consistency.) Store icing, covered, with plastic wrap directly on surface of icing. **Spoon** icing into a piping bag, decorate cookies as desired, and serve, or store in an airtight container at room temperature up to 1 month.

Best-Ever Scottish Shortbread

Makes 24 to 36 cookies, depending on size

Pulverized sugar plus a smidgen of rice flour and slow baking are the tricks to making these perfectly sandy-textured cookies. Instead of rolling the dough and cutting out the cookies, you can also roll the dough into a log, roll the log back and forth in crushed nuts and brown sugar, and then slice and bake.

¾	cup sugar	1	tablespoon rice flour
1	cup unsalted butter, softened	¼	teaspoon salt
2	cups all-purpose flour		

Stack two baking sheets together and line top sheet with parchment paper.
In a food processor, pulse sugar to finely pulverize it, about 10 seconds.
Remove and place sugar in a mixer with butter. Beat on low speed until well blended and then add all-purpose flour, rice flour, and salt and blend to make a firm dough.
Knead on a lightly floured work surface about 1 minute to make dough very firm. Flatten dough into a disk, wrap well, and refrigerate 30 minutes.
Preheat oven to 325°F. Roll out dough gently and cut into cookies or sticks that are ½ to ¾ inch thick.
Place cutouts on prepared baking sheets. Place in oven, and immediately reduce oven temperature to 300°F. Bake until lightly browned, about 40 to 50 minutes.
Cool well. Keep in a cookie tin; shortbread improves with age.

Shortbread Molds

The nicest thing about shortbread, aside from its amazing pure buttery taste, is the fact that it tends to hold its shape without leavening, making it ideal to press into specialty shortbread molds. *Rycraft* and *House on the Hill* are two of the best places to find great shortbread molds; they will even customize a mold of your own design if you want to create a new family tradition or give this recipe with a mold as a gift. Another great shortbread mold comes from the legendary *Hartstone Pottery* company. Molds such as this are usually found in vintage stores.

Classic Pumpkin Pie

Makes 6 to 8 servings

You can double this recipe and make it in a 10-inch quiche pan for large gatherings. This pie is plain, old-fashioned, and so good—and it never fails. Why fiddle with perfection?

½ cup firmly packed light brown sugar

½ cup white sugar

1 teaspoon ground cinnamon

Tiny pinch salt

¼ teaspoon ground ginger

¼ teaspoon ground cloves

2 large eggs

1 (15-ounce) can pure pumpkin puree or 2 scant cups homemade pumpkin puree

1 (12-ounce) can evaporated milk

1 unbaked 9-inch deep-dish pastry shell

Preheat oven to 425°F.

Combine both sugars, cinnamon, salt, ginger, and cloves in a small bowl. Beat eggs lightly in a second bowl. Stir pumpkin puree and sugar–spice mixture into eggs. Gradually stir in evaporated milk. Pour mixture into pastry shell.

Bake 15 minutes. Reduce oven temperature to 350°F. Bake another 40 to 50 minutes or until a knife blade inserted near center of pie comes out clean. Cool on a wire rack 2 hours. Serve at room temperature or refrigerate.

Offer with custard, whipped cream, or vanilla ice cream.

White Chocolate and Vanilla Bread Pudding

Makes 8 to 12 servings

This recipe can be made one to two days ahead and refrigerated until needed. It is good hot (from the oven or microwave) or chilled (as a cheesecakelike dessert for a party or holiday brunch).

10 cups leftover challah, brioche, or egg bread, cut into chunks or cubes
1½ cups light cream or half-and-half
1 cup milk
½ cup heavy whipping cream
7 large eggs, lightly beaten
1 cup sugar
½ cup unsalted butter, melted
2 teaspoons pure vanilla extract
1 teaspoon ground cinnamon
2 teaspoons baking powder
¼ cup all-purpose flour

⅛ teaspoon salt
1 cup coarsely chopped white chocolate
½ cup currants or frozen raspberries

Finishing Touches

Confectioners' sugar and ground cinnamon, for sprinkling
Whipped cream or Bourbon-Spiced Crème Anglaise (page 271)
Raspberries

Preheat oven to 350°F. Lightly grease a 13- x 9-inch pan or baking dish.
In a large mixing bowl, place bread chunks. In a separate bowl, mix together light cream, milk, heavy cream, eggs, sugar, melted butter, vanilla, cinnamon, baking powder, flour, and salt. Pour over bread and let stand 10 minutes or so to absorb. Fold in white chocolate and currants or frozen raspberries.
Spoon into prepared pan. Bake until firm to the touch, about 35 to 45 minutes. Dust top with a little confectioners' sugar and cinnamon.
Offer with whipped cream or Bourbon-Spiced Crème Anglaise on the side, if desired, or garnish each serving with confectioners' sugar, whipped cream, and raspberries.

Pure ambrosia: chunks of bread soaked in a batter of eggs, cream, vanilla, and cinnamon and studded with chunks of white chocolate. Raspberries are optional but lovely.

The Big Honey Cake

Makes 24 to 30 servings

This is, regardless of which holiday you celebrate, a huge, totally awesome, exceptionally flavorful honey cake. It lasts up to a week just covered or two to three months if frozen. Use leftovers to make bread pudding.

Honey Cake History

Some bakeries sell huge honey cakes that are cut into mammoth slabs. Sometimes they are baked in industrial baking pans, their sides lined with greased brown baker's paper. I like the look and generous cuts that result. Here is a homestyle version that features great homemade taste with the wonderful commercial look of a real bakery-style honey cake.

7	cups all-purpose flour
2	tablespoons ground cinnamon
1½	teaspoons ground cloves
1½	teaspoons ground allspice
2	tablespoons baking powder
½	teaspoon baking soda
¾	teaspoon salt
2	cups vegetable oil
1	cup honey
3	cups white sugar
1	cup firmly packed dark brown sugar
1	tablespoon pure vanilla extract
1	teaspoon pure orange extract or orange oil
7	large eggs
1⅓	cups brewed coffee or tea
1	cup cola
½	cup orange juice

Finishing Touches

1	cup slivered almonds, optional
	Confectioners' sugar, for dusting

Preheat oven to 350°F. Line bottom of a 13- x 9-inch pan with parchment paper. Spray paper and inner sides of pan with nonstick cooking spray. Cut out pieces of brown paper (do not use recycled paper) to line the inner sides and make a cake collar for the pan, letting pieces extend 3 to 4 inches above pan. This is a cake "girdle" that will support the cake as it rises high. Spray paper collar with nonstick spray. Line a baking sheet with parchment paper and place pan on it.

In a very large mixing bowl, hand-blend flour, cinnamon, cloves, allspice, baking powder, baking soda, and salt. Make a well in center and add, in order, oil, honey, white and brown sugars, extracts, eggs, coffee or tea, cola, and orange juice; blend well. Scrape sides and bottom of bowl occasionally to ensure batter is evenly blended.

Pour or spoon batter into prepared pan. Sprinkle with slivered almonds, if desired.

Bake 1 hour and then reduce oven temperature to 325°F and bake 45 minutes. Test cake for doneness, and if not quite done, reduce oven temperature to 300°F and bake until done, another 10 to 15 minutes or until cake is firm to the touch. Cool completely in pan. Dust with confectioners' sugar.

To serve, cut cake lengthwise down center and then into big slabs.

Christmas Black Cake

Makes 24 to 48 servings

Black cake is a unique rum-infused fruitcake. For this cake, you will need baker's caramel to "blacken" the cake to its characteristic dark hue. See "Source Guide" to order baker's caramel. I prefer a 7-inch springform pan and to make four to five cakes with this recipe. This is one very fine, elegant, amazing fruitcake.

1 cup dark raisins	Grated zest of 2 lemons
1 cup golden raisins	2 teaspoons ground allspice
2 cups pitted prunes, chopped	¾ teaspoon baking powder
2 cups currants	½ teaspoon salt
1 cup sweet port	1 pound unsalted butter, softened
⅓ cup dark rum	2 cups sugar
4 cups all-purpose flour	10 large eggs
1½ teaspoons ground cinnamon	1½ cups chopped pecans or walnuts
¼ teaspoon ground mace	3 to 5 tablespoons baker's caramel
¼ teaspoon ground cloves	Rum, for soaking

This cake is unlike any fruitcake you have ever had. It has a fruitcake flavor but features the texture of a fine pound cake. No candied fruit here! You can either make a few small round cakes or loaves, or make a huge cake and slice it into hunks and wrap according to whatever your gift-giving requirements are. Just make sure that you fill the pans two-thirds full with batter.

Three weeks to eight weeks before holiday, marinate fruits in port and ⅓ cup rum in a glass or similar nonreactive container with a cover. Stir fruit every few days.

To prepare pans, spray whatever pans you are using (such as four 8- x 4-inch loafpans, several 7-inch springform pans, or two 9- or 10-inch springform pans) very generously with nonstick cooking spray. After pans are sprayed, line the inner sides with buttered brown paper pieces (do not use recycled paper) or buttered parchment paper, all cut to fit.

Preheat oven to 275°F.

To make cake, hand-blend flour, cinnamon, mace, cloves, lemon zest, allspice, baking powder, and salt in a large bowl; set aside. Remove 1 cup of flour mixture to mix in with fruit.

In a mixer bowl, cream butter and add sugar to make a smooth, fluffy mixture, about 3 minutes on low speed. Add eggs, 2 at a time, and blend well. If mixture looks curdled, add 1 cup of dry ingredients to bind things together. Fold in dry ingredients, fruit, and nuts; drizzle in baker's caramel until mixture is well blended. (Drizzle in only as much baker's caramel as you need, per visual preference.) Batter will be a deep brown color. Stop mixer to scrape sides and bottom well of bowl occasionally. Fill prepared pans two-thirds full with batter.

Place prepared pans on a parchment paper–lined baking sheet and bake 1 hour and 45 minutes to 2 hours for 2 large cakes (turn them halfway through baking). If you bake smaller-sized cakes, bake until cakes spring back when gently pressed with fingertips, 75 to 90 minutes.

Cool cakes 15 to 20 minutes before unmolding and removing to a wire rack to cool completely. To cure and store, wrap fruitcake in cheesecloth that has been lightly soaked in rum, which you should then refresh with a few drops of rum each week for up to several weeks. Keep fruitcake wrapped in tins.

Classic Linzertorte

Makes 8 to 10 servings

This version of the Austrian dessert is dolled up with a trio of nuts and a blend of apricot and raspberry preserves. Toast the nuts for maximum flavor.

Is this a cookie or a tart? A torte or a cake? It is the classic European treat: a nutty shortbread kissed with cinnamon and cloves, topped with raspberry preserves, and crowned by a latticework crust and a halo of confectioners' sugar. While linzertorte is seasonal, it is welcome anytime.

Pastry

½	cup unsalted butter, softened
⅔	cup sugar
1	large egg
2	egg yolks
1	teaspoon pure vanilla extract
½	cup finely ground almonds
½	cup ground hazelnuts
¼	cup ground pecans
1	teaspoon ground cinnamon
½	teaspoon ground cloves
⅛	teaspoon salt
2	cups all-purpose flour

Filling

½	cup apricot preserves
½	cup raspberry preserves
1	teaspoon lemon juice or red wine
1	teaspoon cranberry or plum vinegar, optional
1	tablespoon raspberry *eau de vie,** optional

Finishing Touch

Confectioners' sugar

*Eau de vie means "water of life" and is a clear fruit brandy.

Line a small baking sheet with parchment paper. Generously butter a 9-inch tart pan with a removable bottom.

For Pastry, in a food processor, cream butter and sugar until smooth, 1 or 2 minutes. Add egg, egg yolks, vanilla, and nuts and blend about 40 seconds. Add spices, salt, and flour and process to make a thick, firm dough, about 20 to 40 seconds. Wrap dough and chill 20 minutes.

For Filling, blend all ingredients together in a small bowl and set aside.

Roll out dough to fit bottom and sides of tart pan. If dough breaks, patch together pieces. Spoon filling into tart pan.

Preheat oven to 325°F. Gather dough scraps together and, on a lightly floured work surface, roll to about ⅛ inch thick. Cut into strips, using a knife or serrated pastry wheel. Arrange strips in a crisscross or latticework fashion on top of tart, ending at edges, and pressing slightly with fingertips to hold in place. Place tart on prepared baking sheet and place in oven.

Bake 35 to 45 minutes until nicely browned and preserves are gently bubbling.

Cool to room temperature. Remove torte from tart pan and place on a serving platter. Dust with confectioners' sugar before serving.

Traditional Irish Soda Bread

Makes 6 to 10 servings

The wearing of the green ushers in my personal favorite bit of baking. This is the quintessential St. Patrick's Day treat. Rough-hewn, bulked up with baking powder and baking soda, and lightly acidic with buttermilk, this is a great nonyeasted bread. I also create variations that are sweeter, and I have been known to throw in orange juice or chopped chocolate and dried cherries or use brewed tea instead of buttermilk. Other times, I have also fashioned soda breads with oatmeal, but this classic recipe, which is as traditional as you please, is still the best. When it's not St. Pat's, you can surprise a friend, Irish or not, with this fine holiday tradition.

2	cups all-purpose flour
2	cups whole wheat flour
1/3	cup firmly packed brown sugar
1/4	cup white sugar
1	teaspoon salt
4	teaspoons baking powder
1/2	teaspoon baking soda
1/4	teaspoon ground cinnamon
6	tablespoons unsalted butter, cut into small chunks
1	cup raisins, plumped and dried (see page 18)
1 1/2	cups buttermilk, a bit more or less, as required

Finishing Touch

All-purpose flour or natural bran, for dusting

A well-steeped Irish breakfast tea or a strong blend featuring Assam tea leaves is what you want to serve with this bread.

Preheat oven to 375°F. Stack two baking sheets together and line top sheet with parchment paper.

Place all dry ingredients in a food processor and process briefly to blend. Add butter and pulse to cut fat into dry mixture. Turn out into a large bowl and fold in raisins. Then add most of buttermilk and stir, using a Danish dough whisk (see pages 24 and 25) or a fork, until mixture just holds together. Add more buttermilk, if required, a few tablespoons at a time.

Turn out dough onto a lightly floured work surface and knead briefly to make a soft but firm dough. Shape into a 6- to 7-inch mound.

Slash dough 1/2 inch deep, making an "X" on top of dough with a sharp paring knife. Dust top with all-purpose flour or natural bran. Place on prepared baking sheets.

Bake until medium golden brown all over, about 35 to 40 minutes. Cool 10 to 15 minutes before serving. Offer with butter or honey.

Best-Ever Chanukah Rugelach

Makes 48 pastries

After making and creating tons of rugelach recipes for years, this one is still at the top of the heap.

These are just about the best pastries you will ever bite into.

Dough

2	cups unsalted butter, melted
1/3	cup sugar
1/2	teaspoon salt
1/4	teaspoon baking powder
2	cups sour cream
4½	cups all-purpose flour

Filling (repeat these ingredients four times)

1/3 cup or so raspberry or apricot jam

1/2 cup firmly packed brown sugar
1 teaspoon ground cinnamon
1 cup finely chopped nuts, optional
1 cup raisins, plumped and dried (see page 18)

Finishing Touches

1 large egg
Pinch white sugar
Confectioners' sugar, for dusting

For Dough, in a mixer bowl, blend all ingredients in order given on low speed with paddle attachment until a ball forms. Turn out dough onto a lightly floured work surface and roll in a bit of additional flour, if required, to make a soft but manageable dough. Divide into four portions, press each into a flattened disk, and wrap in wax paper. Then place in a zip-top plastic bag. Chill 1 to 2 hours or more.

Preheat oven to 350°F. Stack two large baking sheets together and line top sheet with parchment paper. You will need to repeat this procedure for each batch.

On a generously floured work surface, roll out each portion of dough into a 12-inch circle. Smear on jam and then sprinkle on remaining Filling ingredients. Using a pastry or pizza wheel, cut into 12 wedges. Roll each wedge up snugly and place on prepared baking sheets. Whisk egg and pinch of white sugar in a small bowl. Brush pastries with egg wash.

Bake 30 to 40 minutes until pastries are nicely browned. Cool completely on a wire rack and dust with confectioners' sugar, if desired. Dough freezes well, as do unbaked wedges and baked pastries.

Be Mine Valentine's Day Cherry Blossom Cookies

Makes 24 to 32 cookies

Scrumptious and also gorgeous, these make a great gift cookie for the winter holidays or Valentine's Day. No one ever forgets these.

1	cup unsalted butter, cut into chunks	2	tablespoons half-and-half or light cream
1	cup white sugar		2½ to 3 cups all-purpose flour
2	teaspoons pure vanilla extract	¼	teaspoon salt
½	teaspoon pure almond or cherry extract	24	to 32 chocolate-covered cherries
			Confectioners' sugar, for dusting, optional

Stack two baking sheets together and line top sheet with parchment paper.
In a food processor, pulse butter with white sugar until well blended. Add next 5 ingredients, holding back some flour until you see if you need it, and pulse; then process to make a soft dough. Pat dough into a disk, wrap in wax paper, and chill 30 minutes.
Preheat oven to 350°F.
On a well-floured work surface, roll out dough to ¼-inch thickness, and cut out heart-shaped cookies. Place on prepared baking sheets and bake until golden around edges, about 18 to 22 minutes.
Leave cookies on baking sheets and deposit a chocolate-covered cherry in center of each cookie. Let melt a bit, carefully pressing chocolate down to assist melting. Chill cookies on tray in freezer 15 to 20 minutes and then dust with confectioners' sugar, if desired.

You know those milk chocolate cherries you get on Valentine's Day? OK, imagine this: You bake heart-shaped, delectable, buttery sugar cookies that taste like shortbread but roll like *Play-Doh*. As the baked cookies sit cooling, you plop a chocolate-covered cherry onto the center of each one. The cherries slowly melt and ooze their delectable cherry fondant until you are left with a thin veneer of cherry glaze that has a slight pink shimmer over a cookie base. In the center of each cookie, the chocolate casing sinks down like an inverted volcano and almost creates a 'rose' effect. Once finished, let the cookies set and then dust with confectioners' sugar, if desired. Wrap each one in wax paper, chill, and then pack in a tin.

grainy
goodness

Nutritionists, dietitians, and bakers are learning more about the basics of food—particularly grains—all the time. Carbs have been in, then out, and then in again but with an awareness that was always there. This awareness is that multigrains and alternatives to white wheat flour have much to offer home bakers who choose to bake with added nutrition (see "Benefits of Whole Grains," page 293).

The message about complex carbs and making the carbs we eat count is slowly getting through. It doesn't mean converting your entire approach to baking nor always incorporating multigrains or baking without fat. It means having choices.

As a mindful baker, I also appreciate things that are from our past being conceptually linked to what is new and current. Some of the grains in this chapter, such as spelt and kamut, have been around for centuries and are still as appropriate and tasty on today's table. Baking with a grainier mind-set is simply about making and breaking bread with a nod to the broader spectrum of interesting grains that are widely available to us. It is mostly a matter of using them in recipes that make them perform the best, given the criteria of taste, texture, and nutrition.

But before you give that bag of white all-purpose flour a suspicious eye, it's good to know that white flour has its positive attributes. In fact, all flour, but particularly unbleached all-purpose flour, has merit and is a boon to baking decadent treats. But for many other things, it is the underused, underappreciated grains of old that offer far more to a healthful diet in the way of taste and benefits. These are the grains that fall nicely into the category of complex carbohydrates.

Over time, I have accepted more whole grains into my mainstream efforts of traditional baking. I am a baker who embraces *all* grains. There is something inherently reverent about baking with ancient grains. They may not have the gluten or the loft of white flour, but they almost "speak" to the baker in you and inspire you to new heights.

The Grainy Mind-Set

The first-generation whole-grain baked goods that fueled the complex carbohydrate movement tended to be heavy and tasteless, giving whole grains a bad rap. In reality, stoneground and multigrain goodies offer new dimensions in flavor and texture to savvy bakers—it's just a matter of knowing how to use these grains to make them sing. To start with, it is helpful to know that the most commonly used flour comes in two varieties:

- **Whole wheat**—100% of the grain, nothing taken away, nothing added.
- **White flour**—75% of the wheat with most of the bran and germ removed; it contains the highest percentage of protein or gluten. White flour is usually enriched with vitamins, since flour is a perfect vehicle for carrying added nutrients.

Within these categories, there are unbleached as well as naturally aged flours, organic flours, and factory-milled or stoneground flours.

I like to mix stoneground or organic products with regular unbleached white flours or regular whole wheat flour. Organic flours have their benefits and nutrition but are heavier and drier to bake with. They simply do not have the gluten, i.e., body and structure, on their own to provide the loft and crumb we are accustomed to when baking with white flour. These grains greatly benefit when combined with some unbleached all-purpose flour, which provides structure to baked goods. Think of organic or naturally aged white flours as the supporting cast of multigrain flours. Remember, too, that in bread baking, the small flakes of bran and germ are like tiny splinters cutting through the strands of gluten in the bread, adding wonderful texture.

For the best flavor, try to find a source for freshly milled whole grains. Or grind your own grains using a home mill.

Healthy Baking Tips

- Use sea salt or kosher salt for the most natural flavor.
- Use unpasteurized (raw) honey for its taste, traces of nutrients, and performance in baked goods (it helps with browning and preserving freshness). Resorting to prune puree or applesauce, sweeteners like Splenda, or natural sweeteners such as stevia are options that call for baking experimentation. Replacing everything in baking (especially key ingredients such as fats and sweeteners) with alternative ingredients often makes for compromised baking that is possibly healthy—if only you could get someone to eat it.
- Add nuts, ground flax or bran, and dried or fresh fruit to increase the nutrients, fiber, taste, or sweetness.
- Aside from grains, seeds, rye, oats, barley, amaranth, bulgur, white whole wheat flour, and legumes such as teff are good choices. White whole wheat flour contains all nutrients associated with regular whole wheat flour but is a sweeter, nuttier flour.
- When using dried fruit, you can experiment with organic. When using organic or regular dried fruit from the supermarket, presoak the fruit to hydrate and plump it by covering it in boiling water or very hot fruit juice. Let it stand 5 to 10 minutes and then drain, pat with paper towels, and use as called for. Many new dried fruits are available. Vary your baking by experimenting with dried strawberries, mango, kiwi, banana, peach, and pineapple.
- When using flax seed, use ground if you want the digestive benefits or use whole flax seed as a nutty textural component.
- When using such grains as cracked wheat or millet, cover them in boiling water to hydrate, promote flavor, and produce a more moist grain to be used in dough or batter.
- When using sesame seeds, toasted seeds taste best. Always taste them for freshness. The same is true for nuts. Vary the nuts you use. Try pine nuts, pistachios, or chopped Brazil nuts instead of using walnuts or pecans all the time. Consider unskinned almonds or hazelnuts for more roughage, extra flavor, and a more rustic appeal.
- For the best results, when you bake with whole grains, work by hand, take your time, and stay in the moment. Savor the wholesome effort as well as the final wholesome tastes that result when baking the grainier way.

Whole Wheat, Date, and Orange Muffins

Makes 9 to 12 muffins

These old-fashioned muffins are heavenly. They are delicate and absolutely packed with nutrition and flavor, and they have a gorgeous crumb with a gently crisp top cap. If you have something against dates, use raisins or cranberries.

½ cup unsalted butter, softened
½ cup white sugar
½ cup firmly packed brown sugar
2 large eggs
¾ cup buttermilk
1 cup natural bran
1 cup organic whole wheat flour
1 cup all-purpose flour

¼ teaspoon baking soda
¼ teaspoon salt
2¼ teaspoons baking powder
¼ teaspoon ground cinnamon
½ cup walnuts, finely chopped
Zest of 1 small orange, finely minced
1 cup dried dates, finely diced

Preheat oven to 350°F. Line 12 muffin cups with paper liners. Place on a baking sheet lined with parchment paper.

In a mixer bowl, cream butter with both sugars. Add eggs and blend well. Then stir in buttermilk, bran, and remaining ingredients to make a soft batter. Make sure nothing is stuck on bottom of bowl.

Using an ice-cream scoop, scoop batter into prepared muffin cups, filling almost full.

Bake until puffed up and set and muffins spring back when gently pressed with fingertips, about 25 to 28 minutes.

Fresh Is Best

Using freshly milled grains is a way of ensuring that the grains you use are really fresh and fragrant for your baking. There are a few brands of grain grinders available. Otherwise, using a grain grinder that is an attachment to a stand mixer you already have is good way to get great grains at a better price and utilize your own mixer.

Earth and Moon Whole Wheat Sandwich Bread

Makes 2 small loaves or 1 large loaf

One of my first jobs was as head baker for a health-food holistic café and restaurant called *Terre Etoile*. Color me green beans—but while all else was healthy and wholesome, my dessert creations were sheer decadence. Yet no one complained! The bakery took off, and all sorts of famous people, from celebrities to National League baseball players, dropped by for one delight or another. My desserts were outdone only by the sandwiches that *Terre Etoile* made their reputation on. These sandwiches were massive, towering affairs of sprouts and fillings packed on a throne of fluffy, moist whole wheat bread. The sandwiches were out of this world. I know because in addition to creating the full bakery menu, I eventually created all the fillings to go in the sandwiches. This recipe makes a beautifully hued, moist, and lofty-grained wheat bread reminiscent of that amazing bread.

This is the sort of bread that craves sprouts, grainy mustard, hothouse tomatoes, Swiss or Havarti cheese, and then some sort of vegetarian filling or smoked turkey shavings. I love this bread for its fragrance, moistness, and gorgeous color. It's nutritious enough for health-food nuts and is simply great bread for the toast-and-sandwich crowd. Cut it into lofty slices, pile it high, and serve forth.

2	cups warm water (100°F to 110°F)
2	tablespoons rapid-rise yeast
1	cup white bread flour
2½	teaspoons salt
3	tablespoons honey
3	tablespoons brown sugar
5	tablespoons canola oil
2	teaspoons baker's caramel*
4	to 5 cups whole wheat, all-purpose, or bread flour, or mixed, preferably organic
½	cup sunflower seeds
⅓	cup sesame seeds

*See "Source Guide," page 316.

Stack two baking sheets together and line top sheet with parchment paper.

In a mixer bowl, hand-whisk water and yeast together and let stand 2 to 3 minutes to dissolve yeast. Fold in white flour and then add salt, honey, brown sugar, oil, baker's caramel, and half of whole wheat flour and mix briefly. Let dough stand 15 minutes and then, with a dough hook, knead on lowest speed of mixer, adding additional whole wheat flour as required to get a soft but cohesive, somewhat tacky dough, 8 to 10 minutes.

Remove dough hook and spray dough with nonstick cooking spray. Cover entire mixer and bowl with a large clear plastic bag. Let dough rise about 45 to 90 minutes until almost doubled in size.

Turn out dough onto a lightly floured work surface and gently deflate. Divide dough in two. Sprinkle work surface liberally with sunflower seeds and sesame seeds. Roll or press each portion on board and then shape each portion into an oblong loaf and place in two 9- x 5-inch loafpans generously sprayed with nonstick cooking spray. Place loafpans on prepared baking sheets. Alternatively, shape into one or two oval shapes and place on prepared baking sheets to bake free form. Spray dough with nonstick cooking spray, cover loosely with plastic wrap and let rise until quite puffy, about 45 to 90 minutes.

Preheat oven to 375°F. Bake breads 15 minutes and then reduce oven temperature to 350°F and bake until they are well browned. Cool in pans 10 minutes; then invert onto wire racks to cool completely.

Date-Apricot-Raisin Pinwheel Cookies

Makes 2 to 4 dozen cookies, depending on size and style of cookies

Sometimes nothing is more satisfying than a rustic, sweet thing like this date cookie. This apricot-tinged date cookie is too good to appreciate until you make a batch. These are so old-fashioned and hearty, with vitamin-packed dried fruit and fiber-rich oats. Check out the fold-over version (below) of these cookies, too.

Fruit Filling

1   cup chopped pitted dates
½   cup golden raisins
½   cup chopped dried apricots
    (preferably Californian)
¼   cup sugar
½   cup water or orange juice

Cookies

½   cup unsalted butter, softened
1   cup firmly packed light brown
    sugar
½   cup white sugar

2   large eggs
2   teaspoons pure vanilla extract
2½ cups all-purpose flour
½   teaspoon baking soda
¼   teaspoon salt
1½ cups quick cooking oats
Milk, as required

Finishing Touches

Melted butter, for glazing
Milk or water
Sugar

For Fruit Filling, in a medium saucepan, simmer dates, raisins, apricots, and sugar in water or orange juice, adding more liquid as needed (in case fruit sticks) until thick, about 15 to 20 minutes. Remove from heat; cool well. **Stack** two baking sheets together and line top sheet with parchment paper. **For Cookies,** in a mixer bowl, cream butter with both sugars until fluffy. Blend in eggs and vanilla. Fold in flour, baking soda, salt, and oats to make a thick dough, adding only a little milk to make it hold together. Wrap dough and chill 30 to 60 minutes.

Roll out dough to a 10- x 8-inch rectangle. Spread filling over dough. Using parchment paper as an aid, roll up dough, jellyroll fashion. Wrap well and chill 4 hours or freeze 1 to 2 hours.

Preheat oven to 350°F.

On a lightly floured work surface, cut dough into ½-inch slices. Place on prepared baking sheets. Brush with melted butter. Bake until done, and edges of cookies are starting to brown, about 14 to 18 minutes. Let cool on baking sheets 10 minutes before allowing to cool on a wire rack.

For Fold-Over Cookies, on a lightly floured work surface, roll dough to ¼-inch (maybe a bit less) thickness. Cut into 4-inch circles. Deposit some fruit filling in middle. Paint edges of cookies with milk or water and then fold over and seal or crimp. Brush top with milk and sprinkle with sugar. Bake until done, about 15 to 20 minutes. Cool on baking sheets.

Benefits of Whole Grains

Whole grains seem to have real staying power, and your body partakes of that complexity in a myriad of beneficial ways. News about health and nutrition changes by the hour, but there never seems to be any debate as far as whole grains are concerned:

- They help in digestion.
- There are indications that whole grains can lower cholesterol.
- They have been shown to protect or offer some prevention against certain diseases—from cancer to heart disease.
- People allergic to wheat may be able to tolerate grains such as spelt and kamut. Be sure to check with your health-care provider before making any changes in your diet.
- Many grains contain large amounts of dietary fiber, iron, calcium, minerals, and amino acids.
- Most refined flours have been stripped of 80% of their nutrients by the time they arrive at the supermarket. Look for the term *enriched* on the product label. This means certain B vitamins and iron are added back after processing. Unbleached white flour is a better choice. Organic unbleached flour is a better choice again.

Honey, Fruit, Pine Nut, and Almond Traveler's Bars

Makes 12 bars; also pictured on page 288

There is evidence that even the Crusaders carried granola bars in hand (or in the saddle) for the road. The bars lasted well, so they were often used in ancient baking. This version is a totally scrumptious granola bar that does a body good.

Even the uncooked batter of this recipe is delicious. If you are out of one ingredient or another, substitutions are fine. Add an egg for more iron and protein if you like, but then don't nibble on the uncooked batter.

½	cup light olive oil or unsalted butter, melted
½	cup honey
¼	cup firmly packed brown sugar
2	cups granola cereal or rolled oats
1	cup puffed brown rice
⅓	cup pine nuts
½	cup sweetened shredded coconut
⅓	cup chopped dates
⅓	cup dried strawberries, dried mango, or dried cherries, minced
¼	teaspoon ground cinnamon
⅛	teaspoon salt
2	tablespoons unbleached all-purpose flour or whole wheat flour
2	tablespoons toasted sesame seeds
½	cup coarsely chopped unskinned almonds

Preheat oven to 350°F. Line a 9-inch square pan, or, preferably, an 11- x 7-inch brownie pan with parchment paper. Leave some overhang. **In a large bowl,** stir together oil or butter and honey. Blend in brown sugar, granola or rolled oats, puffed rice, pine nuts, coconut, dates, dried fruit, cinnamon, salt, flour, sesame seeds, and almonds. Mixture will be sticky. Using wet hands or a wet flat spatula, press mixture into prepared pan. Place pan on a baking sheet.

Bake on lower rack of oven about 18 to 22 minutes or until top seems set. Refrigerate about 1 hour before cutting into bars. Turn out onto a board and cut with a sharp knife. Best stored individually wrapped in wax paper and frozen.

Whole-Grain Halvah Scones

Makes 12 to 14 small-to-medium scones

These are delectable and nutritious scones that are sweetened with halvah and honey and studded with dried fruit. The halvah is optional but offers a taste of the past, updated in a contemporary treat. These are wonderfully rustic and delectable to the very last crumb.

2½ teaspoons baking powder
½ teaspoon baking soda
½ teaspoon salt
½ cup firmly packed brown sugar
½ cup spelt or kamut flour
2 cups whole wheat flour
½ cup, approximately, unbleached all-purpose flour
½ cup unsalted butter, cut into chunks
⅓ cup honey
1 large egg
½ cup, or as required, loose, plain yogurt or buttermilk

½ cup finely chopped vanilla halvah*
⅓ cup rolled oats
¼ cup chopped sunflower seeds
½ cup dried strawberries or blueberries, or raisins
½ cup blueberries (instead of or in addition to dried fruit)

Finishing Touches

Melted butter or milk, for glazing scones before baking
Warm honey, for brushing on baked scones

*Halvah is Middle Eastern sesame seed candy. Find it at most large upscale markets or health-food stores near bulk nuts.

Preheat oven to 400°F. Have an oven rack set up in upper third oven position. Stack two baking sheets together and line top sheet with parchment paper.

In a large bowl, blend baking powder, baking soda, salt, brown sugar, spelt or kamut, whole wheat, and white flours. Cut in butter to make a grainy mixture. Make a well in center and add honey, egg, and most of yogurt. Mix it halfway through and then fold in halvah, oats, sunflower seeds, and fruit. Stir with a fork to make a soft dough.

Turn out onto a lightly floured work surface and gently knead until you can pat dough into a round, adding more white flour as required to firm it up if required. Alternatively, leave dough softer, and use an ice-cream scoop to deposit scones on prepared baking sheets.

For traditional hand-cut scones, cut into small triangles, about 1½ inches thick. Place on prepared baking sheets. Brush with butter or milk before baking.

Bake 18 to 22 minutes until scones are nicely browned. Brush with warm honey as scones come out of oven.

If you prefer, use canola or light olive oil instead of butter in these scones. Butter is a natural fat, and considering that this recipe makes 12 to 14 scones, the end result is a mere trace of butter per scone. Plus, the flavor of butter is unrivaled. If you don't have the halvah, you can leave it out. The scones are equally good without it.

BetterBaking.com's Famous Breakfast Scones

Makes 12 to 14 small-to-medium scones

Yes, Virginia, there is a scone version of the Breakfast Cookie! This is a great idea from one of my Web site visitors, whose e-mail subject line was simply: Loved the Breakfast Cookies; Begging for a Scone! So here it is, created to order.

If you prefer, you can use spelt or kamut to replace some of the whole wheat flour. These noble grains will be a bit more rustic. Vary the fruit as you wish. These scones are nicely crusty on the outside, amber colored within, and are, despite their health pedigree, rather delicate. OK, I cannot stop bragging: These are simply wonderful.

Zest of 1 small orange
2½ teaspoons baking powder
½ teaspoon baking soda
½ teaspoon salt
¼ teaspoon ground cinnamon
½ cup firmly packed brown sugar
2½ cups whole wheat flour*
½ cup unsalted butter or canola oil
¼ cup honey
2 tablespoons maple syrup
2 large eggs
1 cup, or a bit more, buttermilk or soured milk or loose, plain yogurt
1 cup granola cereal (your choice of brand but go for a really fiber-filled one)
⅓ cup rolled oats

¼ cup cornmeal
2 tablespoons ground flax seed
¼ cup sunflower seeds
¼ cup chopped almonds
½ cup raisins, plumped and dried (see page 18)
½ cup dried sour cherries or cranberries
½ cup frozen raspberries or blueberries or diced apple

Finishing Touches

Milk, for brushing
Flour or granola, for dusting
Brown sugar or flax seeds, for dusting
Warm honey, for drizzling after scones come out of oven

*You can use part spelt or kamut or both.

Preheat oven to 400°F. Have oven rack set up in upper third oven position. Stack two baking sheets together and line top sheet with parchment paper.
In a large bowl, blend orange zest, baking powder, baking soda, salt, cinnamon, brown sugar, and whole wheat flour. Cut in butter or drizzle in oil.
Make a well in center and add honey, maple syrup, eggs, and most of buttermilk. Mix it halfway through and then fold in granola, oats, cornmeal, flax seed, sunflower seeds, nuts, and fruit. Stir with a fork to make a soft batter, adding more buttermilk at this point if mixture seems dry and does not hold together.
If you want drop scones, use an ice-cream scoop to deposit scones on prepared baking sheets. If you prefer cut scones, turn out dough onto a floured work surface and gently knead, taking in a bit more flour as required to make a dough you can shape into a ¾-inch-thick round. Cut into small triangles.
Brush with milk or dust with flour or granola or brush with milk and dust on some brown sugar or flax seeds or leave plain.
Bake 17 to 22 minutes until scones are nicely browned. Brush with warm honey as scones come out of oven, if desired.

Little French Bakery Corn and Multigrain Muffins

Makes 12 medium muffins

Here's my version of another bakery treasure I found once at a fancy French bakery. The originals were baked in conical molds with brown paper inserted inside them like a sleeve so that the finished muffins, which were tied with small cords, looked like little muffin "haystacks." I use a miniature springform pan (but you can use a muffin pan) and make collars of parchment paper. Once baked, I tie ribbon around each muffin. Silly but charming and oh so French. The muffins themselves are filled with corn and whole wheat goodness. And they have a totally surprising delight of taste and texture—grainy, crusty, tender, and sweet.

¼ cup corn or canola oil	2½ teaspoons baking powder
¼ cup unsalted butter, softened	¼ teaspoon baking soda
½ cup white sugar	½ teaspoon salt
¼ cup firmly packed brown sugar	⅓ cup chopped sunflower seeds
1 tablespoon honey	2 tablespoons wheat germ or ground flax seed
1 large egg	1 cup buttermilk
½ cup stoneground cornmeal	¾ cup raisins or currants, plumped and dried (see page 18)
1½ to 2 cups multigrain flour or stoneground whole wheat flour	
½ cup unbleached all-purpose flour	

Arrange a rack in oven to upper third position. Line a baking sheet with parchment paper. Line 12 muffin cups each with a collar of parchment paper, extending 2 to 3 inches above rim of muffin pan surface. Spray inside of each liberally with nonstick cooking spray.

Preheat oven to 375°F.

In a mixer bowl, cream oil, butter, both sugars, and honey until smooth. Blend in egg and then fold in cornmeal, flours, baking powder, baking soda, salt, sunflower seeds, and flax seed, drizzling in buttermilk as batter mixes on low speed of mixer. The batter should be like a thick cake batter. If it is very liquidy, add some multigrain flour, a few tablespoons at a time, until mixture is like a muffin or carrot cake batter. Fold in raisins.

Spoon into prepared pan. Place pan on prepared baking sheet. Bake 17 to 22 minutes or until muffins are just browned on top.

Cool in pan 10 minutes before gently removing. Once you can handle them comfortably, tie each with ribbon.

Sesame Snap and Halvah Macaroon Cookies

Makes about 2 dozen cookies

This unique, buttery, delectably crisp-tender cookie has a macaroon pedigree. It features pockets of just-melted halvah and sesame snaps, as well as sesame seeds, kamut flour, and honey. Sun-dried strawberries make this ambrosial, but dried sour cherries or cranberries are a fine option. These cookies are heavenly and healthy. Sesame snaps are like sesame brittle and are often in health-food stores as well as the kosher-food section of supermarkets (they are imported from Israel). Cookies such as these are truly treats, and they satisfy in a big way. One cookie with green tea or espresso during an afternoon break will carry you to supper.

Multigrain Choices

Aside from white all-purpose flour and whole wheat flour, there are interesting, nutritious, and flavorful grains to bake with. They include amaranth, teff, kamut, barley, spelt, cornmeal, groats, brown rice, wild rice (which is not really rice but another grain), flax, rye, buckwheat, and millet. All are available on the health-food aisle in most supermarkets and online via various whole-grain suppliers.

½	cup unsalted butter, melted, or light olive oil
½	cup firmly packed brown sugar
¼	cup warm honey
2	large eggs
2	tablespoons lemon juice
2	teaspoons pure vanilla extract
¾	cup kamut or multigrain flour or spelt flour
¼	cup all-purpose flour
¼	teaspoon salt
1	teaspoon baking powder

2	tablespoons toasted sesame seeds
3	tablespoons sunflower seeds
½	cup dried strawberries or cranberries
2	cups rolled oats or natural granola (or half and half)
1	cup coarsely chopped vanilla halvah
2	to 3 cups coarsely crumbled sesame snaps

Preheat oven to 350°F. Stack two baking sheets together and line top sheet with parchment paper; spray with nonstick cooking spray.

Blend everything together in a mixing bowl in order given. For each cookie, form into 2-tablespoon lumps and press down ever so slightly on prepared baking sheets.

Bake until nicely golden brown, about 15 to 18 minutes; the more baked they are (without burning them), the nicer the taste and texture.

The Skinny-Jeans Cookie

Makes 10 to 15 cookies

Health-food stores always have neat (but expensive) big cookies just near the cash register to tempt you. I found the "skinny cookie" in such a place and bought it. One bite and I couldn't believe such flavor and chewy goodness was "skinny." Here is my version. It has no butter, no eggs, very little flour (and it is spelt, to boot), and tons of oats. It is about the best thing you will ever indulge in.

1⅓ cups firmly packed brown sugar

½ cup water or orange juice

1½ teaspoons pure vanilla extract

½ cup canola oil

¾ cup spelt flour

2 tablespoons cornstarch

3 cups rolled oats

¾ teaspoon baking soda

½ teaspoon salt

¼ teaspoon ground allspice

½ teaspoon ground cinnamon

1 cup raisins, plumped and dried (see page 18)

1 cup *Bran Flakes* cereal

Preheat oven to 350°F. Stack two baking sheets together and line top sheet with parchment paper.

In a mixer bowl (or by hand), blend brown sugar, water or orange juice, vanilla, and oil. Fold in spelt flour, cornstarch, oats, baking soda, salt, allspice, and cinnamon. Fold in raisins and cereal. You will have a thick, gloppy batter.

Deposit heaping ⅓-cup mounds of batter 2 inches apart on prepared baking sheets, pressing down slightly with wet hands.

Bake until nicely browned and dry or set to the touch, 15 to 20 minutes. Cool on baking sheets 15 minutes before removing. The longer you bake these, the more crisp they'll be. They will further crisp as they cool, but these are big, chewy cookies.

Cracked Wheat Bread

Makes 1 large loaf

Cracked wheat (also known as kasha or bulgur wheat) gets thrown in here for the most fragrant, moist, lofty, and flavor-packed rustic bread ever. You can mix this dough in the bread machine, but bake it in the oven.

½ cup cracked wheat or bulgur wheat

¾ cup boiling water

1¼ cups warm water (100°F to 110°F)

2½ teaspoons rapid-rise yeast

1½ cups stoneground whole wheat flour

2 tablespoons honey

1¼ teaspoons salt

1 to 2 cups, or as required, white bread flour

Cracked wheat, cornmeal, and bran, for dusting counter

In a medium bowl, cover cracked wheat with boiling water and let stand 20 minutes.

In a mixer bowl, hand-whisk warm water and yeast together and let stand 2 to 3 minutes to dissolve yeast. Add whole wheat flour, honey, salt, and soaked bulgur and mix well. Add most of white bread flour and then knead with dough hook on lowest speed of mixer, adding more white flour as required to make a soft dough, kneading on low speed 6 to 8 minutes.

Remove dough hook, spray dough with nonstick cooking spray, and cover entire mixer and bowl with a large clear plastic bag. Let dough rise until almost doubled, 45 to 60 minutes. Gently deflate and roll to shape into a large ball on a work surface generously dusted with cracked wheat, cornmeal, and bran.

Preheat oven to 375°F.

Shape into a ball (you can also bake it as a 9- x 5-inch loaf). Place on a parchment paper–lined baking sheet, spray lightly with nonstick cooking spray, and cover loosely with plastic wrap. Let rise 30 to 45 minutes.

Bake until done, 35 to 45 minutes.

Natural Bran-Banana-Buttermilk Muffins

Makes 12 medium muffins

Natural bran is available in bulk, boxed by *Quaker*, or from health-food stores. It makes for a lighter bran and banana muffin that is slightly crusty on the outside, moist inside, and simply delicious.

1	cup very hot buttermilk	1	tablespoon baking powder
1	cup natural bran	½	teaspoon baking soda
¼	cup wheat germ	¼	teaspoon salt
¾	cup pureed banana	½	cup raisins or chopped dates, plumped and dried (see page 18), optional
2	large eggs		
1	teaspoon pure vanilla extract		
2	tablespoons honey or molasses		**Finishing Touch**
¾	cup firmly packed light brown sugar		Slivers of banana for tops of muffins
½	cup canola or safflower oil		
1½	cups unbleached all-purpose flour		

Preheat oven to 375°F. Line a baking sheet with parchment paper and spray 12 muffin cups with nonstick cooking spray and then line each one with a muffin liner. Set on prepared baking sheet.

In a medium bowl, stir hot buttermilk with bran and wheat germ and let stand 5 minutes. Add bran mixture and pureed banana to a large bowl and stir in eggs, vanilla, honey, brown sugar, and oil and blend well. Fold in flour, baking powder, baking soda, and salt to make a soft batter, adding only a touch more flour if it seems too wet and gloppy versus seeming like a batter. Fold in raisins or dates.

Using an ice-cream scoop, deposit batter equally into muffin cups. Top each with a thin sliver of banana.

Bake until done and muffins spring back when gently pressed with fingertips, about 22 to 25 minutes.

Flax Seed Luncheon Rolls

Makes 16 small luncheon buns or 12 larger sandwich rolls

The first thing you would notice about these delightful luncheon or salad rolls is how good-looking they are. Then you would sink your teeth into crusty, nutty (but no nuts) bronze-crumbed wonders and be carried away by the outer crust and inner crumb. Then you might notice the flax seeds, sesame seeds, molasses (just for color, not for flavor), and touch of whole wheat flour and bran and think—wow—this is health food? If you make these large, use them as brown-bag lunch rolls.

> **Ground flax seeds are easily digested, whereas whole flax seeds provide roughage. I use whole flax for a nice nutty taste and texture in these rolls.**

2	cups warm water (100°F to 110°F)
1	tablespoon rapid-rise yeast
2	tablespoons flax seed oil or canola oil
2	teaspoons toasted sesame seed oil
1	tablespoon fresh lemon juice
2	tablespoons honey
2	tablespoons molasses
1	tablespoon salt
2	tablespoons rye flour
1	large egg
½	cup flax seeds
2	tablespoons sesame seeds
1	cup whole wheat flour
½	cup natural bran
3	to 4 cups white bread flour

Finishing Touches

⅓	cup each, white bread flour and natural bran, for dusting tops

Spray interior of a mixer bowl with nonstick cooking spray. Line a large baking sheet or two smaller ones with parchment paper.

In a mixer bowl, hand-whisk water and yeast together and let stand 2 to 3 minutes to dissolve yeast. Briskly whisk in flax seed oil, sesame seed oil, lemon juice, honey, molasses, salt, rye flour, egg, flax seeds, sesame seeds, whole wheat flour, and natural bran. Stir well to blend. Fold in 2 cups of white bread flour and blend with a wooden spoon a few minutes. With dough hook, knead on lowest speed of mixer, adding remaining bread flour, as required, to make a sticky but cohesive dough, about 8 to 10 minutes.

Remove dough hook, spray dough with nonstick cooking spray and cover entire machine and bowl with a large clear plastic bag. Let dough rise until almost doubled, 45 to 60 minutes.

Turn out dough onto a lightly floured work surface and gently deflate. Let dough rest, loosely covered with a tea towel or plastic bag, 15 minutes. Divide dough into 16 portions and shape each into a ball. When you have formed all balls, spray them with nonstick cooking spray. Roll each ball first in flour and then in bran.

Preheat oven to 375°F. Place rolls, spacing them about 2 to 3 inches apart, on prepared baking sheet.

Bake rolls 18 to 20 minutes or until nicely browned all over and crusty. Dust with natural bran or flour, if desired, as rolls come out of oven. Cool on baking sheet. Freeze extras or keep a few out for up to 2 days.

Honey-Nut Infused Cookies

Makes about 34 to 40 cookies

Densely nutty shortbread cookies are saturated with a honey, lemon, and vanilla syrup after baking. Serve in confectionary cups as a decadent treat. These are similar to baklava in flavor yet are easier to make in this cookie form.

¾ cup sugar

½ cup whole almonds

½ cup walnut halves

½ cup pistachios

1 cup unsalted butter, softened

¾ cup light olive oil

Zest of 1 orange, finely minced

¾ cup fresh orange juice

½ teaspoon salt

4 teaspoons baking powder

6 cups, approximately, all-purpose
   flour

Honey Syrup

1 cup sugar

1 cup water

¼ cup unpasteurized honey

½ teaspoon ground cinnamon

1 tablespoon fresh lemon juice

2 teaspoons pure vanilla extract

Finishing Touch

Ground pistachios or almonds,
   optional

Preheat oven to 350°F.

Stack two baking sheets together and line top sheet with parchment paper. In a food processor, grind sugar and 3 types of nuts together, pulsing to make a nutty/sugar mixture.

In a mixer, blend butter with nut mixture and cream well. Add oil and blend well. Then add orange zest, juice, salt, baking powder, and most of flour. Blend well to make a thick dough.

Form walnut-sized rounds and press onto prepared baking sheets. Alternatively (and far nicer), pack dough into a tiny tart shell, about 2 inches wide and ½ inch deep. Tap briskly on a counter to release the formed cookie and then place on prepared baking sheets. Repeat with remaining dough.

Bake until just browning around edges, 25 to 35 minutes. Cool well.

Meanwhile, for Honey Syrup, simmer all ingredients together on low heat 8 to 10 minutes. Cool.

Dip baked cookies in Honey Syrup and then place them on a clean sheet of parchment paper. Repeat with all cookies. Place each cookie in a paper muffin liner. Dust with ground pistachios or ground almonds, if desired, and then drizzle on remaining syrup if there is any (this will allow cookie to soak further and be more thoroughly infused).

Multigrain Moist Pita Breads

Makes 10 to 12 pitas

I like pita bread and enjoy its rustic character and sandwich sensibility, but I am not keen on those dry, thin rounds you have to eat within the hour. By contrast, these are thick and moist, and you can slice them horizontally to make sandwich pitas. Pitas like this often come in other versions (multigrain, whole wheat, flax, etc.), and all freeze well. Some are made with a sourdough starter. These are equally flavorful and a touch quicker to make.

2	cups warm water, preferably spring water (100°F to 110°F)	¼	cup ground flax seed
2½	teaspoons rapid-rise yeast	¼	cup spelt or kamut flour
2	tablespoons honey	1	teaspoon malt powder
2	teaspoons salt	2	cups organic whole wheat flour
2	tablespoons whole flax seeds	1½ to 2½ cups unbleached white bread flour	
¼	cup *Bran Flakes* cereal or natural bran		

Stack two baking sheets together, line top sheet with parchment paper, and set aside.

In a mixer bowl, hand-whisk water and yeast together and let stand 2 to 3 minutes to dissolve yeast. Briskly whisk in honey, salt, flax seeds, bran cereal, ground flax seed, spelt or kamut flour, malt, whole wheat flour, and half of bread flour. With a dough hook, knead on lowest speed of mixer 6 to 10 minutes, adding more flour as required to make a very tough, slick dough. Cover loosely with plastic wrap and let rest 20 minutes.

Turn out dough onto a lightly floured work surface. Divide dough into 10 to 12 sections. Form each into a 6- to 8-inch flattened round pita. Arrange pitas on prepared baking sheets. Cover with another inverted baking sheet.

Preheat oven to 450°F.

Bake until nicely browned, turning once, about 15 to 20 minutes, removing inverted baking sheet for last 5 minutes of baking.

Red River Valley Bread

Makes 2 medium breads

This recipe makes two amazing loaves—gently crusty on the outside, freckled with whole grains inside, and, overall, moist, fragrant, and almost springy with body, making them superbly fresh days later. This is a great choice for morning bread or sandwiches. Happily, this bread, like most multigrain breads, freezes well.

2 cups *Red River Cereal* (or similar product)	2 tablespoons honey or maple syrup
2¾ cups boiling water	2 tablespoons molasses
2 tablespoons rapid-rise yeast	1 tablespoon brown sugar
1¼ cups warm water (100°F to 110°F)	2¾ teaspoons salt
1 cup stoneground whole wheat bread flour	¼ teaspoon ground cinnamon
3 tablespoons softened butter or canola oil	4 to 6 cups white bread flour

Finishing Touch

Flour or wheat germ, for dusting

In a medium bowl, cover cereal with boiling water. Stir once and let stand 30 minutes. Line a large baking sheet with parchment paper.
Place soaked cereal in a mixer bowl. In a glass measuring cup, whisk yeast and warm water together and let stand 2 minutes to dissolve yeast. Add yeast mixture and 1 cup whole wheat flour to soaked cereal and mix. Add butter, honey or maple syrup, molasses, brown sugar, salt, and cinnamon and stir. Fold in most of white bread flour and mix with a wooden spoon. Let stand 12 minutes.
Then with dough hook, knead on lowest speed of mixer, adding more white bread flour as required until dough just holds together and is somewhat bouncy, about 8 to 10 minutes. The amount of flour you have to add will depend on how much water the cereal absorbed to begin with.
Remove dough hook and spray dough with nonstick cooking spray. Cover entire mixer and bowl with a large clear plastic bag and let rise until almost doubled, about 45 minutes.
Turn out dough onto a lightly floured work surface and gently deflate. Then divide dough in half and shape each into a ball. Place each ball on prepared baking sheet and dust with flour or wheat germ. Cover loosely with plastic wrap and let rise until almost doubled, 30 to 45 minutes.
Preheat oven to 350°F. Place breads in oven and bake until done and medium brown, about 30 to 40 minutes.

This bread is made with Canada's legendary *Red River Cereal*, which was originally formulated in Manitoba's Red River Valley. The cereal is vintage health food in this era of whole grains, and it contains the grain of the moment: flax seed. There are a few places that sell it online; see "Source Guide" for how to order. This is a wonderful cereal containing flax, rye, and cracked wheat. You can substitute most multigrain cereals in this recipe.

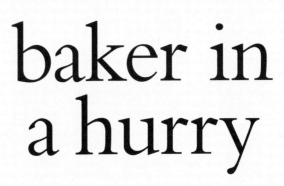

baker in a hurry

Sometimes we all need things quicker than lightning, yet we still want to present something freshly baked and home assembled, even if not wholly homemade. Quick-and-easy baking, or shortcut baking, does have its charms. I am not one to recommend that using convenience mixes and premade doughs be your default baking style, but these are ingenious quick fixes that will do you proud nonetheless.

Quick and easy means being inventive—using a premade piecrust or store-bought frozen white bread dough and some other convenience ingredients along with your own scratch ingredients. Some of these recipes are favorites, and I make them as often as I do more traditional treats (Smash Apple Pie, page 310, is one example).

Still other quick-and-easy recipes offer gift or convenience-mix ideas, such as the layered brownie mixes, pages 308 and 309, that do double duty as a quick mix or a great gift for someone who would appreciate an all-natural gourmet mix from your home kitchen. It's all good, and it's all quite fun.

Baking is about being old-fashioned, but part of the whole broad picture is being able to mix and match techniques and ingredients and then factor in your busy life and come up with some neat tricks. The bottom line is still flavor over speed, but the speed and the ease of preparation do not hurt these recipes' appeal.

Chocolate Chip Cookie Mix in a Jar

Makes 2 to 3 dozen cookies

Pass on the joy of baking. A cookie mix in a jar with a recipe card attached is a perfect gift. You can make a few of these gift jars at a time; it takes the same effort, and multiple gifts are the result.

Dry Mix

2   cups all-purpose flour
¾   teaspoon baking soda
½   cup white sugar
2   cups semisweet chocolate chips
1⅓ cups firmly packed brown sugar

Add-Ins

1   cup unsalted butter, softened
2   large eggs
1   teaspoon pure vanilla extract

In a large bowl, blend flour, baking soda, white sugar, and chocolate chips. Put half of mixture in a large Mason jar. Top with brown sugar and then remaining dry mix of flour, baking soda, white sugar, and chocolate chips. Seal and tie with a ribbon and recipe card.

Recipe card text:

To make cookies, dump mix into a bowl. Blend in 1 cup softened unsalted butter, 2 large eggs, and 1 teaspoon vanilla. Stir well. Deposit heaping tablespoonfuls of cookie dough on a parchment paper–lined baking sheet. Bake at 350°F for 15 to 18 minutes.

Fudge Brownies in a Jar

Makes 2 dozen brownies; pictured as mix on page 306

Brownie mix is the easiest thing to create and give. Incidentally, I pack this mix in Mason jars or dollar-store decorative jars. Ribbon and a card are all you need to finish this gift.

If I, like Oprah, ever did a 'my favorite things' show, Fudge Brownies in a Jar would be on the hit list. Everyone who visits BetterBaking.com would get a jar.

Dry Mix

2½ cups sugar
⅔   cup premium-quality cocoa powder
½   cup chopped nuts, optional
⅛   teaspoon baking soda

⅛   teaspoon salt
1¼ cups all-purpose flour

Add-Ins

¾   cup unsalted butter, melted
4   large eggs, lightly whisked

To prepare, pour sugar into a large Mason jar or other large jar. Add cocoa, nuts, baking soda, and salt. Spoon flour on top and press down. Seal jar.

Recipe card text:

To make brownies, dump mix into a large bowl. Stir in ¾ cup melted unsalted butter and then 4 eggs. Spread batter in a lightly greased 13- x 9-inch or 11- x 8-inch pan. Bake at 350°F for 25 to 30 minutes. Cool at room temperature 20 minutes. Refrigerate 30 minutes and then cut.

Double-Fudge White Chocolate Chunk Brownies in a Jar

Makes 2 to 3 dozen or 10 to 14 large brownies; pictured in jar on page 307

As with all of my layered mixes, this gets packed into a pretty Mason jar and tied with a ribbon, with a recipe card attached. Adding a brownie pan to the gift makes it the perfect baking ensemble. This is a great kids' gift, as well as being just the thing for the beginning baker.

Layered Mix

2   cups sugar
½   cup premium-quality cocoa powder
1   cup all-purpose flour
¼   teaspoon baking soda
¼   teaspoon salt
½   teaspoon finely pulverized instant coffee granules, optional

1   cup white chocolate chips or chunks
½   cup chopped pecans
1   cup semisweet chocolate chips

Add-Ins

1   cup unsalted butter, melted
4   large eggs
1   teaspoon pure vanilla extract

To create the layered angled appearance of the mix in the jar, simply tilt the jar and add each ingredient through a funnel (made of paper) while the jar is tilted.

In a large jar or Mason jar, layer sugar, cocoa, flour, baking soda, salt, coffee, and then white chocolate, nuts, and chocolate chips at an angle (see note at right).

Recipe card text:
To make brownies, dump mix into a large bowl. Stir in 1 cup melted unsalted butter and then add 4 eggs and 1 teaspoon vanilla. Blend well. Spread batter in a lightly greased 13- x 9-inch pan. Bake at 350°F until done, 40 to 50 minutes. Cool well and then refrigerate before cutting.

Quick Brownie Pie

Makes 6 to 8 servings

This is good warm or cold, either on its own or topped with whipped cream or ice cream. It makes a great picnic dessert. You can fold chocolate chips, white chocolate chunks, toasted pecans, or coconut into the brownie batter.

1   (9-inch) frozen pastry shell

1   (19.5-ounce) package brownie mix

Preheat oven to 350°F. Line a baking sheet with parchment paper and place pastry shell on it.
Prepare brownie mix and spoon into pastry shell.
Bake until brownie filling is set, about 25 to 35 minutes.
Cool a little before serving. This pie is good chilled, warm, or at room temperature.

Smash Apple Pie

Makes 6 to 8 servings

This is a flash of a pie that is as good as the best pastry-shop offering. It uses two frozen piecrusts, shredded apples, and an oven—all for a pie that is ready in barely an hour. You can make Smash Pie with peaches, apricots, blueberries, or almost any fruit filling you choose.

2   (8- or 9-inch) deep-dish frozen pastry shells
5   large apples, shredded (unpeeled)
½   cup cranberries, coarsely chopped
½   teaspoon ground cinnamon
1   tablespoon fresh lemon juice
¾   cup sugar

Finishing Touches

Milk, as required
Sugar

Preheat oven to 375°F. Line a baking sheet with parchment paper. Place one frozen pastry shell on prepared baking sheet.

Place a sheet of wax paper on a work surface. Shred apples, stopping just before you get to core (**photo 1**). Place shredded apples in a large mixing bowl. Add cranberries, cinnamon, lemon juice, and ¾ cup sugar. Toss well. Spoon fruit filling into bottom pastry shell. Brush a tiny bit of water around edge of pastry shell; then gently invert second frozen pastry shell onto filled pie, using foil piepan as a guide (**photo 2**). Remove or peel away foil piepan on top and discard. Let pie stand 10 to 15 minutes to partially thaw pastry shells enough to be able to crimp edges. Pressing gently, "smash" top pastry shell onto filling just slightly and then crimp edges with fingertips or fork tines to seal.

Brush pie with milk and sprinkle with sugar (**photo 3**).

Bake until fruit begins to produce juice, about 45 to 55 minutes.

Peach and Pear Strudel Tart

Makes 6 to 8 servings

Here's the easiest, prettiest tart ever—a variation on a recipe I make often with all sorts of fruits, particularly apples.

6   peaches, peeled and diced

6   pears, peeled and diced

¾   cup sugar

Juice of half a lemon

¼   cup golden raisins, plumped and
     dried (see page 18)

1   teaspoon ground cinnamon

2   tablespoons all-purpose flour

½   cup unsalted butter, melted and
     cooled

12   sheets of filo dough

Finishing Touch

Confectioners' sugar, for dusting

Generously spray a 10-inch deep-dish tart pan with a removable bottom with nonstick cooking spray. Place it on a parchment paper–lined baking sheet. Preheat oven to 375°F.

Prepare fruit and toss in a large bowl with sugar, lemon juice, raisins, cinnamon, and flour.

Brush pan with melted butter. Lay 1 sheet of filo on top and press into pan, allowing sides to drape over edge of pan. Brush with butter. Repeat with another 4 sheets of filo, buttering each one.

Spoon fruit into tart pan, pressing gently. You should have enough fruit to mound nicely (slightly over edge of pan). Fold in overlapped ends of filo onto fruit filling.

Brush 1 sheet of filo with melted butter and lay (buttered side up) on top of fruit. Repeat with 1 more sheet of filo. Fold in filo overlap onto fruit. Cut remaining filo into 3 circles the size of tart pan. Brush each with butter and gently place on top of fruit. Be sure to brush top layer with melted butter so that top browns. Make small knife marks in filo through to fruit to allow steam to escape.

Place tart in oven on lowest oven rack. Reduce oven temperature to 350°F and bake until pastry puffs and fruit begins to produce juice (40 to 50 minutes). Cool well. Just before serving, sift lightly with confectioners' sugar.

Smithsonian Soda Cracker Buttercrunch

Makes 8 to 10 servings

Years ago, my recipe for Matzoh Meal Buttercrunch (similar to this recipe) made it to the Smithsonian in a speech about the culture of foods and how certain recipes just get passed around.

35	unsalted soda crackers	1	cup coarsely chopped chocolate
1	cup unsalted butter		(dark, milk, semisweet combo)
2	cups firmly packed brown sugar	½	cup chopped toasted almonds

Preheat oven to 350°F. Lay crackers out on a parchment paper–lined rimmed baking sheet.

Gently heat butter and brown sugar over medium heat about 3 minutes. Pour over crackers. Bake 15 minutes and then reduce oven temperature to 325°F and bake another 10 minutes. Remove from oven and sprinkle with chocolate. Let stand 10 minutes; then smear chocolate a bit. Sprinkle on nuts. Let set. Break into pieces to serve.

Commuter's Grain Bars

Makes 16 to 20 bars

These jam-filled cake mix and oatmeal–based goodies whip up in minutes and yield a nice batch of wrap 'n' go bars that are ideal for a snack on the run, a brown-bag lunch, or a coffee break. A bake-sale winner, too.

1	(18.25-ounce) package gold or white cake mix	2	teaspoons lemon juice
2½	cups quick-cooking oats		Pinch ground cinnamon
½	cup firmly packed brown sugar	1½	cups raspberry or strawberry
¼	cup vegetable oil		preserves or jam mixed with 1 to
1	large egg		2 tablespoons water

Preheat oven to 375°F. Lightly spray a 13- x 9-inch pan with nonstick cooking spray. Have a baking sheet lined with parchment paper ready.

In a large bowl, combine dry ingredients. Add oil, egg, lemon juice, and cinnamon and, using a fork or fingers, mix until crumbly and mixture just barely holds together. Measure out two-thirds of this mixture and pat into bottom of prepared pan, pressing firmly into pan to cover bottom. Combine preserves and water; spoon over crumb mixture in pan and spread evenly. Cover with remaining crumb mixture. Gently pat down crumb mixture on top. Place pan on prepared baking sheet, place in oven, and reduce oven temperature to 350°F.

Bake 20 minutes or until top is light brown. Cool completely and semi-freeze before cutting into bars.

Garlic Bubble Bread

Makes 1 loaf

A bottle of garlic-infused oil and some frozen bread dough make this recipe easy. This zesty bread would be great with chicken cacciatore or a bowl of hot minestrone.

1	pound store-bought frozen bread dough, thawed
⅓	cup garlic-infused oil
⅓	cup unsalted butter, melted, or olive oil
2	tablespoons finely minced fresh parsley
2	tablespoons finely minced fresh garlic

Salt and pepper to taste (or seasoned salt)

½ cup pieces or lumps of chèvre cheese

½ cup grated Parmesan cheese

Sesame seeds, as garnish

This is hands-on food all the way. Serve warm and simply pull apart sections to serve.

Generously spray a 9- x 5-inch loafpan with nonstick cooking spray. **Divide** dough into small chunks to form 1½-inch balls and set aside. Whisk together garlic oil and butter (or olive oil), parsley, and garlic. **Dip** dough balls in garlic oil/butter mixture. Layer all dough balls on each other in prepared loafpan. Sprinkle salt and pepper between layers, dot with chèvre cheese, and sprinkle with grated cheese. Top bread with sesame seeds, if desired.

Cover loafpan loosely with plastic wrap and let dough rise until almost doubled, about 45 minutes.

Preheat oven to 350°F. Place loafpan on a baking sheet and place in oven. Bake until browned and crusty, about 30 to 40 minutes.

Cool about 15 minutes before serving.

metric equivalents

The recipes that appear in this cookbook use the standard U.S. method for measuring liquid and dry or solid ingredients (teaspoons, tablespoons, and cups). The information in the following charts is provided to help cooks outside the United States successfully use these recipes. All equivalents are approximate.

Metric Equivalents for Different Types of Ingredients

A standard cup measure of a dry or solid ingredient will vary in weight depending on the type of ingredient. A standard cup of liquid is the same volume for any type of liquid. Use the following chart when converting standard cup measures to grams (weight) or milliliters (volume).

Standard Cup	Fine Powder (ex. flour)	Grain (ex. rice)	Granular (ex. sugar)	Liquid Solids (ex. butter)	Liquid (ex. milk)
1	140 g	150 g	190 g	200 g	240 ml
¾	105 g	113 g	143 g	150 g	180 ml
⅔	93 g	100 g	125 g	133 g	160 ml
½	70 g	75 g	95 g	100 g	120 ml
⅓	47 g	50 g	63 g	67 g	80 ml
¼	35 g	38 g	48 g	50 g	60 ml
⅛	18 g	19 g	24 g	25 g	30 ml

Useful Equivalents for Dry Ingredients by Weight

(To convert ounces to grams, multiply the number of ounces by 30.)

1 oz	=	¹⁄₁₆ lb	=	30 g
4 oz	=	¼ lb	=	120 g
8 oz	=	½ lb	=	240 g
12 oz	=	¾ lb	=	360 g
16 oz	=	1 lb	=	480 g

Useful Equivalents for Length

(To convert inches to centimeters, multiply the number of inches by 2.5.)

1 in				=	2.5 cm		
6 in	=	½ ft		=	15 cm		
12 in	=	1 ft		=	30 cm		
36 in	=	3 ft	=	1 yd	=	90 cm	
40 in				=	100 cm	=	1 m

Useful Equivalents for Liquid Ingredients by Volume

¼ tsp				=	1 ml	
½ tsp				=	2 ml	
1 tsp				=	5 ml	
3 tsp	=	1 Tbsp	=	½ fl oz =	15 ml	
		2 Tbsp	=	⅛ cup =	1 fl oz =	30 ml
		4 Tbsp	=	¼ cup =	2 fl oz =	60 ml
		5⅓ Tbsp	=	⅓ cup =	3 fl oz =	80 ml
		8 Tbsp	=	½ cup =	4 fl oz =	120 ml
		10⅔ Tbsp	=	⅔ cup =	5 fl oz =	160 ml
		12 Tbsp	=	¾ cup =	6 fl oz =	180 ml
		16 Tbsp	=	1 cup =	8 fl oz =	240 ml
		1 pt	=	2 cups =	16 fl oz =	480 ml
		1 qt	=	4 cups =	32 fl oz =	960 ml
					33 fl oz =	1000 ml = 1 l

Useful Equivalents for Cooking/Oven Temperatures

	Fahrenheit	Celsius	Gas Mark
Freeze water	32° F	0° C	
Room temperature	68° F	20° C	
Boil water	212° F	100° C	
Bake	325° F	160° C	3
	350° F	180° C	4
	375° F	190° C	5
	400° F	200° C	6
	425° F	220° C	7
	450° F	230° C	8
Broil			Grill

many thanks

My salute and special bow of gratitude to Ellen Fuss, my fearless, flawless, and seemingly unfatigued in-house Test Kitchen Manager. A million thank-yous and fat-free hugs.

A very special salute to my "baking godmothers" (aka *A Passion for Baking* testers): Linda Behrens, Karen Brenker, Ellen Gold, Ann Harste, Brenda Jackson, Regina Joskow, Leone Lamb, Samantha Langer, Judith Lessler, Michelle Louie, Dana Martin, Jill Moncarz, Doris Ruth Oppenheimer, Mary Pfeifer, Ann E. Ring, Denise Roig, Ann Ryan, Nancy Schofer, Jodi Smith, Amy Stromberg, and Jen Topp.

My thanks to the following companies for their assistance and support: All-Clad Metalcrafters; Boyajian Inc.; The Harneys of Harney & Sons Fine Teas; Hollingsworth Custom Wood Products, Inc., Canada; Nielsen-Massey Vanillas; Scharffen Berger Chocolate Maker, Inc.; and Weber-Stephen Products Co.

My warmest thanks and appreciation for their unique support of my work on this book to Tom Payne and Clabber Girl Corporation, Brian Maynard and KitchenAid, and Matt Nielsen of Nielsen-Massey Vanillas. Without this trio and their generosity in countless, consistent ways, *A Passion for Baking* would not be as glorious as it is.

Warmest gratitude to John MacKenzie, Paul MacKenzie, and Alex Zakher of Elehost Web Design Inc., Toronto, Canada, for keeping this author and BetterBaking.com online and looking beautiful.

A very special thanks to the team at Oxmoor House: Jim Bathie, photography director; Katherine Eckert and Kay Clarke, photo stylists; Kelley Wilton, food stylist; and Melissa Clark, senior designer. And to photographers Beau Gustafson and Lee Harrelson for making my recipes look so gorgeous.

My heartiest thanks and respect to Julie Gunter, editor, baking midwife, and editorial partner in crime, for her meticulous attention to detail, spirited teamwork, adventurous nature, and discerning palate concerning anything decadent and chocolate. She has turned hard work into sheer fun and helped ensure you will not only bake with passion but with success.

My warmest thanks to Susan Payne, executive editor at Oxmoor House, who was the first to suggest on that fateful day one May that I bring my "passion" to the fore and to the editorial powers that be at Oxmoor House. Thank you for your warm welcome and uncanny vision, and for your careful stewarding of this book from proposal to print. Not only do you shine on authors and help create great books, you also dance. What more could I have asked?

Special thanks to Brian Carnahan, vice president and publisher at Oxmoor House, for the courtesy of his professional regard and belief in me as an author.

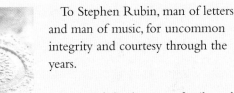

To Stephen Rubin, man of letters and man of music, for uncommon integrity and courtesy through the years.

A special thanks to my family and friends, particularly my Aunt Beryl and Uncle Ralph Goldman for their warm care, interest, and encouragement of their youngest niece and her sons. I dedicate this book in loving memory of my Uncle Ralph, an inspired champion and supporter of the arts and artists, including his baker/writer niece.

Warm appreciation to my baking readers who have waved me on through the years.

A huge smile, a wingspan of hugs, and both pride and love beyond measure to my three sons, who have praised and critiqued every crumb and crust of each recipe in this book. Thank you for being the tireless sounding board and for the applause of each triumph, both small and grand. Life is indeed magic and filled with passion.

source guide

For specialty items or particularly endorsed products and brands, check out some of Marcy's recommended sources.

• Ingredients

American Spoon Foods
1668 Clarion Avenue; P.O. Box 566; Petoskey, MI 49770-0566; 888-735-6700 (to order); www.spoon.com
▶ High-quality **dried fruits** and **nuts**, as well as **preserves, sauces,** and **chutneys.**

Arla Foods USA
645 Martinsville Road; P.O. Box 624; Basking Ridge, NJ 07920; 800-243-3730; www.arlafoodsusa.com
▶ *Lurpak* Danish butter is **European butter** from a 100-year-old butter company. It has an intense buttery taste and is packed in special *alufoil,* which protects the product from light, ensuring optimal freshness.

Boyajian
144 Will Drive; Canton, MA 02021; 800-965-0665 or 781-828-9966; www.boyajianinc.com
▶ Maker of pure **citrus oils,** including orange, tangerine, lemon, and lime.

Burnbrae Farms
1-800-666-5979; www.naturegg.com
▶ **Omega-3-enriched eggs** for baking.

Fleischmann's Yeast
ACH Food Companies, Inc.; 800-777-4959; www.breadworld.com
▶ Major yeast company offering **fresh** as well as **active dry** and **instant dry yeast.**

Hodgson Mill, Inc.
1100 Stevens Avenue; Effingham, IL 62401; 800-347-0105; www.hodgsonmill.com
▶ Excellent **grains** and **multigrain flours;** also offers **white whole wheat flour.**

Hulman Company
P.O. Box 150; Terre Haute, IN 47808; 812-232-9446; www.bakewithlove.com
▶ Fine-quality **baking powder** with the *Clabber Girl, Davis,* or *Rumford* brand name.

King Arthur Flour
The Baker's Catalogue
135 Route 5 South; P.O. Box 1010; Norwich, VT 05055; 800-827-6836; www.kingarthurflour.com
▶ A unique source for dedicated home bakers, this company is a treasure chest of **commercial bakeware, specialty salts, sugars, extracts, flour, malt powder, mixes, yeasts, mixers, bread machines,** and **unique tools** (such as the Danish dough whisk).

Molini Pizzuti
www.molinipizzuti.it
▶ Italian company famed for their production of the fabulous **perfect-for-home-pizza flour, "00" Flour.**

New York Cake and Baking Distributor
56 West 22nd Street; New York, NY 10010; 800-942-2539 or 212-675-2253; www.nycake.com
▶ For the baker, cake decorator, and home pro, **all manner of things associated with baking** and **decorating.**

Nielsen-Massey Vanillas
1550 Shields Drive; Waukegan, IL 60085; 800-525-7873 (U.S. only); 847-578-1550; www.nielsenmassey.com
▶ If not *the* best, one of the best vanilla manufacturers in the United States, offering **single-** and **double-strength vanilla** in Madagascar Bourbon, Mexican, or Tahitian extracts and vanilla blends. *Nielsen-Massey* vanillas can also be ordered through *King Arthur Flour,* as well as the *Penzeys, Ltd. Spice House.*

Penzeys, Ltd. Spice House
19300 West Janacek Court; Brookfield, WI 53045; 800-741-7787; www.penzeys.com
▶ One of the best sources for **quality spices,** with a stellar selection.

Red Star Yeast
P.O. Box 737; Milwaukee, WI 53201-0737; 877-677-7000 or 800-445-4746; www.redstaryeast.com
▶ Major yeast company specializing in **fresh, active,** and **instant dry yeast.**

Robin Hood Multifoods
Smucker Foods of Canada Company
Consumer Services Department
80 Whitehall Drive; Markham, ON L3R 0P3 Canada; 800-268-3232; www.robinhood.ca; www.redrivercereal.com
▶ Canadian **flour** company and maker of *Red River Cereal* (for specialty breads).

Saco Foods, Inc.
P.O. Box 620707; Middleton, WI 53562-0707; 800-373-7226; www.sacofoods.com
▶ This company offers superb baking **cocoa** and **buttermilk powder.**

Scharffen Berger Chocolate Maker
914 Heinz Avenue; Berkeley, CA 94710; 800-930-4528; 510-981-4050; www.scharffenberger.com
▶ Renowned source of high-quality **chocolate.**

Spices Etc.
P.O. Box 2088; Savannah, GA 31402; 800-827-6373; www.spicesetc.com
▶ Fine spices and natural **flavorings,** such as **vanilla, butter, coconut, pineapple, toffee,** and **mango.** Dried **fruit,** quality **teas, dry cheese,** and **buttermilk powder.**

• Equipment and Supplies

All-Clad Metalcrafters
424 Morganza Road; Canonsburg, PA 15317; 800-255-2523; www.allclad.com
▶ Premier manufacturer of **cookware** and superb **bakeware.**

Ares Kitchen & Baking Supplies
514-695-5225
▶ Canada's largest kitchen and baking supplies store, featuring Marcy's *Cuisine D'Or* **rolling pin.**

Beehive Kitchenware
One West Street; Fall River, MA 02720; 508-678-4335; www.beehivekitchenware.com
▶ A great source for **specialty measuring cups** and **spoons.**

Beryl's Cake Decorating Equipment
P.O. Box 1584; North Springfield, VA 22151; 800-488-2749 or 703-256-6951; www.beryls.com
▶ Extensive line of British, European, and American **cake-decorating supplies, specialty ingredients,** and **molds.**

Bridge Kitchenware Corporation
711 3rd Avenue; New York, NY 10017;
212-688-4220; www.bridgekitchenware.com
▶ Commercial American **bakeware**, as well
as imported **molds** and **other small wares**.

Cuisinart
150 Milford Road; East Windsor, NJ 08520;
800-726-0190; www.cuisinart.com
▶ Renowned for their **food processors** and
many other **upscale kitchen appliances**,
including **bread machines**.

Cumberland General Store
P.O. Box 4468; Alpharetta, GA 30023-4468;
800-334-4640; www.cumberlandgeneral.com
▶ Retro and contemporary **baking pans** and
other **kitchen tools**.

Golda's Kitchen
700 Matheson Boulevard West;
Mississauga, ON L5R 3T2 Canada;
866-465-3299 or 905-712-1475;
www.goldaskitchen.com
▶ This Canadian-based retailer has a vast
online offering, including **rolling pins**, **baker's
caramel**, and a full line of best-quality
bakeware, **cookware**, **mixers**, *Zojirushi* **bread
machines**, **tools**, and **small wares**.

Hearth Kitchen Company
226 Selleck Street, Suite B;
Stamford, CT 06902; 800-383-7818 or
203-325-8800; www.hearthkitchen.com
▶ This company offers a hearth **baking
stone** for superior homemade pizza.

House on the Hill, Inc.
650 West Grand Avenue, Unit 110;
Elmhurst, IL 60126; 877-279-4455;
www.houseonthehill.net
▶ Replica **wood molds** of historical and
artistic cookie designs used in shortbread, butter cookies, and gingerbread
houses.

James Sloss/French Butter Dish
www.frenchbutterdish.com
▶ American-made **French butter crocks**.

J.K. Adams Company
1430 Route 30; P.O. Box 248;
Dorset, VT 05251; 800-451-6118;
www.jkadams.com
▶ Solid hardwood **rolling pins** with plastic
bearings, as well as **pastry boards** and
spice racks.

KitchenAid
Customer Satisfaction Center;
P.O. Box 218; St. Joseph, MI 49085;

800-541-6390 (for countertop appliances);
800-422-1230; www.kitchenaid.com
▶ Full line of **stand mixers**, as well as **refur-
bished mixers**, **food processors**, **blenders**,
large appliances, and **electric grain mills**.

La Cuisine Kitchenware
323 Cameron Street;
Alexandria, VA 22314-3219;
800-521-1176 or 703-836-4435;
www.lacuisineus.com
▶ An excellent source for upscale **bakeware**,
decorating equipment, and anything associated with the art and craft of baking and
cooking.

Lee Valley Tools Ltd.
P.O. Box 6295, Station J;
Ottawa, ON K2A 1T4 Canada;
800-267-8735 (U.S.); 800-267-8761
(Canada); www.leevalley.com
(search gardening/kitchenware)
▶ Many fine **cutlery** products but, in particular,
a source for the original **stainless-steel rasp**,
now commonly known as a Microplane®, used
to zest citrus and grate chocolate.

Leon Neal
3506 Carriage Drive; Raleigh, NC 27612;
919-789-4338; bowlman-neal@nc.rr.com
▶ Authentic **wooden bread** or **biscuit bowls**.

Nordic Ware
Highways 7 and 100;
Minneapolis, MN 55416-2274;
800-328-4310 or 877-466-7342;
www.nordicware.com
▶ Renowned original maker of the trade-
marked **Bundt pan**; also makes many
varieties of **specialty bakeware**, such as
brownie and scone pans.

Plugra
800-535-5371; www.plugra.com
▶ High-performance **baking butter**.

Rochow Swirl Mixer Company, Inc.
P.O. Box 10405; 1900 University Avenue;
Rochester, NY 14610-0405;
585-244-1120; www.rochowcutters.com
▶ The heaviest-duty, most commercial
biscuit, **scone**, and **donut cutters** to be
found.

RoyalBag
www.royalbag.com/trash_liners.asp
▶ Large clear garbage **bags** (Marcy puts
them over her mixer when proofing dough).

Rycraft, Inc.
9234 East Valley Road, Suite D; Prescott

Valley, AZ 86314; 800-479-2723;
www.rycraft.com
▶ An unusual source for unique heirloom
ceramic **cookie stamps** suitable for shortbread and other holiday cookies. They also
do **custom stamps**.

Sur La Table
5701 Sixth Avenue South, Suite 486;
Seattle, WA 98108; 800-243-0852;
www.surlatable.com
▶ This extraordinary mail-order supplier
distributes a baker's and cook's catalogue
offering **imported bakeware**, as well as
nested *Matfer* **cookie cutters**, **heavy-duty
aluminum cakepans**, *Kugelhopf* **molds**,
Zojirushi **bread machines**, and **ceramic
pizza stones**.

Sweet Celebrations Inc.
P.O. Box 39426; Edina, MN 55439-0426;
800-328-6722 or 952-943-1661;
http://www.sweetc.com
▶ This mail-order company, formerly known as
Maid of Scandinavia, has **everything for the
home baker**, such as hard-to-find **parchment
paper loafpan liners**. Look here to find
unusual **bakery-** and **pastry-related items**,
as well as many standard but hard-to-find
necessities.

Thorpe Rolling Pin Company
336 Putnam Avenue; P.O. Box 4124;
Hamden, CT 06514; 800-344-6966
▶ Classic, quality hardwood **rolling pins with
ball bearings**, available nationwide in
culinary stores.

Vic Firth Gourmet, Inc.
77 High Street; Newport, ME 04953;
800-894-5970; www.vicfirthgourmet.com
▶ Specializes in outstanding **rolling pins**, as
well as **pepper mills** of all descriptions.

Williams-Sonoma
877-812-6235; www.williams-sonoma.com
▶ Premier supplier of **tools**, **ingredients**, and
kitchen appliances.

Wilton Industries
2240 West 75th Street;
Woodridge, IL 60517; 800-794-5866 or
630-963-1818; www.wilton.com
▶ Wilton offers a full line of specialty and
standard **cakepans**. Offers a few different
lines, **nonstick pans**, **anodized aluminum**
(a treated aluminum pan), as well as
Wilton Pro, a more **heavy-duty baking pan**.
Available nationwide at cake decorating
stores, gourmet shops, and housewares
departments.

index

Italicized entries reflect subject categories.